1 MONTH OF
FREE
READING

at
www.ForgottenBooks.com

By purchasing this book you are eligible for one month membership to ForgottenBooks.com, giving you unlimited access to our entire collection of over 1,000,000 titles via our web site and mobile apps.

To claim your free month visit:
www.forgottenbooks.com/free265966

ISBN 978-0-265-89319-7
PIBN 10265966

SMITHSONIAN INSTITUTION
BUREAU OF AMERICAN ETHNOLOGY
BULLETIN 65

ARCHEOLOGICAL EXPLORATIONS IN NORTHEASTERN ARIZONA

BY

ALFRED VINCENT KIDDER

AND

SAMUEL J. GUERNSEY

WASHINGTON
GOVERNMENT PRINTING OFFICE
1919

LETTER OF TRANSMITTAL

Smithsonian Institution,
Bureau of American Ethnology,
Washington, D. C., February 27, 1917.

Sir: I have the honor to submit herewith a memoir on "Archeological Explorations in Northeastern Arizona," by Alfred Vincent Kidder and Samuel J. Guernsey, and to recommend its publication as Bulletin 65 of the Bureau of American Ethnology.

Very respectfully,

F. W. Hodge,
Ethnologist-in-Charge.

Dr. Charles D. Walcott,
Secretary of the Smithsonian Institution,
Washington, D. C.

Approved:
C. D. Walcott, Secretary.

3

CONTENTS

II

ILLUSTRATIONS

8

PLATES—continued

ARCHEOLOGICAL EXPLORATIONS IN NORTH-EASTERN ARIZONA

By Alfred Vincent Kidder and Samuel J. Guernsey

INTRODUCTION

THE present report records the investigations in the Kayenta district of northeastern Arizona, carried on in the summers of 1914 and 1915 by the Peabody Museum of Harvard University, under the authority of permits granted by the Secretary of the Interior. In the first section of the paper the sites are described in the order of their excavation; the second is devoted to a consideration of the specimens recovered; and the third consists of a preliminary discussion of the archeological problems encountered. Although our explorations in the region are still being carried on, it seems best to publish the results of the first two years' work at the present time, in order that they may become available to students as soon as possible.

The opening up of the immensely fertile archeological field of northeastern Arizona is due to the initiative of Prof. Byron Cummings, whose first expedition into the district was made in 1908. Since then he has done a great amount of thorough and painstaking work in the ruins. The Peabody Museum, feeling that the field was essentially his, asked his permission before undertaking their explorations. This was most cordially given. The authors wish, accordingly, to express their most hearty thanks to Professor Cummings for his generous cooperation.

The liberality of the following friends of the Museum provided a substantial addition to the somewhat scanty funds available for the work: Miss Madeleine Mixter and Messrs. Augustus Hemenway, John E. Thayer, Bayard Thayer, William North Duane, Lawrence Grinnell, Bronson M. Cutting, Charles P. Bowditch, Clarence B. Moore, and J. M. Longyear.

Thanks are due also to Mr. and Mrs. John Wetherill and Mr. Clyde Colville, of Kayenta, at whose trading post the expeditions made their headquarters. Their hospitality has always been unfailing, and we grew to look forward with the greatest pleasure to our periodical returns from camp to their little oasis of civilization. To

13

the Navaho. Clayton Wetherill, our guide, rendered us the same cheerful and intelligent help that has done so much to make successful other archeological expeditions, particularly those of Dr. T. Mitchell Prudden.

The expedition of 1914 was under the joint leadership of the authors; in 1915 Mr. Guernsey was in charge, assisted by Dr. R. G. Fuller. Mr. Charles Amsden, of Farmington, New Mexico, a student of archeology, was with us on both trips; Mr. John W. Edwards was on the second trip. The field work was done during the months of June and July of each year, and the parties reached Kayenta by wagon via Shiprock, New Mexico, and the trading post of Teecnuzpos.

The Kayenta trading post was founded by Mr. John Wetherill in 1909 and therefore is shown on only the more recent maps. It lies in the northeastern corner of the Navaho Reservation, not far south of the Utah-Arizona line, and is situated in the broad valley of Laguna Creek, 9 or 10 miles below the mouth of Marsh Pass. North of the post rise the jagged red-sandstone peaks of the "South Comb," over which may be seen the top of "El Capitan," an enormous isolated pinnacle of black basalt. To the south the valley is closed in by the flanks of the Black Mesa (the "Zilh-Le-Jini" of the maps). Between the Kayenta district and the Colorado River to the west and northwest is the Navaho Mountain plateau, from which radiate numberless tortuous and steep-walled canyons. The exploration of these canyons has scarcely been begun, but the energy of Mr. Wetherill and Professor Cummings has already disclosed in them such archeological treasures as the cliff-houses of Sagi and Nitsi Canyons and such geological wonders as the Rainbow Natural Bridge.

As the Sagi and Nitsi cliff-houses were, and still are, being investigated by Professor Cummings, the authors chose for their work the Monumental Valley district to the north of Kayenta. About the middle of the first season, however, the water supply in the Monuments failed, and at the suggestion of Professor Cummings, who happened to be at Kayenta at the time, we took up the exploration of the Skeleton Mesa and Marsh Pass regions. This occupied us during the second half of the first season and the whole of the second.

I. FIELD WORK

SEASON OF 1914

PROVISIONING at Kayenta, the party first took up the exploration of the territory lying between the great Capitan Rock ("Agathla Needle" of the maps) and the "Monuments," a cluster of enormous eroded pillars of sandstone lying about midway between it and the San Juan River (pl. 1; fig. 1).[1]

Several short but many-branched canyons head in the plateau north of El Capitan and run down to the lower or Monument bench, where they open out and merge into a great barren "flat" that stretches away toward the San Juan. There are neither permanent springs nor streams in these canyons, but save in years of exceptional drought water is carried over from the spring rains until those of midsummer in numerous deep pockets in the sandstone cliffs. The vegetation is of the usual semidesert type, cedar and piñon predominating, while box elder and scrub oak are found in certain favorable localities; the commoner small growths are sage, greasewood, cactus, and the narrow-leaved yucca. While none of them occur in the immediate vicinity, spruce, pine, and quaking aspen are to be found on the high mesas 15 or 20 miles to the south, and cottonwoods grow abundantly in the valley of the San Juan, about the same distance to the north. Navaho families live here and there in the canyons, each one with its flock of sheep and goats, and its sandy corn patch situated in some sheltered bay or draw of the cliffs where long experience has shown that there is a maximum of underground water with a minimum of wind.

In this region there are no large ruins, either of cliff-houses or pueblos. There are, however, numerous one- and two-roomed structures and a few more pretentious buildings. The former were made by simply walling up the fronts of small natural caves or crannies in the rocks (pl. 2); their floors are not leveled, their roofs are seldom smoked, and there is little in the way of rubbish or potsherds in or about them to indicate that they were ever used as dwelling places. For this reason and because they are never found in groups or clusters, but are scattered up and down the canyons with no apparent

---

[1] For general descriptions of the region see Prudden, 1903, and Cummings, 1910.

relation.to one another, it seems probable that these structures were used as temporary storage places for harvested corn awaiting transportation to the winter habitations. Of the larger structures six were found and excavated.

RUIN 1

This is a small cliff-house built in a recess about 20 feet up the side of a detached rock hummock in the canyon bottom (fig. 1 and pl. 3). The exposure is southeast. The cave floor slopes rather steeply from front to back, and the rooms are clustered in the eastern end of the cave, leaving a considerable clear space at the west. The house consisted originally of six or eight rooms (fig. 2), but is in an advanced stage of ruin, the walls being much fallen and no roof timbers left in place. This condition is rather difficult to account for, as the over-

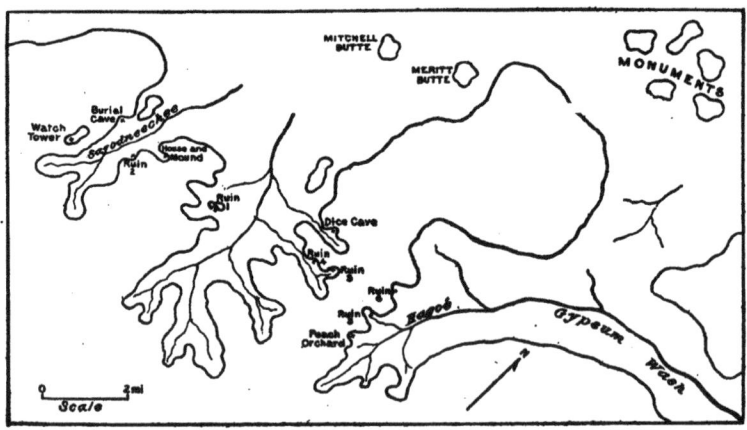

FIG. 1.—Sketch map of the Monuments district.

hanging roof of the cave completely shelters the buildings from rain and, outside of one quarter, there is no sign that the place was ravaged by fire. The masonry is composed of irregular slabs of sandstone, roughly coursed, set in adobe mortar and abundantly spalled. The best work is seen in the front wall of room 6, which is built along the shelving edge of the cliff and stands very true and even, 8 feet high (pl. 4). The precarious position of this wall, its insecure footing, and the fact that it formed the support for several structures behind it, necessitated careful and solid construction. That this was provided shows that the more careless work on the other rooms was not due to inability to produce better. No data as to size or architecture of doorways or method of roofing could be gathered.

Rooms 1 and 2 have almost completely fallen away, only two courses of the south wall appearing. Their former shape is clearly indicated, however, by adobe mortar still adhering to the rock along

MARSH PASS

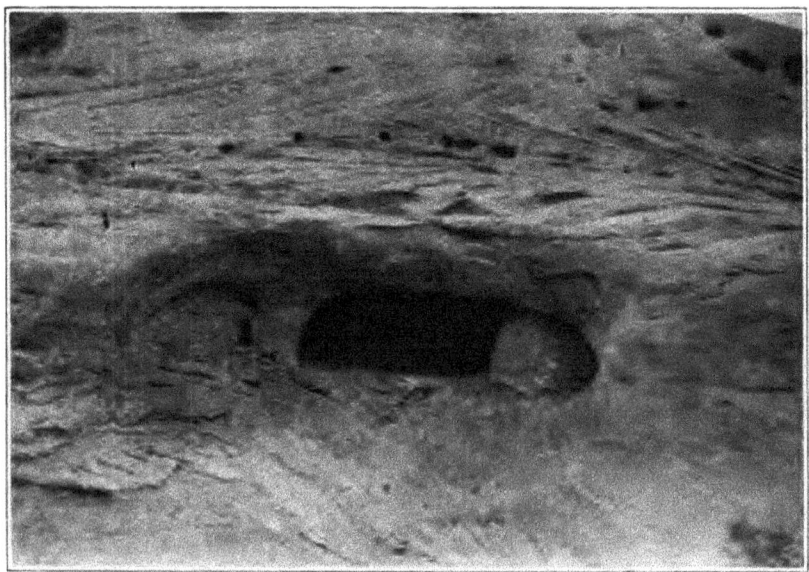

GRANARIES

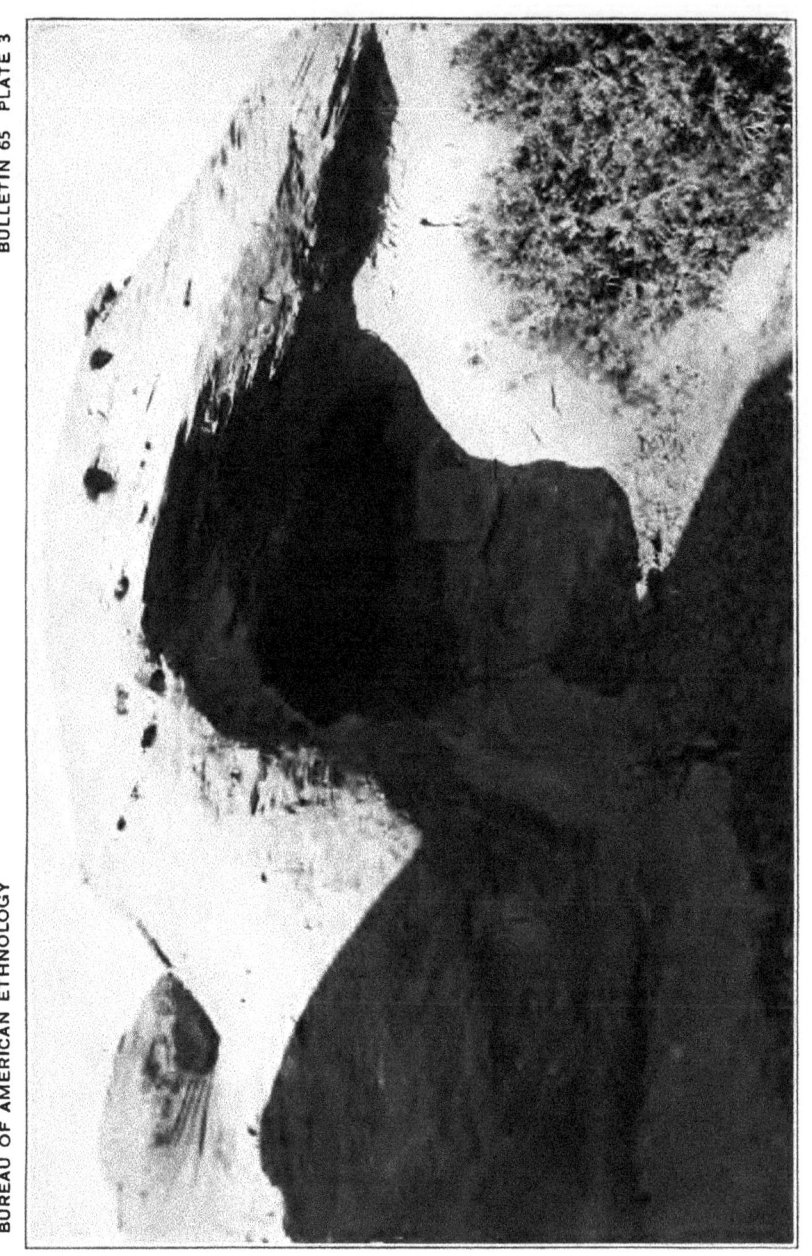

RUIN 1

EAST END OF RUIN 1

the lines where the walls joined the roof of the cave. The rock is also heavily smoked within the spaces marked out by the adobe, showing that fires had been used in these chambers. Room 3 is also much ruined, but probably once extended to the roof of the cave. Room 4, somewhat better preserved, and roughly elliptical in shape, had a former height of 5 feet 6 inches. One jamb of the doorway, faced and rounded off with adobe, is still in place. Just below the door there is incorporated in the wall a short, thick log of piñon wood, set horizontally and apparently so placed to strengthen and tie the masonry. There was here 2 to 3 feet of débris, blown sand,

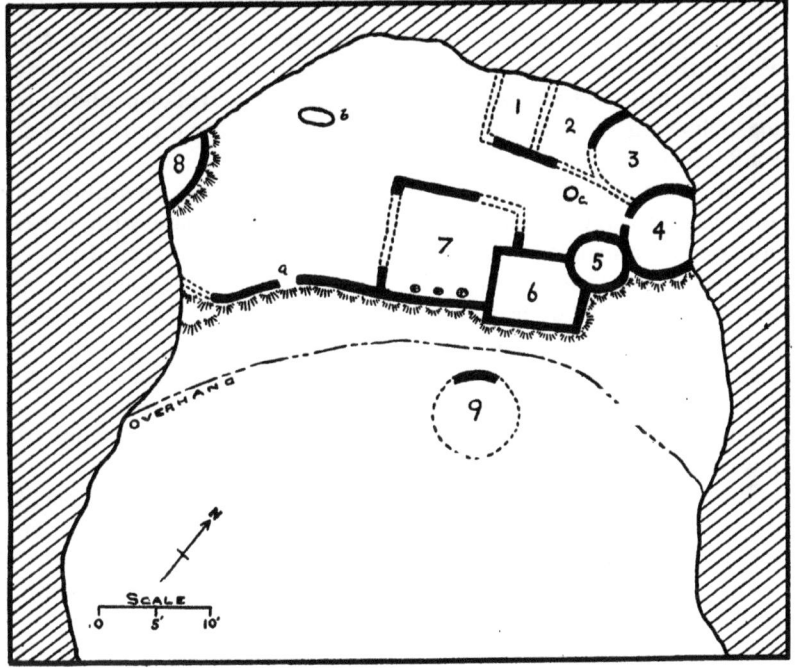

FIG. 2.—Plan of Ruin 1.

fallen building stone, and rubbish of occupation. Near the probable floor level and lying against the wall were two wooden digging sticks in a remarkably perfect state of preservation. (See pl. 47, d, e.)

Room 5, round and 4 feet in diameter, was probably a storehouse or granary. Its rubbish contained two bone awls. Room 6 was filled to a depth of 3 feet with blown sand and débris of occupation. In the northeast corner lay a small corrugated jar. There must once have been an artificially leveled floor in this room, as the bottom of the cave slopes very steeply. The same conditions obtained in room 5, but in neither case could such a floor be distinguished.

The six chambers just described were apparently the only true inclosed and roofed rooms of the house. The space No. 7 was, in all probability, an open court or terrace. Its front wall is shown in the foreground of plate 4. Having been merely a retaining wall, it probably never stood very much higher than it does at present. Just inside it were set three short cedar posts, 9 inches in diameter, and from them to the north side of the room ran three poles about 6 feet long. At the north end these poles rest on other poles, laid horizontally. Below and around this logwork is packed earth and rubbish thrown in presumably as filling material. The whole had been reduced to charcoal by so severe a fire, burning from above, that even part of the rubbish below the logs was charred and scorched. There was a layer of unburned rubbish above the logs, showing that the house was inhabited for some time after the conflagration.

The western part of the cave is closed in by a low retaining wall and was principally bare rock leveled here and there with packed adobe containing charcoal, corncobs, cedar bark, and other refuse. In the rear of this space at b (fig. 2), and again nearer the rooms at c, are fireplaces, rounded depressions in the cave deposit $2\frac{1}{2}$ feet in diameter by 8 inches deep, coped and lined with stone slabs and plastered up and rounded over with mud. Each of them was filled to the top with white wood ashes. Room 8 was once a small storage cist or granary, formed by masoning up a cranny in the rock; all but the lowest course of the wall, however, has now fallen away.

Entrance to the cave must have been gained by ladder, a doorlike gap, which can still be made out in the front retaining wall or bulwark (fig. 2, a), having undoubtedly been the place against which the ladder was set. The pole by which we climbed to the ruin runs up to this entrance and may be seen in plate 3.

On the ground below the cave there is a small section of curving wall (fig. 2, No. 9); it has been almost completely destroyed by water falling from the rocks above. This undoubtedly marks the site of the kiva.

On the cliff west of the kiva there is a pecked petroglyph, a "mountain sheep" (see pl. 89, m), and around the point of the rocks some 500 yards farther west there is a large series of pictographs, ancient ones deeply pecked and much weathered, and recent incised drawings, probably Navaho, of men on horseback hunting deer (see pl. 97, b, c). Directly in front of this group, about 20 feet from the rocks, there is a large, low mound of dark soil which contrasts sharply in color with the red adobe earth of the region. On it were many potsherds, broken stone implements, and chips, and its whole appearance strongly suggests the burial mounds of the mesa ruins, north of the San Juan. A series of trenches run through the dark deposit to the undisturbed red substratum failed, however, to disclose any skeletons. Potsherds on the surface and in the earth were not noticeably different from those of the cliff-house.

Within a radius of half a mile from Ruin 1 were four small granaries, a group of ancient pictographs, and several Navaho drawings. Laid in a cranny behind the back wall of one of the granaries there was found a series of switchlike implements made by tying together at the butts a number of little twigs. There were three finished specimens and materials for making another. All were most perfectly preserved and are more fully described in section 2.

After completing the excavation of Ruin 1, we moved into the next canyon, about 2 miles to the west, and camped at a place called by the Navaho *Sayodnecchee*, "Where the red rocks run under," in reference to a noticeable dip in the red sandstone strata.[1] Here one of our party, while exploring a few days previously, had found a second cliff-house.

RUIN 2

Ruin 2 lies in a cave about 65 feet deep by 70 feet across the mouth (pl. 5). It is accessible only from below, where there is a sheer drop of 22 feet to the sloping lower rock; from there to the valley bottom there is a less abrupt slope of rock 50 feet in vertical height. We made our entry by lashing two poles together, raising them to the edge of the cave, and steadying them with ropes while Clayton Wetherill climbed in and fastened hand-ropes. It required much daring and great skill in handling himself for this first adventurer to work from the end of the top pole, which barely reached the lip of the rock, up over the steep incline to the safe footing of the cave proper (pl. 6, *a*). We were, without question, the first people to enter this cave since its final desertion by the occupants. The buildings themselves were much ruined, a condition attributable primarily to destruction of the roofs and timbers by fire, and secondarily to the elements. While the whole interior is perfectly sheltered from rain, southerly and westerly winds, which blow in this region with great violence, scour and whirl the sand round and round in the cave, producing an almost constant attrition that cuts away the adobe mortar from between the building stones and ultimately brings down the walls themselves. To such wind-erosion may be

---

[1] For this and other Navaho names and their meaning, as well as for much other information in regard to the Navaho, the authors are indebted to Mrs. John Wetherill.

attributed, we think, much otherwise inexplicable decay of cliff-dwellings.

The house contains two kivas and nine or ten small cell-like rooms of irregular shape (fig. 3). The two kivas were built side by side in the lower front slope of the cave, and were probably only semi-subterranean, as the cave deposit is relatively shallow. Their rear or eastern sides were sunk into the earth, while the sides toward the mouth of the cave doubtless stood free. If they had been made entirely subterranean a heavy retaining wall and much filling would have been necessary, and although this was done for some of the kivas of Cliff Palace and other Mesa Verde buildings there is noth-

Fig. 3.—Plan of Ruin 2.

ing to show that it had been attempted here. The rear of the kivas lay enough underground to bring the roofs to a level with the floor of the cave behind (fig. 4).

Kiva I (fig. 5), the eastern and larger of the two, is a plain circular room without niches; diameter, 14 feet. The front or southwestern wall has fallen away; the débris seems to show that large flat slabs of stone had once been set vertically in it, and it was further strengthened by two upright posts of cedar. The rear wall still stands to a height of nearly 5 feet. The masonry on the inside is solid, but not carefully or precisely laid, there having been no cutting

RUIN 2

c. WATCHTOWER

b. MASONRY OF KIVA 1

DETAILS OF RUIN 2

a. ENTERING RUIN 2

or shaping of the stones. The coursing is primitive, and a large amount of adobe mortar and spalls (chips of stone and potsherds) are in evidence (pl. 6, *b*). These defects were undoubtedly concealed by a coating of plaster, but this had been entirely removed by the severe sand-scouring of the southerly winds. The exterior of the wall is very rough and not brought to any uniformity of face.

The floor is partly made from the bedrock of the cave, pecked and chipped down, in a rather unsuccessful attempt at leveling; partly of adobe. Where the adobe floor remains, it is hard-packed and level, and shows repeated top-coverings; it is, however, so badly

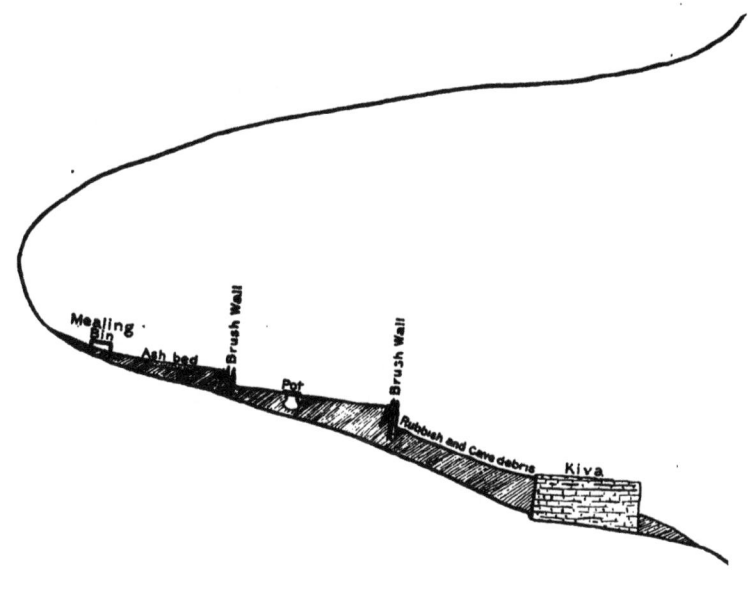

Fɪɢ. 4.—Section of Ruin 2, showing kiva, terraces, etc.

broken and disintegrated that the round fire pit is the only "floor feature" that could be distinguished; it is 2 feet in diameter, 5 inches deep, lined and coped with stones and adobe, and filled with white ashes. Whether or not a deflector or a sipapu (ceremonial opening) had ever been present cannot be determined. The ventilator opening sets 2 inches above the floor and is unusually small (11 inches high by 9 inches wide). Its edges are neatly rounded off with adobe, and it has a little step or sill made from a stone slab projecting 3 inches into the room. The vertical shaft rises directly behind the kiva wall, its inner side being the outer side of the latter. It is circular, 12 inches in diameter, and is broken away some distance below its former outlet.

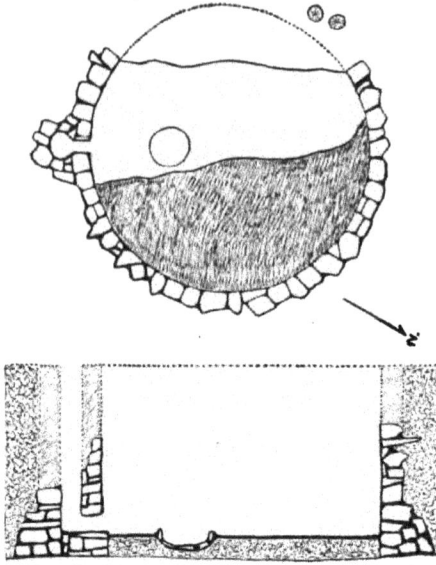

FIG. 5.—Plan and section of Kiva I, Ruin 2.

No trace of roofing remains, but in clearing the floor we found a layer of charcoal and lumps of hard-baked adobe that probably had come from the burned roof. Over this there was a deposit 2 to 3 feet thick, composed of light rubbish—corn husks, cobs, fragments of string, worn-out sandals, feathers, and bits of wood. All this seems to have been blown into the kiva after desertion and gradually bedded down, though it is possible that it was thrown in while the house was still in use and the kiva burned and abandoned. We found nothing above the charcoal layer, however, too heavy to have been blown in.

Kiva II (fig. 6), diameter 12 feet, is, with the exception of the floor, in a better state of preservation than Kiva I. The walls, having been less sand-scoured, still retain some of their original adobe plaster. The points of interest are: The incorporation of large vertically placed sandstone slabs in the masonry of the lower part of the wall (indicated on plan); the presence of some slight evidence as to the method of roofing; and a recess on the north side opposite the ventilating flue.

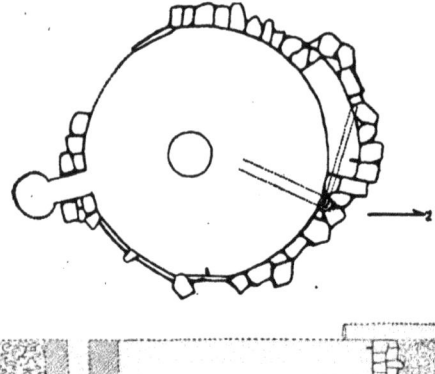

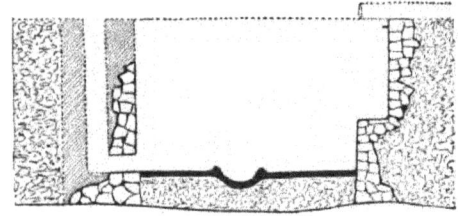

FIG. 6.—Plan and section of Kiva II, Ruin 2.

The roof, as in Kiva I, had been entirely burned away, and much charcoal littered the broken and crushed adobe floor. Near the east end of the niche, however, there is an upright post incorporated in the wall. It is charred wherever it protrudes from the adobe plaster; but its top, 6 feet above the floor, is cut squarely off, and in the adobe surrounding it is the mark or cast of the end of a horizontal beam, 10 inches through, which must have crossed the room from southwest to northeast (fig. 6). Another mark above this one shows a smaller beam to have spanned the niche obliquely to its center. This evidence is slender enough, but the roofing of kivas is a point of considerable interest and importance. The top of the wall at other parts of the kiva is unfortunately so ruined that the termination-sockets of these rafters cannot be found.

The niche is 5½ feet long, 1½ feet deep, and 2 feet 7 inches above the floor. It is flagged with sandstone slabs, and the corners and angles are neatly rounded off with adobe. The burnt end of a peg protrudes from its back wall at the east end near the top.

In this kiva, again, the floor was so much broken that no trace of a deflector or a sipapu (if they ever were present) could be found. The fire pit occupies its usual place, near the middle of the floor. The ventilator entrance is again small (10 inches high by 15 inches wide); the vertical shaft is completely destroyed.

It should be noted that in each of these kivas the ventilator opens from the south side rather than directly toward the mouth of the cave.

Aside from the two kivas and remnants of some wattlework walls there was little of architectural interest. The small rooms ranged about the sides of the cave were much ruined, had lost their roofs by fire, and because of their small size and irregular floors appear to have been little more than storage places. The walls of the two chambers at the back were, however, heavily smoked, and in one of them were found parts of a large rush mat (see pl. 44, *f*), much like the bed-mats of the modern pueblos, so that it seems probable that these rooms were used for sleeping.

The principal living place of the people, then, appears to have been the open central and rear quarters of the cave behind the kivas. The cave floor runs up and back in three or four natural terraces, which have been emphasized by low retaining walls of brush and stone. On these terraces there was a thin accumulation, seldom more than 1 foot to 18 inches deep, the débris of occupation, composed of corn refuse, leaves, twigs, potsherds, and worn-out utensils of various sorts. At the back of the cave there was found a bed of white wood ashes roughly 4 feet square and 4 inches to 6 inches deep; above it the roof was much smoked. A double mealing bin of sandstone slabs lay just behind the ashes; the metates had been removed. Near by was an adobe-lined pot-shaped storage hole 18 inches deep.

Only the buried lower parts of the brush walls remain, the tops having been burned off even with the ground level. The two lower ones just back of the kivas are simple affairs, composed of oak brush and twigs broken from the bushes and stuck into the floor of the cave. Their height is now about 1 foot and from the size of the twigs could never have been more than 3 feet. The leaves on the brush, though of course dry, are still green. The upper wall is more pretentious; it is made of pairs of stakes set 2 feet apart (2 inches between the stakes in the pairs) and filled with bundles of grass, cedar bark, and oak brush, all laid horizontally and tied in at intervals with yucca leaves. These walls were not mudded up as were the true "wattle-and-daub" constructions of other regions, but were reinforced and backed on their upper sides with stone slabs. (See fig. 4.)

Although the débris of occupancy in this ruin was neither extensive nor deep, several interesting finds were made. A considerable number of light objects were found in Kiva I, a few in Kiva II; the majority of the specimens, however, were taken from the open terraced spaces in the body of the cave. Pottery vessels were here discovered as follows: At *a*, figure 3, lying below the light accumulation of rubbish and covered with a flat piece of sandstone, was a small red jar about half full of squash seeds and kernels of corn, most perfectly preserved and appearing as fresh as if harvested within the year. This was probably a seed-cache (see pl. 34, *c*). At *b*, *c*, and *d*, respectively, were found three large gray-ware ollas, each one empty and covered with a sandstone slab; at *e* and *f* were large jars of black-and-white ware, also covered with rough stone lids. All these vessels were so sunk in holes pecked into the soft, shaly cave floor that their tops were just level with the ancient living surface. All of them were cracked or otherwise damaged, crudely mended with gum and reinforced with ligatures of yucca string, and finally set in the floor, doubtless for use as storage vessels.[1] The little red jar had clearly been overlooked at the time of the abandonment, but the larger pieces, too frail for transportation, had evidently been emptied of their contents and deliberately left behind. At *g*, just outside one of the rooms and beneath 8 inches of closely packed rubbish, lay a cap of yucca yarn. (See pl. 34, *a*.)

OTHER SITES AT SAYODNEECHEE

Mound.—A third of a mile below Ruin 2 a small side-canyon enters from the east. In it lies a one-room cliff-house and a mound of the same type as the one noticed near Ruin 1. (See fig. 1.) The

---

[1] See section 2 for description of these jars (pl. 53).

mound is irregularly circular, about 100 feet in diameter, 4 feet high at the center, and becomes thinner toward the peripheries. We trenched this deposit thoroughly and found it to be composed of dark earth full of potsherds, charcoal, and fragments of animal bones. Through it, here and there, are distinct lenses of white ash about 1 inch thick and of varying size; between the lenses (vertically) are layers of clean sand or dark mound earth. At a depth of 4 feet 6 inches beneath the surface, at the middle, the undisturbed red soil was encountered.

Superficially and in cross-section (the ash-lenses excepted) this mound, like that near Ruin 1, has exactly the appearance of the burial mounds of Alkali Ridge.[1] No skeletons, scattered or burnt human bones, or other indications of burials could be found. We have observed mounds of this type in the vicinity of Kayenta, in Sagi Canyon and its branches, in Sagiotsosi, the lower part of Laguna Creek, and in the Chinlee. They are almost always built in open and exposed situations, usually at or near the mouths of canyons. We have never seen remains of stone houses, either walls or building stones, upon any of them, although the two here described are the only ones in which we have gone below the surface.

Mr. John Wetherill, of Kayenta, whose knowledge of the ruins of the San Juan drainage is equaled only by that of his brother Clayton, believes these mounds to have been the sites of adobe houses similar to those described by Cummings from Nitsi Canyon.[2] We found, however, no trace at all of adobe walls, floors, or fireplaces, and it is scarcely conceivable that such remains should have entirely disappeared without even leaving red streaks in the earth. At the very old adobe ruin of Agua Fria near Santa Fe, New Mexico, where no sign of the building can be observed above ground, the interior of the mound contains walls and floors in almost perfect preservation. Another instance of the lasting qualities of adobe is shown in Professor Cummings's description of a ruin at Moab, Utah, where adobe walls and floor were discovered in a mound containing pottery of a very crude and presumably ancient type.[3] We are inclined to believe, therefore, that these mounds were summer residences of the cliff-dwelling people, where they lived in perishable brush houses like the Navaho summer shelters of to-day. If this were the case, the layers of sand between the ash-lenses might be attributed to winter storms. The pottery of the Sayodneechee mound and of the mound near Ruin 1 is identical with that of the near-by cliff-ruins.

Cliff-house.—One hundred yards from the mound there is a one-room house in a little cave at the ground level. Its walls had originally reached the roof of the cave, but are now much broken down, and the room was full of drift sand and the accumulated refuse of

---

[1] Kidder, 1910, p. 356.   [2] Cummings, 1910, p. 27.   [3] Cummings, ibid., p. 18.

countless rats' nests. A wooden slab, an incised flat stone, and a few potsherds were the only artifacts found. Smoke stains on the cave roof and the presence of a number of animal bones in the refuse behind the rear wall seem to show that this house had been a living place rather than a granary. On the cliff a few yards farther up the canyon were pictographs of serpents, a mountain sheep, and numerous handprints, all done in white paint. (See pl. 95, a.)

Watchtower (?) (see fig. 1).—Watchtowers, so common in the Mc-Elmo, Mesa Verde, and Montezuma Creek regions, seem to be rare in the Monuments district. A possible one was found, however, on the top of the southernmost of three high buttes that rise from the mesa opposite Ruin 2. A photograph taken from the Ruin 2 cave (pl. 7) shows these buttes and gives also a good idea of the broken character of the country. The place was chanced upon while we were searching for a vantage point from which to secure a panoramic photograph of the valley. The top of the butte is flat, the sides for the last 40 feet precipitous or even overhanging, and the summit attained only by a difficult scramble of 10 or 15 feet up a crack in the rocks. Although the site would seem to have been quite safe from attack without any fortification, low walls of rough slabs were built on each side of the entryway (fig. 7), perhaps to give protection from arrows. The lookout proper, if such it was, is a little round structure, 4 feet 6 inches in diameter, backed up against a jut of the rock. Its walls are 20 inches thick, made of rough stones piled on each other without mortar; they now stand 18 inches high, and from the small amount of fallen stones can never have exceeded 2 feet (pl. 6, c). The opening, or doorway, faces northwest. There had evidently never been a roof, the low walls having served merely as a windbreak. In the enclosure were a couple of inches of blown sand and a few rocks from the walls. A careful search of the whole summit revealed only a few quartz chips and a single plain gray potsherd.

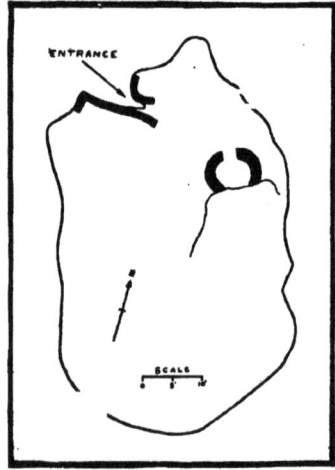

FIG. 7.—Plan of watchtower.

This structure was probably either a lookout place or a shrine. It would have answered admirably for the former purpose, as it commands an unparalleled view out over the whole region and is quite impregnable. On the other hand, the tendency of the ancient people of the Southwest to select elevated sites for their shrines is well known, and a low circular wall seems to have been a favorite type of shrine enclosure. No trace of offerings could be found, but these might well have been perishable objects, such as feathers, sticks, or carved wooden images.

SAYODNEECHEE BURIAL CAVE

On the same side of the canyon as the "watchtower" and nearly opposite Ruin 2, there is a deep, narrow cave (see fig. 1). It lies at the foot of a high cliff at the level of the valley bottom and its mouth is almost hidden from view by a large dune of blown sand. No evi-

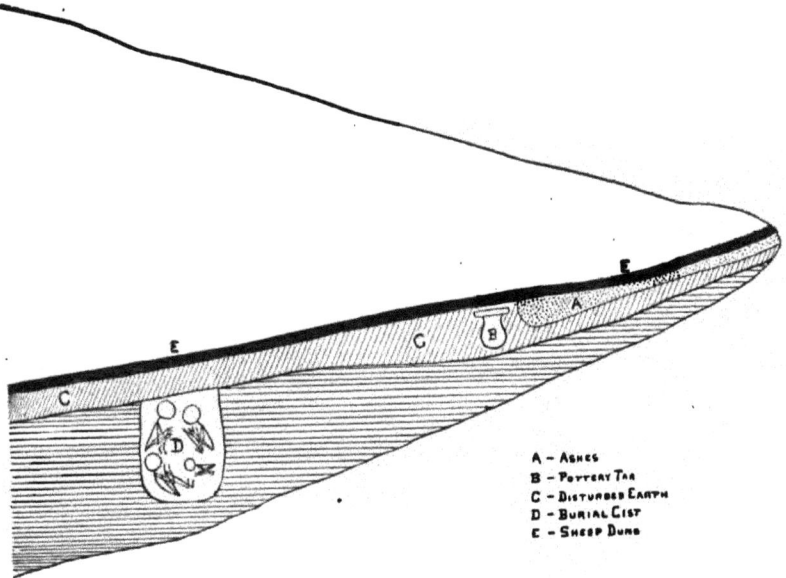

A – ASHES
B – POTTERY JAR
C – DISTURBED EARTH
D – BURIAL CIST
E – SHEEP DUNG

FIG. 8.—Section of cave, Sayodneechee.

dence of occupancy appeared on the surface, but the roof was much smoked and a fragment of a burnt human jaw was picked up by one of the party at the rear of the cave; these signs led us to excavate. The cave had evidently been used for a long time by the Navaho for a sheep corral, as the surface is covered with a closely compacted layer of dung, 3 to 4 inches thick (fig. 8). Below this lies a stratum, 1 foot to 18 inches thick, of disturbed soft, red, sandy earth (probably sloughage from the cave roof) mixed with charcoal, decayed organic material, a few corncobs and animal bones, and a very few coiled and gray potsherds. Below this is the hardpan extending to an undetermined depth and composed of red earth so homogeneous and compact that it could be shoveled only with difficulty.

It was here that the burials were found. They lay in jar-shaped
cavities dug in the hardpan, which was so solid that there had been
no need of strengthening or lining the cists beyond the introduction
of a few stone slabs along their lower sides. The digging had been
done with sharp-pointed implements that had left their marks on the
sides of the holes.

Cist A (fig. 9), the nearest to the front of the cave, was 3 feet
6 inches deep, 3 feet wide, 4 feet long, and had a flat bottom. In it
were seven skeletons—four adults and three children. Skeleton 1
was the topmost, an adult female, flexed on the left side and covered
with rotted textile fabric, a bit of which we preserved in paraffin.
About the neck was a string of hemispherical stone beads. No. 2, a

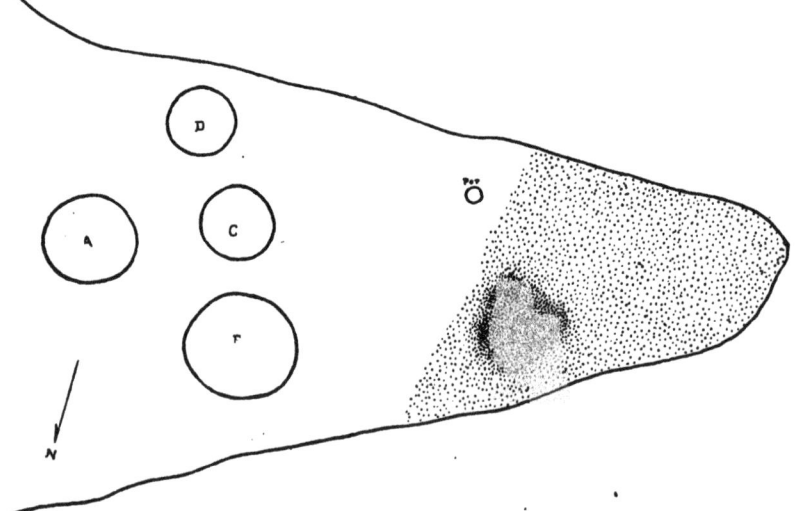

Fig. 9.—Plan of cave, Sayodneechee.   Scale : ¼ inch=5 feet.

very large adult male, lay close under No. 1, flexed on the right side.
On the left pelvic bone there was a part of a twined bag that had
formed a portion of the wrapping; this also was preserved in paraffin.
The skeleton itself was too much decayed for removal. No. 3, an
adult of doubtful sex, was flexed on the left side partly underlying
No. 2. A bowl-shaped basket, greatly decayed, was inverted over the
head, and a string of dark beads with a few green beads as a pendant (see pl. 70, *l*) was about the neck. At the hips was a deposit of five
chipped points, and at the side of the head were small plates of shell
perforated for suspension. The skeleton was badly rotted, but the
skull, which was not in contact with the bones of other skeletons, was
in good condition. In front of the face of skeleton 2, and therefore
just below the hips of No. 1 and over the elbows of No. 3, were the

much decayed remains of an infant of about one year. Near the head, but in exactly what position could not be determined, were some small cylindrical beads of asphaltite. Skeleton 5, an adult female in a bad state of preservation, was directly below No. 2, and therefore side by side with No. 3. It was flexed on the right side, with the head under the pelvis of No. 2. Remnants of baskets could be seen over the knees and under the hips. Among the ribs and just above the pelvis of this body were the bones of a very young child, probably unborn. Skeletons 6 and 7 were young children; No. 6 with its head on the pelvis of No. 5; No. 7 with its head at the sternum of No. 5. Under the chin of No. 6 were a pendant of greenstone and one of abalone shell, and a quantity of olivella shells.

Cist B was found 4 feet behind Cist A, and a little to one side of it. While its structure was exactly the same and it was only a little larger (4 feet 6 inches deep by 4 feet in diameter), it contained the skeletons of no fewer than 19 individuals—8 adults and 11 children, under 5 years of age. There is no possibility of this remarkable deposit having been an ossuary, or repository for bones stripped of their flesh, for all the skeletons lay in order (pl. 8, *a*). It appeared to us that the cist must have been filled at one time, perhaps to hold the dead from some particularly virulent epidemic. The bodies could hardly have been packed in so tightly, and yet show so little disturbance, if they had been put in one by one and the cist closed up between times. An example of a later interment was found in Cist C, and in that case the evidence was quite clear (see below). No signs of violence, no crushed or cut skulls, no bones apparently broken before death, were noted; a massacre theory seems untenable.

The bodies were all tightly flexed and packed in together in all kinds of positions. Great pressure seems to have been exerted in cramming them down. All the skeletons were badly decayed and so fragile that few complete crania could be recovered. Those at the bottom of the pit were much more poorly preserved than those near the top; this was not due, we think, to greater age of these skeletons, but to the decomposing effect of the bodies above them. It was noticed in Cist A that the skeletons were most badly rotted where they came in contact with others; those in Cists C and D, on the other hand, which were not crowded and did not touch one another, were excellently preserved, some so well that portions of the hair and tendons still adhered to the bones.

The remains in Cist B lay in fine red earth which was so loose that the skeletons would not hold together, but had to be removed bone by bone; this, and the fact that they were so tightly packed and so decayed, precluded the possibility of recording the exact position of each body.

With almost every skeleton could be made out traces of baskets, a few fragments of which were recovered; they appeared to have been laid over the hips and heads, sometimes below the back. Bits of textile fabric were also paraffined and are of interest for comparison with those found in the cliff-houses. With many of the skeletons were beads of stone, shell, or bone, most of these occurring near the necks; the percentage of such ornaments was much higher with the bodies of children than with those of adults. Two groups of small objects were found. One, from just below the shoulders of a large adult male (or perhaps on the breast of another skeleton lying directly underneath), consisted of 13 chipped points, several smooth pebbles, a bone whistle, and a few small beads; there were also parts of the jaws of two prairie dogs (?) and a lump of red ochre. The whole seemed to have been inclosed in a skin pouch, portions of which could be seen in the earth. The second lot came from the back of the skull of an elderly male; in it were chipped points, a bone whistle, a stone pipe, olivella shell beads, and a gray substance which appears to be meal. This material may also have been in a bag, though no traces of a bag remained; a rotted basket of indeterminate shape, found in contact with the objects, may perhaps have been the container.

At the top of Cist B, above the highest of the burials, there was a pocket of burned human bones, broken up in small pieces. They were apparently the remains of a single adult. In the flattish bottom of the cist there was a circular depression 1 foot 5 inches across and 10 inches deep (pl. 9). Wedged down in this, but of course more than filling it, was the much rotted skeleton of an elderly . female, lying in a flexed position with the face down. In the bottom of the depression, under the body, lay a round, flat cake of an earthy yellow substance. This had been made by grinding ochreous sandstone, mixing it with a little clay for a binder, and molding it into its present form. Faint finger marks may be seen on its surface. Diameter, about 6 inches; thickness, 3 inches. The cake is shown in situ in plate 9.

Cist C (pl. 8, *b*, left side of picture) was 4 feet deep and 2 feet 8 inches in diameter. Like A and B, the pit was roughly jar-shaped and had been cut down into the hard, homogeneous cave-earth with a digging tool, the marks of which, in the form of vertical grooves, were visible all about the sides. In this cist there were no stone slabs about the bottom. The filling around the bodies was soft, fine, red earth such as may be produced by crumbling the hardpan. Skeletons 1 and 2 were adults; No. 1 was in a semireclining position with the head against the east side of the cist (this is the skeleton which appears in pl. 8, *b*); the knees were drawn up, but the flexion was less

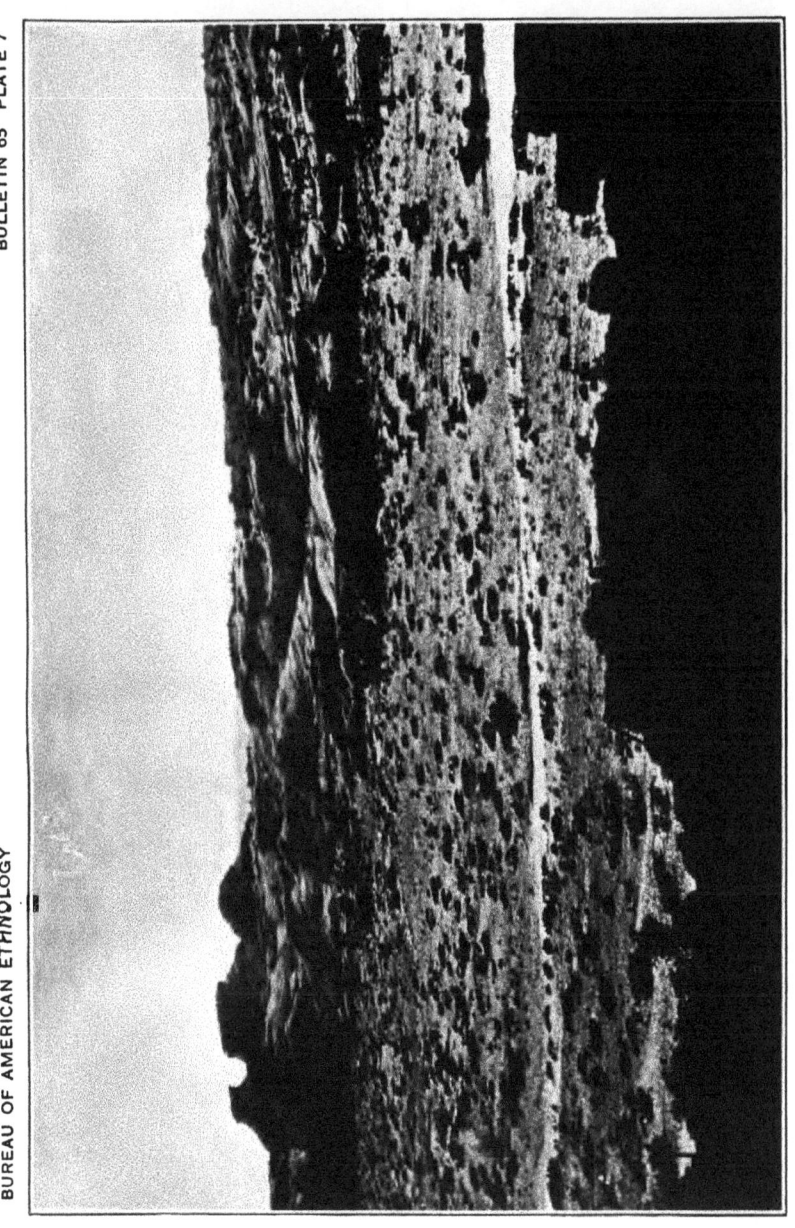

WATCHTOWER BUTTE FROM RUIN 2

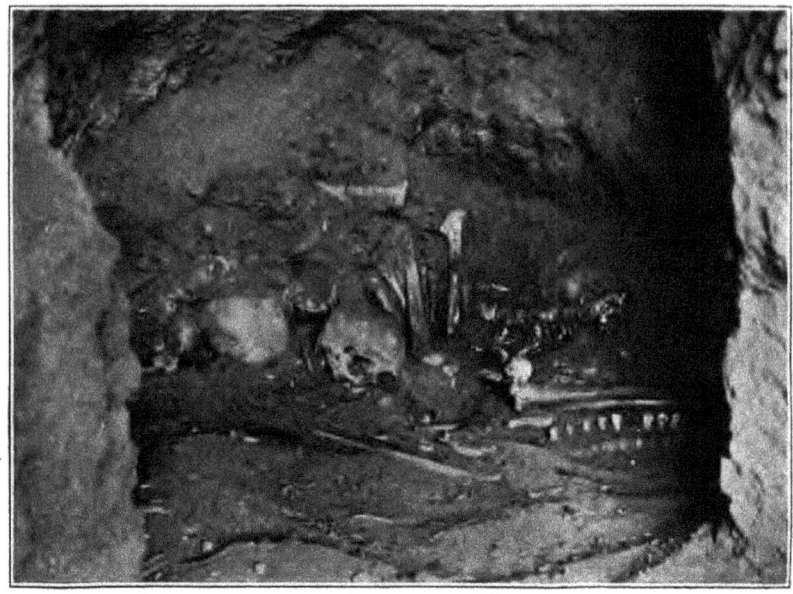

a. CIST B, PARTLY CLEARED

b. CISTS B AND C

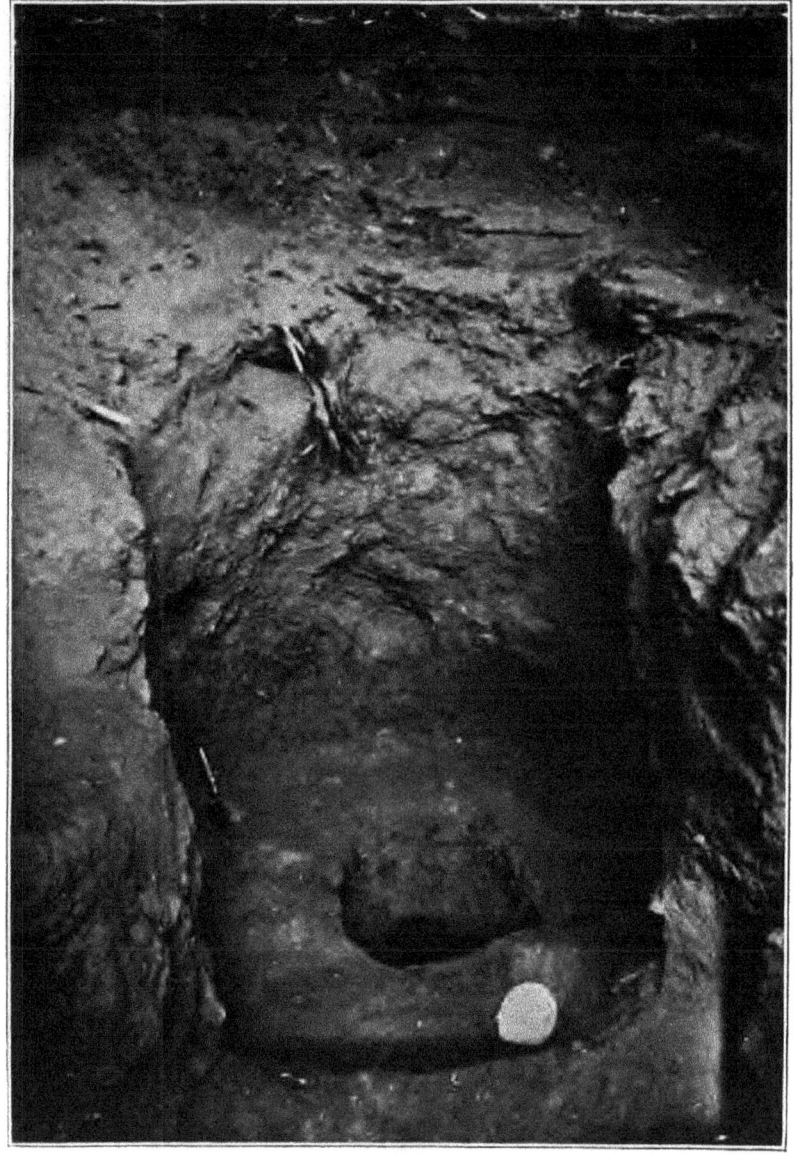

CIST B, CLEARED

a. RUIN 4

b. HAND PRINTS IN RUIN 4

than in the other burials. No. 2, beside it, was in an almost identical attitude, but had the head against the back wall of the pit. Under No. 1 lay the head of No. 3, also an adult; this skeleton, as well as No. 4 (an infant), had been disturbed and pushed against the north side of the cist. Some of the bones were in natural order, others were mixed and disarranged; the infant skeleton was almost entirely disarticulated. These two bodies had evidently been the primary burials and had originally occupied the lower central part of the cist; when the other two (Nos. 1 and 2) were interred they pushed aside and crowded down the original burials. Scattered among the bones of Nos. 3 and 4 were 50 or 60 olivella-shell beads. Each of the four bodies had been accompanied with one or more baskets.

Cist D was the smallest of the four. It measured 2 feet 6 inches at its point of greatest diameter, and was 3 feet 6 inches deep. It had three stone slabs against the lower sides, and showed the usual vertical pick-marks. In it were the skeletons of two children—No. 1 flexed on the back, and having at the neck a small loaf-shaped stone, afterwards identified as an atlatl weight (see p. 180 and pl. 83, c); No. 2, which lay flexed and face down, had at the chin two beads of abalone shell and one of satin spar. Baskets had been used to cover these bodies, but, as in the other cists, they were completely decayed.

No further burial places were found, although the rest of the cave was cleared to hardpan. As over the cist zone, there was also over the whole rear of the cave a layer of disturbed dark soil containing charcoal, animal bones, some corncobs, and a few potsherds, principally corrugated, one black and white. Nine feet behind the cists, and with its top just below the crust of sheep dung, was found a jar of rough dark ware, bearing broad, flat coils at the neck; it had been cracked and mended with piñon gum, and the neck bound, for greater strength, with yucca leaves. The cover, a rough sandstone slab, was in place, but the vessel was empty. Close by was a hole in the dark soil, presumably dug to hold another jar.

The last 10 or 12 feet at the back of the cave were covered, below the sheep dung, by a layer of ashes very uniformly a foot thick (see fig. 8, a). This ash bed was somewhat puzzling, as it was so evenly laid down and extended so far back into the cave and so far under the sloping sides that it seemed scarcely possible that it could be lying as deposited. While there were no defined fireplaces in it, the layer was somewhat thicker and heavier toward the front on the north side (see fig. 9); possibly the fires were made at this point and the ashes were redistributed by wind. The roof of the cave is heavily smoked above the whole bed. The ashes contained one or two potsherds (none were in the disturbed layer below the ash bed), a small coiled basket lacking the bottom, and several pieces of burned human bones; among the latter were a fragment of a jaw and the head of a large femur. As there were a number of rat holes in the hardpan about the cists, we believed at first that these bones had been brought up by rats from the pocket of cremated remains above Cist B; but as that pocket seems to have contained the remains of only one individual, and as the bit of jaw (left side and part of the ascending ramus) is duplicated in the fragments from the pocket, we reached the conclusion that the two lots were not directly related. Perhaps the cave was used as a crematory at a time subsequent to the building of the cists; if such was the case, the Cist B pocket may not have been synchronous with the inhumations below it. Chemical analysis of the ashes, to see if they contain bone residue, may throw light on the question.

The method of burial observed in this cave, the natural or undeformed condition of the crania, and the nature of the mortuary offerings, all present features foreign to the normal cliff-house culture of the region. The only objects of cliff-house make found were the storage jar and the few potsherds. The former was buried in the disturbed earth layer (see fig. 8), its bottom not reaching the hardpan; the latter all came from the upper parts of the disturbed earth and from the ashes, none from the disturbed earth below the ashes, and none from in or about the burial cists. Aside from the pottery, the finds in this cave agree very closely with those made in Grand Gulch, Utah, by the Wetherill brothers and assigned by them to an older culture which they named " Basket Maker."[1] The question of the cultural affinities of the Sayodneechee cave remains will be more fully discussed in Section III.

RUIN 3 (FIRESTICK HOUSE)

Ruins 3 and 4 are situated in a short, deep canyon entering the main valley from the east, a little way below Ruin 1 (see fig. 1). As water could not be obtained in this branch, we pitched our camp by a Navaho sheep reservoir in another canyon a mile below.

Ruin 3, " Firestick House," as we called it, has a magnificent setting. It lies in an enormous cave at the head of a small box canyon with walls rising absolutely sheer to a height of 250 feet. The cave itself is sculptured on colossal lines; it is a great hollow in the cliffs, with a narrow shelf running along its rear part, some 70 feet above the valley bottom; on this ledge is perched the ruin (fig. 10). The last climb of 30 feet to the houses is perpendicular, and we accomplished it only after much labor, by hauling two logs over the steep slopes below, lashing them together, and raising them with ropes until the topmost could be lodged in a crack of the ruin ledge. The

---

[1] See Pepper, 1902.

ancient people used for an entryway a vertical fissure at the north end, up which there was pecked a series of shallow foot and hand holds. From the top of the fissure to the first of the rooms, footholes had been cut along an unpleasantly tilted and crumbly ledge 18 inches wide, with a 30-foot drop and a 70-foot slide below. Before guying up our poles directly into the rooms, we had climbed to the top of the fissure and attempted the ledge. We found, however, that the ancient steps were too much worn down and shallowed by sand erosion for us to use. It was evident that no one had entered this cliff-house since its abandonment as a dwelling place, although two or three little granary rooms on the lower benches had been used by the Navaho as caches.

FIG. 10.—Ruin 3.

Once in the ruin, we found it to consist of a single line of 10 living rooms with a continuous front wall, built flush with the edge of the cliff. The back part of the cave slants up too steeply to have been available for buildings (fig. 11). There is no kiva, nor could we find any trace of one in the valley below. The rooms are of two quite distinct types: at the southern end come four chambers built of the usual adobe-laid masonry of the region, each having one or more doorways and each having once undoubtedly been roofed; beyond these the rooms are somewhat larger and have walls varying from 18 to 28 inches thick, made of large irregular slabs of sandstone piled up without mortar and depending for stability entirely on their weight. At present the walls at the south end of the line average

3 to 4 feet high, nor were they ever, apparently, much higher; at the north end they are much broken down. There were no doors in the series of rough-walled rooms. These doorless inclosures were seemingly never roofed over, and were probably outdoor living rooms, used in preference to the open cave space in order to have a level floor and to afford protection from the wind.

The two bits of wall on the upper level at the rear were attempts at terracing abandoned before completion. Behind the southern one there is an empty metate bin of stone slabs.

The only features of architectural interest are furnished by the more carefully built tier of four rooms. The first three of these are large enough for habitation; the fourth, a little closetlike chamber, was used presumably for storage purposes. Each of the first

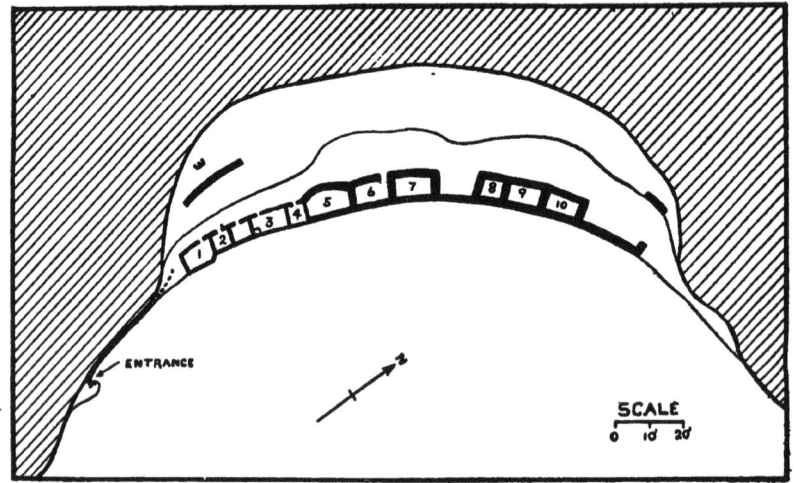

Fig. 11.—Plan of Ruin 3.

three has two doorways opening upon the narrow passageway between the rooms and the rock ledge behind; in room 1 and room 3 one of the two doors is sealed up with masonry; in room 2 both are open. The purpose of so many entrances is rather puzzling, but may perhaps be explained by the presence in room 2 of traces of an adobe wall which once divided it into two small square apartments. This wall had evidently been removed before the house was abandoned, but both doors were left open. In the other two rooms there were probably also such partitions cutting the chambers in two and necessitating double entrances; when the partitions were taken out one of the useless apertures was closed. The doorways themselves are in excellent preservation, differing from each other only in very minor details of measurement, and are typical of the doors of all the ruins examined.[1] The average of the six·belonging to rooms 1, 2, and 3 is 23 inches high by 17 inches wide. For sills, slabs of sandstone were used. The jambs are rounded off with adobe and the lintels are double; an overlintel of stone with a wooden lintel of slim oak or cedar rods set 1 inch below it (fig. 12). Stone slabs do not seem to have been used to close these doors, as there is neither recessing of the jambs to receive them[2] nor any sign of staples to hold them in place (cf. Cummings, 1910, p. 23). The doorway in room 4, very considerably smaller (18 by 13 inches), was of similar construction.

Evidence as to roofing was very meager; no beams were found either in place or in the refuse. It was quite evident that this building was not destroyed by fire, nor could the beams have rotted away. We must therefore conclude, as in the case of Ruin 1 and many other cliff-dwellings, that the beams were removed by the owners when the house was abandoned, or by other house-building people of ancient times who did not wish to undertake the labor of cutting and shaping new ones. The Navaho's well-known dread of ruins of habitations is quite sufficient to acquit them of any hand in the matter.[3] In each short wall of room 2 are four 3-inch beam sockets, and along

FIG. 12.—Doorway in Ruin 3.

the long walls at about 2-foot intervals are holes for the reception of smaller cross sticks. These are at a height of only 4 feet from the floor, making the apartment a very low-studded one. In room 3, although the outer wall stands to a height of nearly 6 feet, the beam rests are not visible. The southeast corner of room 3 was occupied by an ash bed, and the adjacent walls showed so much smoking that, although there was no pit or inclosed space, it was evidently the location of a regularly used fireplace. In the outer wall at this point and at the level of the floor is a draft or ventilating hole, 6 inches in diameter.[4]

There was very little rubbish in the cave, either in the open passageway between the line of the rooms and the rock ledge behind or

---

[1] No tau-shaped doors were seen in any of the ruins examined during the summer, nor have any such as yet been reported from the region by Fewkes or Cummings.

[2] See pl. 12, a, a doorway in Ruin 6.

[3] This question of the presence or absence of beams may eventually help us in a minor way to determine the sequence of houses in a given locality.

[4] Not before recorded for cliff-dwellings, but found at Puyé and Tyuonyi, northwest of Santa Fe, N. Mex.

in the chambers themselves. This is perhaps to be accounted for by the fact that the rooms were built directly on the edge of the cliff, so that a convenient dumping place was immediately at hand, and also because no terracing work was done. Open terraced spaces in cliff-houses usually seem to have been filled gradually with débris of occupancy rather than by deliberate grading with sand or adobe. The passageway and each room contained a few inches to a foot of rubbish, and over this a heavy layer of slough from the cave roof, stones from the walls, and sand blown up from the valley bottom. Objects found in the central and northern rooms were rather badly decayed as the result of a slight seepage of water from the back of the cave. The floor of room 1 was covered to a depth of 14 inches with corncobs, in all about two barrelfuls. They were all fresh, clean, and evidently lay just as thrown after the kernels had been removed. Many of them had bits of stick inserted in their butts, and there were a few pairs of cobs fastened together butt to butt on single sticks (see pl. 34, d). The ruin received the name " Firestick House " from a fire-making outfit, drill and hearth, found tied together as if for traveling (see pl. 50, f). It came from the next to the last room at the north end. All the other objects collected were taken from the rubbish in the rooms and passageway, nothing being found in the bare back slopes of the cave.[1]

RUIN 4 (PICTOGRAPH CAVE)

A third of a mile below Firestick House there is a little group of rooms built against the cliff (pl. 10, a); they are partly overhung by a 200-foot precipice and partly sheltered from storms by a great shoulder of rock. For some distance on each side of them the cliff is covered with hundreds of pictographs: ancient ones, some painted in white, some pecked into the soft sandstone; and modern charcoal and scratched drawings of the Navaho. These were really the most interesting feature of Ruin 4, called by us " Pictograph Cave." The painted examples were of two styles—large, square-shouldered human figures with peculiar headdresses; and handprints, many hundreds of them, of all sizes, from those of babies up (pl. 10, b; see also pls. 96, 97, and figs. 100, 101). There are single rights, single lefts, and pairs; the majority are in white paint, a few in red. All but a dozen or so stenciled ones were made by dipping the hand in liquid paint and slapping it against the smooth rock. The large human figures occupy flat places on the cave walls, and because of their more exposed situation are rather badly weathered. The highest of them are 15 feet above the present ground level, and as there is no

---

[1] The exact locations of all specimens may be found in the Peabody Museum catalogue.

evidence of rooms ever having been built below them, they would seem to have been made by people standing on poles or scaffolding.

Our exploration commenced with a series of test pits sunk through a top layer of sheep dung, deposited by Navaho flocks that had evidently sheltered here through many winters; they revealed turkey droppings, potsherds, and other rubbish typical of cliff-dweller occupancy. Excavations were accordingly begun behind a pile of huge bowlders and were continued at various points along the cliff and in the rooms themselves (fig. 13).

The rooms now standing form a little cluster at the western end; they are of the usual rough masonry of such houses and offer nothing of architectural interest. It was noted, however, that the painted handprints extended underneath the walls where they abutted against the cliff, proving that they were made before the building of the rooms. The roofs have entirely disappeared. On and under the

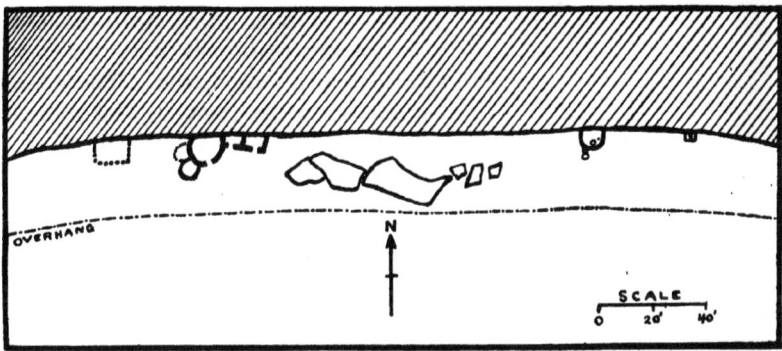

Fig. 13.—Plan of Ruin 4.

floors, all about outside and along the cliff behind the fallen rocks, there was a layer of débris varying in depth from a few inches to 2 feet. Although this deposit was dry and in good condition for the preservation of specimens, it yielded a rather small quantity of material. In it was an unusually large quantity of turkey droppings and turkey feathers, as well as a number of animal bones. A wooden skinning knife (see pl. 49, *l*), bloodstained about the end, and a yucca sandal in process of manufacture (see pl. 37, *b*), were the most interesting finds. From just below the sheep-dung layer near the rooms there were taken a fragment of a leather moccasin and a small bow, the latter apparently whittled out with a metal knife; these two objects are presumably of Navaho origin.

To the east of the pile of large rocks the rubbish practically terminated, appearing again here and there in small pockets. In this direction, 115 feet from the house cluster, was discovered a kiva; it lay entirely below ground, backed up against the cliff wall, and was not visible before excavation, the top of its wall having been hidden under the stratum of sheep dung. It was filled with cave slough and blown sand, and held no débris beyond half a dozen corrugated and red-and-yellow sherds, and a few building stones that had fallen from the upper part of the walls. In shape it is roughly square with well-rounded corners, and its diameter of 7 feet 6 inches makes it the smallest kiva yet recorded (fig. 14). Although the upper parts of the walls had fallen, the floor was excellently preserved. The body of the room and the horizontal passage of the ventilator proved to have been dug out of the solid, undisturbed hardpan at the base of the cliff and simply coated with adobe. The upper wall above the hardpan was of masonry to retain the looser top soil. Over the walls were many thin coats of plaster, each one heavily smoked.

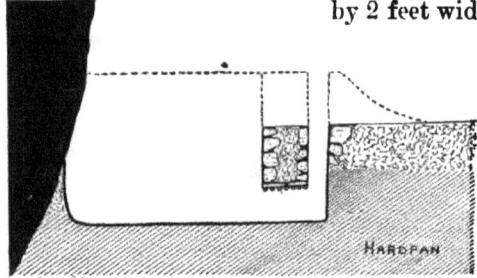

FIG. 14.—Plan and section of kiva, Ruin 4.

Of the typical kiva features there were present in this example the ventilator, fire pit, and sipapu. There is no banquette, nor are there any cubby-holes. The ventilator enters at the floor level through an opening 1 foot 5 inches high by 2 feet wide. The horizontal passage, whose bottom and sides are cut from the hardpan and merely coated with adobe, is roofed with a series of small oak (?) rods, above which are flat slabs of sandstone. Its total length is 2 feet 10 inches. As the ascending shaft runs through the soft upper earth it is inclosed in masonry. At its present top it is 8 inches square. It will be noticed in the plan that the ventilator opens into the kiva near the southwest corner. A more usual position for it would have been in the middle of the south side. The fire pit and sipapu are also arranged in an unusual way. In normal kivas on both the north and the south side of the San Juan a line drawn at right angles out from the center of the ventilator shaft passes first through the center of the fire pit and then through the sipapu. Here, however, the fire pit, instead of occupying its customary position directly in front of the ventilator, is placed well to the eastern side of it. The conventional requirement that ventilator, fire pit, and sipapu shall be in alignment is, however, fulfilled by placing the latter still farther to the east and almost against the side wall. The fire pit has an adobe curbing raised a few inches above the floor, and, as seems to be the invariable rule in all kivas, no matter how they may differ otherwise, it was full of tightly packed white wood ashes. The sipapu is sunk through the adobe floor into the solid hardpan beneath, and its edges are carefully smoothed and rounded off with mud.[1] As was the case in the kivas of Ruin 2, no deflector was in position; by the southwestern side of the fire pit, however, and between it and the ventilator entrance, there were found many fragments of hard-baked adobe bearing the marks of twigs or reeds (see dotted area in fig. 14). These may have been part of the roofing, but as no such fragments were found elsewhere on the kiva floor it may be that they are bits of a deflector built of "wattle-and-daub." The floor at this spot is so much broken that it is impossible to tell whether or not posts to support such a contrivance had been set in it.

No sign of the former height of the roof was afforded by smoking of the overhanging cave wall or by adobe marks, for the erosion by blown sand has effectually removed all such traces. The height of the room could hardly have been less than 6 feet; the walls at present stand 3 feet 10 inches, and as the ground throughout the cave does not seem to have been lowered since the abandonment of the ruin, this kiva appears to have been only semisubterranean.[2] The cave wall at the rear below the ground level is much smoked; this coating extends down behind the rear filling-up wall of the kiva, showing occupancy of this part of the cave previous to the building of the ceremonial room.

Thirty feet eastward from the kiva, and, like it, set against the cliff, there was found a grass-lined hollow 18 inches in diameter and 1 foot deep, surrounded on three sides of a square by a wattled fence. This last was burned off at the old ground level, so that its former height could not be determined. It was suggested by Clayton Wetherill that this might have been a nest for setting turkey hens. He informs us that nests very similar to this one, sometimes containing eggshells, were found by him and his brothers in the Mesa Verde ruins. Although no bits of shell were recovered here, there were some turkey droppings and feathers in and about the inclosure; not more, however, than were found in the general digging throughout the cave.

---

[1] Dimensions: Fire pit, diameter 1 foot 10 inches, depth 8 inches; sipapu, diameter 6 inches, depth 4 inches.

[2] We have seen a kiva in Grand Gulch, with its roof still in place, which is only about one-third subterranean. The upper part of its walls, where they stand clear of the ground, are very roughly finished, and the whole gives the appearance of a tumbled heap of rocks.

In the earth just west of the "nest" was uncovered a small fragment of a human occipital bone. Following this clew we dug extensively all along this part of the cliff in a futile search for burials.

With Pictograph Cave we finished our work in the westernmost of the canyons that run down toward the "Monuments" from the Capitan Plateau. In a country so broken and containing so many ramifying side valleys our survey was necessarily superficial, but that we missed any ruins of considerable size is not likely. There are, however, literally hundreds of caves which were not examined, and it is probable that some of them contain burials, caches, or sand-covered deposits left by people who did not build houses. Such a cave not far from our camp showed no superficial sign of occupancy, but yielded on exploration a number of shallow ash beds containing cracked bones and part of a sandstone metate. There were also picked up in this cave a hank of yucca fiber prepared for spinning, and a small bone lozenge with incised crosshatching on one side; there were no potsherds.

HAGOÉ

Our next move was to Hagoé Canyon, a gorge running roughly parallel to the one we had just left (see fig. 1). Its head is also in the Capitan Plateau, and it ends directly among the "Monuments." Although its source was apparently not more than 2 or 3 miles from our last camping place, as the crow flies, we had to ride 15 miles through the "Monuments" to reach it. The scenery of Hagoé, especially about its lower end, where erosion has been particularly freakish, is as extraordinary as any that can be found in the Southwest. The "Monuments" themselves, shafts, and towers of wind-and-water-sculptured sandstone, guard its entrance (pl. 11, a, b); in its upper reaches the red and gray and yellow cliffs with their sheer faces, rounded domes, and small, high-perched natural bridges are superb beyond any description. The Hagoé Valley is dry and sandy; there are neither running streams nor springs; the few Navaho families who inhabit the region procure their water from tanks and reservoirs in the rocks. We camped by one of these at the head of the canyon. Just below, in a deep bay of the cliffs, partly overhung by the upper strata and well sheltered from the wind, there is a Navaho peach orchard. Its 150 or more trees, heavy with fruit just ripening, seemed surprisingly green and flourishing in so barren a setting. There is evidently an underground seepage of water at this place which the Indians have cleverly held back and concentrated on their trees by means of a series of cross-ridges of earth and rocks. Almost hidden in a cranny above the orchard is a one-room cliff-house. Its interior and its roof (which is supplied by the cave) are heavily smoked. On a smooth rock face at one side is a very large pecked representation of a mountain sheep (see pl. 89, *j*).

RUIN 5 (FLUTEPLAYER HOUSE)

The only ruin of considerable size that we were able to find in Hagoé lies in a cave in a short western branch of the canyon. Its exposure is to the south, and, as is always the case with sheltered caves at the ground level, the whole place was covered with a 3 or 4 inch layer of compact sheep dung, which had to be broken to pieces and moved away before any work could be done. On the rocks on either side of the mouth of the draw where the ruin is situated are most interesting and elaborate series of pecked pictographs (see pl.

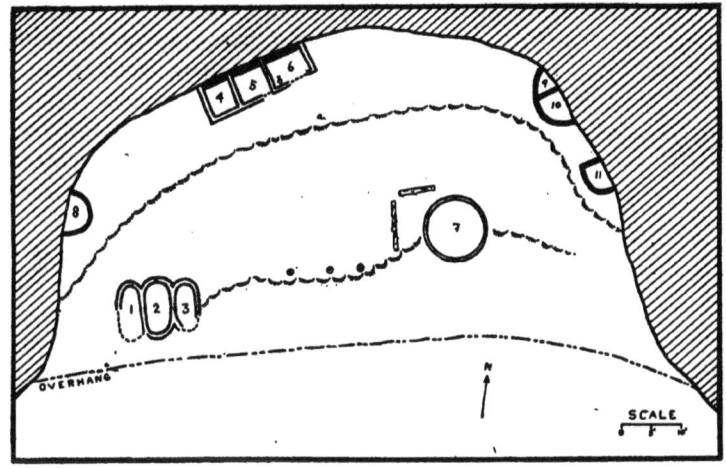

FIG. 15.—Plan of Ruin 5.

93, *b*, and fig. 96). One group consists of hump-backed creatures apparently blowing on musical instruments. These suggested the name "Fluteplayer House" for the ruin itself.

Though not promising at first glance, Fluteplayer House was the most instructive site excavated during the season's work, for it contained clear evidence of two distinct ancient cultures, one superimposed upon the other. The cave that shelters these remains is 100 feet long and 50 feet deep (fig. 15), its floor sloping evenly up from the ground level to the back, a rise of from 15 to 17 feet. A seepage of water from the strata along the back of the cave has wet the lower measures of the culture deposit, and jimson weed and box elders, both of which need some extra degree of moisture, grow about the mouth.

A trench cut into the deposit at almost any part of the cave gives the cross section shown in figure 16. The top layer just under the sheep dung consists of dirt and light, dry rubbish—corn husks, reeds, cedar bark, string, bits of feather and fur cloth, together with many sherds of corrugated, black-and-white, and red-and-yellow wares, all of the Kayenta style. Below this to the cave floor is a thick stratum of earth, containing a great deal of wood ash and charcoal, many animal bones, flint chips, and bone implements. Most, if not all, of the perishable objects in this stratum have disappeared through decay. The potsherds are radically different from those above; we found none coiled or indented, but instead a coarse, plain, black ware that showed either no coiling or a few broad, flat coils about the necks of vessels. With it was much black-and-white ware of surprisingly good quality and elaborately ornamented, but entirely different in all respects from that of Kayenta. (See pls. 63, *b–h*, 64, *e*.) In some places this stratification is vague; in others, notably in the front part of the cave, it is well defined and further accentuated by the intercalation of a thin layer of clean blown sand topped by 1 to 2 inches of unmixed ashes.

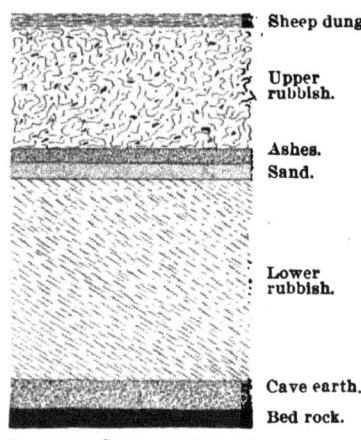

Sheep dung.

Upper rubbish.

Ashes. Sand.

Lower rubbish.

Cave earth. Bed rock.

Fig. 16.—Cross section of deposit in Ruin 5.

The difference in culture is also seen in the house structures. There are four chambers built about the periphery of the cave (walls indicated on the map in solid black), the masonry of which is in no respect different from that usually found in the normal Kayenta cliff-dwellings; this means that it is made of rough blocks and slabs of sandstone laid up with much adobe mortar, the interstices liberally spalled with smaller bits of stone. These four rooms are all set on the solid rock. Their rear walls and roofs were provided by the cave itself. The seven other rooms (light walls on the plan) differ from these very radically. They occur in two groups of three each, with one room lying by itself. One group is set well out toward the front of the cave at a place where the floor slopes up rather steeply. Its three units are oval in shape, or, perhaps more correctly, rectangular with rounded corners. Their walls are now much broken down, but enough is preserved to show that they had been semisubterranean chambers whose rear or uphill ends were completely sunk into the cave deposit, while the front or downhill parts were perhaps exposed to one-half or two-thirds of their height.

The bottoms of the walls are made of large, flat sandstone slabs set on edge in the earth, and the building was carried up by means of adobe "turtlebacks," masses of clay averaging 15 inches long, 5 inches wide, and 3½ inches thick, which were put on wet and pushed and patted down over the series below (fig. 17). An occasional stone was introduced among the adobes; after the structure had dried and settled together the irregularities and cracks were filled and smoothed over with more clay, making a firm, enduring, good-looking wall. These rooms were entirely filled with earth, ashes, and other refuse, the lower levels of which produced pottery of the non-Kayenta type.

The second group of three rooms is built against the back of the cave, a slight ledge of which was evened up with stones and clay to make a low bench at the back of each chamber. In shape they are more nearly rectangular than those in front, but in construction the two assemblages are identical, as the rear rooms are now, and always were, semisubterranean. Large slabs set on edge form the foundations, and the upper parts are of adobe "turtlebacks." No clue could be obtained as to the method of roofing in either group.

 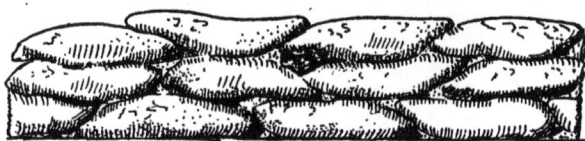

FIG. 17.—Adobe "turtlebacks" in Ruin 5.

The seventh room (fig. 18) stands by itself, both in position and in structure. It is nearly circular,[1] and except for its front part, where, because of the downward slope of the cave floor, the wall probably protruded slightly above ground, was entirely subterranean. It had been dug from the compact hardpan and completed by simply coating the sides of the excavation with plaster. An occasional stone was introduced to fill a chink. The front or south side, where the earth had apparently not been firm enough to serve as a wall, was built up of large stone slabs; presumably its upper portion had been made, as in the rooms just described, of adobe. From the floor the walls rose to a height of 3 feet 6 inches, where they were set back 8 inches, and then rose again for 1½ feet to what was evidently the floor level of the cave at the time of occupancy. The 8-inch offset seemed to have been designed to receive the ends of the roof beams, but as it was less than 4 feet above the floor we were somewhat puzzled as to the method of roofing until we made a more careful examination of the offset and discovered the charred butts of 2 to 3 inch poles driven slantingly into the hardpan at such an angle

---

[1] Dimensions: East and west, 11 feet 7 inches; north and south, 10 feet 9 inches.

that if extended they would meet over the center of the room at
about 6 feet above the floor, forming a flattish conical roof. Over the
poles there had been a layer of reeds and grass, parts of which, completely oxidized, were found adhering to what was left of the rafters.
The middle of the roof was probably slightly above the old ground
level, as indicated in figure 18. A hatchway must have been used for
entrance. At first sight this room had all the appearance of a kiva,
but excavation showed that there was no ventilating apparatus, no
fire pit, sipapu, or any of those features which seem essential to cliff-
dwelling kivas.

FIG. 18.—Round room in Ruin 5.

The logs and the three posts shown in figure 15 form part of a
piece of terracing work, belonging probably to the earlier occupancy.
The culture deposit behind the posts and nearly up to the three
back rooms was the deepest in the cave, but was too moist except
at the top to contain anything but objects of bone, stone, and pottery. The lower levels held, as elsewhere in the cave, the crude
black ware and the unfamiliar style of black-and-white ware; it was
also noticed that there were many more chips of stone and whole
and broken flaked implements in these lower levels than in the upper
rubbish. The percentage of bone implements was also greater; in
particular there were found two bone implements with perforated
butts (see pl. 64, c, d); another was taken from the floor of the round
room.

Just in front of the three rear rooms, and extending all around the back of the cave, is an upper terrace made by a natural rise of the rock. The deposit here is shallow and consists largely of ashes. At *a*, figure 15, we uncovered a coiled and indented olla of the normal cliff-dwelling variety, bound with yucca harness and covered with a flat stone. The covering slab lay directly beneath the sheep-dung layer at the level of the last occupancy. Save for a handful of white powdery substance, it was empty. At *b*, figure 15, on the floor in the corner of the easternmost of the three back rooms was found a bowl made from the bottom of an old olla. Inverted over it, but pushed to one side and crushed down by the pressure of the earth, was a small jar with flat coiling at the neck, containing a large hank of decaying yucca string. The fragments of the upper jar were saved; the bowl was too much rotted to handle. The string, of fine quality, very evenly twisted and apparently more than 100 yards long, was put carefully aside in an attempt to dry it sufficiently for preservation. It was forgotten when we packed the other specimens. The two pieces of pottery were both of the type found in the lower levels; from their position on the floor of the room, their advanced state of decay, and because of the fact that dry rubbish, including a sandal and a pot ring, was found lying directly above them, we believe them to have belonged to the early occupancy.

Room 5 was so full of turkey droppings (in places nearly 2 feet deep) that it seems probable that it was used, presumably by the later inhabitants, as a turkey pen. Room 4 was quite full of dry, well-preserved rubbish, with red-and-yellow and Kayenta black-and-white sherds. Here were found several sandals, bits of cotton cloth, wooden implements, and a problematical object woven of yucca (see fig. 40).

It is unfortunate that none of the rooms of what we have called "normal cliff-dwelling" masonry should have been built directly above the semisubterranean adobe structures which are considered to have belonged to the first occupancy of the cave. If they had been, the relative age of the two would be settled beyond question. The finds in the lower parts of the sunken rooms, as distinguished from those made in their upper parts, agree so closely with the character of the stratification throughout the body of the cave as to leave no doubt in our minds that the sunken rooms were used, partly filled with rubbish, and abandoned, before the erection of the stone-built rooms by the people who made the Kayenta red-and-yellow and black-and-white pottery.

Although some trenching was done at the front of the cave in the hope of finding skeletons, none were discovered.

Ruin 6

A morning's work was sufficient to clear the only other house investigated at Hagoé. It is situated three-quarters of a mile below Fluteplayer House, on the same side of the canyon. The cave that gives it shelter is hollowed from the foot of the cliff at the top of a rocky talus; its outlook is east. There are but four rooms (fig. 19), all of them much ruined., The only one containing rubbish was the southern of the two front chambers; this was probably a kiva, as it has carefully rounded corners, the walls bear several coats of blackened plaster, and there is a small round fire pit in the middle of the floor. No sipapu could be found, while the ventilator, if there ever had been one, has fallen away with the east wall. The rear stands 4 feet high, the bottom 2 feet having been cut from the cave formation and stuccoed up in the same manner as in the kiva of Ruin 4 and the round room of Ruin 5. Room 2, like the two back rooms, had nothing in it but sand and building stones; the doorway of one of the latter (No. 3) was neatly made, having a countersinking worked into the masonry to hold a door slab (pl. 12, a).

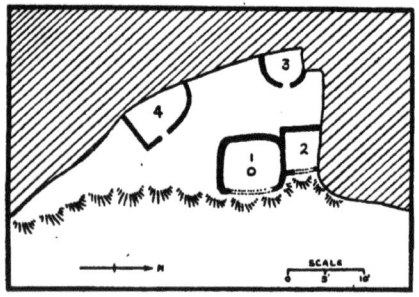

FIG. 19.—Plan of Ruin 6.

Across the side wall of the cave there extends a series of sandal prints, stenciled in white, alternating right foot with left as a man would walk. This series, with some of the many stenciled handprints that also adorn the rock, are shown in plate 92. The pottery was typically Kayenta in style.

Laguna Creek

With the ruins just described our work in Monumental Valley was brought to a close. We desired to investigate a group of caves in the lower part of Hagoé Canyon in which, according to the Navaho, there are signs of ancient occupancy, but we were prevented from so doing by lack of water. It is hoped that we may be able to explore these caves in the near future.

Leaving Monumental Valley, we proceeded to the east, passed a group of canyons which were then being investigated by Professor Cummings, crossed the drainage of Gypsum Wash, and camped at a ruin in the "South Comb" in the Laguna Creek drainage, 7 or 8 miles below Kayenta.

a

b

THE MONUMENTS

a. DOORWAY IN RUIN 6

b. UPPER TIER ROOMS, RUIN 7

The South Comb, a great fault in the sandstone formation, extends from San Juan River to Marsh Pass. To the north, beyond the river, it continues as far as Elk Ridge in San Juan County, Utah, where Comb Wash takes its name from it. It is a long line of sandstone cliffs, abrupt on their western sides, sloping to the east, their jagged and toothed summits readily suggesting the name that has been given them by settlers.

While there are a number of small surface ruins along both sides of the comb from the river up to within 5 miles of Kayenta, its walls in that stretch seem to contain few caves suitable for cliff-dwellings. Water is also very scanty. In 1912 one of the authors rode its whole length on the western side and along a good part of its eastern face without finding any houses, nor does Mr. John Wetherill know of any beyond a few in the neighborhood of Kayenta.[1] The ruin at which we worked is, therefore, so far as we know, the northernmost cliff-house of any size in the South Comb proper.

At this point there is a break in the cliffs, leaving a narrow gulch that twists through the jagged and tilted sandstone strata. It is one of the few places in the whole length of the comb where horses may be got across and is consequently much used by the Navaho as a route from the broad open plains of Laguna Creek to the more broken country to the westward. At several places among the ledges there are seep springs; close by, along Laguna Creek, lies abundance of good corn land; one part or another of the winding gulch or its branches offers shelter from any wind that can blow, and, all in all, this little nook in the comb must have been an almost ideal home site from the cliff-dweller's point of view. That it was thoroughly appreciated is shown by the remains of a surface ruin on a sand knoll in the main gulch, and by the cliff-house just mentioned.

Ruin 7 (Olla House)

" Olla House," as we called it, was very prolific in specimens. This was due to the fact that the house was not only entirely protected from rain by the roof of its sheltering cave, but also because there was no seepage of water from the rear of the cave itself. Furthermore, the place seems to have been inhabited for a considerable time, so that large beds of refuse accumulated in the open spaces in front of the rooms.

Plate 13, *a*, a photograph taken from the opposite side of the little rocky draw, shows the site, a " double-decker " house, as it is called in the Southwest; the main group of living rooms below, a walled-up ledge for storage and defense above. The ruin in the lower cave was larger than any of the houses previously examined; it contained

---

[1] These have been examined by Professor Cummings.

16 ground-floor rooms, five or six of which had once been two stories high, and two kivas (fig. 20). As usual, the rooms are arranged about the back of the cave, the kivas are set in front, and low retaining walls convert the remaining space into living terraces; the larger at the front of the cave, the smaller at a slightly higher level, behind the kivas and between two groups of rooms. On the back walls of the cave there are numbers of pictographs, a few pecked, but the majority painted in red and yellow.

Architecturally Olla House is precisely like all the other cliff-dwellings thus far described. The masonry is of rough stones of all sizes and shapes, vaguely coursed, laid up with a great deal of adobe mortar and heavily spalled. While the walls average only 8 inches thick, they are surprisingly firm and solid. In some parts of the building the outer surface of the walls was evidently finished

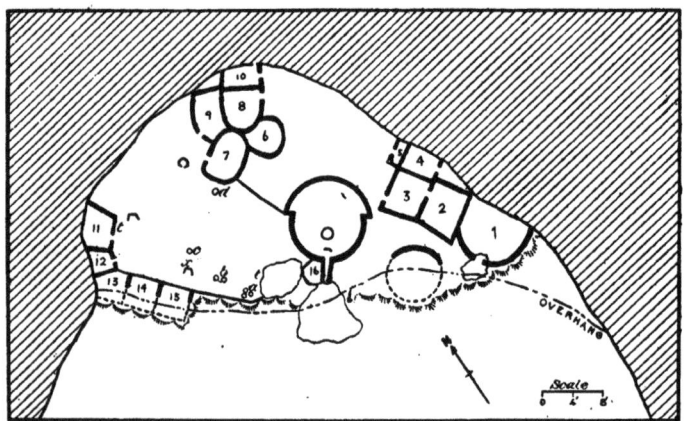

Fig. 20.—Plan of Ruin 7.

with adobe plaster, traces of which can be seen in plate 13, *b*, on the wall of the left-hand room. All walls, however, were not so treated, nor was the interior of the rooms commonly plastered. Although there is no evidence of fire, all the roofs have disappeared; the sockets for the beams, however, show the use here, as in Firestick House, of two or three large timbers, crossed at right angles by seven or eight small ones. Where second stories are present, the upper and lower rooms each have doors of their own. The doorways themselves average 23 inches high by 14 inches wide at the top and 15 inches at the bottom. They are provided with lintels made of wooden rods and stone slab overlintels; the slab forming the sill projects in a number of cases to form a little ledge or step (see pl. 13, *b*, left-hand room).

With the exception of room 1, whose floor had apparently been leveled with refuse, the rooms contained little but blown sand and

a. RUIN 7

b. ROOMS IN RUIN 7

ROOMS AND KIVA IN RUIN 7

a few potsherds. Rooms 14 and 15, lying outside the terrace wall and only partly protected from the weather, have been almost entirely destroyed; they contained in their rear portions small deposits of rubbish.

The most interesting feature of Olla House is the kiva (pl. 14). It is excellently preserved, the walls standing from 6 to 7 feet high all around. As usual, it occupies a position well toward the front, is sunk in the cave deposit as deeply as possible, and was furthermore banked about with débris of construction and of occupancy. The upper two or three feet probably stood clear, the building having thus been only semisubterranean. The room is an almost perfect circle, the average diameter being 11 feet 4 inches (fig. 21). A niche,

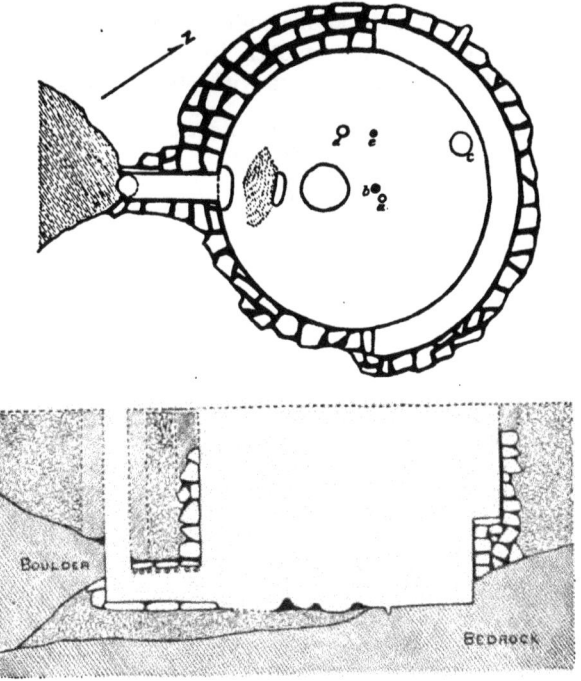

FIG. 21.—Plan and section of kiva, Ruin 7.

3 feet 2 inches above the floor and 1 foot 4 inches deep, extends nearly halfway around the room on the eastern side. The ventilator opens 3 inches above the floor level; the horizontal passage is 4 feet long, paved with sandstone slabs and roofed with cedar rods set in the masonry on either side; above the rods are more slabs. The stonework about the inner end of the horizontal passage is carefully done; toward the outer end it is heavy and coarse. The vertical shaft has completely fallen away, but one side of it, the farthest from

the kiva, is indicated on an adjacent large bowlder, the side of which has been pecked down and vertically grooved to conform to the round shape of the ascending shaft. In front of the ventilator lies what was apparently some form of deflector. It is now a mere adobe ridge 14 inches long by 3 inches high, carefully finished off and so smoked that it seems unlikely that there was ever any structure built over it. It may perhaps have served as a support or a rest for some sort of movable screen; the floor between it and the ventilator, however, is so much broken that it cannot be seen whether or not there was ever a groove or a series of holes to receive the lower end of such a contrivance.

The fire pit, directly behind this peculiar " deflector," is remarkably symmetrical and is neatly coped about with adobe. Behind the fire pit the floor of hard-packed adobe ends, the rear half being supplied by the bedrock itself, made smooth by pecking away the protuberances and filling up the hollows with clay. The sipapu, a round

FIG. 22.—Loom loop in kiva floor.

hole 3 inches wide and $3\frac{3}{4}$ inches deep, is sunk into the solid rock (fig. 21, a); $2\frac{1}{2}$ inches from it we noticed, while brushing off the floor, a faint ring in the plaster, and, on cutting around it, opened up a sealed sipapu (b) of finer construction and greater depth than the other. It was filled with clean sand, plugged with adobe, and then plastered over. We do not hesitate to call it a sipapu, because it lies exactly in the normal position of that ceremonial opening, back of the fire pit and on the line drawn from it through the center of the ventilator opening. Why it should have been closed and a second one made so close beside it is a mystery.

There are three other holes in the kiva floor—c, a shallow depression near the wall, pecked out, perhaps, for a pot rest; d, an excavation 2 inches deep, 4 inches in diameter, less carefully shaped than the sipapu; e, containing a loop of braided yucca anchored in the adobe floor by means of a cross-stick and so placed that the top of the loop was just below the floor level (fig. 22). The underside of the top of the loop shows such wear as would have been caused by the play of a string or rope running through it. It is possible that *c* and *d* also once contained loops, and with *e* formed part of a series of loopholes such as were later found in other kivas.

On the wall seven or eight thin coats of plaster may be counted, each one blackened with smoke. This renewing of the plaster in thin layers seems to be characteristic of all kivas, not only here but in Canyon de Chelly, Mesa Verde, Chaco Canyon, and the Rio Grande. There are no recesses or cubby-holes in this kiva; the single large niche is edged and flagged with flat pieces of sandstone (pl. 15). In the masonry at the top of the back wall of the niche, and 2 feet 9 inches above its floor, there is a smooth, level surface about 3 feet long; while not distinctly defined at either end, it is conceivable that this smooth area may indicate the former presence of an entryway at this place. The smooth appearance may, however, be quite accidental, and it is much more probable that entrance was gained by a hatchway in the ceiling. No sign of roofing was visible, although the wall on the southeast side stands 7 feet high. In the masonry on the northwest side, 6 feet from the floor, are sockets left by two sticks, 2 inches in diameter, 8 inches apart; being too small for roof beams, these probably represent the former location of wall pegs.[1]

What seems to have been a second kiva has, unfortunately, been almost entirely destroyed by water falling from the cliff above. There remain only a segment of curved wall and traces of a niche or bench.

Between the large rock mentioned as having formed part of the back of the vertical shaft of kiva 1 and another bowlder lying to the northwest of it is a cist or inclosure of large sandstone slabs (fig. 20, No. 16). When first uncovered it was thought that it might have some connection with the adjacent kiva, but no relation between the two could be made out, and it proved on excavation to be filled with earth, rubbish, and a quantity of turkey droppings.

The two open spaces or terraces occupied most of our time, as the deposit in them was 2 feet to 3 feet deep and was so filled with specimens of all kinds as to require excavation almost entirely with a trowel. It consisted of the usual cliff-dweller débris—corn husks, cobs, leaves, sticks of wood, bits of cloth, bone, turkey droppings, and ashes. In it were two fairly well defined living surfaces, one at 14 inches, the other at 18 inches above the cave floor. They were distinguishable by the compact character of the general refuse, and were covered in some places with a thin coating of adobe and ashes. The levels were not constant throughout the mass, having been

---

[1] In Mesa Verde kivas short pegs are regularly found protruding from the front of the pilasters near their tops.

broken up here and there by ancient diggings, but they could be determined with certainty in many places. No difference in culture was ascertainable, the potsherds and other artifacts being of the same character from all depths.

The first objects were found just inside the outer retaining wall of the lower terrace, where there were uncovered three large corrugated ollas, their tops on the lower living surface. They were not covered, and contained nothing but earth (pl. 16, *a*). Three feet from them, and a little farther in from the wall, were two others, their tops on the upper level, covered with rough stone slabs, one having a piece of rush matting between the lip of the jar and the lid (pl. 16, *b*). Both were empty. A sixth vessel of the same type, also empty, was found still farther to the rear; the levels were vague at this point, so that its vertical position could not be determined. It was harnessed with yucca leaves, and its bottom, from which a piece had been lost, was strengthened with a coil of feather-cloth string. The seventh and last of this fine series of corrugated jars was the largest. Its top seemed to lie a little below the second-floor level. A sandstone lid covered it, and inside was a yucca ring-basket half full of shelled corn. In the bottom of the vessel were shriveled remains of flesh, apparently dried rabbit meat, judging from the shreds of fur adhering to them.

At *x*, figure 20, on the upper level was found a small yucca ring-basket, also containing pieces of meat. Almost directly below it, on or just beneath the lower floor level, was a worn-out basket of the same make, but much larger, flatter, and more loosely woven.[1] Besides these large objects there were recovered a number of yucca sandals of all kinds of weaves; many pieces of rush matting; implements of wood, such as awls, arrow foreshafts, fire-drill sticks, and agricultural tools; fabrics of yucca and cotton thread, and potsherds in considerable abundance.

The permanent fixtures, so to speak, of this terrace consisted of "turkey nests" and fire pits. The "turkey nests" are shown on the plan at *t, t*, figure 20. In making them, a hollow had been scooped out of the rubbish and neatly faced with adobe until it was about a foot in diameter and 8 inches deep. In and about each of these "nests" was found much more than the usual amount of droppings and feathers; there was no inclosing fence such as was noticed at Ruin 4. Three fire pits were found, all sunk in excavations made in the rubbish, and all built of slabs set on edge and so plastered together as to form roughly boxlike inclosures. Each one was paved with slabs, open at the top and partly full of wood ashes. The largest, a four-sided structure, was 2 feet square and 2 feet deep; the small-

---

[1] Probably a winnowing or sifting basket; see pl. 43, *c*.

DETAILS OF KIVA, RUIN 7

a

b

CORRUGATED JARS IN SITU

est, a very neatly made little hexagonal affair (pl. 17), had slightly flaring sides 8 inches long. The adobe used to bind together the slabs of this latter fireplace was burned very hard and was full of the tiny seeds of some species of grass.

The débris on the upper terrace was not so thick as on the lower; no fire pits were found in it, but it produced a perfect harvest of worn-out sandals, some so caked with mud that it was obvious that their owners, after some journey in the rain, had discarded them rather than attempt to clean them. Directly behind the kiva, in a bed of turkey droppings, were uncovered the somewhat decayed remains of a beautifully made cradle (see pl. 42). Near it, just under the layer of sheep dung, was a piece of buffalo hide, tanned with the hair on; as it was not covered by the ancient rubbish, it must be placed in the doubtful class as possibly of Navaho origin.

The buildings on the ledge above and to one side of the main ruin have the appearance of a mere fortification and storage place. The shelf that they occupy was reached in ancient times by a row of foot- and hand-holes pecked in the lower cliff and by a sort of balustrade wall above. (See pl. 13, *a*, right-hand side.) The steps are now so sand-blown, and the rocks so shaly and rotten, that our entry was effected with great difficulty. Once up, we found that the place was a long, narrow, sloping bench, the front of which was walled up, partly with good solid masonry, partly with rough stones piled upon each other without mortar. That it was designed as a stronghold seems plain from the elaborate system of loopholes cut in the higher wall at the northern end. They are 3 to 3½ feet from the floor, 2½ inches in diameter, and are cut through the wall at such angles as to command the canyon bottom, the approach to the main ruin below, and the ascent to the upper ledge itself. A very neat bit of building is seen in the little storage room at the back of this upper tier. (See pl. 12, *b*, right-hand side.) It is cemented against the sloping cliff like a swallow's nest, and is as solid and perfect as the day it was built. It has a well-made door (not visible in the photograph), 20 inches high by 13 inches wide, with wooden lintel and stone slab overlintel as usual. Its chief peculiarity lies in the method of its construction; its walls are made of long, thin rods of sandstone that crack naturally out of the ledge at this place. The average dimensions of these stone "poles" are: length 54 inches, width 4½ inches, thickness 2½ inches. They are laid up "log-cabin-wise," the ends crisscrossing at the corners, and the chinks between filled with adobe and spalls. This is, of course, an exceptional bit of work, made possible by the nature of the rock cleavages along this particular ledge; it shows, nevertheless, the readiness of these prehistoric masons to turn to their advantage every freak of their environment.

Few artifacts were found in this upper story. Behind the loop-holed wall was a bed of dry grass under blown sand, and beneath the grass were a fragment of matting, an arrow foreshaft, fragments of two bowls and an olla. The bowls were of normal Kayenta style, one red-and-yellow, one black-and-white; the olla was quite different, strongly resembling the pottery from the lower levels of Fluteplayer House and that from the ruins on the rock bench next to be described.

RUINS ON THE ROCK BENCH

Opposite the mouth of Olla House draw the canyon broadens out a little and is almost blocked by a dome-shaped, sandy hill. At its northern foot there is a spring; beyond this the canyon wall rises in a series of rocky benches, or steps, on the second of which, as well as on the sand hill in the valley, are the remains of a former extensive settlement.

The ruins on the bench consist of thirty or more round or oval inclosures, scattered irregularly over the whole slope. The circles, which vary from 6 to 10 feet in diameter, are made of large sandstone slabs set on edge. Excavation showed that each house had a hard floor of packed adobe, seemingly without a regular fireplace. The wall slabs are sunk into the ground from 5 to 8 inches below the floor. There do not seem to have been lateral doorways, the inclosure being usually unbroken. In some cases the rooms are partly sunk into the side hill, making them semisubterranean. As there is practically no fallen building stone in or about them, we think it probable that their upper parts were of the same "turtleback" adobe construction that was observed by us in similar round rooms with slab foundations at Fluteplayer House. This view is further strengthened by the type of pottery found in the foot or so of sand, charcoal, and ashes which covered the floor of each inclosure. It is of exactly the same style, both black-and-white and coarse black with broad flat coils about the neck, as that found at Fluteplayer House. In the rooms themselves we found no Kayenta sherds, and very few of them among the thousands of fragments that litter the surface of this bench.

The sand hill is also covered with identical sherds, chips, and other signs of occupancy. There were apparently many of the slab-circle rooms here, but they have practically all been undermined by the blowing away of the sand, and the slabs have toppled over in all directions. On the crest of the hill are the remains of a series of rectangular cells—a single row, to all appearances, 50 feet long by 8 feet wide. The walls, where they are visible, stand about 2 feet high, are of solid stone construction, and, from the amount of fallen blocks, they had at least one story of good masonry. This group of rooms we believe to have been built by the Kayenta people at the same general period as Olla House. The few fragments of pottery found at this spot were of the Kayenta styles.

A little trenching in likely spots failed to disclose any burials. A much larger force of men than ours would be necessary for a proper exploration of the bench and the hill, as the ruins cover a great deal of ground and at some places are buried deep under sand dunes. Our work hereabouts was accordingly brought to a close, and we returned to Kayenta.

MARSH PASS

The remaining weeks of our field season were spent in a preliminary survey of the Marsh Pass district (see pl. 1). Marsh Pass proper is a narrow defile between the great Black Mesa (Zilh-le-jini of the maps) and the high, broken sandstone country to the west. A good road, recently constructed by the Indian Bureau, leads from Kayenta through the pass and on via Cow Springs or Vakishibito to Tuba City. Leaving Kayenta, one follows this road up the broad valley of Laguna Creek, with the high, dark cliffs of the Black Mesa on the left. After 8 or 9 miles the valley narrows, as the slopes of Skeleton Mesa close in from the north and west. A mile or more and one reaches Marsh Pass itself, a narrow, rough defile, bordered on each side by high cliffs; on the right is the mouth of Sagi Canyon, a majestic red gorge with precipitous walls. Another mile and one is clear of the pass and in a most beautiful long, grassy valley, half a mile to a mile wide, walled in uncompromisingly on the south by the Black Mesa and bounded on the north by sloping ledges of red sandstone (see pl. 21, b). The scant drainage from this defile runs down through the pass, where it is joined by a more constant flow from the Sagi system, the two forming Laguna Creek and ultimately emptying into the Chinlee.

Although there is no flow of water in these upper reaches of Marsh Pass comparable with that in Sagi Canyon, there is a plentiful rainfall at certain seasons of the year; every storm that crosses this part of the plateau seems to swing along the face of the Black Mesa and deliver part of its rain upon the valley. The vegetation, while still strictly of the dry-country type, is more luxuriant and varied than about Kayenta and in the " Monuments;" particularly is this true of the little side canyons that lead up into the red sandstone on the northern side, where hollows and pockets in the rock hold supplies of stored rain water so large that they probably last through the dry seasons of all but exceptionally dry years.

The valley is a level plane covered with bee plant, grass, sage, and greasewood. Its southeastern wall, as stated above, is formed by the steep, rough, piñon-clad face of the Black Mesa; the rise of the northwestern escarpment is much more gradual and its total height considerably less: it consists of tilted sandstone strata, sparsely wooded with the inevitable piñon and cedar. Along the base of these slopes are mounds. and hummocks of sandstone, some bare. some drifted over with dune-like accumulations of sand. This whole northern side of the Marsh Pass Valley, with its warm southern and southwestern exposure, abundant water holes, and broad sweeps of good adobe soil for corn culture, must have been well situated for the homes of the ancient agriculturists, and the remains of their villages are scattered thickly along the edge of the flat land. from the lower gorges, where Sagi enters, to the point 3 miles above, where our exploration closed.[1]

Our camp at Marsh Pass was made on the rock slopes about 2½ miles above the mouth of Sagi Canyon. Directly opposite a reddish butte stands in the valley near the foot of the Black Mesa, and just behind us opened a narrow. gorge-like canyon, in which was situated the cliff-dwelling that we intended to excavate.

RUIN 8

This house was visited by Dr. Fewkes in 1909, while on his way to the ruins in Sagi Canyon, and is described and figured by him in his "Report on the Ruins of the Navaho National Monument" under the name of "Cliff-house B." Dr. Fewkes's description of the house and its surroundings is quoted entire:

This picturesque ruin occupies the whole floor of a narrow, low cave situated in an almost vertical cliff forming one side of a canyon which extends deep into the mountain; the entrance is between low hills on the left, where the road ascends [sic] to Marsh Pass. The ruin can be seen for a long distance, but as one approaches the canyon in which it lies the site is hidden by foothills. The accompanying view [see our pl. 18, a] was taken from the opposite side of the canyon, it being impossible to get an extended detailed view of the ruin from above or below. Beyond the ruin the canyon forms a narrowing fissure with precipitous sides; its bed is covered with bushes, stunted trees, and fallen rocks. No flowing water was found in this canyon, but in the ledges near its mouth, below the ruins, there are pockets and potholes which contained considerable water at the time of the writer's visit.

This cliff-dwelling is difficult to enter, the walls of the canyon, both above and below and on the sides, being almost perpendicular. A pathway extending along the side of the cliff on the level of the cave approaches within 20 feet of the ruin; from its end to the first room of the ruin this trail is continued by a series of footholes pecked in the rock, making entrance hazardous at this point. Although the walls of this cliff-dwelling are more or less destroyed and their foundations deeply buried, there still remains standing masonry of a square tower (?) reaching from the floor to the roof of the cave. One corner of this

---

[1] Consult Fewkes, 1911, for ruins observed by him farther to the west.

FIREPLACE IN RUIN 7

a. RUIN 8

b. ROOMS IN RUIN 8

tower is completely broken out, but the remaining sides show that this building was three stories high, composed of rooms one above another.

Several other rooms lie concealed under fallen walls and débris. One of the most instructive of these is what may have been a kiva, or ceremonial room,[1] the location of its walls being indicated by stakes projecting out of the ground. Lower down, where the wall was better preserved, sticks or wickerwork were found interwoven in the uprights, the whole being plastered with adobe, a form of wall construction common in prehistoric ruins of Arizona.[2]

As soon as our excavations were begun in Cliff-house B we found that the ruins were in bad condition. A strong seepage issues from horizontal cracks along the back of the cave, which, judging from the appearance of the rocks and earth, must at times almost amount to a flowing spring. This has so thoroughly soaked the culture deposits throughout the dwelling that for the most part they have decayed to a black, loamy substance mixed here and there with ashes. The underflow has also weakened the foundations of some of the walls, so that a number of them, although well protected from rain, have fallen completely into ruin.[3] The whole place, too, is encumbered with fragments of rock fallen from the roof of the cave since the building of the house.

We cleared the front rooms at the eastern end and sunk trenches and test pits into the deposit at the back in a vain attempt to find dry rubbish. We did not dare to excavate about the base of the tower or in the rooms immediately adjacent to it, as their underpinning was in such a precarious condition that the tower itself might easily have been brought down on the workmen. (See pl. 18, *b*.)

Rooms 1 and 2 (fig. 23) contained a little rubbish, in which we found fragments of a black-and-white jar and two much-decayed wooden weaving (?) tools. Room 3, an irregular little apartment, had been closed in on the eastern side by a " wattle-and-daub " wall, the remains of which protruded above ground. It was this room that Dr. Fewkes very naturally thought might be a kiva. The two kivas lay, however, completely buried just to the west of it. A handsome little black-and-white bowl with a handle, broken into many fragments, was found in a recess in the north corner.

The most striking piece of masonry in the ruin is presented by the walls of room 9, a three-story tower well toward the front (pl. 18, *b*). Its whole southern wall and parts of the sides have fallen, yet it still stands 19 feet above the present rubbish line and reaches to the roof of the cave. The height of the first-floor room from ground to roof beam holes is 7 feet; the second story 6 feet 8

---

[1] No other rooms that could be called ceremonial were recognized in Cliff-house B, but the writer's examination of the ruin was not very thorough and. their existence may have escaped him.

[2] Fewkes, op. cit., pp. 10–11.

[3] Similar conditions exist in Balcony House, Mesa Verde, where there is also a spring at the rear of the cave.

inches; the third, which was probably only a small storage chamber, about 3 feet. At x (fig. 23), just behind room 9, may be seen the remains of an old wattle wall deeply sunk in the rubbish; over it is a layer of rat dung, and above this again is built a wall which extends back to room 6. This upper wall and the walls of room 6 itself are of masonry much superior to that of the rest of the house. The stones are large, well matched, rubbed smooth, and carefully coursed, suggesting strongly the masonry of the surface ruins of the pass which we investigated later. The wattle wall was built after the completion of the tower, room 9, as its edge is modeled up against it; the upper wall and room 6, therefore, were constructed at a still later date. It is regretted that the unstable condition of the high tower forbade more clearing at this interesting spot. The

FIG. 23.—Plan of Ruin 8.

door of room 6 is much larger than the average. Its height is 2 feet 7 inches; breadth, 1 foot 5 inches; it has a lintel of wooden rods with a slab overlintel set slightly above it (pl. 19, a).

Room 12 (pl. 19, b) is in perfect preservation; its back wall and roof are provided by the cave. The door differs slightly from the normal in that its wooden lintel, made of three cedar slats, sets directly against the stone slab lintel instead of half an inch to an inch below it. Built into the walls are several stones bearing incised designs (pl. 19, b, lower left-hand corner). That the decorations were cut on the stones before they were introduced into the masonry is shown by the fact that the adobe mortar runs over the designs in several instances. One block pictured in plate 20 is even more conclusive; it was broken in two and the halves were built into different

a. DOORWAY IN ROOM 6, RUIN 8

b. ROOM 12, RUIN 8

INCISED SLAB BUILT INTO WALL, RUIN 8

courses of the wall.[1] At some time after the completion of this room it so settled into the ground that the tops of the walls sagged away an inch or so from the cave roof; the space thus formed was stopped up all around with adobe of a different color from that used in the original masonry.

Although nowhere in Ruin 8 were any roofs in place, fragments of roofing were found in the débris. Over the beams had been laid twigs or cedar bark,[2] and upon this was spread a coat of adobe mortar, over which were laid bunches of long grass, more adobe, more grass, and finally a last layer of adobe, making a total thickness of about 4 inches. We have not observed this grass-layer

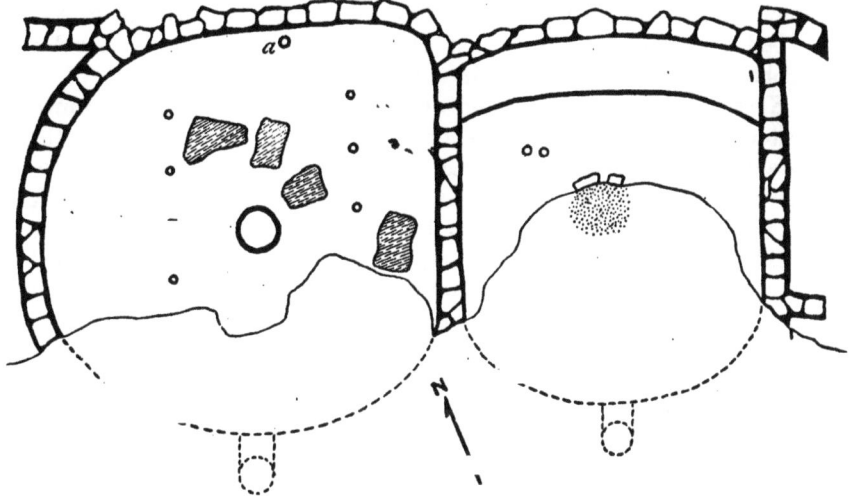

Fig. 24.—Kivas 1 and 2, Ruin 8.

method in any other ruin, nor have we seen it described. It makes a very strong and springy covering, and pieces of the mixture will stand a blow which would shiver an equal amount of unmixed adobe.

Of the two chambers on the eastern front, K 1 is probably, and K 2 is surely, a kiva (fig. 24). Both are in poor preservation, water from the cliffs above having so entirely destroyed their front walls that their ventilating shafts, if they had them, have quite disappeared. Both had once occupied a semisubterranean position, with their rear or northern portions well sunk in the cave deposit, their southern walls probably standing partly free.

---

[1] For the designs see fig. 97, a, b, c.

[2] We saw neither reeds nor slats. The former were found in Ruin 2, and the latter observed in place in the roof of a cliff-house in Devil's Canyon, San Juan County, Utah (see Kidder, 1910).

No sign of flooring could be found in excavating kiva 1, but that it once did have an adobe floor some 2 feet above bedrock in front and connecting with the bedrock at the back seems to be shown by smoke marks on the side walls. The room is identified as a possible kiva because of the bench at the rear, the multiple layers of plaster still adhering to parts of the masonry, and the presence of two small, carefully made holes (3 inches in diameter by 3 inches deep; 2 inches in diameter by 2 inches deep, respectively) cut into the bedrock at the rear. These little holes suggest sipapus very strongly. They may have been covered by the adobe floor, the level of which can not be exactly made out at this spot; but, on the other hand, the bedrock itself may have formed the floor at this point, in which case they would have been exposed. Toward the center of the room was a bed of white ashes and part of the underpinning of a circular adobe structure, all that remained of the fire pit.

Kiva 2, adjoining this room on the west, is comparatively much better preserved, most of its hard-packed adobe floor being still intact. In shape kiva 2 is roughly rectangular with rounded corners; it measures 12 feet east and west, and was presumably about 10 feet across from north to south. There is no bench. The walls still retain much of their plaster; at one spot eight heavily smoked layers could be counted. The fire pit is circular, slightly raised, and coped as usual with adobe; it was full of clear, white ashes. Directly south and east of it there lay on the broken floor a compacted mass of adobe and fragments of sandstone, possibly the remains of a fire screen. There are four slabs of sandstone laid flat and cemented flush with the floor; their upper surfaces are well smoothed as if by long use. Three of them were taken up in excavation; the fourth, left in situ, can be seen in plate 21, a. The same photograph also shows eight small holes sunk into the adobe. As a, figure 24, is a plain, cylindrical cavity, occupying approximately the prescribed position for the sipapu, it is provisionally identified as such. The other seven holes are arranged in two parallel alignments, one on each side of the fire pit; the western range has four, the eastern three holes. They have neatly rounded edges, and vary from 1½ to 3 inches in diameter. All but one contained loops resembling that found in the kiva of Olla House. These loops are made of bent twigs, except in a single case, where a doubled yucca string is employed. As all were left in position, the method of anchoring could not be observed, but it was, perhaps, by means of a crosspiece, as in Olla House (fig. 22). It will be noticed that the holes in each series are in almost exact alignment. Whether or not a fourth hole existed at the south end of the eastern series could not be determined because of the bad condition of the floor. There can be little doubt that these series of loop holders served as attachments for the lower bars of looms.

a. DETAILS IN KIVA 2, RUIN 8

b. MARSH PASS FROM RUIN 8

a. RUIN A

b. MASONRY OF RUIN A

Both kivas were full of building stones, rocks sloughed off from the cave roof above, and mixed débris containing an unusually large number of potsherds. Most of this rubbish seems to have fallen and slid into them from the rooms behind. Much of it was charred, but the loops in the floor of kiva 2 are quite untouched by fire. In the débris of kiva 2 was found a small cylindrical cup of cottonwood, showing faint traces of an incised design (fig. 46); on the floor was part of a black-and-white bowl containing the carbonized meats of piñon nuts.

SURFACE RUINS IN MARSH PASS

The remainder of our time in Marsh Pass was spent in examining the ruins of villages in the open. All along the northeastern side of the valley at the foot of the rock slopes are swells or hummocks of sandstone, some almost bare, some partly covered with red adobe earth (pl. 21, *b*). Upon these, at varying heights above the valley bottom, a few even on the flat, but always close to the rocks, are to be seen tumbled piles of building stone, with here and there a protruding fragment of wall (see pl. 1). About these former village sites, and particularly on the slopes below them, are fragments of broken pottery in the most extraordinary quantities. In some places, where the water has washed away the sand and gathered them together, they lie as thick as the shingle on a beach. The houses about which these sherds are strewn are apparently all of very much the same type, but with one exception the heavy rains and fierce winter winds of the pass have completely leveled them.

RUIN A

This favored exception is a ruin standing on a rocky eminence about 3 miles above the place where Sagi Canyon enters the pass (pl. 22, *a*). It is figured by Professor Cummings[1] and described as follows:

Frequently a large building that has served as a fort or place of assembly, and perhaps both, was surrounded by many smaller structures grouped about it, as in the case of a large ruin near Marsh Pass, in northern Arizona. The main building was a rectangular structure, 90 feet long and 10½ feet wide, that evidently was two stories in height. Parts of the walls above the first story still stand and some of the timbers that supported the floor of the second story are yet in place. All about are found the ruins of smaller structures, and the ground is full of broken pieces of pottery of excellent manufacture in corrugated ware and in the smooth white ware decorated in black and the red ware decorated in black and yellow.

---

[1] Cummings, 1910, pp. 28, 29.

Dr. Fewkes, in his Navaho Monument paper, also gives two views of the structure, which he calls Ruin A.[1] He thus comments upon it:

The first ruin of considerable size that was visited is situated to the left of and somewhat distant from the road, a few miles west and south of Marsh Pass. As this ruin stands on an elevation it is visible for a considerable distance across the valley, especially to one approaching it from the southwest. The standing walls rise in places to a height of 10 feet, showing indications of two stories, some of the rafters in places still projecting beyond the face of the wall. The two walls highest and most prominent are parallel, inclosing a long room or court; in one place a break has been made through these walls, as appears in the illustration. The remnants of foundations of other walls back of these show that Ruin A was formerly very much larger than the walls now standing would indicate.

The walls are composed of roughly laid masonry, bearing evidences on the inside of adobe plastering. An exceptional feature is the large number of the component stones, decorated on their outer faces with deeply incised geometrical figures, apparently traced with some pointed implement. [See fig. 97, *d–g.*]

Professor Cummings's identification of this structure as a central fort or place of assembly surrounded by smaller structures, is, we think, wrong. We are of the opinion that Ruin A is an example of the ordinary type of dwelling of this region and that the other ruins on this hill and those at other points along the valley were built in the same manner as this solitary standing example. In other words, we believe that it owes its preservation not to the superiority of its construction but to its situation on the crest of the ridge, where its foundations were safe from the undermining action of surface drainage. This belief is based on the evidence afforded by the eastern wall, which at one point has fallen away for a space of 15 to 20 feet long (pl. 22, *a*). The wall has fallen outward almost as one piece and, lying flat on the ground, has been so covered by drift sand that if the other walls were not standing, no one would suspect that there had once been at this place a structure 15 feet or more in height. With this fact in mind we examined the other ruins grouped about Ruin A, those of numbers of other houses farther down the pass, and still others on a mesa at the mouth of Sagi Canyon, with the result that we could often make out, partly buried in the earth, sections of wall that had formerly stood to a height of from 10 to 12 feet, fallen quite flat on the ground and giving, at a superficial examination, no clue to the size of the buildings of which they had once formed parts. It seems, then, that Ruin A is typical of the domiciliary structures of the Marsh Pass district, and also probably of certain large houses on the top of Black Mesa described to us by the Navaho. The build-

---

[1] Fewkes, 1911, p. 10.

ings seem to have been from 30 to 100 feet long, 8 to 10 feet wide, and usually two stories high. These units are sometimes so placed as to make rectangular inclosures, sometimes merely set close to each other without touching.

To return to Ruin A, the building was, as Professor Cummings and Dr. Fewkes point out, probably two stories high. The roof beams, 7 feet 3 inches above the present ground level, are set 3 feet apart and are bedded in holes in the masonry, the butts and ends running clear through the walls. In saying that the masonry is roughly laid, Dr. Fewkes does the builders a little less than justice, for the stonework is superior to nine-tenths of the masonry of the Southwest, ancient or modern. The wall, 23 inches thick, is double-faced, with a hearting of adobe and rubble. It is constructed of large, fairly well-matched stones, distinctly coursed and with some attempt both at breaking joints and bonding corners. The interior is less carefully finished than the outside, probably because it was covered with a layer of plaster; the faces of the stones on the exterior have been carefully rubbed down to an even surface (pl. 22, *b*). There is one doorway in the standing part of the eastern wall; probably another in the section that has fallen. The door is much larger than those of the cliff-dwellings, but does not otherwise differ from them.[1]

While there are no surface indications of cross walls to divide the long building into chambers, we have no doubt that excavation would disclose them. All the houses along the pass appear to have had heavy outer walls and more lightly built inner partitions. The question of the interior arrangement of the long corridor-like units could be settled by a little digging. This we were unable to do, as our somewhat limited time was entirely taken up with general exploration of the different sites, clearing a surface kiva, and excavations in the burial places.

The result of our general exploration was the discovery of an almost continuous line of villages from Ruin A, the southernmost limit of our work, to the mouth of Sagi Canyon. All these groups are as nearly alike as the variations of the topography allow. The houses are built on the hummocky lower skirts of the sandstone ledges; between them and the valley bottom are sandy inclines covered with potsherds, broken stone implements, and other débris of occupancy. Here lie the burials. Where there was sufficient soil the kivas were sunk into the ground near the houses, but when, as is often the case, the house site is practically bare rock, they are placed

---

[1] Measurements: Height 32 inches, width at top 26 inches, at base 28½ inches. Stone lintel 46 inches long, 2 inches thick. Wood lintel of cedar poles set 1 inch below stone lintel. Compare door measurements in room 6, Ruin 8; the wall of that room is of masonry much like that of Ruin A.

farther downhill or even in the valley bottom.[1] Back of the
houses come the broken, piñon and cedar covered sandstone slopes.
There are a few buildings even here, such as the one mentioned by
Dr. Fewkes on page 11 of his report and called by us the "Tower
House." Standing on a spur of rock just below Ruin 8, it was
once a considerable structure, but is now all fallen except 5 feet
of the northwestern wall. As in Ruin A, the masonry is double-
faced, rubble filled, plastered within and neatly smoothed without.
Some previous digger has cut a hole in the lower portions, showing
the interior to be choked with earth and stone; a number of slim
oak and elder twigs visible in the dirt probably once formed part
of the roofing.

Near the Tower House and at several other places among the
ravines are remains of reservoirs, built to supplement the natural
water pockets that abound in these rocks. To make the reservoirs,
walls of heavy, rough stones were thrown across little gullies and
banked with earth. The central parts, probably once 6 or 7 feet
high, have now been cut away by the water, but the wings, crossing
the sides of the gullies, can still be made out (pl. 23, a).

The kiva that was excavated lies about half a mile below Ruin A
and a few feet to the south of its parent ruin (see pl. 1). Although
part of the southwestern side had been cut away by an arroyo, it
was otherwise in excellent preservation. It is roughly circular, 10
feet 6 inches in average diameter, and had evidently been entirely
subterranean, as the top of its wall, 6 feet 9 inches high, is buried
a foot or more below the present ground level.

The masonry is inferior—large, irregular stones set into the
earth; this was, however, entirely masked with plaster. The floor,
lower walls, and parts of the benches still preserve this coating,
specimens of which show as many as 13 layers. As may be seen
in the ground plan and elevation of this kiva (fig. 25), it differs
somewhat from the kivas previously described. The most striking
features are the large southeastern niche, under which extends the
horizontal passage of the ventilator, and the long banquette which
seems to have extended at least three-quarters of the way around the
room. The two offsets do not quite meet. The horizontal passage
enters the chamber 7 inches above the floor level; it was roofed with
cedar slats, now rotted away. The ascending passage is just behind the rear wall of the deep recess, but is so much broken down
that no measurements could be taken. The packed adobe floor was
very firm and smooth; when cleared it was found to be covered with
half an inch of fine, clean sand, which had presumably sifted in
after the desertion of the place, but before the roof fell. The de-

---

[1] Kivas were apparently never incorporated directly in the house cluster, but were
built as near it as convenient; this statement, however, is based merely on surface
indications.

a. REMAINS OF RESERVOIR

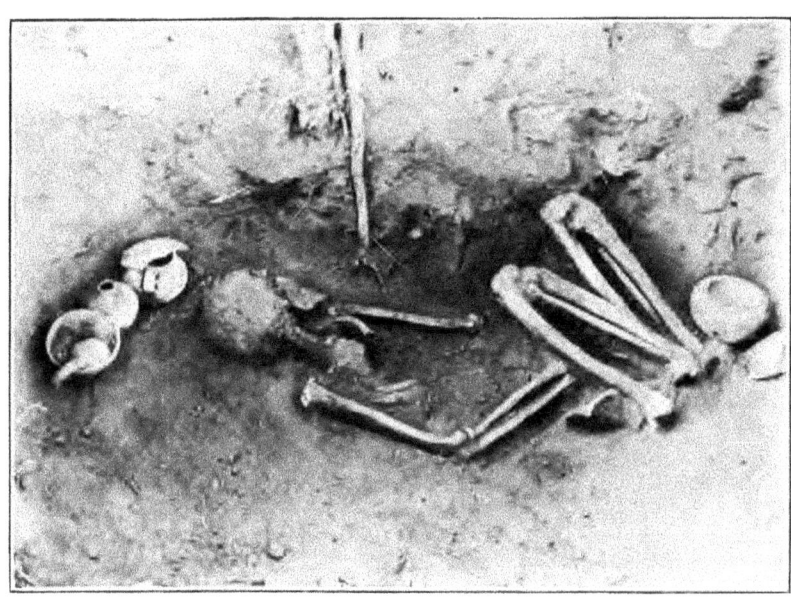

b. SKELETON 1

a. SKELETON 2

b. SKELETON 3

flector is a slab of stone a little more than an inch thick, the upper parts of which were broken off and could not be found. Near it, let into the floor, was a flat piece of granitic rock, very smooth and somewhat hollowed out on the upper surface, as if by use as a shallow mortar. The fire pit is square, an unusual shape, coped with stone slabs and, as always, full of white ashes. Directly behind it is a well-made hole, 10 inches in diameter, 8 inches deep, rather larger than most sipapus; another hole near it is more nearly of the conventional size, 3½ inches in diameter. Close by the wall, just below where the long banquette joins the deep southeastern one, is a third depression in the floor; it is oval, 6½ inches wide, 11 inches long, and 3 inches deep. The roof has been completely destroyed by fire. The only artifacts found in the kiva were half of a red-and-yellow bowl, a bone awl (fig. 51, *f*), and a small arrow point.

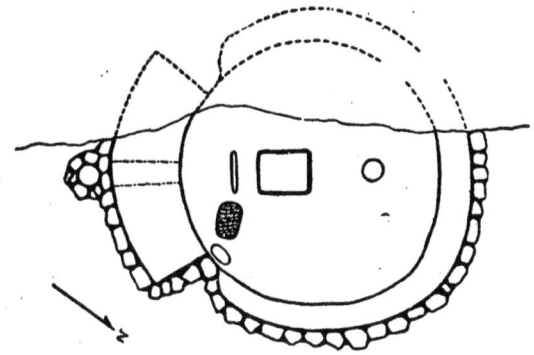

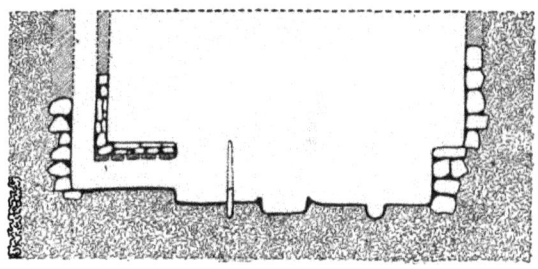

FIG. 25.—Plan and section of kiva in Marsh Pass.

BURIAL PLACES

As was stated above, the cemeteries were found in every case in the sandy slopes below and usually to the east and south of the house clusters. These slopes have suffered a considerable amount of denudation, so that a number of the cemeteries appear to have been completely washed away. Others are now being denuded, so that exposed skeletons and single bones may be found after every heavy rain at half a dozen places between the mouth of Sagi Canyon and Ruin A. Much pottery has undoubtedly been brought to light in this way, picked up by the Navaho and sold to traders,[1] but no regular digging by either whites or Indians has apparently ever been done.

---

[1] We consider it probable that a number of the pieces in the Keam collection, now in the Peabody Museum, were brought in by the Indians from this vicinity. Keam's post, in Keams Canyon in the Hopi country, was, at the time this collection was made, the nearest store to Marsh Pass.

We took out partly exposed skeletons at six or seven different places, and did systematic trenching at two localities—the "Camp Cemetery" and "Pottery Hill" (see pl. 1).[1]

CAMP CEMETERY

The Camp Cemetery, a little above the entrance of the ravine that shelters Ruin 8, is a sherd-covered slope crowned by the ruins of several house units. The burials were located by finding human bones scattered about the mouth of a badger hole. A trench, cut to bedrock, was run north and south at this point. The surface here is covered by a layer of loose drift sand, 6 inches to 1 foot thick, overgrown with sagebrush and rubber weed. Under this and extending to bedrock, 3 to 4½ feet below, is a fine-grained, sandy adobe, so very closely compacted that it had to be broken up with the pick before it could be shoveled. About 2 feet below the surface was a wavy half-inch stratum of ashes and charcoal. Charcoal, potsherds, and bones of deer, turkeys, and rabbits were scattered through the hardpan to the bottom. So hard was the ground that it took four men four days to dig a trench 42 feet long, 10 to 12 feet wide, and 3 to 4 feet deep. We found six skeletons, and there are probably others in the immediate neighborhood.

As few burials from northeastern Arizona have hitherto been treated,[2] it may not be amiss to describe these six.

Skeleton 1 (pl. 23, b) lay 35 inches below the surface, 9 inches above bedrock, and was both covered and underlaid by cedar bark. Elderly male. Partly flexed on back and left side, hands at groin, ribs and thoracic vertebræ destroyed by a badger hole, head southwest. A small black-and-white colander lay over the feet, and beside it a broken rubbing stone. Back of the head were four other small pots, one covered with a sherd, another containing the bones of a rodent.

Skeleton 2 (pl. 24, a) lay 2 feet southwest of No. 1 and at the same level. It was an infant of about 18 months, lying on the right side, hands in front of face, thighs at right angle to body, lower legs flexed; head southwest. Before the face were grouped four pieces of pottery and a large sherd.

Skeleton 3 (pl. 24, b) lay 24 feet south of No. 2, 3 feet below the surface and directly upon the bedrock. Adult male. The body was on the right side, legs partly drawn up, hands between the upper thighs, head southwest. In front of the chest was a red

---

[1] "Pottery Hill" is the place spoken of by Fewkes (1911, p. 12) as a probable cemetery; the "rings of small stones suggesting graves," however, proved to have no mortuary significance. They seem to have been cooking places.

[2] Cummings (1910) gives the only information we have on the subject.

pitcher and a red bowl. Pressure from above had broken the left humerus over the lip of. the pitcher, the radius and ulna of the same arm over the edge of the bowl. Over the feet was inverted about half of a red bowl, and in front of the right knee were found fragments of a small clay vessel with ridges on the exterior. Three olivella shells were lying in contact with the left cheek bone; under the chin were four more, and six or seven were found behind the pelvis. The arrangement of these groups could not be made out, but the shells in each case lay end-to-end as though they had been strung. About the right wrist were olivella shells in the form of a bracelet, five strings of shells wide; the lower ones were too decayed for preservation. Traces of cedar logs which had formerly covered the burial could be made out in the sand.

Skeleton 4, adult female, lay 6 feet due south of skeleton 2, 32 inches below the surface, 24 inches above bedrock. Body on left side, knees drawn up to chest, and hands near the groin. Head south. The bones of this skeleton were in bad condition, a badger hole having torn out the ribs and some of the vertebræ. The grave had been covered with cedar sticks 2 inches in diameter and 4 inches long, running horizontally across the body about 1 foot above it. There was no pottery, but in front of the chest and 3 inches above the knees was a pocket or deposit of sixteen flint chips and broken projectile points. Behind the shoulders lay two pebbles worked smooth by use in rubbing. Somewhere near the feet, its exact position not determined, was a small arrow point.

Skeleton 5 (pl. 25), adult male, was found 5 feet east of No. 1, 10 inches above bedrock, 44 inches below the surface. It lay face down, legs tightly flexed, hands at the groin, head south. This grave was overlaid with five cedar logs side by side, parallel with the body and 10 inches above it, making a covering 55 inches long by 18 inches wide. The wood was considerably rotted and bent down into the grave by pressure from above. Beside the body was a piece of cedar 19 inches long, 3 inches in diameter, which appeared to have had a longitudinal groove on one side; it was so decayed, however, that its exact nature could not be determined. On the other side of the body lay a group of offerings running from the head to the feet. By the skull was a large red bowl with a handle, inverted and covering a double handful of piñon nuts; close beside it a broken pottery ladle, a small pitcher, and a rubbing stone. At the knees was a large black-and-white bowl containing a small red bowl; a large sherd lay at the shins, and by the feet was a red pitcher. Set on edge near the latter was a metate accompanied with a hand stone which showed traces of red paint. A large quartz chip was in contact with the left elbow. This skeleton was less crushed and generally better preserved than the others.

Skeleton 6, elderly female, 6 feet southwest of skeleton 5, lay on bedrock 46 inches from the surface, on left side, knees drawn up but not tightly flexed, right hand in front of face, left on breast. Head southeast. The bones were crushed and disarranged by heavy pressure, the left radius and ulna having been pushed 3 inches away from their junction with the humerus, the ribs broken and wrapped down over the vertebræ. Over the grave were three cedar sticks arranged in parallel order as in grave 5. There were no offerings.

All these burials were close to bedrock. The bodies seem to have been placed loosely flexed in oval excavations which were then covered with cedar poles or small logs and probably further protected by cedar bark. When the interments were made the ground was evidently much less hard than it is now, for definite outlines of the graves cannot be made out. The earth all about the graves is discolored and disturbed to the bottom; probably the dead were placed, as they seem to have been in the Montezuma Creek region,[1] in the village midden. All the heads pointed in a southerly direction, up the valley, and those of the outcropping skeletons found here and there in the pass, whose positions could be determined, followed, with one exception,[2] the same rule. This record applies only to eight or nine burials, and may therefore be only the result of coincidence. One further point of interest in connection with these skeletons is the fact that while generous offerings of mortuary pottery were usually deposited, most of the vessels were distinctly poor ones, small, badly fired, cracked, or otherwise imperfect. This is contrary to the general rule in southwestern cemeteries.

POTTERY HILL

During the progress of the work on the Camp Cemetery a heavy rain so filled our trench that digging had to be discontinued. We took this opportunity to send our whole force along the sand banks below the ruins in search of such small objects as usually are found on village sites after a rain. The result was a harvest of arrowheads, pottery disks, beads, pendants, and other like specimens. While thus engaged we found, about a quarter of a mile below the Camp Cemetery, another slope, topped by ruins, literally covered with potsherds and, what was of most interest, showing seven or eight outcroppings of human bones. Work was accordingly begun here when we had finished our other trench. Test pits were dug and a long cut opened which revealed a most peculiar state of affairs. There was a surface layer 8 inches to 1 foot thick, composed of sand, small pieces of broken sandstone (débris of construction?),

---

[1] Kidder, 1910, p. 358.
[2] This skeleton was in an upright sitting position, facing southward.

and many potsherds; in this were quantities of loose human bones, some whole, some broken, none lying in order. Below the top stratum the soil was of the same darkish color as that of the Camp Cemetery, and also contained charcoal, bones, and a few sherds. This deposit was about 4 feet deep, and below it was clear, yellow, hard-packed, and evidently undisturbed sand. A hole 7 feet deep failed to reach bedrock. In the dark earth were found five incomplete skeletons partly in order but evidently more or less disturbed. In one, for instance, the pelvis, first four vertebræ, and right leg lay in order, the lower bones of the left leg were in about the positions they should have occupied, but the femur was 8 inches too high and was half reversed. One incisor tooth was touching the pelvis, and a red jar, crushed flat, lay underneath. All the rest was missing, save a few ribs and finger bones from the earth above and to one side. Traces of a cedar-wood covering could be seen. A second disturbed burial, somewhat nearer the surface, consisted of both feet, fragments of skull, lower jaw, part of the pelvis, and a few ribs, none in order. Among the bones were several olivella shells, a large red jar, a black-and-white bowl, and parts of a cedar wand (?) about 2 feet long, loaf-shaped in cross-section and painted bright blue. Three feet away was a bone whistle. Here again cedar had been used to cover the original interment.

Only one complete burial was taken out. The skeleton was that of an infant of about one year; it lay flexed, head southeast, directly upon the undisturbed lower sand at a depth of 4 feet 6 inches. In front of the face were two bowls and a little pitcher resting upon a sherd from a large black-and-white olla. A selenite pendant was under one of the bowls.

Although we did a great deal of digging on Pottery Hill, hoping to encounter graves that had not been cut to pieces, we found conditions everywhere the same. Two more pots were taken out, as well as several red stone pendants and olivella shells, evidently scattered mortuary offerings. The disturbance of this cemetery was not the work of man, at least not during modern times, as the surface showed no pitting. The only explanation that presented itself was that there had occurred a slight slide of the whole hillside which upset the first arrangement of many of the bodies to some extent. Then arroyos may have formed in the deposit, washed out parts of skeletons, and then themselves filled up again by the caving in of their sides; finally there was, perhaps, a general re-leveling by wind. The top layer of completely confused bones seems to consist of wash from a part of the same cemetery higher up the hill which is now completely denuded.

The day before we left Marsh Pass we discovered burials in a large cave above Ruin A; as it was completely explored the following year, we will describe the finds made on this occasion with those of the 1915 season.

NOCKITO

Our homeward route from Kayenta led down Laguna Creek to the "Cornfields," a Navaho settlement with a large acreage of prosperous-looking corn. Some 2 miles south of the fields on the western side of the creek there is a large surface ruin built on a series of sandstone knolls; the gray rock of which the walls were constructed must have been carried nearly half a mile from the top of a low mesa to the east. The site is little more than a jumble of fallen blocks, with a bit of protruding wall here and there. Quantities of potsherds, apparently representing a mixture of the Kayenta and northern San Juan styles, are to be found below the ruins.

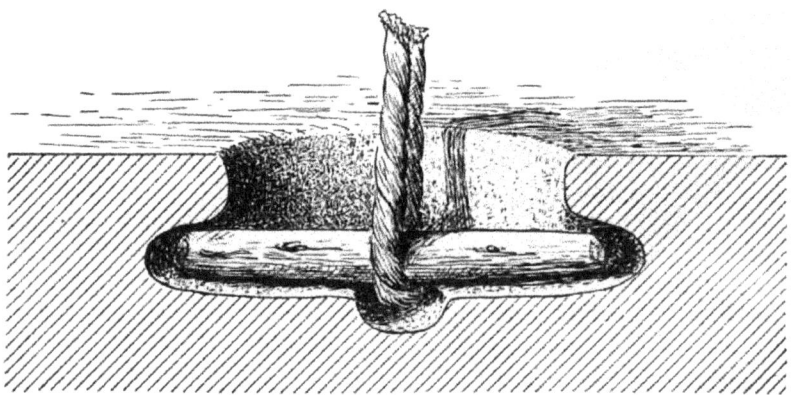

FIG. 26.—Loom-loop hole cut in sandstone ledge.

A few yards north of the houses there is a bare sandstone ledge pitted with numbers of tool-sharpening grooves; there are also two interesting series of holes pecked into the rock. The first consists of a cylindrical excavation 12 inches in diameter and 15 inches deep; running northeast by east from this is a row of five small holes in perfect alignment and exactly 15 inches apart. Their shape is difficult to describe, but, as the illustration (fig. 26) shows, they doubtless served as sockets for wooden crosspieces, which, like the loops observed in the floors of several kivas, held the lower bar of a loom. The second set, 20 feet southwest of these, consists of a long oval hole with two small depressions in its bottom. In the line of its long axis and 22 inches from either end there is a hole 3 inches in diameter and 2 inches deep. We have no hint as to the probable use of this arrangement.

At the Cornfields we crossed Laguna Creek on the rocks above a rapid and followed down the western side. Camp was made 3 or 4 miles below at a place where Laguna Creek drops over a series of ledges, making, when the water is high, an impressive waterfall. About a spring in a deep gully near the falls there is an extensive bed of cat-tail rushes. This was the only place where we found cat-tails growing, although mats made from their leaves were met with in every ruin. Above the spring and commanding the falls there is a 40-foot sandstone bluff overhanging a narrow flat bench with a full southern exposure. Here are potsherds scattered in quantities, the bowlders are scored with tool-grinding grooves, and on every smooth surface along the cliff are pictographs of mountain sheep, lizards, and human figures.[1] No house walls were noticed.

From the camp at the falls to the Chinlee is 8 or 9 miles, over flat mesa, with a final drop down steep ledges to the valley itself. The Chinlee at this point runs through a canyon varying in width from a few hundred yards to three-quarters of a mile, bordered by hummocky, domed, red cliffs and pleasantly shaded with large cottonwood trees. Near a small waterfall there is an unimportant cliff-house with several pictographs along the rocks near it.[2]

Nockito (Navaho, "Mexican water") trading post, 4 or 5 miles below our crossing, is situated in a deep side canyon which enters the Chinlee from the eastern side. Two miles below the post, in the main valley, there is a bay in the eastern cliffs forming an amphitheater-shaped "flat" between the rocks and the river, about three-quarters of a mile long and one-third of a mile wide. At its northern end are the remains of what was once a very large cliff-village.

RUIN 9

The ruins are in a shallow cave set well above the valley bottom, but easily reached from it up a sandy incline. Conditions had not been favorable for the preservation of this ruin from decay, as the overhang of the cliffs is so high that a southerly wind could drive rain or snow clear to the back of the cave; besides this there is a seepage of water from a horizontal fault along the whole length of the house bench, which concentrates in fine bubbling springs at either end of the ruin. The elements and this spring water have together brought about a very complete state of collapse. Few walls stand clear of the rubbish, and the rooms at the front of the cave are almost entirely buried under débris. In spite of these conditions it is obvious that Waterfall Ruin was once a very extensive structure, and one which, moreover, was inhabited for a long time. This

---

[1] See pls. 89, c; 90, c, g, j, l, n, o, p; 91, j; and fig. 102, c.
[2] See pls. 89, e; 90, a; 91, j.

is indicated by the enormous beds of débris of occupancy which encumber the slope below the houses and choke up all those spaces in the rear of the cave not actually covered by rooms.

Unfortunately the pothunters of the nineties did extensive digging at this site.· They completely trenched over a zone of burials that once extended all along the front of the cave on the lower slopes. They also did some pitting and room clearing in the rear, but this apparently was not carried to any great depth; the work, however, was done so long ago that the holes have to some extent filled up and reexcavation would be necessary to determine where disturbance has taken place. In spite of the moisture in parts of the site and in spite of vandalism, the Waterfall Ruin would splendidly repay careful excavation, for there is still left a great deal of untouched dry rubbish (what little we cleared was extraordinarily rich in textiles and wooden implements); it contains at least seven kivas, and probably ten or a dozen; and, moreover, we believe, though without any definite evidence beyond bits of fallen wall and a few potsherds, that under the cliff-house there will be found the remains of a large settlement of the " Fluteplayer " or Slab-house type.

We spent a day and a half here, tested the rubbish beds, excavated one kiva, and examined a small surface ruin on a rock near the waterfall. This surface ruin appears to have been contemporaneous with the last occupancy of the cliff-house. Behind one of its broken walls we found a wooden doll somewhat rotted, which we took to be ancient, but which the Navaho in the valley said had been made and deposited there many years before by their own people. We also photographed or copied a number of pictographs, some painted on the walls of the.cave, some pecked on near-by rock surfaces.[1]

The kiva that we excavated is in the eastern part of the building, well toward the front. There are rooms on each side of it and behind it, but whether or not they actually touch the kiva, we did not determine; we do not think they do. The chamber itself is sunk well into the ground and was probably entirely subterranean. In shape it is a lopsided square with rounded corners (fig. 27). While the wall at one place stands to a height of 6 feet 10· inches, there are visible no sockets or rests for roof beams. We found the place nearly full of débris, the upper 3 feet of which was stone, adobe lumps, and trash thrown in by pothunters who had excavated in the rear. Below this was the ancient deposit of light rubbish, as corn husks, twigs, bits of cotton cloth, broken wooden implements, etc.; the floor was covered with an inch or so of clean sand.

---

[1] See pls. 90, c, 1; 91, h; 94, d.

The walls are roughly made and irregular both in line and plumb, but are covered with many layers of plaster. There are no niches. The regular kiva features present are the ventilator, fire pit, and probably a sipapu. No fire screen is in place, but there were found, at the spot where it should have been, ten or twelve rough stakes whose lower ends showed that they once had been driven 3 or 4 inches into the earth. They may have formed the basis of an adobe-covered screen. The floor at that point was too much broken, however, to add any evidence. The ventilator passage could not be cleared without destroying the wall under which it ran; its entrance is 1 foot wide, 14 inches high. The fire pit is rectangular, its slab coping rising 2 inches above the floor; in it and in a bed between it and the ventilator were the usual white ashes. Hole *a*, diameter 3 inches (fig. 27), was sealed up flush with the floor; on cutting out the adobe plug, it proved to have smooth sides running down 2 inches, but no bottom other than soft cave sand. Hole *b*, diameter 10 inches, was noticed because it was sealed with gray adobe, contrasting in color with the reddish floor; this adobe was filled with small breast feathers of the turkey. The hole itself has irregular, unsmoothed sides and no bottom; probably it was a

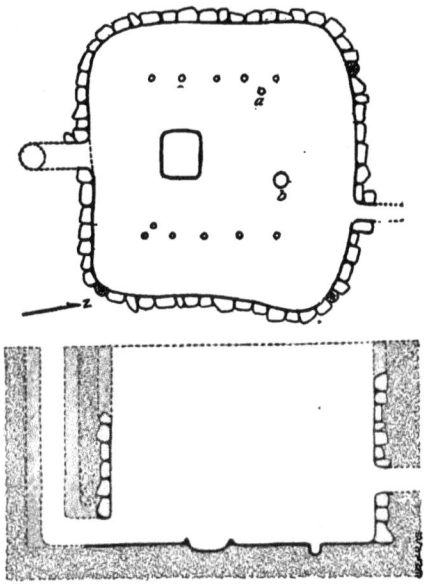

FIG. 27.—Plan and section of kiva, Ruin 9.

patched-up break in the floor. No other apertures occurred that could be considered as sipapus. On each side of the fire is an alignment of five holes containing yucca loops. There are also two odd loopholes between the lines and the fire pit.

In the back or north wall of the kiva, 2 feet 2 inches above the floor, is an aperture 1 foot wide by 13 inches high; it opens into a tunnel of the same size running toward the back of the cave. Time forbade following it to its termination. Eight or nine feet to the rear a round vertical shaft 1 foot in diameter emerges from the rubbish by the side of a room; it is possible that it and the passage out of the kiva may have had some connection. Posts are set vertically in the wall as shown; they have been burned down flush with the masonry on their in-room sides and have been plastered over with red adobe, indicating repair and reoccupancy of the room after the fire. The whole kiva indeed has a patched and mended appearance and was evidently in use for a long time.

Several kivas with banquettes and therefore of more conventional construction can be made out in the front part of the ruin; none, however, has the six-pilaster arrangement of. the northern San Juan region.

SEASON OF 1915

The party provisioned, as in 1914, at Kayenta and proceeded at once to Marsh Pass, where work was commenced in Kinboko ("House Canyon"), a deep, narrow gorge that enters the pass from the west just above Ruin A (see pls. 1 and 26). Camp was pitched high up on the rocks at the mouth of the canyon, drinking water being procured from potholes in the sandstone ledges.

CAVE I

Cave I was discovered and partially prospected during the last days of the 1914 season. It lies in the south wall of Kinboko, about a quarter of a mile above its mouth. The cave is 50 feet above the canyon bed, and is roughly 160 feet wide by 60 feet deep (fig. 28). The entrance is flanked on either side by great dunes of sand, between which there is a steep-banked arroyo formed by storm drainage falling from the cliffs above. The edges of the arroyo and the tops of the dunes are thickly overgrown with a tangle of wild gooseberry and other deciduous bushes.

Within the line of shelter (indicated on the plan by a dotted line) the cave floor rises in a steep slope of sand and broken rock to a sort of rear platform or bench, which itself rises, though much more gently, to its junction with the back wall of the cave. The continuity of the rear bench is broken at its middle by a group of large, rough blocks of sandstone fallen from the roof. Some of these have evidently lain in their present positions for a very long time; others, which show smoking on their under sides, have evidently dropped since the ancient inhabitants built their fires in the cave. The sloughing off of the ceiling is still going on; many parts of the roof are now in a precarious condition, particularly over the large rocks and along the eastern edge of the rear bench. One morning, indeed, just as the party was turning out of the canyon to climb up to the works several big scales crashed down on the upper bank. For this reason digging was not attempted under that spot, nor in one or two other places where inspection of the roof disclosed loosening fragments.

SKELETON 5

KINBOKO ("HOUSE CANYON")

Before the cave was excavated the signs of human occupancy
were not impressive: the roof was somewhat smoked; on the walls
were painted a large zigzag in red and a nondescript figure in faint
white; in addition to these ancient pictographs there were at two

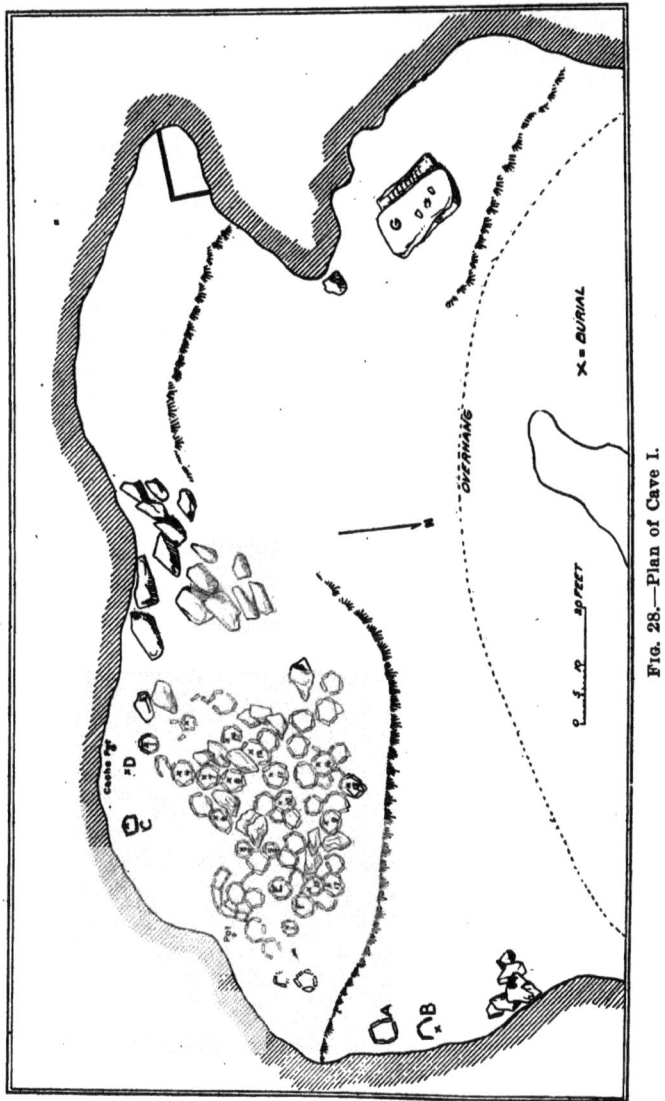

FIG. 28.—Plan of Cave I.

places groups of Navaho drawings, crudely done in charcoal and
representing men on horseback, in wagons, and on foot, and also cattle and sheep. On two fallen rocks at the northwest front was a set
of grinding grooves and a series of pecked hand prints (pl. 92, *b;*

fig. 28, *g*). In a bay at the west end of the rear bench stood the foundations of a small cliff-dweller building. The most promising indication, however, was the presence of two or three shallow holes in the sand, from which some recent intruder had thrown out the bones of several different skeletons.

The systematic exploration was begun by opening a trench through a level spot in the east front, at the foot of the steep bank which rises to the rear bench. This was within the line of shelter, nearly dry, and was free from the bushes that grow so thickly outside. Six inches below the surface was encountered loose rubbish, running to a depth of 2 feet 6 inches; it lay on a well-packed floor, below which there was a second rubbish stratum 1 foot thick, resting on hardpan, the latter showing no trace of disturbance.

Fragments of basketry, worn sandals, and broken implements were found in both rubbish layers, though more commonly in the upper one, which also contained many scattered bones from the skeletons of adults, adolescents, and very young children. Bones also were found lodged against the up-hill sides of some large rocks. Apparently most of the bones and débris forming the upper stratum had worked down from higher up. The trench at this point exposed a zigzag pecking on the cave wall a few inches under the surface sand.

As digging progressed, rocks were encountered in such quantities that only the end of the trench directly against the east wall was carried to the top of the bank. This ran through the spot where, in 1914, were found a skull and parts of two "mummies" (see p. 82). A little above this was uncovered a stone slab cist (fig. 28, *A*) 4 feet long and 18 inches deep. At the bottom, under the general rubbish that filled and covered it, there was found nearly a bushel of corn-cobs (pl. 27, *a*). The kernels had evidently been removed before the cobs were thrown into the cist. Three coils of basket splints were taken from the trench near the top of the bank (see pl. 75); these specimens did not seem to be part of the rubbish, but had apparently been placed in a hole and covered up for safe-keeping.

Reaching the top of the bank and the floor proper of the cave, we removed a circle of loosely piled stones 12 feet in diameter and 2 feet high (not shown on plan), assuming at the time that it was the work of Navahos, who sometimes build structures of this kind to corral kids and very young lambs. Traces of fires noted inside it, however, led Mr. Clayton Wetherill to suggest that it might have been made by wandering Utes, who occasionally seek shelter in caves and erect similar constructions for temporary dwellings. The complete excavation of the level area in this section of the cave showed it to be nearly filled by a group of cists which in arrangement much resembled a huge honeycomb. Before considering this cist area, however, we will complete the description of the other parts of the cave.

Reference to the plan will show a space along the east and southeast walls where no cists were found. Here the face of the trench disclosed a surface layer, 6 to 8 inches deep, consisting of sand, sheep droppings, and broken stone from the ceiling. Under this was an accumulation of rubbish composed of grass, corn husks, and bark mixed with sand; it was 3 feet 6 inches deep, and through it, at a depth of 3 feet, could be traced an old floor level of closely packed rubbish. This same floor level appeared again on the western side of the cist area, but here it was mudded over and covered a rubbishy stratum of grass, husks, and bark mixed with charcoal and ashes. The débris above this floor contained more grass than did that below it.

Beyond the large rocks there is another flat area; this was not completely excavated; test holes, however, showed loose rubbish but no cists. The foundations of the cliff-house structure at the extreme western end of the cave were fully exposed and found to rest on undisturbed hardpan. This was disappointing, as we had hoped to recover some stratigraphical evidence at this point. At the western front, about the two rocks with the grinding grooves (fig. 28, *g*), there is a small, level space which was covered, below the surface sand, with a thick layer of ashes and charcoal. This section, it may be noted, is the only one that receives the sun for any length of time during each day.

Pottery vessels, presumably deposited by the cliff-dwelling people, were found at two places; one, a small black olla, was taken from the surface sand near the east wall; the other, a handsome little black-and-white jar with a single horizontally placed handle, lay close to the back wall and only 8 inches below the surface (fig. 28). It was covered by a large sherd and proved to contain an interesting and valuable cache of small objects; these are described on pages 147–151.

To return to the cists: These were almost all grouped together on the gently sloping eastern end of the rear bench and differed very little one from another. They were all roughly circular in shape, averaged 2 feet 6 inches in diameter, and were about 2 feet 6 inches deep. They were made of large unworked sandstone slabs, set on edge or on end and generally leaning a little outward (pl. 27, *b*). The slabs usually met, sometimes overlapped. The cist bottoms were often filled with packed adobe, and many of them were lined with soft grass or bark. Grass was also frequently used to calk open spaces or poor joints between the slabs. In general the tops of the cists were found just below the surface layer of sand, and must, therefore, originally have stood somewhat above the ancient floor level; they were thus probably only semisubterranean. As the plan shows, they were placed more or less at random in the occupied area, some being quite independent, others (as at the clusters about Nos. 10 and 15) having walls in common with their neighbors. The only approach to a planned arrangement was observed at the southeastern side, where nearly encircling a well-built cist were two rows of slabs 12 to 18 inches apart, the inner row being the same distance from the central cist. Single slabs had been used to subdivide into small compartments the space between the rows, and that between the inner row and the central cist.

There were nearly 60 of the inclosures in all; of these, 20 were surely identifiable as burial places; a number of others contained traces of organic matter, rotted fur-string blankets, and scattered human bones, which might indicate a like use. Uncertainty in this regard is due to the fact that, with very few exceptions, the cists were found in a very badly disturbed condition; almost all had been plundered in early times, their contents removed from the cave, or scattered and mixed with the general rubbish; only in remote corners or in the deepest parts of the cists were burials or objects found untouched. Because of these conditions we were unable to determine whether or not all the cists were intended for mortuary purposes. Some, as has been stated, contained definite evidence of burials; others may have held bodies, but have been so badly pulled about by the plunderers that their case is doubtful; still others were quite empty when excavated, and appeared to us to have been so at the time of the abandonment of the cave. All so closely resembled each other structurally that repetition may be avoided by describing a selection of those which showed unusual features of construction, or contained objects of special interest.

Cist 1 (1914), diameter 3 feet, depth 2 feet 4 inches, held some scattered bones of a young adult. Against one side at the bottom was the " mummy " of a baby, whose inconspicuous position had protected it from the looters. It was wrapped in fur cloth and covered with a piece of hide. In the disturbed cist filling was a small twined bag (see pl. 79, *b*) and several fragments of coiled basketry.

Cist 3 was built against the back wall of a larger cist and was about 2 feet deep; in it was found the " mummified " body of a baby (pl. 28, *a*) propped up against the side wall in a sitting position and wrapped in a much-rotted fur-string robe. The knees were bound together with many turns of a fine light-colored string, probably made from dog hair, and in the lap was a quantity of fiber string loosely tied in small hanks (see pl. 66, *b*). A lump of white, chalky substance lay near the remains; a large stone bead and fragments of a coiled basket were found above them. In the upper part of the

a. CIST A

b. TYPICAL CIST

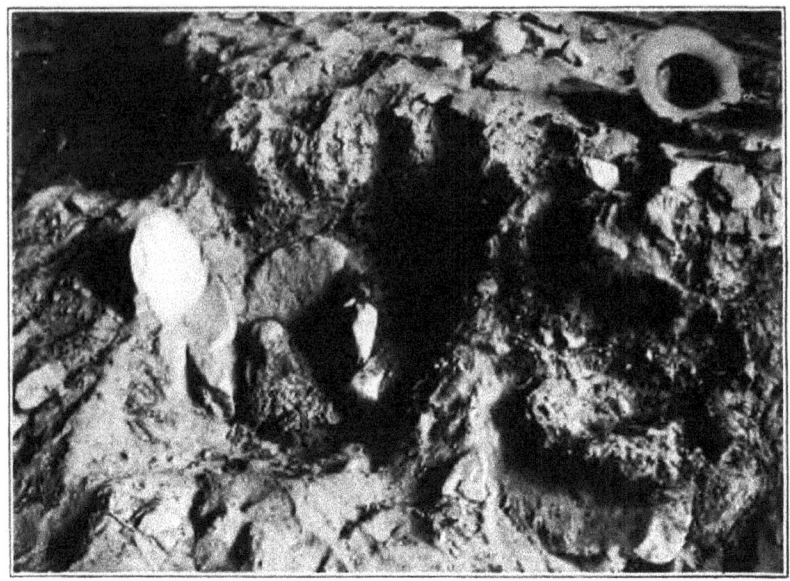

a. CIST 3

b. CIST 4 AND ADJACENT STRUCTURES

a. CIST 9

b. CIST 16

b. CAVE II

a. UPPER KINBOKO

cist were a few bones from the skeleton of an adult and pieces of a decayed woven bag.

Cist 4 was 3 feet in diameter, 20 inches deep, and nearly 2 feet below the surface. It had not been deep enough, however, to escape the early diggers, and there were left in its bottom only parts of the skeleton of an adult, an adolescent, and an infant. These fragments were partly held in place by adobe, with which the bodies had apparently been mudded in. Shredded flesh and torn and twisted ligaments adhering to the long bones of the adult indicated that the missing portions of the body had been ruthlessly wrenched away. From the few bones of this skeleton that lay undisturbed, it was seen that the corpse had been placed in the cist in a reclining position, resting against the side wall. The feet bore square-toed sandals (see pl. 69), and at one side were two elaborately woven sandals tied together by their laces. The remains of the child and of the adolescent were so scattered that nothing regarding their original positions could be learned. At the bottom of the cist was a peck or more of Coreocarpus seeds, solidified by partial decomposition into a compact mass; there were also the usual rotted fragments of fur-cloth robes and twined bags. Plate 28, *b*, shows the cist with the loose filling brushed away to expose the bones.

Cist 6.—The burial in this cist had been disturbed and only a few bones remained. These were encased in adobe and under them were traces of a fine twined bag which appeared to have been originally of good size; above the bones lay the rotted remains of a coarser fabric and part of a cedar-bark bag. This part of the cave was slightly moist, and few specimens in good condition were found in it.

Cist 9, 3 feet wide, 3 feet 6 inches long, 20 inches deep, held the skeleton of a child covered with cedar bark and fragments of a coiled basket. The remains had been placed in a large coiled basket of which but little was left. Parts of a fur-string blanket were found under the body, and about it were bits of a feather string that may have served to hold the cedar bark in place around the body. At the bottom of the cist lay some small remnants of a twilled mat, or possibly of a twilled basket. Most of these crumbled at a touch. The bones and wrappings were completely encased in adobe. In another part of the cist were a few bones of an adult, a "mummified" foot, a small toy cradle of grass, and a lignite bead. The photograph reproduced in plate 29, *a*, shows the adobe mass that contained the child's body, the foot, and the toy cradle, all in situ.

Cist 10 was slightly more than 3 feet in diameter at the top and 2 feet 6 inches deep; its saucer-shaped bottom was of hard adobe 1 foot thick. The upper part was filled with loose rubbish, from which were taken two sandals, part of a large woven bag in splendid preservation (see pl. 79, *f*), and fragments of a large coiled basket. On the bottom lay a shallow bed of coarse charcoal mixed with adobe, in which were a few bones from the skeleton of an adult (see cross section, fig. 29). On completely clearing out the cist and brushing clean the adobe lining at the bottom, an atlatl, or spear thrower, was exposed near the wall at one side, its upper face flush with the hard surface of the adobe; the specimen as it rested in place was slightly bent and twisted to conform to the shape of the bottom of the cist, and was so firmly embedded that it was necessary to cut away the adobe about it with a pocketknife before it could be taken out. After removing the atlatl, a white object with

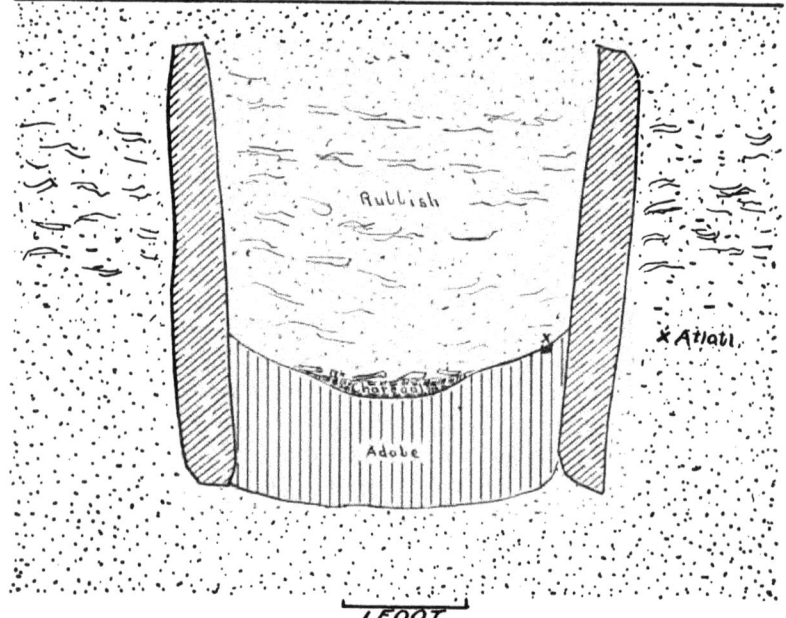

Fig. 29.—Cross section of Cist 10.

a flat upper surface was observed in the adobe matrix. The atlatl was returned to place and the position of the new find noted; the latter was then also removed and found to be a peculiarly shaped piece of worked limestone that had been bound to the under side of the atlatl by means of wrappings, faint traces of which can still be made out. A fuller description of these specimens is given on page 178.

Cist 16 was 4 feet 10 inches long, 3 feet 6 inches wide, 3 feet deep, and 1 foot below the surface. In it were a number of specimens evidently overlooked by the ancient plunderers, and the " mummified " upper half, including the head, of a girl of about 18 years of age.

Except for one detached foot, the legs had completely disappeared. As will be seen in plate 29, *b*, and figure 30, the remains rested in a reclining position against one of the slabs forming the cist wall. The body had been wrapped in a fur-string robe, a few ends of which remained, as did also part of a string apron or skirt found near the hips. Lying on the breast, parallel with the left arm, which was close against the side, the hand resting in the lap, were a number of reeds; these lay flat and close together and had perhaps once been fastened together, though all traces of binding had disappeared. They may be seen in plate 29, *b*. About the neck was a double string of olivella shell beads supporting a flat white stone pendant with a band of natural red coloring through its center (see pl. 70,*e*). The hair

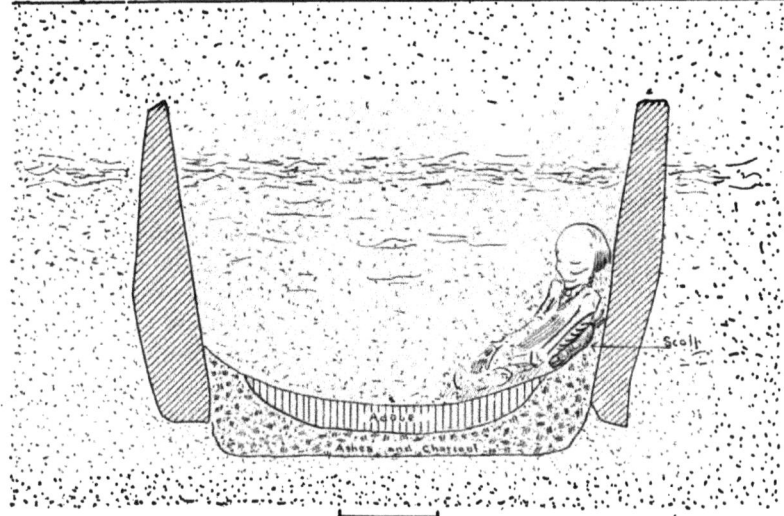

FIG. 30.—Cross section of Cist 16.

on the back of the head was about 8 inches long and showed no dressing; that on the crown and about the forehead seemed to have been cropped close. At the side of the body and partly under the right arm were fragments of a cradle made of small reeds crossed on each other, interwoven with hair string, and fastened to a wooden hoop. On and about the cradle were scattered bones of a baby and ends of fur-string. On removing what remained of the large "mummy," a trophy made from the skin of a human head (see pl. 87, *a, b*) was found below it under the left shoulder. This specimen lay face upward and showed faint traces of a woven fabric that had been between it and the corpse; fastened to it were remnants of two strings, the ends of which extended in the direction of the "mummy's" neck. When the trophy was taken out, the underside was found to have the hair still attached to it and to be arranged in a very elaborate coiffure. A fuller description of this object is given on pages 190–191.

The upper filling of the cist showed a thin stratum of compacted rubbish a few inches below the top; in the débris below this were a sandal, fragments of skin pouches, and a small coiled basket (see pl. 76, *l*) containing a three-pendant neck ornament and a flint flake. Above the compacted stratum, just under the surface sand, lay a single sandal. All these specimens had apparently been dislodged from their original positions by the looters. When the cist was entirely emptied, the bottom was found to be filled with a thick, saucer-shaped cake of adobe, laid on a foundation of charcoal and ashes mixed with sand (fig. 30).

Cist B (1914).—This cist was near the eastern wall of the cave, on the slope below the main cist area. Only a few stones of the inclosure remained. In it was part of a "mummified" adult torso, lacking the head. It was apparently in its original position, as bits of its fur-cloth wrappings were about it and it lay in sand presumably darkened by its own decomposition. Near by in the sand were found fragments of another adult, pieces of two very coarse baskets (see pl. 76, *a*), and the cranium and mandible of an elderly male. This skull probably belonged to one of the broken "mummies."

Cist C (1914) lay a little outside of the main group and close to the cave wall. Its preservation from disturbance is probably due to this fact. It was a small slab inclosure of the usual type and was not roofed over in any way. Under the sand which filled it was the desiccated body of a female infant lying on its back, wrapped with fur cloth, and covered with a piece of mountain-sheep hide tanned with the hair on. Further covering was supplied by part of an old cradle of cedar bark and yucca leaves, and over all lay a large, flat coiled basket (see pls. 73 and 76, *h*).

Cist E, a circular slab inclosure, had evidently been plundered; there remained in it, however, a stone pipe (fig. 94, *a*), part of a clay pipe (fig. 94, *d*), a small brush of stiff fibers (pl. 74, *e–f*), and a portion of a purse or pouch of tanned skin. From this cist also came a bundle of feathers tied up with string; the identification of the feathers will be found on page 177.

Cist F was interesting in that it had quite surely never been used for burial. This was proved by the fact that it was covered when found by an undisturbed roof of small limbs topped by several inches of brush. It was entirely empty, except for clean sand that had sifted in. Its greatest diameter was 3 feet; its depth 2 feet 6 inches; it lay 3 feet below the surface; to this more than usual depth it probably owes its escape from disturbance.

The only burial not in a cist was uncovered at *d* (fig. 28); it was the skeleton of a very young baby lying at a depth of 1 foot 6 inches and protected only by a single flat slab placed close above it. The burial was accompanied by the decayed remains of a fur-cloth blanket and of a coiled basket, and below was an almost completely rotted cradle made of thin twigs tied together with ornamental lashings of human hair.

Summing up the evidence as to burial customs, we find that the bodies were placed, often in reclining positions, in the bottoms of the cists. No attempt at roofing the graves seems to have been made, sand merely having been heaped in over the corpses. Wrappings of fur cloth were almost invariably used, supplemented occasionally, as nearly as we could tell, by portions of worn-out or deliberately cut-open twined bags. Offerings were numerous and varied, but the one standard gift to the dead seems to have been coiled basketry; wherever we found burials at all well preserved they were always accompanied by at least one such basket. As to the number of bodies per cist, our evidence from Cave I is not very reliable, owing to the generally confused condition of the cemetery. It may be said,

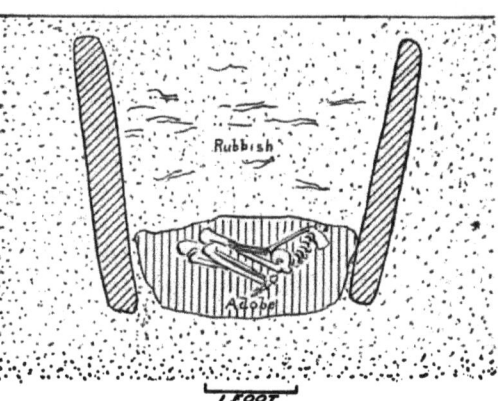

Fig. 31.—Cross section of Cist 6, showing bones encased in adobe.

however, that no such packing in of bodies as was noted at Sayodneechee took place here. On the other hand, most of the cists in Cave I undoubtedly held more than a single corpse. The commonest allotment seems to have been one adult and one or two infants.

Some of the bodies were evidently mudded into the cists at the time of interment, as many bones and partly "mummified" limbs were found incased in masses of hardened adobe (fig. 31). This hardening could scarcely have been due in every case to the action of liquids freed from the bodies during decomposition, since many of them were desiccated rather than decayed. Mr. John Wetherill, who visited the cave while the work was in progress, told us that he had seen similar adobe packing in some of the Basket Maker burials in Grand Gulch.[1]

---

[1] Fewkes (1914, p. 5) reports mudded-in burials from the lower Mimbres in southern New Mexico.

The culture represented by the finds in Cave I is, without much question, that of the Basket Makers, the method of burial, the undeformed type of skull, and the objects found in the graves, all being foreign to the cliff-dwelling culture, but closely similar to the Basket Maker remains from southeastern Utah described by Pepper. In all the digging in this cave there was found but a scant handful of potsherds, and these were all from the surface sand. The rarity of potsherds, the most common mark of cliff-dweller occupancy, would seem to indicate that the cave had been but little used by them. The cliff-dweller structure in the western corner was apparently never finished; this may perhaps be accounted for by the dangerous condition of the ceiling, or by the presence of burials of which the people were not aware until after they had commenced to build their house.

There is at present no evidence as to when or by whom the cists were plundered. The Navahos' well-known fear of the dead acquits them of any share in it. It might have been the work of Utes or of some other wandering tribe, but suspicion falls most naturally on the ancient cliff-dwelling people whose most extensive settlement in this region was situated at the mouth of Kinboko close to the cave (Ruin A). As has already been suggested, beads and other ornaments were probably the prime motive for digging. To reach these the heads of the bodies would first have been pulled from the cists, when, owing to their round shape, they would soon have rolled down the steep front bank and out into the canyon bottom. This might account for the fact that but two adult skulls were found (near Cist B, and on the Cist 16 "mummy"). Another possible explanation of the lack of skulls is that the plunderers may have carried away the crania for some ceremonial purpose. If the skulls had been merely thrown aside and had later rolled down the sloping front and so out of the cave, some of the jaws would probably have remained on the upper levels. As a matter of fact, only two jaws were recovered, and these lay with the two crania above mentioned.

CAVE II

Cave II is situated in the northern wall of Kinboko, near its head, less than 2 miles above Cave I. Here the canyon is quite narrow and between 300 and 400 feet deep (pl. 30, *a*); its bottom is covered with thick clumps of box elder whose vigorous growth is due probably to the underground moisture which emerges in a spring of good water a little lower down. The cave lies at the top of a steep slope of talus that reaches more than 100 feet up the canyon wall. Its entrance is partly hidden from below by the apex of a cone-shaped segment of the talus, which rises some 10 feet higher than

the cave floor directly in front of the opening, though some distance
out from the cliff (pl. 30, *b*).   The cave was apparently formed by
the falling out of large pieces of rock which broke off from the
cliff along the line of cleavage.   Débris from above has filled the
lower part of the break and formed a base for the floor.

The entrance is a triangular opening 50 feet wide at the base and
20 feet high at the apex.   Reference to the plan (fig. 32) will show

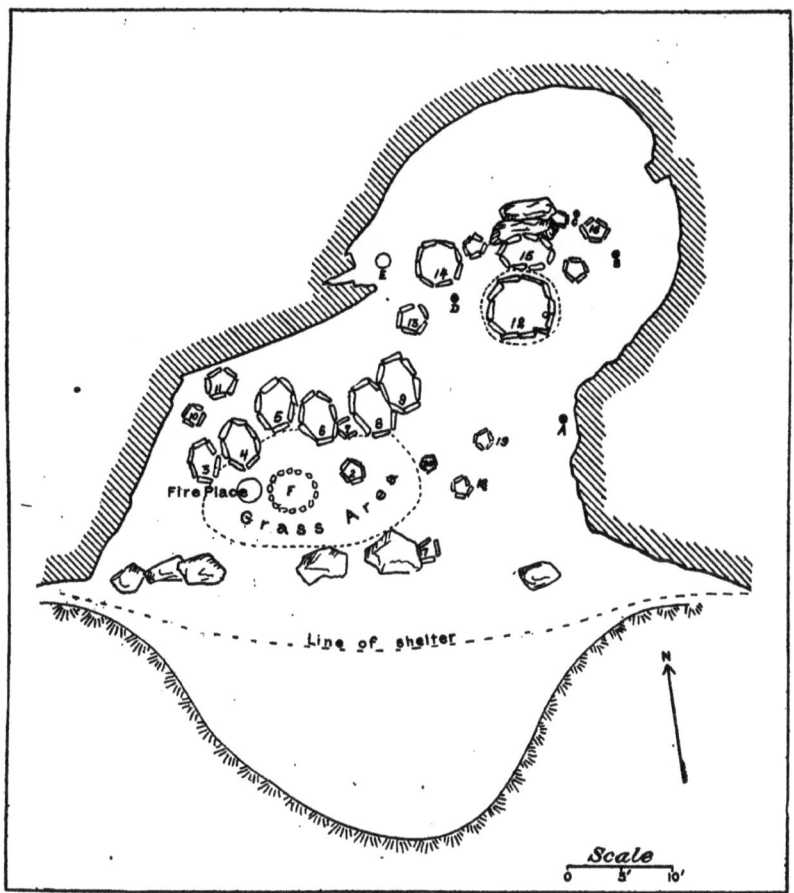

Fig. 32.—Plan of Cave II.

a bend in the eastern wall; and a reentrant angle in the west wall
opposite the bend partly divides the cave near the center, thus forming a front and a rear room.   The extreme depth, measured from
a point directly under the entrance, to the back of the rear room is
50 feet; the line of shelter extends some 20 feet beyond this.   The
opening faces the south.   Irregular arches form the roof, which
slopes gradually to where it meets the floor at the rear.

The whole cave is well lighted and free from moisture. The floor was covered with fine, clean sand, built up by eddying winds into a low drift near the middle of the rear room (pl. 31, *a*). In the western side and front of the outer compartment a quantity of ashes and charcoal, only partly covered by sand, gave evidence of relatively recent fires. On a smooth section of the rear wall of this room are a number of pictographs, square-shouldered human figures in white paint, handprints in red, and curious geometrical designs also in red (see pl. 97, *a*) ; a number of Navaho drawings in charcoal are on the same wall. The lower parts of some of the square-shouldered figures were covered by sand that had accumulated on the old floor level. The remains of fires, the smoked ceiling, and the pictographs were the only signs of occupancy to be seen on entering the cave, the smooth sand floor giving no hint of the existence of a number of interesting cists and objects which its complete excavation yielded. The surface sand was found to have an average depth of 8 inches; under it a floor level of packed rubbish and dirt could be traced throughout, except where there occurred cists or other things to break its continuity. Rubbish in varying quantities extended to a depth of 3 to 4 feet, sometimes showing other strata that probably marked earlier floor levels.

The western half of the outer room contained a group of six well-built slab cists, nearly uniform in size and shape (fig. 32, Nos. 3, 4, 5, 6, 8, 9). Their average dimensions were 4 feet 6 inches long, 2 feet 6 inches wide, 18 inches deep; five were just below the upper old floor level; Cist 6 differed from the others in having a dome-shaped roof built of small sticks overlaid with cedar bark, corn husks, and oak leaves, the whole held in place by small stones. All these cists were lined with grass or shredded bark. South of and in front of this group, and from 18 inches to 2 feet deeper, much loose grass was found in which were five nest-like bunches of grass, each holding either a rude yucca net filled with grass or bark, or a cedar-bark bag. About the sides of the lowest of these nests or beds (Cist F) had been placed stones the size of paving blocks, possibly to hold back the loose sand. West of Cist F was a bowl-shaped fire hole; it was 2 feet in diameter and 16 inches deep, measured from the surface; the bottom was filled with coarse charcoal. A layer of grass ran under this pit, separated from it by 6 inches of clean sand. A small space, perhaps 5 feet across, on the upper old floor level between Cist F and the fire hole was mudded over with a 2-inch layer of adobe. The situation here was somewhat confusing. The whole area containing the grass and nests being filled with loose blown sand, it could not be determined whether the grass nests occupied individual holes or whether they were arranged about the sides and bottom of a large basin-shaped depression excavated in the cave floor. Conditions about the fire

a. INTERIOR OF CAVE II

b. CISTS 12 AND 14

a. THE COMB AT THE HEAD OF KAYENTA VALLEY.

b. THE COMB SHOWING CAVE V

hole would indicate that a part of this section had been filled up above an old floor level while the cave was still in use. This part of the cave held a large accumulation of ashes and charcoal, mainly on the upper old floor level back of the cists and along the side wall. .

In addition to the large cists, this section contained six small cists of slabs, two in the grass and nest area (fig. 32, Nos. 2 and 20), two near the back wall (fig. 32, Nos. 10 and 11), and two in the eastern side of the room (fig. 32, Nos. 18 and 19). These held nothing of special interest and had no unusual features of construction; their locations and sizes are shown on the plan. Two feet from the east wall, at *a* (fig. 32), a small seed-jar-shaped coiled basket was found bottom up in a hole 18 inches deep, dug in the hardpan of the cave floor. In the basket was a small disk or plaque of coiled basketwork and part of a skin pouch that had contained red paint; two large pieces of bird skin with the feathers still on them lay at one side (see pl. 77). Another hole beside the large rock at the front (fig. 32, No. 17) held a small yucca net and part of a grass bag. These were covered with a thin, flat slab of stone on which red and yellow paint had been ground, the underside showing a thick coat of each. A third hole (fig. 32, No. 7) at the side of Cist 6 contained a coil of rope (see pl. 75, *e*). In the general digging back of Cist 6 were found three large potsherds of the same ware as that common about the surface ruins in the valley. They were nested together and lay barely covered by the surface sand well above the old floor. Apparently they had been used to hold or grind paint, one of them still showing traces of a brilliant green pigment. Near this spot also were found a few bones from the skeleton of a very young child and fragments of badly rotted woven fabric.

The rear room contained three large slab cists and four smaller ones; the latter were like the small cists in the outer room and need no description. Cist 12 differed in some respects from any yet encountered (pl. 31, *b*). It was a circular structure built of long slabs of stone set on end, sometimes overlapping each other, either to provide extra strength or to close up the joints. The entire upper part of this structure was reinforced by an outer wall of adobe 10 inches thick, the edges of which, though badly crumbled, still held in place a number of small, flat stones, evidently set in the mud while it was still soft to strengthen or finish off the rim. The whole was covered by a roof constructed as follows (fig. 33): four log rafters, 4 to 5 inches in diameter, were laid across the cist with their ends resting on the rim; as will be seen on the drawing, the end of the log nearest the front of the cave was set in the crotch of a thick upright stick standing against the inner wall. This support appeared superfluous, as the beam was of ample length to span the opening and of sufficient strength to support its share of the roof. A wide space from this beam to the front of the cist was half covered with small sticks placed with one end resting on the wall, the other on the beam and at right angles to it. This arrangement left a small open space, probably an entrance or hatchway, near the upright crotched log. For this reason perhaps the crotch was introduced as an extra strengthener. The exact dimensions of the hatchway could not be determined, as the adobe portion of the roof was much crumbled. The roof beams were covered with sticks, which in turn were covered with cedar bark, small stones, and a layer of adobe. The interior was completely filled with clean sand containing no trace of rubbish. The inside dimensions were as follows: diameter at top, 5 feet; at bottom, 4 feet 6 inches; depth from underside of roof beams, 3 feet 6 inches. The roof was 2 feet 6 inches below the present surface. The largest slab used was 4 feet long, 2 feet 4 inches wide, and 4 inches thick; the average slab was somewhat less in width, but of about the same length.

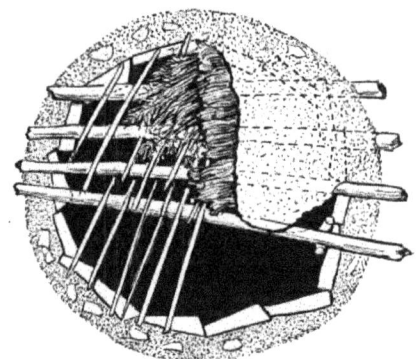

FIG. 33.—Plan of Cist 12.

A layer of oak leaves was found some 5 feet below the surface in this part of the cave; below it there was no rubbish, and above it several inches of clean sand.

Cist 14, between Cist 12 and the west wall, was built with unusual care of large, thin, apparently selected slabs (pl. 31, b, upper part of picture). The joints were carefully closed and smoothed over with adobe, and the junction of the floor and sides was neatly rounded with the same material. The top was finished with a rounded rim of adobe in which had been set several round, smooth sticks 2 to 3 inches in diameter by 12 to 18 inches long. The remains of a roof of small sticks covered with adobe lay in the bottom; under these was found a square-toed sandal. Nine inches below the bottom of this cist appeared the hard-trodden rubbish of a floor, and still deeper the stratum of oak leaves previously noted. The great care shown in the construction of this cist might justify one in thinking it to have been intended for the storage of water; it would have served that purpose well, and from our own experience in clambering up and down from the spring to the cave, would have been a great convenience to the ancient people if used in this way. It is interesting to note, in this connection, that at d (fig. 32), just in front of this cist, there was uncovered a large water-carrying basket (see pl. 78, a, b).

Between Cist 14 and the side wall (fig. 32, *e*) three or more pecks of shelled corn were found carefully cached in a pit 3 feet 8 inches deep and 2 feet in diameter dug in the hardpan. The cache was covered with: first a layer of fine grass; then coarse grass and a cedar-bark cradle; the whole weighted down by a flat slab of stone. The top had been used for a fire hole, judging from a quantity of ashes and charcoal found 9 inches below the surface and directly over the stone slab.

Back of Cist 12 and on a level with its roof was uncovered a shallow, carelessly built cist (fig. 32, No. 15), which in general resembled the six long cists in the outer room and, like them, was lined at the bottom with bark (pl. 31, *b*, upper right). Irregular flat stones had been used in its construction, and no care had been exercised to make good joints. Its dimensions were 4 feet 6 inches by 2 feet 10 inches. The small cists indicated on the plan in this room were like the small ones in the outer chamber.

Two vessels were taken from this part of the cave. One, a small black jar, was found at *b* (fig. 32); in it was a little gourd-shaped ladle of red ware; the pot had no cover and was filled with sand. The second vessel was near Cist 16, at *c* (fig. 32); its mouth had been sealed with a bunch of moss held in place by a thin flat stone. It contained a gourd-shaped ladle of yellow ware. Both were buried in the surface sand. (See pl. 58, *a–d*.)

To sum up the finds made in Cave II: The purpose or use of the large cists and grass nests can be only a matter of conjecture, but it seems reasonable to suppose that they served as sleeping bins or bedding places, since as regards exposure they are situated in the most livable part of the cave, a fact attested to by the later visitors who built their fires here. As to whether the cists and the objects found in them were the work of the Cliff-dwellers or of the Basket Makers, there may be some question, but it should be noted that aside from the three large sherds, two or three fragments of black-and-white ware, and the two black pots, all from the surface sand, nothing found here was in any way typical of the Cliff-dweller culture. This seems all the more significant when it is remembered that the talus in front is covered with small blocks of stone perfectly suited to the construction of cliff-houses, and that with very little labor the cave could have been transformed into a desirable living place.

It seems possible that in early times there may have been some surface indication that would have served to distinguish a purely domiciliary cave such as this one from one used for burial; for there were no traces here of such disturbance as was found in Cave I, though this cave could hardly have escaped the notice of the industrious diggers who plundered the burials of Cave I in search of beads and other mortuary offerings.

SURFACE RUINS IN MARSH PASS

A short time was spent in examining surface ruins above the section explored in 1914. They were found to occupy practically every desirable site on both sides of the valley to its head, and were also scattered through the piñon growth on the first bench of the Black Mesa. As a rule these ruins were much dilapidated, few walls showing above the surface, though it is probable that considerable portions of foundations or other walls may be covered by sand and earth. There appears to be no difference between the pottery from one ruin and that from another, except that about the villages at the foot of the valley red ware seems to preponderate, while at the upper end black-and-white and red occur in nearly equal quantities.

Three graves were excavated, one at the head of the valley and two at separate sites about one mile above Ruin A.

Skeleton 1.—Adult in a good state of preservation. Flexed, with the hands in the lap; head south, face east. There were no mortuary offerings. This burial was in rubbish, as the earth about it was full of potsherds.

Skeleton 2.—Adult. The bones lay close against the rocks that form the side of the valley; denudation had partly exposed the skull and carried away the pelvis and legs. The head pointed south and faced west; near it was a small corrugated mug.

Skeleton 3.—Adult in good preservation. Flexed on left side, head south, face east. Between the knees and the chin lay a black-and-white bowl containing a small pitcher of the same ware.

The skulls of skeletons 2 and 3 had been exposed by washing, and our attention was called to them by a Navaho who disliked to pass the spot and who asked us to remove them.

BLUE CANYON CAVE

A brief visit was made to the head of Blue Canyon (see pl. 1), where a Navaho had reported a large cave with many pictographs on its walls; one he described as an "owl." The trip was an interesting one, the route leading up a steep Navaho trail to the top of the Black Mesa and down an equally precipitous path into the head of the canyon. The return was made by a different way over a rough and very obscure trail said to have been used by the Navaho many years ago to escape war parties of the Ute. The cave itself proved a disappointment. It was situated in the canyon bottom and offered no inducement for excavation. The pictographs consisted mainly of hand prints in white. The " owl " is shown in plate 95, *b*. On the top of the Black Mesa the broad-leaf yucca was seen for the first time in this region.

SURFACE RUINS AT THE HEAD OF KAYENTA VALLEY

The work of excavating the caves in Kinboko and the other investigations in that district having been completed, camp was moved to below the mouth of Marsh Pass, where the rest of the field season was spent in exploring a part of the uptilted and broken " comb " lying between Skeleton Mesa and Kayenta Valley (see pl. 1). Owing to the rugged character of the country, this could be accomplished only on foot, which limited the area examined to a radius of not more than 5 miles (pl. 32, *a, b*).

Opposite the new camp, which was pitched on the east bank·of Laguna Creek at the entrance to the pass, were remains of quite an extensive surface ruin. These lay along the perpendicular escarpment of a detached portion of the comb. No walls were visible on the surface, but a number of low mounds covered with building stones probably conceal the foundations of rooms. At this place there is also a granary made by walling up the front of a small recess under a large, irregular rock standing alone some distance out from the cliff. Its doorway is a rectangular opening 17 by 19 inches. The most interesting feature of this neighborhood is the great number of pictographs worked in the smooth face of the cliff; sketches of a few of the most striking ones are given in plates 89, *h, i;* 91, *c, e, f, g*.

CAVES III AND IV

Climbing up and through a narrow break between the section of the comb back of the surface ruin and the next segment, two small caves were found (see pl. 1). The first, which can be seen from the bank of the creek, contained no cliff-house structures. The low roof was much blackened by smoke. As the floor was saturated with moisture from a seeping spring at the back, no digging was attempted. The second cave is near the top of the comb and was reached by passing through a narrow fissure and up a rough talus composed of huge blocks of stone. The cave itself is a crevice in the rock, 35 feet deep, 30 feet wide, and 20 feet high at the front. Its back is completely closed in by a well-built wall, forming a room 11 feet deep and 8 feet wide at the front; access to this chamber is gained through a doorway 17 inches wide and 19 inches high (pl. 33, *a*). Two long, narrow slabs of stone serve as lintel and as sill. Two small sticks cross the top of the doorway just under the lintel;

their ends, penetrating the jambs a few inches, hold them securely in place. This door was found blocked with stones; on removing them the room was seen to be the repository of a quantity of Navaho belongings which, judging from their dilapidated condition, had evidently been cached there for many years.[1] Among the articles noted were a large basketry water bottle, a tray-shaped basket like those now in use by the Indians, and a number of long, double saddlebags of rawhide whose contents were not examined as it was thought best to leave the cache untouched rather than risk incurring the ill-will of the Navaho, with whom the party were on very good terms. In the front at the right of the entrance there remains part of the foundation wall of a room. There was but little rubbish here, and none whatever in the rear room. On the side wall were four hand prints in white and, written in charcoal, " Richard Wetherill and ——— Billings, 1895."

CAVES V AND VI

Two caves occur about 1 mile below the entrance to Marsh Pass. One of these, which can be seen from the road, is situated halfway up the side of the comb, in a break facing the valley (pl. 32, b). The second was discovered in climbing to the first, and is in the bottom of a small wash which has at some time carried away the greater part of the earth floor. In one end, however, there remains some rubbish, which, with a much blackened ceiling, furnish evidence that it was once inhabited. The upper cave was reached by climbing up a steep ledge. It is a shelter about 85 feet long, 40 feet deep, and 20 feet high, facing the southwest. A great quantity of shale-like flakes from the roof cover the floor, which falls at a sharp angle from the back to the front, being merely a continuation of the steep slope by which the cave is entered.

In the western half, near the back, a low wall can be traced, and in front of this part of a crescent-shaped wall, both of rather crude workmanship, so far as observed. In the outer half of the cave the tops of two stone slab cists appear above the floor. The old surface of the ceiling has nearly sloughed away, but wherever it remains it is blackened by smoke.

Owing to lack of time, these caves were not further investigated.

SUNFLOWER CAVE

This cave is situated in the top of a jagged section of the comb almost directly back of the two caves just described (see pl. 1). It

---

[1] We later learned from a young Navaho that these goods had been the property of his father, now dead, who placed them in the cave 20 years ago.

is well concealed and can be seen only from a few points on the rocks that would scarcely be reached by an ordinary visitor to the country.

The approach from Laguna Creek is through a narrow ravine which connects the valley with one of the huge basins that lie back of the comb. From the bottom of the ravine the cave is approached by climbing up a rather steep ledge strewn with débris from the

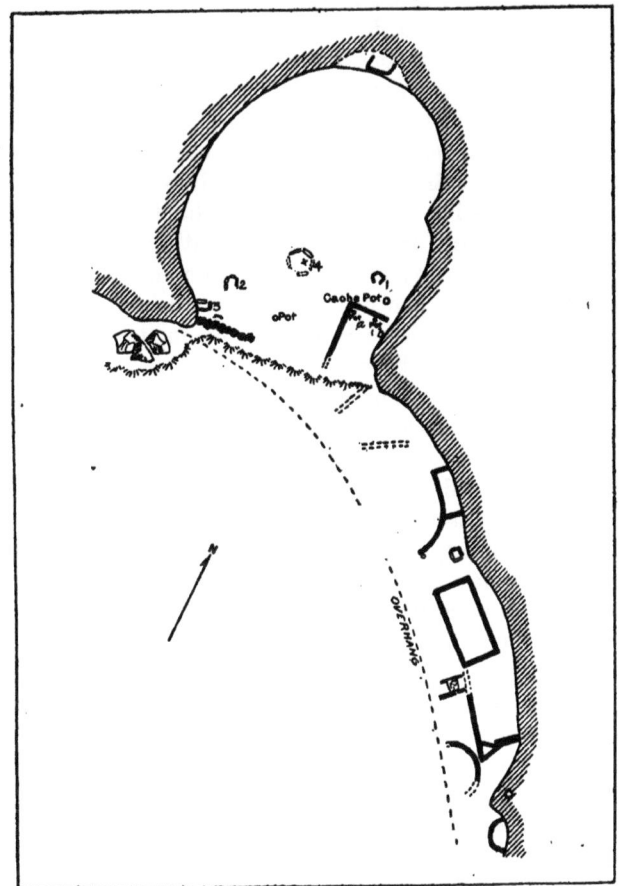

FIG. 34.—Plan of Sunflower Cave.

cliff above. The entrance is a ragged break in the rock, back of which opens a space 30 feet wide and 40 feet deep, with perhaps 18 feet between the floor and the highest point in the dome-shaped roof. The opening faces the south and is flanked on one side by an overhanging cliff, beneath which are the much fallen walls of several cliff-house rooms (fig. 34). Within the cave, at the right of the entrance, the foundation walls of a room 10 feet long and 7 feet wide rise a few inches above the surface. From the opposite side a rough wall, 1 foot 6 inches high, built of irregular stones, extends nearly halfway across the front. There are remains of a small storage room on a ledge at the extreme rear. The cave is absolutely dry and the roof is heavily coated with the smoke of many fires.

The first work here was the opening of a test hole back of the small room at the front. This was done with a trowel, the only implement available at the moment. Rubbish was found just below the surface sand, and at a depth of 1 foot a flat stone was encountered, which proved to be one of two slabs covering what was supposed to be a large corrugated pot with a broken rim. On removing one of the stones there was disclosed the edge of a wooden " sunflower " and several cone-shaped objects coated with pitch; these were partly covered with sand which had filtered in (pl. 33, b).

Further investigation was deferred to the following day when, with proper equipment, the work of excavating the cave was commenced by clearing away the rubbish from about the pot. The latter was found to be the upper half of a large, bottomless, corrugated olla placed rim down in a hole dug in the hardpan floor of the cave. This hole had been lined at the bottom and on the sides with cedar bark, forming a nest for the jar. The contents proved to consist of 26 painted wooden " sunflowers," 25 varnished cone-shaped wooden objects, one carved and painted wooden bird, and two pieces of tanned skin, cut and painted to represent " sunflowers." All these objects had been placed in the pot with great care, first the two skin " flowers," the larger at the bottom nearly closing the neck of the jar; the bird lay back down on these; the wooden " flowers " and cones were so arranged about the sides and center of the pot as to make the best use of the very limited space. A petal was missing from each of two " flowers," otherwise the specimens were in the most perfect condition and appeared as fresh and clean as if made yesterday.

The exact location of the find with reference to the room and to the side wall of the cave is shown in the plan (fig. 34), and a more detailed description of the objects themselves will be found in Section II (pls. 60, 61).

The front wall and a portion of the side wall of the room at the right of the entrance had fallen down a steep slope, 6 to 8 feet high, leading up to the cave. On clearing away the débris at the top of this slope, the foundations of the room were found to have been laid on an old, much-used, and very hard floor which itself rested on hardpan. In the room a second floor had been built over an accumulation of rubbish 6 or 8 inches deep (fig. 35). This floor was paved with thin slabs of stone leveled off and mudded in

a. CAVE IV

b. SUNFLOWER CACHE IN SITU

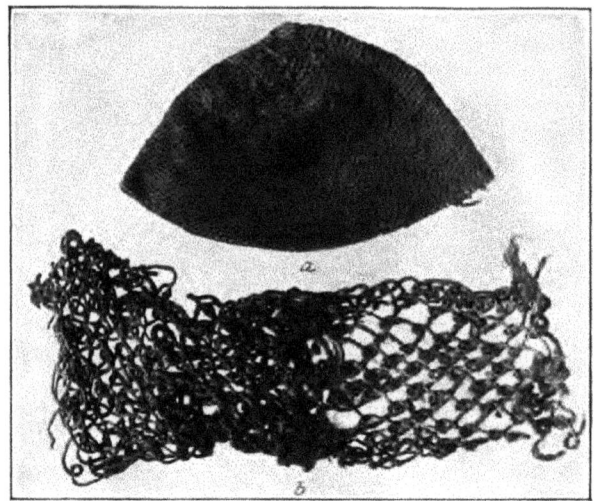

a. CAP. *b.* LEGGING

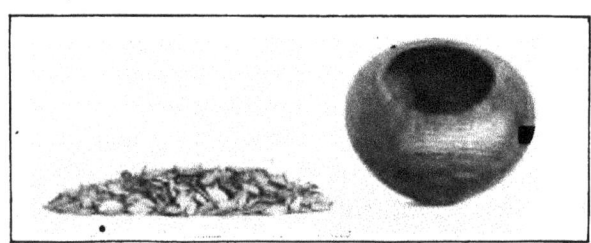

c. STORE OF SEED CORN AND SQUASH SEEDS

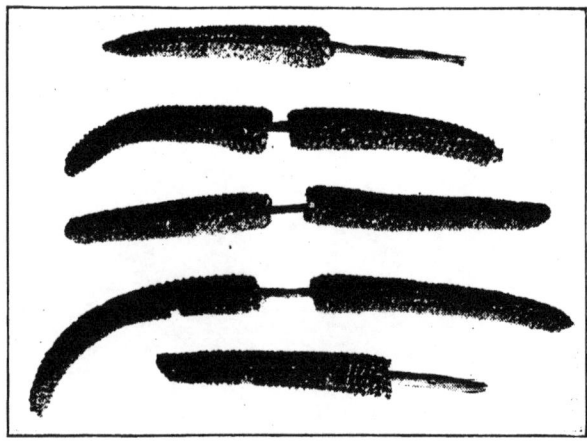

d. CORNCOBS ON STICKS

with adobe, and joined to the walls with rounded corners; above
it were a few inches of rubbish and the surface sand. The complete clearing out of the room was rewarded with a large corrugated olla (see pl. 58, *g*), a spherical black jar (see pl. 59, *a*), and
several typical cliff-house specimens. The first pot (fig. 35, *b*) was
at the back of the room near the side wall of the cave. It had
been placed in a hole apparently dug through both floors, though
neither floor was as well defined here as in other parts of the
chamber, probably because the slanting wall of the cave afforded
but little headroom at this point. Flat stones had been placed
about the sides of the hole to protect the jar, and a flat stone had
been used to cover it, failing, however, to keep out the sand with
which it was filled when found. The second pot (fig. 35, *a*) lay bot-

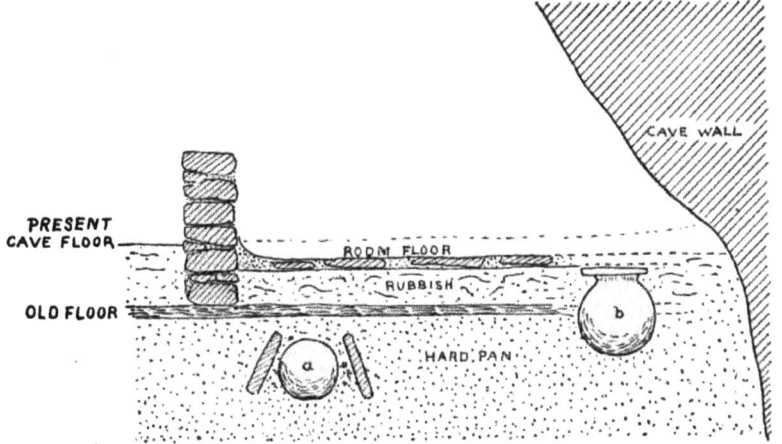

FIG. 35.—Cross section of room in Sunflower Cave.

tom up and empty under the unbroken lower floor. It was surrounded by four flat stones, the tops of which inclined somewhat
inward. The space between the slabs and the pot was filled with
compacted sand and broken stone which had to be picked away before the jar could be removed. There seems good reason to believe
that the presence of the pot was unknown to the builders of the
cliff-house structure. In trenching the main floor of the cave, four
cists were found.

Cist I was apparently an ordinary cliff-house storage hole; it was
2 feet in diameter by 18 inches deep, and contained nothing of
interest.

Cist II was a small depression that had been completely lined
with a hard, gray, cement-like substance, nicely smoothed on the
interior to form a cup-shaped receptacle 14 inches in diameter and

12 inches deep; a good portion of it had been broken away and what remained was badly shattered. Embedded in the outer side of the "cement" was a sherd of black-and-white ware which proves the cliff-house origin of the structure. The material used in making this cist is apparently the same as that employed in the construction of a fire pit in Ruin 7 (1914; see p. 53 and pl. 17).

Cist III was a well-built rectangular slab bin, 21 inches long, 18 inches wide, and 18 inches deep. It was, perhaps, a mealing place.

Cist IV.—The outlines of this cist could be traced by a disturbed area showing in the face of the trench. It had originally been a stone enclosure, though but two of the slabs were still in place. A few bones from the skeleton of a child were found in its upper part; near the bottom were a few badly preserved bones of an adult. Lying on the bottom at the side nearest the back of the cave were two decorated bone-tubes (see pl. 86, *f*). Imprints of coiled basketry could be seen in hard lumps of the adobe filling, but nothing of the basket itself remained. This cist gave us the impression that it had been a Basket Maker burial chamber which had been pulled to pieces, partly emptied, and then filled in with rubbish during the cliff-house period.

Two floor levels were visible through the digging in the rear of the cave, the complete excavation of which we were unable to make at this time. The rubbish contained much ashes and, in some places, quantities of turkey droppings. From the general digging came a square-toed fringed sandal (see pl. 68, *b*). This is a perfectly typical Basket Maker specimen; its position in the cliff-house rubbish would seem to lend color to our theory that there had been an early Basket Maker occupancy of this cave, and that their remains had been disturbed and scattered about at the time of the construction of the cliff-house. It is possible that the spherical black jar from under the floor of the room is also a Basket Maker product; it is unlike any cliff-house pottery that we have seen.

Of the house structures along the cliff outside the cave, there remain portions of the walls of four well-defined rooms and a part of a circular foundation that may have been a kiva. The architecture is like that of the other ruins of the district and their excavation yielded nothing unusual. The positions of these rooms and their dimensions are shown on the plan.

A little below the mouth of the canyon leading to Sunflower Cave there is a surface ruin. Its most prominent feature is the foundation of a building 25 feet long and 10 feet wide, of which the walls stand 4 feet high. All about are fallen walls and much broken pottery. This structure is of the same type as Ruin A in Marsh Pass.

ROCK FORD RUIN [1]

In the course of our return trip to the railroad a preliminary reconnoissance was made of a cliff-house ruin on the west bank of the Chinlee a few miles above Mexican Water and Ruin 9 of the 1914 expedition. The dwelling is situated in a shallow cave in the low cliffs which here line the valley. The exposure is to the south. There remain parts of several rooms, and portions of a thick, buttressed front wall behind which lies a plaza 40 feet long by 25 feet wide. There seems to be much dry rubbish, and the site would probably well repay excavation.

---

[1] This ruin was cleared in 1916.

II. MATERIAL CULTURE

IN this section are described the minor antiquities recovered during the two seasons' work. The specimens are assigned to three groups: Those from the cliff-houses, those from the lower level of Ruin 5, and those from the Basket Maker caves. The recognition of two distinct cultures—the Cliff-house and the Basket Maker, with the addition of the somewhat more doubtful Slab-house culture based on the finds from Ruin 5—is thoroughly believed in by the authors. As to the correctness of this grouping the reader may judge for himself after a consideration of the evidence of the major remains (houses, burial places, etc.) presented in the preceding section, and of that of the minor antiquities about to be described. The objects from all the cliff-houses are discussed together, and the same has been done with the material from the three Basket Maker caves. The Peabody Museum catalogue number of each specimen mentioned but not figured is given in the text, and each is referred to its proper ruin or cave; the locations and catalogue numbers of figured specimens may be found in the Appendix.

A. CLIFF-HOUSE CULTURE [1]

FOOD

VEGETAL

Corn was apparently the staple food of the people. A large part of the rubbish in every house consisted of corn husks, stalks, and cobs. On the specimens submitted to him for examination, Mr. G. F. Will, of Bismarck, North Dakota, has given us some interesting notes, which for convenience in comparison are placed with his remarks on Basket Maker corn (p. 154). Stores of shelled corn (presumably for seed) were found in Ruins 2 (pl. 34, *c*) and 7. Long ropes of braided husks and the butts of ears strung together on yucca leaves show that the ancients hung up their maize to dry exactly as do the modern Pueblo Indians. Cobs with rough sticks inserted in their butts came from several sites, and from Ruin 3 pairs of cobs fastened together, butt to butt, by means of small sticks (pl. 34, *d*). The purpose of this practice is unknown.

Beans, both plain red and red-and-white, were extensively used. We have not yet succeeded in having botanical identifications made.

---

[1] Ruins 1 to 9, inclusive, Sunflower Cave and Marsh Pass surface sites.

Squash seeds, stems, and pieces of rind were uncovered at every site; the species, according to Prof. F. W. Waugh, of the Canadian Geological Survey, is probably *Cucurbita maxima*, or Hubbard squash. Bits of the rind were sometimes worked into round disks for use as spindle whorls.

Gourds.—A small variety, probably, according to Professor Waugh, *Cucurbita pepo*, was recovered in considerable quantities, particularly in Ruin 5.

Grass-seed is gathered and used as a grain by the modern Paiute and other Plateau tribes. It also apparently formed a part of the food of the Cliff-dwellers. In Ruin 1 was found a mass of grass seed (A–1150) which had been stored in a corrugated jar. Cummings reports from Sagiotsosi caches of the seed of a " coarse bunch grass " and a " finer grass seed." [1]

ANIMAL

While it is probable that the principal diet of the people was vegetable, the number of mammal and turkey bones found in the ruins show that animal food was much used.

Domesticated turkeys were seen by the Spaniards at the Pueblo towns in 1540,[2] and they seem to have been kept by the ancient people of northern Arizona as well. Quantities of feathers, bones, and droppings were present in all the ruins that we excavated, and we also saw, in Ruins 4 and 7, constructions which might have been used as brooding places (pp. 39 and 52). Turkey feathers for making feather cloth were undoubtedly of as great importance as was the flesh; Castañeda, indeed, states that turkeys were not eaten at Cibola.

Game.—From our excavations came bones of the following animals, most of which were probably used for food:[3]

Mule deer (*Odocoileus hemionus*).
Mountain sheep (*Ovis canadensis*).
Pronghorn antelope (*Antilocapra americana*).
Coyote (*Canis estor*).
Large dog or wolf (*Canis* sp.).
Western fox (*Vulpes macrourus*).
Texan jackrabbit (*Lepus californicus texianus*).
Warren's cottontail rabbit (*Sylvilagus auduboni warreni*).
Woodchuck (*Marmota* sp.).
Pocket gopher (*Thomomys* sp.).
Arizona bushy-tailed woodrat (*Nestoma cinera arizonæ*).

---

[1] Cummings, 1910, p. 14.
[2] Castañeda, see Winship, 1896, pp. 491, 521.
[3] We are indebted to Dr. Glover M. Allen, of the Museum of Comparative Zoölogy, Harvard University, for the specific identifications.

Bones of the mountain sheep, cottontail, and jack rabbit were by far the commonest; deer and pronghorn antelope occurred rather sparingly.

DRESS

BODY CLOTHING

As to the body clothing of the people we gathered very little data. Feather- and fur-cloth blankets were probably the standard over-garments for cold weather, but we found no trace of jackets of feather cloth such as are reported by Hough from the upper Gila.[1] The cotton cloth, of which so many rags were collected, seems to have been used for shirt-like garments, as many of the pieces show cutting on the bias, sewing together of edges, apertures for armholes and other evidences of tailoring. Bits of deerskin and mountain-sheep hide, some dressed with the hair on, some without, show signs of sewing with sinew thread as if for use as fitted clothing; nothing large enough for description was collected. From Ruin 9 came part of a breechclout of fiber (A–1705); it is identified as such by means of perfect examples (presumably from the Canyon de Chelly) in the Peabody Museum. A skullcap (?) of coiled work without foundation in yucca cord was discovered in Ruin 2 (p. 24 and pl. 34, *a*). It is, so far as we know, the only textile cap that has yet been found in the Southwest. Nordenskiöld, however, describes a leather cap found on the head of a "mummy" at Step House, Mesa Verde.[2]

FOOTGEAR

For the study of footgear much material was gathered in the form of leggings, moccasins, and particularly sandals.

Leggings, or fragments of them, were found in Ruins 2, 5, and 9. They are all of the same type and weave, tubular stockings netted with the stitch called by Mason "coil work without foundation." The best preserved example (pl. 34, *b*, Ruin 9) is of child's or small adult's size, 12 inches long. It reached to the knee and is shaped to fit the calf of the leg. The upper part of the foot is also shaped and was probably designed for attachment to the border loops of a sandal. The material is yucca string wound with feathers. The fragmentary specimens (A–1396 and A–1541, Ruins 2 and 5) seem to have been similar, but perhaps larger; they differ, furthermore, in that the string of which they are netted contains deer or mountain-sheep hair so twisted between the strands that it fluffs out in all directions. This hair has now been almost wholly eaten away by

---

[1] Hough, 1914, p. 72, and figs. 149, 150.   [2] Nordenskiöld, 1893, pl. xix, 2.

insects, but when new the fluff string, like the feather cord, must have made up into a soft, warm fabric. These specimens may be parts of sock-like shoes or bootees such as are contained in the American Museum collection from Grand Gulch, Utah;[1] these are made in one piece, in the same weave and of the same fluff string as our pieces.

Moccasins are represented in our collection by a single specimen of somewhat doubtful antiquity (A–1318, Ruin 4, see p. 37). It is made of heavy leather, and is exactly like the examples used by the Navaho to-day. Moccasins were, however, made by the Cliff-dwellers, having been found on " mummies " and in the ruins.[2]

Sandals were the standard footgear; we obtained about 100 specimens. They may be classified as follows:

Type I.—Yucca leaf.	Type II.—Cord.
a, Twilled weaving.	*a*, Wickerwork.
1, Coarse.	*b*, Twined weaving.
2, Fine.	*c*, Coil without foundation.
b, Wickerwork.	

Type I, *a*, 1 (pl. 35). Coarse twilled weaving of whole yucca leaves. The typically square heels of these sandals have a pad made by turning back the butts of the leaves after the actual weaving has been completed. The plaiting starts at the toe, which is usually square, sometimes a little rounded, rarely shaped for right or left foot. Eight or nine leaves are used and doubled to make sixteen or eighteen elements. These are laid side by side and braided together, over two under two, until the desired length is reached. Then a transverse element, usually a short bit of yucca (fig. 36), is laid across the leaves, every other one of which is brought about it in a half-turn, pulled through, and folded back over the top of the sandal, where it is left uncut as a pad for the heel. The odd elements run under the transverse bar and are held in place by it. They are usually trimmed off short, but in some cases the transverse bar is made double and the odd elements are turned back about it underneath the sandal, thus making a stouter heel. As the component leaves usually run the whole length of the sandals and back again (fig. 36), the length of the sandals is limited to less than half the length of a single leaf; hence they are seldom more than 8 inches long and must, therefore, have been worn chiefly by children.

Type I, *a*, 2 (pls. 36, 37). This type was also made of whole leaves and is also of diagonal over-two under-two plaiting. It differs from the other type, however, in that the examples are much more finely woven and in the fact that the component leaves do not

---

[1] A. M. N. H. no. H–12938. The collection in the American Museum from Grand Gulch contains material from both Cliff-dwelling and Basket Maker caves.

[2] Cf. Fewkes, 1909, fig 37 ; Nordenskiöld, 1893, pl. xix, 2.

run the entire length of the piece. Work is begun at the toe in the same way as before, but with from 20 to 30 elements. As the weaving is finer and there are more elements the leaves do not, of course, run the whole length of the sandal, but are replaced, as they run out, with new leaves. Each added leaf is woven for a few stitches beside the old one in order to set it in solidly; then the old one is brought out on the underside and there left protruding. As the weaving progresses a number of these ends of leaves are left on the underside, and when the sandal is finished they are all trimmed off evenly about half an inch long, making, when somewhat shredded by wear, a soft and strong layer of fiber covering the whole sole. Plate 37, *b*, a sandal finished but never trimmed, shows the leaves protruding on the underside; the top (pl. 37, *a*) is entirely free from "work ends." In this finer woven type the toe is neatly rounded off and shaped for right or left foot; some examples have a little jog or offset (pl. 36, *a*), the use of which is not clear. In all cases the heel as well as the toe is carefully finished and the ends are so worked back into the weave and brought out on the bottom as to make it difficult, in the finished and trimmed piece, to tell where the work begins and where it ends. The edges of some of the sandals are plain, as in the first class (pl. 36, *a*); others have a single

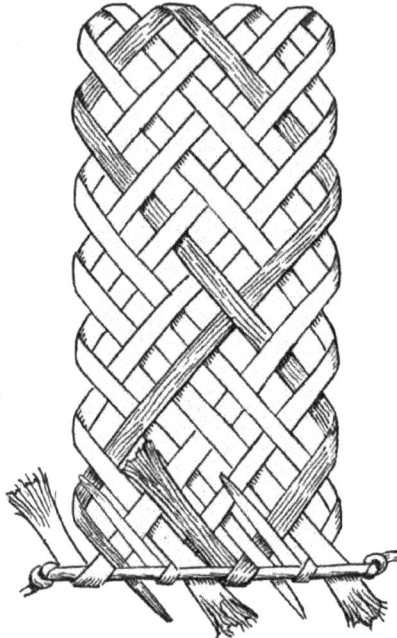

Fig. 36.—Simplified drawing showing weave of Type I, *a*, 1, sandal.

or double border (pl. 36, *b*), which appears to be made of a different and more involved weave than the simple over-two under-two method employed in the bodies of the pieces. Careful examination, however, shows that these borders are of exactly the same weave and were produced by pulling the elements, as they approached the edge, so tightly that they rolled up on each other, making a thickened selvage. There is, of course, no structurally imposed limit on the length of these sandals; they range from children's size, 6 inches long, to large examples, 12 inches in length. There is one specimen in the collection (pl. 36, *c*) that has yucca fiber cords woven into the lower surface in a geometrical pattern. This was probably done to give

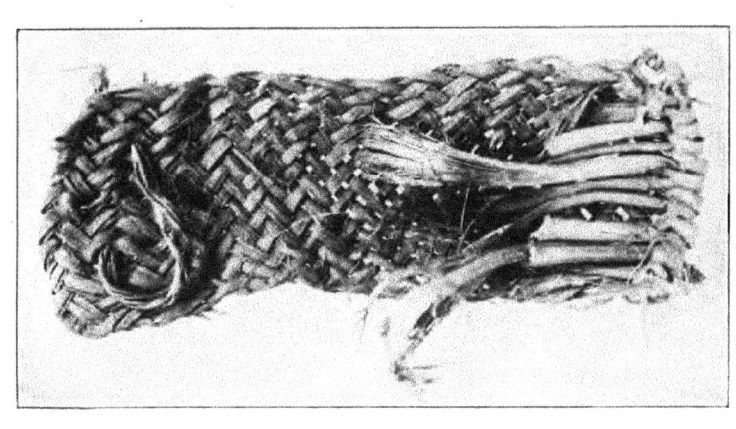

a. UPPER SIDE

b. UPPER SIDE

TYPE I, a, 1, SANDALS

c. SOLE

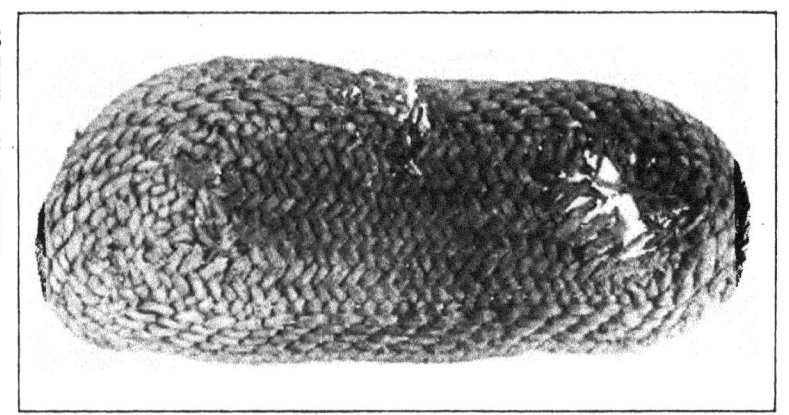

a

c

b

TYPE I, a, 2, SANDALS

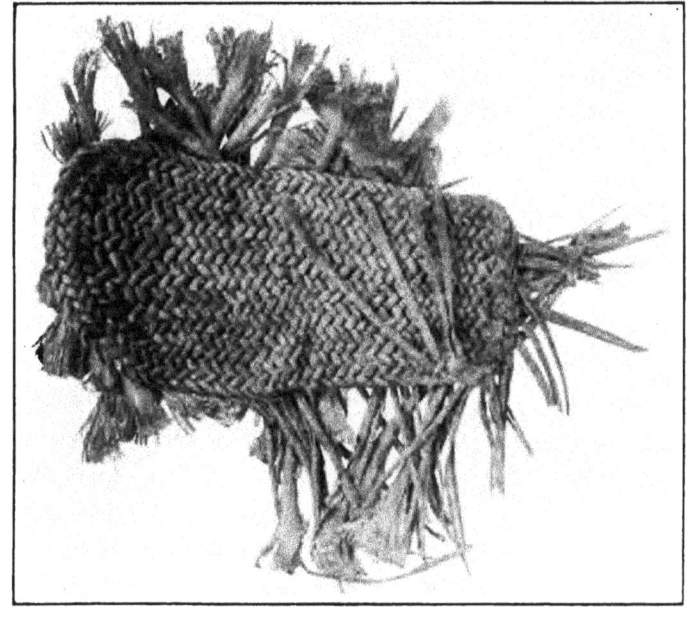

a

b

TYPE I, a, 2, UNFINISHED SANDAL

c. SOLE

b. UPPER SIDE

a. UPPER SIDE

extra wearing qualities to the sole, and also, perhaps, the ridges of the pattern helped to provide the foot with a better grip on smooth rocks.

Type I, b (pl. 38). Wickerwork of whole leaves woven over two heavy yucca-leaf warp-strands tied together at either end. The cross-woven elements, or weft-strands, are started on the upper surface of the sandal, where the small end is left; the strands pass under one warp, back over it, and under the other (fig. 37). They are then cut off, leaving the larger ends on the sole of the sandal, where they are shredded out to form a cushion-like pad of fiber (pl. 38, c). In some cases the weft-strands are woven back and forth several times, but the small ends are always left on top and the large ends always carried through to the bottom and shredded. This type of sandal is of a long, oval form and is never shaped for right or left foot, neither is there any difference between heel and toe other than the presence of the added heel and toe attachments. Mason figures[1] a sandal analogous to these, but it is woven, according to the description, over four warps and the shredded butts are left on the upper surface. In our collection there are a few examples similarly made over four warps; the ends, however, as in all the two-warp specimens, are brought out on the bottom.

FIG. 37.—Weave of wickerwork sandal, Type I, b.

Type II, a (pl. 39, a). Wickerwork of cords over a four or six strand warp made by looping either two or three cords, the open ends of the loops being at the heel, the closed ends forming the toe. The warps are of heavy, well-twisted two-strand yucca cord; the weft is of very much heavier and more loosely twisted cord, also of yucca. It is laced back and forth over and under the warp elements and crowded together so tightly that the resultant sandal is a strong, heavy fabric three-eighths to one-half inch thick; it is considerably more flexible, however, than the whole-leaf sandal and must have had far greater wearing qualities. The specimens are neatly made in rights and lefts and shaped to conform to the outline of the foot; the toe is brought to a rather sharp point, the heel is sometimes square, sometimes rounded. The ends of the warps are occasionally used to form the heel attachment loop.

Type II, b (pl. 39, b, c). Twined weaving of twisted (apocynum?) fiber over a many-stranded warp of yucca strings. The soles have a raised pattern. The warps in the example dissected (no. cat. number,

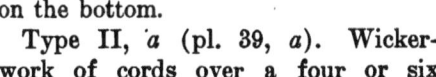

---

[1] Mason, 1897, p. 678, fig. 4.

Ruin 7) are 18 in number, made of 9 looped yucca cords, their open ends at the heel. The warp pattern, as shown in figure 38, is an elaborate one, the elements being laid out in the form of the foot with the same little jog on the outer side that was seen in the better grade of plaited sandals (pl. 36, *a*). The framework of the jog is formed by a single warp-loop. The complicated tie at the heel, where all the warp-strands are made fast, is accomplished by bringing down the central strands, turning them back (i. e., toward the toe) and coupling each one with the descending part of the strand next to it. These couples (descending strand and turned-back end of the next one) are held together by weaving, over and back, the outer strands, which are unraveled into their two component twists of fiber, each twist becoming a separate element and being joined with its mate to form a pair of twined weft elements. In the drawing this terminal tie of the warp is magnified out of its proper proportions in order to show

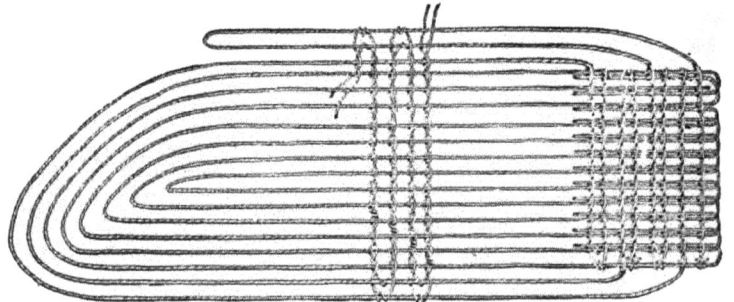

FIG. 38.—Weave of Type II, *b*, sandal.

the method of insertion of each of its strands. In the original sandal the tie is not over one-half inch deep. The first true weft element of the softer (apocynum?) fiber (counting from the heel) is woven over all the warps and pulled tight; as a result of this, the outer warp-strands on each side being somewhat longer than the central ones, the heel and adjacent sides of the sandal are slightly drawn up, making a sort of cup-shaped pucker that must have fitted snugly bout the heel of the wearer. This can not be shown in the diagrammatic drawing, but appears in the photograph (pl. 39, *b*).

The above description of the terminal fastenings of the warp was worked out by pulling to pieces a fragmentary example. The only other sandal of this type in our collection is finished off in the same general way, but has some minor differences which can not be studied, so tight is the weave, without destroying the specimen. We must therefore wait for more material before we can make further notes on this interesting tie.

The warp prepared, the weft is run in. Its weaving is extraordinarily fine, there being no fewer than 22 strands to the inch (8 warp-elements to the inch). In spite of this closeness of weave, it is not probable that any frame or loom was used to hold the warp in place, although a small comb might have been employed to push or work down the weft-strands snugly against each other. In this connection, a statement of Mr. Richard Wetherill is of interest:

> Sandals have been found (in southwestern Colorado and southeastern Utah) in great numbers partially completed, from fine threads of yucca to the whole leaf, and all seemed to be worked offhand. Those made of fine thread and unfinished have been found with the loose ends tied in a bunch to keep from tangling until time could be had to complete them. The coarser kinds merely had the ends sticking out at all angles. In all cases the toe was made first.[1]

In the body of the sandal, where the sides are parallel, the weft is merely run across from side to side. At the toe the process is somewhat complicated by the looping of the warp. The difficulty is, however, very neatly overcome, the weft-elements at the toe being kept from going slack as they radiate, by the introduction of short "fillers" run from the edge to the center and back again.

The normal weave of the sandal body is shown in the drawing (fig. 38). It is ordinary twining. The edges are given a tight and even binding by taking a double turn with one of the weft-strands about the outer warp, its paired strand taking a single turn about the warp just within. The raised pattern or underside strengthening, so characteristic of this type of sandal, is not an added or imbricated feature, but is produced, as the drawing shows, by taking a double turn of one of the paired twined elements about the other in such a way that it appears only on the underside. These knots are arranged in geometrical patterns. Their purpose was probably to strengthen the sole and roughen it for gripping smooth rocks.[2]

This sandal type suggests a possible use for certain flat stones, shaped like "jog-toed" sandals, that have been commonly found in the ruins of the San Juan drainage. These stones have always been called "sandal lasts," but their large size, and the fact that none of them have any holes or grooves for the attachment of strings, have made the method of their employment uncertain. Their form, however, is so exactly that of the "jog-toed" sandals that it seems certain that they must have had some connection with the making of them. Their identification as sandal stones is made even more positive by the existence of a pottery "sandal last" in the possession of Mr. M. C. Long,[3] which bears on its surface the intaglio imprint of the knot-

---

[1] Wetherill, 1897, p. 248.
[2] Consult, however, Cushing in Snyder, 1899, in which are discussed possible magical concepts connected with these raised patterns.
[3] Figured by Snyder, 1899, p. 7 and fig. 3.

patterned bottom of a twined sandal. In our collection there is a small fragment of a similar object (A–1385, Ruin 5). It will be remembered that there are two types with the offset or jog, one plaited of whole leaves (I, *a*, 2), the other the twined type just discussed (II, *b*). For the former a pattern would have been convenient in order to measure the proportions of the growing sandal, place the jog correctly, etc., but it would not have been necessary. For the latter, with its complicated series of concentrically looped warps (fig. 38), a measure of some sort must have been almost indispensable for the correct preliminary laying out of the strands so that they should be of the right lengths and have the proper curves. During the weaving in of the weft-strands, also, a standard pattern, such as would have been provided by the stones, must have been a great help in keeping a check on the proportions of the growing fabric. Dr. Snyder's[1] theory as to the use of the stones is as follows:

A long strand of yucca fibre was first wrapped around the stone from one end to the other at intervals of half or three-quarters of an inch. This preliminary step served as a basis for securing the intertexture of prepared material, as the stone served for a guide for shaping the form. Upon these transverse filaments the work was commenced and prosecuted, first on one side of the so-called last and then on the other, by the " over and under " method of broad plaiting. When this process of interweaving the damp and flexible strands had been conducted sufficiently far on both sides of the model to fix by it the shape and dimensions of the sandal, they were probably cut apart and finished separately.

An examination of sandals of any type, however, shows this idea to be erroneous; none have been made in pairs and cut apart, and in no case does the warp run otherwise than longitudinally.

A word as to the distribution of " sandal stones." They are common in the Mesa Verde ruins, and are figured by Fewkes[2] and Nordenskiöld,[3] Morley reports them from the McElmo,[4] and Professors Cummings and Kidder excavated several on Alkali Ridge, San Juan County, Utah, in 1908. Mr. Richard Wetherill states[5] that they occur in Marsh Pass, Chaco Canyon, Grand Gulch, Allen Canyon, and Montezuma County, Colorado. We know of no case of their having been found outside the San Juan drainage.

Type II, *c* (pl. 40, *a*). Of this class we found but one specimen, a very fragmentary sandal, apparently of child's size. The sole is made of stout yucca string in coil without foundation. The twists are pulled very tight, giving a flat, even texture. Netted to the edges of the sole are shreds of what was evidently an attached " upper " or, more probably, a sock-like legging. The stitch is the same, coil without foundation, but is very much looser. The thread of

---

[1] 1897, pp. 129, 130.
[2] 1909, pl. 21, *j*.
[3] 1893, pl. xxxix, 6.

[4] 1908, pl. xxxix, *s*.
[5] 1897, p. 248.

c. TYPE II, b, SANDAL, SOLE

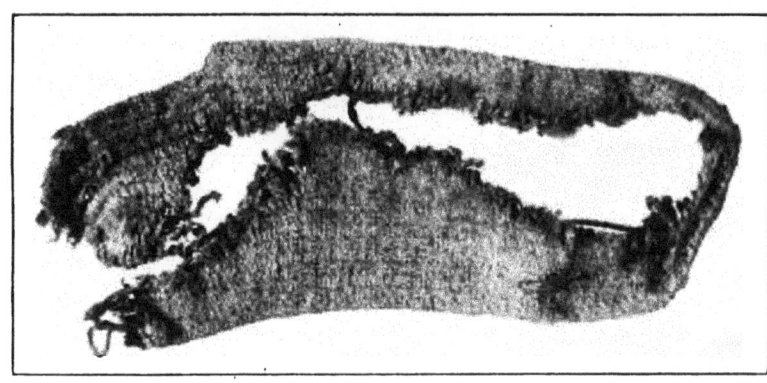

b. TYPE II, b, SANDAL, UPPER SIDE

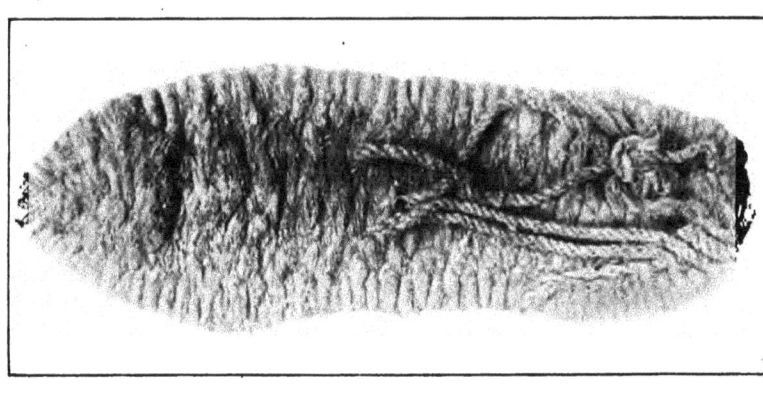

a. TYPE II, a, SANDAL

b. SIDE-LOOP TIE

a. TYPE II, *c,* SANDAL

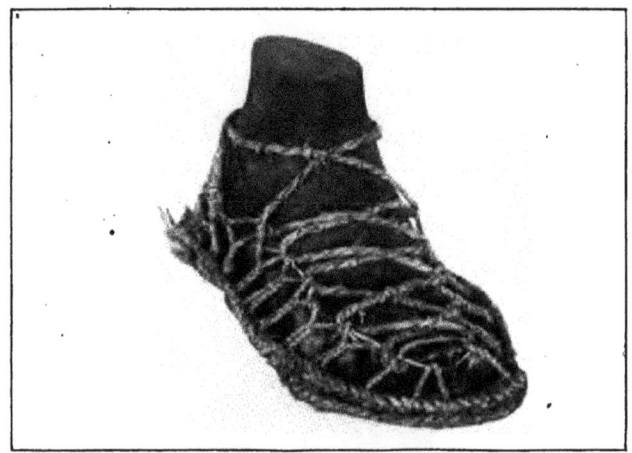

a. SANDAL-LOOP TIE ON FOOT

b. TOE-HEEL LOOP SANDAL TIE

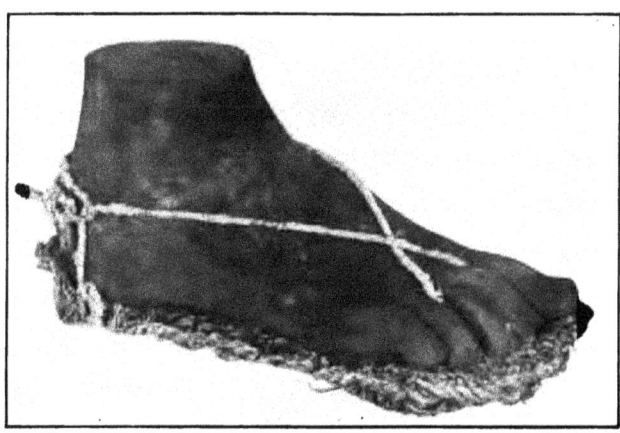

c. CRISSCROSS SANDAL TIE

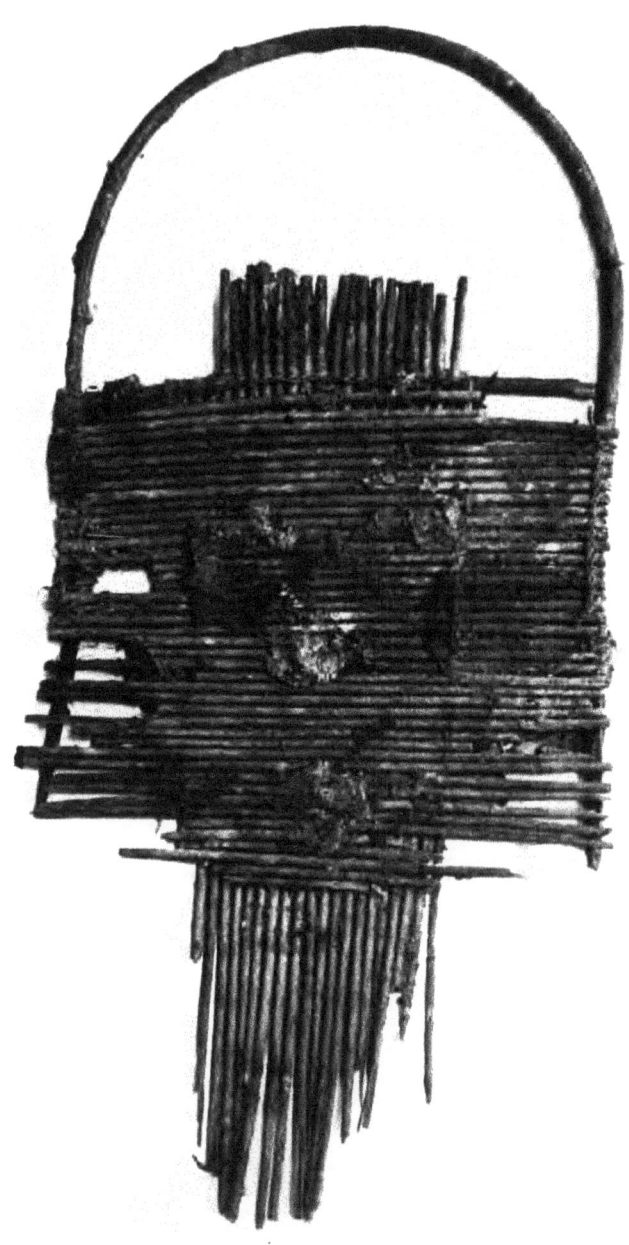

CRADLE

which it is made is apparently cotton with woolly brown animal hair
so worked into it in spinning as to fluff out on all sides of it and much
increase its thickness and warmth, while adding practically nothing
to its weight.

Sandal ties.—There were two methods of attaching sandals to the
feet: by edge loops, and by toe-heel loops. In the first case, loops
of string or yucca leaf were fastened all around the edge of the
sandal (pls. 40, *b;* 41, *a*). By means of strings rove through these
loops, laced over the toes and instep and about the ankle, the footgear was held firmly in place. Padding of cedar bark or corn
husks was commonly introduced under the lacings and between the
foot and the sole. Edge-loop attachment is found on sandals of all
types except those of coarse yucca-leaf wickerwork (I, *b*), which
have no edge suitable to hold the loops.

The toe-heel loop attachment is made up of toe loop, heel loop,
and tie string (pls. 38, *a;* 41, *b*). The tie string begins on the
instep, is turned about the toe loop, brought back and turned about
the heel loop on the right, over the instep and about the heel
loop on the left, back to the instep and made fast (pl. 38, *a*). The
heel-and-toe loops are worked into the body of the sandal. The toe
loop usually takes in the second and third toes, but we have one specimen (A–1682, Ruin 9) which is provided with two loops, one to hold
the great toe, the other to engage the second and third toes. A variation in the toe-loop attachment is shown in plates 35, *b;* 41, *c;* the second and third toes are held by a crossing of the tie string, which is run
through the body of the sandal in front, crosses above the inclosed
toes, runs back over the instep and about the ankle, being caught
through the body of the sandal at the heel. A short string about the
back of the heel serves to hold the tie cord taut.

The loops and tie strings are generally of yucca cord or of whole
yucca leaves, less commonly of braided yucca, feather cord, or rags
of cotton cloth. No ties of human-hair string, so commonly present
on Basket Maker sandals, were found in the cliff-dwellings.

HOUSEHOLD APPURTENANCES

Cradles were found in Ruins 3 and 7. The specimen from the
former site (A–1285) is merely a peeled stick half an inch thick,
bent into an open loop, 26 inches long by 10 inches wide, and
laced across and across with an open mesh of yucca leaves. Although this is undoubtedly a cradle, it was presumably only a
makeshift affair, as it is much inferior in workmanship to the
one from Ruin 7 (pl. 42). Although battered by use and probably discarded as worn out (it was found in the rubbish covered
with turkey dung), this cradle still shows the excellence of its

construction. It is 23 inches long by 10¼ inches wide. Its main support is a hoop made from a stout unpeeled oak twig. The lower parts of this are broken away so that one cannot tell whether or not the ends were brought around into a loop at the bottom. The filling consists of two sets of carefully smoothed willow sticks. The longitudinally running series of 21 sticks is attached above to a crosspiece, the ends of which are bent about the sides of the frame; the lower end of the series of longitudinal sticks was probably lashed to a second crosspiece, now missing, or perhaps to that part of the frame that is gone. The lateral series of sticks forms the upper surface of the cradle. Forty-five of its elements remain, and probably half as many more have disappeared. They have a double fastening, their ends being held by yucca-string ties to the outer frame and their central parts being fastened to the longitudinal series by ornamental wrappings of fine human-hair cord. The design seems to have embodied large diamond-shaped figures.

Screens of wooden rods held together by yucca strings running through perforations in them are very common in the ruins of the Mesa Verde and Chaco Canyon (explorations of the authors; and see Nordenskiöld, 1893, pl. xix, 2). During our excavations we were constantly on the lookout for fragments of them, but found only a single broken rod (A–1457, Ruin 7). From Ruin 9 came part of a screen made of large reeds held together by twined weaving of yucca strips (A–1599).

Torches.—Long, thin bunches of cedar bark bound with yucca-leaf strips and showing signs of burning at their ends were collected in Ruin 2 (pl. 45, 4 and 5). (For fire-making apparatus, see under "Objects of Wood," p. 120.)

Brushes.—A brush made by bundling together a quantity of straight, tough grass stems and tying them near one end with a bit of yucca string, was found in Ruin 1 (A–1152). Exactly similar brushes have been seen in use by the authors among the Navaho, the Rio Grande Pueblos, and the Zuñi. The short ends serve in dressing the hair; the longer, flexible parts for cleaning pots, dusting out basketry meal trays, and sweeping the floor.

BASKETRY

Yucca ring baskets.—We procured a few perfect specimens and many fragments of baskets of this class. They are in essence nothing but pieces of matting attached to rings of willow or some other pliable wood, but whether they were made as small mats and then fastened to the rings, or whether they were woven directly on the rings, we do not know. The ends of the elements that make up the mat are bent over the ring outward in bunches of two or four, made fast by a pair of horizontally running twined strands and clipped off. A drawing in Mason's Basketry (1904, fig. 61, *a*, *b*) shows the process very clearly.

The mat is made of yucca leaves or yucca strips, twilled weave, over two under two. The strands are so manipulated, in all the examples recovered by us, as to produce in the weave a pattern of concentric diamonds (fig. 39). The center of the pattern is always at the bottom of the basket. We found only one fragment (A–1715,

Fig. 39.—Pattern of twilled yucca baskets.

Ruin 9) showing coloring of the strands to accentuate the design; in the Wetherill collection in the Colorado State Museum at Denver, however, are several specimens from the Mesa Verde bearing handsome figures in dark and light strands; Nordenskiöld figures two similar ones from Spruce-tree House.[1]

The smaller baskets, 8 to 10 inches in diameter (pl. 43, *a*, *b*, Ruin 7), are bowl shaped and tightly enough woven to hold corn or beans, but too open to carry meal, grass seed, or other fine substances; the larger ones, 15 to 20 inches in diameter (pl. 43, *c*, Ruin 7) are so

---

[1] 1893, pl. xliv, 1, 2.

shallow and of so open a weave that it seems probable that they were used as winnowing trays.

Coiled basketry.—Although no whole pieces were obtained, a few fragments of shallow, tray-like coiled baskets were collected in the rubbish heaps of the cliff-houses. All the specimens belong to a type not included by Mason in his classification,[1] which may be called "two rod and bundle." It is analogous to Mason's two rod and splint and three rod types. Another difference between these speci- mens and any noted by Mason is that the sewing elements do not interlock. This feature will be more fully discussed in the section on Basket Maker coiled baskets (p. 169).

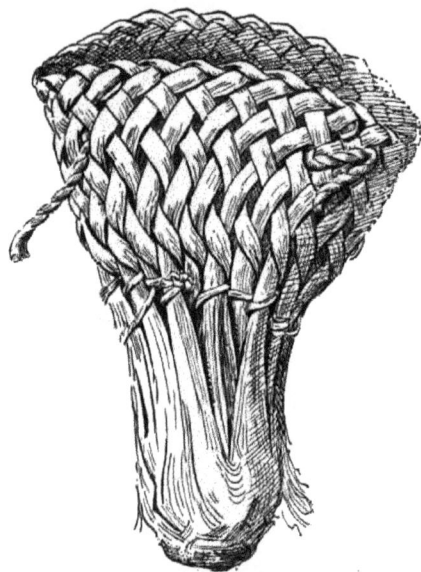

Fig. 40.—Yucca-plant basket.

The foundation of the coil consists of two willow rods of equal size placed side by side; above them is a bundle of fibrous material. The sewing splints from below inclose all three elements. The splints from the next coil above are sewn through the bundle, usually taking in about half of it (for illustrations, see fig. 80 in the Basket Maker section). The bundles, being soft, pack down between the paired rods and so fill up the interstices between the rods of one coil and those of the next that the resultant weave is ex- traordinarily tight. The best examples would certainly be water- tight without coating of any kind. The finer specimens average 5 coils and 18 stitches to the inch; a coarse one has 4 to 4½ coils and 8 to 10 stitches. In all cases the foundation is entirely concealed..

Materials employed in manufacture, so far as we can tell, are: For rods, willow, peeled or unpeeled; for bundles, strips of yucca leaf partly shredded into fiber; for sewing strands, fine splints of wood, probably willow or sumac. A coil of these splints prepared for use was found in Ruin 2 (A–1223).

A little basket, made from a single yucca plant, was taken from the rubbish on the upper level of Ruin 5. The stalk is cut off just below the origin of the leaves, which latter are woven together, as shown in figure 40, to form a cornucopia-shaped receptacle 2½ inches

---

[1] 1904, p. 247.

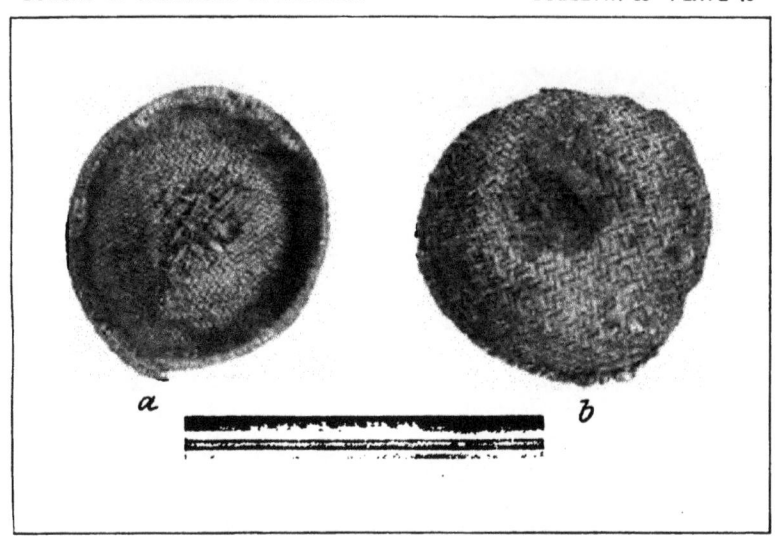

SMALL TYPE OF RING BASKET

c. LARGE TYPE OF RING BASKET

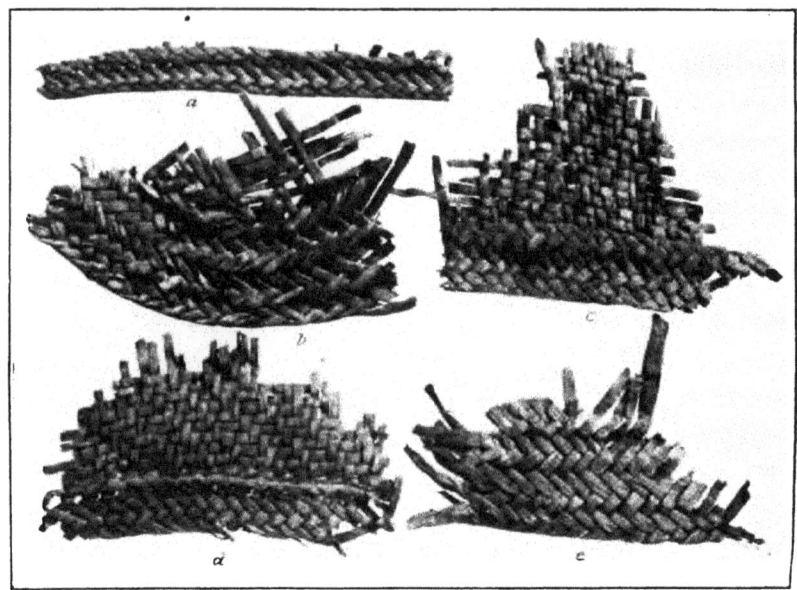

SELVAGES OF RUSH MATS, RUIN 7

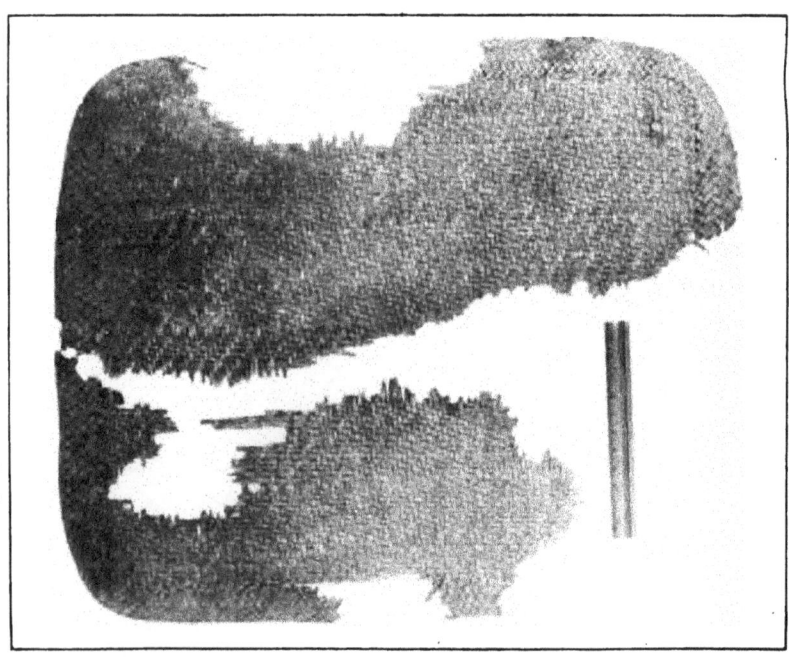

_f._ RUSH MAT

deep. Two loops of string were attached to one side; one is still in place, the other has come loose. The bases of the leaves are held together by twined woven strings. In the American Museum of Natural History, New York (cat. no. H–14251, "southeastern Utah") there is the exact duplicate of this little contrivance, even to the two loops of string; Mr. John Wetherill possesses a similar specimen, probably from Sagi Canyon. All three evidently belong to a well-defined type, as to the use of which we can offer no suggestion.

MATTING

From the number of fragments that occur in the rubbish of the cliff-houses it would appear that mats must have been in very

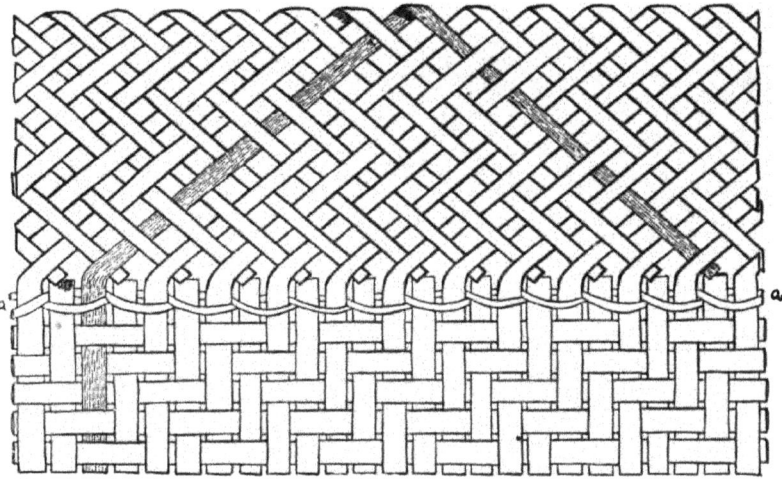

FIG. 41.—Rush-mat selvage.

common use. Although no complete specimen was recovered, large parts of one were found on the floor of a room in Ruin 2 (pl. 44, *f*). All our specimens are made of cat-tail rushes and all are woven in the same way—twilled work, over two under two. Each mat has a twilled border or selvage (pl. 44, *a–e*), 1 inch to 3 inches wide, woven at a different angle from the body elements and made up of every other one of them. The chief interest in these mats lies in the working of the borders. As may be seen in the diagrammatic drawings (figs. 41, 42), every other strand is cut off at the edge of the body. The ends are held in place by a pair of twined rushes (*a–a*, fig. 41). The projecting or uncut ends are plaited together for a short distance, turned at the edge, and brought back to the body where they are tucked under the strands that emerge at that place, or are more securely fastened by being turned back again toward the edge and locked under the elements following them in the series (fig. 42). These are the common methods. We have two specimens showing variants of the same styles: one, A-1702, Ruin 7, with a double border made by bringing the elements back from the edge, past the junction of body and selvage to a second edge, and then back again to the junction where they end as usual. The other (A-1515, Ruin 7): the odd elements in this case, instead of being merely cut off, are carried, before ending, a few turns to the right, thus supplementing the twined binders and giving greater strength to the fabric (pl. 44, *d*).

These rush mats all appear to have been square or rectangular with rounded corners. Their size was fairly uniform, having been

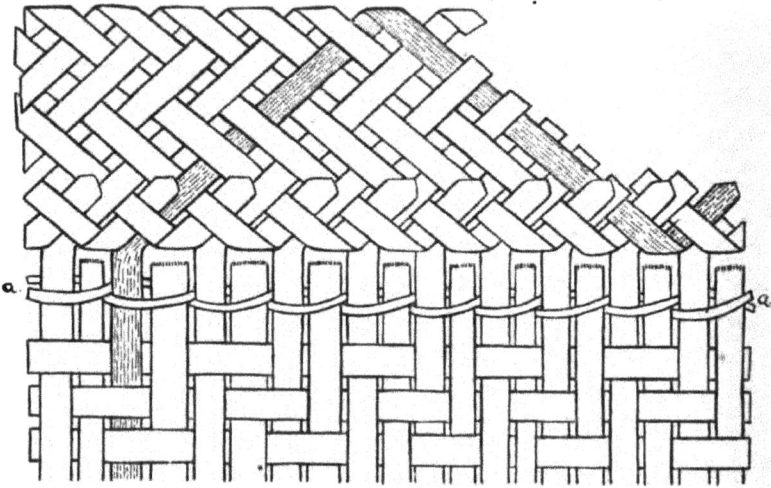

Fig. 42.—Rush-mat selvage.

limited by the length of the component rushes. Our nearly complete specimen (Ruin 2) measures 3 feet 2 inches in one direction and seems to have been nearly square. A similar mat from Sprucetree House, Mesa Verde, figured by Nordenskiöld[1] is square and measures 1.2 by 1.2 meters. Cummings[2] gives a description of one that is 3 feet by 2 feet 6 inches.

TWISTED ELEMENTS, STRINGS AND THREAD

Cotton.—Cotton string was used for practically nothing but the weaving of cloth and the sewing of garments. The finest of it is single strand, about one-fiftieth inch in diameter. This was employed in the better grades of cloth, but was not strong enough for sewing,

---

[1] 1893, pl. xlviii, 4.   [2] 1910, p. 35.

a somewhat heavier string, usually two-stranded, having been used for that purpose. The stoutest cotton cord in the collection is one-tenth inch in diameter; but, like all the other products of this fiber, it is not closely twisted. Cotton threads were sometimes dyed red (A-1551, Ruin 7), or black (A-1286, Ruin 3). A large hank of cotton thread, prepared for weaving (A-1621), was found in a charred condition in one of the kivas of Ruin 8.

Whether cotton was grown in northern Arizona or whether it was obtained in trade from the south has not yet been definitely decided. We know that the plant was cultivated at Zuñi and seemingly by the Hopi in the sixteenth century,[1] and there is no reason why it should not grow in favorable localities in the San Juan district. We had the good fortune to recover from a rubbish heap a large wad of cotton waste, bunches of the fiber, and uncombed cotton still containing the seeds (88322). This should practically settle the question, as raw materials of this sort would hardly have formed an article of trade.

Yucca.—Yucca fiber was the most important of all cordage materials, probably nine-tenths of all the twisted cord employed having been made from it. In the particular region investigated by us, the only common yucca plant seems to be the "narrow leaf" (*Y. angustifolia*), and this was apparently also the case in former times, as all the identifiable leaves found in the rubbish or worked into baskets and sandals belong to that species. The broad-leaf yucca grows on the top of the Black Mesa, also on the Mesa Verde. Both these localities are higher and moister than the Monument country.

Every stage in the production of yucca string is illustrated in the collection: sheaves of whole leaves, chewed or pounded leaves with the parenchyma partly removed, and lastly, hanks of the cleaned fiber ready for spinning (pl. 45, 6–11). Yucca string is very stout, specimens that have escaped moisture being still quite as hard to break as modern twine of the same weight. The majority of the specimens range in diameter from one-twentieth to just less than one-fourth of an inch in diameter; the cord most commonly found is about one-tenth of an inch in diameter. Examples over one-fourth of an inch are rare; our largest specimen (A-1693, Ruin 9) is not quite one-half inch. The standard string is two-strand, each strand twisted clockwise, the two twisted together anti-clockwise. Three and four strand strings are found, but are not abundant. Some very stout cords are made of two strands, each one of which is two-

---

[1] Coronado, Winship, 1896, pp. 489, 550, 558. Espejo saw many cotton "towels" (kilts?) at Tusayan in 1583. Consult Lewton, F. L., The Cotton of the Hopi Indians: A New Species of Gossypium, *Smithsonian Miscel. Coll.*, vol. 60, no. 6, Washington, 1912.

stranded. Very few two-strand strings are twisted clockwise; there are, in our collection of several hundred pieces, only four or five such examples.

Yucca strings seem to have been made very long, rolled into hanks or balls, and cut off in lengths as required. The rotting mass of cordage found in a jar in Ruin 5 could hardly have contained less than 200 yards. Nordenskiöld figures a hank of fine two-strand string from Step House, Mesa Verde, that is over 400 meters long and weighs but 277 grams.[1]

Apocynum (?).—While the majority of strings were made of yucca, there also occur examples that appear to have been twisted of other fibers. What these are we cannot say, but one type, which produces a whitish string, less harsh and rather more pliable than that made of yucca, is not uncommon. The fibers are finer than those of yucca, and become, with wear, fluffy and woolly. The material is, perhaps, some form of apocynum.

Human hair.—This was occasionally used. Our best specimen (A-1549, Ruin 7) is a two-strand, clockwise twist. Most examples of hair string are found worked into netted textile or used as lashings for cradles.

BRAIDING

Cotton was plaited round for cord, flat for tape. Both of these products seem to have been employed as tassels, fringes, and other ornamental additions to belts and clothing; round braids also served as draw strings for bags (p. 149). One tassel begins with a flat, twilled braid of 32 very fine strands; these are ultimately doubled up to form 16 heavier elements, which are braided together in the same way for an inch or so; they are then worked into a square braid 3 inches long, the whole ending in a round, fluffy ball (A-1557, Ruin 7). Another (A-1559, Ruin 7) is a flat, twilled braid of 24 strands, which ends in four round-braided cords of six strands each. Two bits of round-braided cord, made of some kind of animal hair in eight strands, four white and four black, were found in Ruin 4 (A-1274). A similar piece (A-1360) came from the near-by Ruin 3, and a third from "Sunflower Cave" (A-2611).

Yucca, both fiber and leaf, apocynum (?), corn husk, cedar bark, and other vegetal substances, are all found braided in various lengths and thicknesses. The commonest and apparently the most useful type is a narrow three-strand flat braid of shredded yucca leaves (not prepared fiber); this makes a stout cord that was employed, among other things, for rafter loops and for pot harness. Burden bands, one of yucca, one of rushes, both braided flat, are shown in plate 45, 1, 2 (Ruins 1 and 2).

---

[1] 1893, pl. xlix, 4.

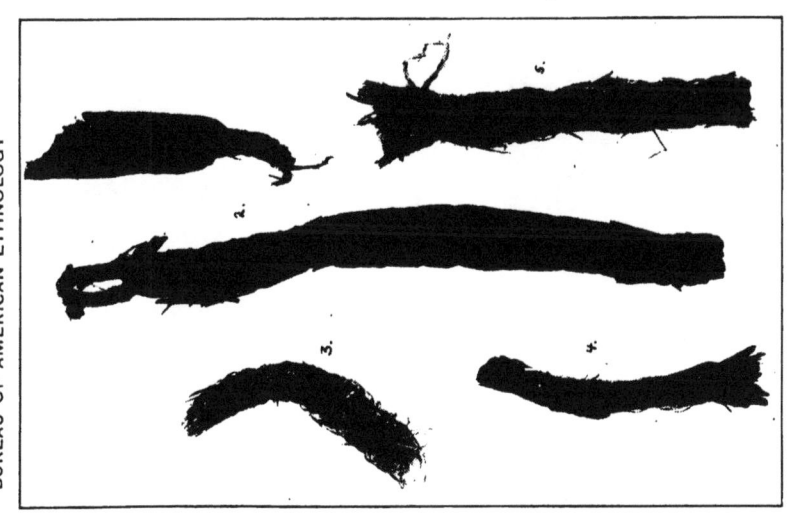

STRING-MAKING SERIES

BURDEN STRAPS AND TORCHES

1. MAGNIFIED PHOTOGRAPH OF COTTON CLOTH

2. END OF BURDEN STRAP

3. COIL WITHOUT FOUNDATION

4. HANK OF FEATHER CORD

Although it is not braided, a singular little object from Ruin 2 may be mentioned here.   It is made of a single continuous flat splint knotted about two supporting strands in the manner shown in figure 43.   Its length is 3 inches.

CLOTH AND OTHER FINE-CORD TEXTILE FABRICS

Cotton.—Rags of cotton cloth were found in the rubbish of every ruin excavated; none of them, however, were large enough to give any idea as to the nature of the garments of which they once formed parts or of the original size of the pieces of fabric.   The specimens are of two kinds, the plain and the striped, the former much the more abundant.   The thread of both warp and weft of all the specimens is single-strand and loosely twisted.   Thread for binding and sewing is somewhat stouter and is always two or three strand. Plain cloth is made in the simple checkerboard weave (pl. 46, *a*) and is of two classes—that in which the warp and weft are of equal thickness, and that in which the weft is much heavier than the warp. As is shown in the accompanying table of elements to the

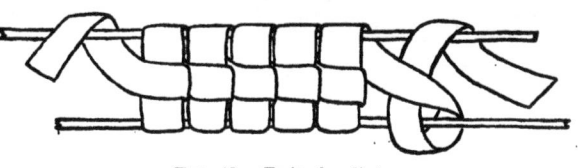

FIG. 43.—Twined splint.

inch in a series of 26 specimens chosen at random, the examples within the groups differ from each other only in fineness of weave.   It will be noticed also that the heavy weft cloth averages somewhat coarser than that in which the warp and weft are of equal weight.

EQUAL WARP AND WEFT			HEAVY WEFT		
Warps	Wefts	Examples	Warps	Wefts	Examples
20	24	1	16	20	1
24	24	1	20	24	2
24	28	4	24	24	4
28	32	3	24	28	2
28	36	2	28	28	1
32	34	1	28	32	1
32	56	1			
36	40	2			

Of striped cloth we have only two specimens; the weave in both cases is twilled, in one it is over two under two, in the other over two under one.   The former (A–1620, Ruin 8) has alternate stripes of

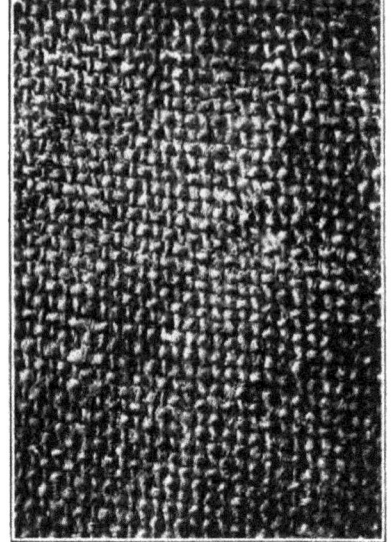

a. MAGNIFIED PHOTOGRAPH OF COT-
TON CLOTH

b. END OF BURDEN STRAP

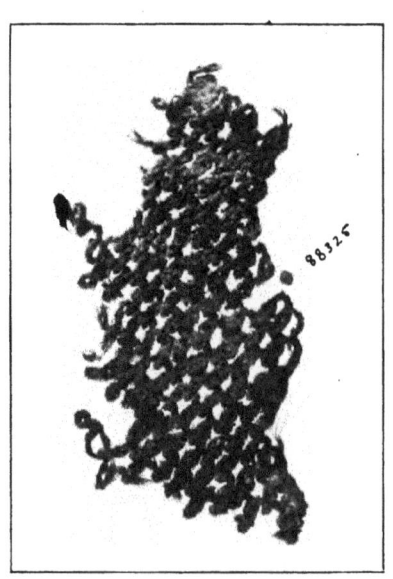

c. COIL WITHOUT FOUNDATION

d. HANK OF FEATHER CORD

Although it is not braided, a singular little object from Ruin 2 may be mentioned here. It is made of a single continuous flat splint knotted about two supporting strands in the manner shown in figure 43. Its length is 3 inches.

CLOTH AND OTHER FINE-CORD TEXTILE FABRICS

Cotton.—Rags of cotton cloth were found in the rubbish of every ruin excavated; none of them, however, were large enough to give any idea as to the nature of the garments of which they once formed parts or of the original size of the pieces of fabric. The specimens are of two kinds, the plain and the striped, the former much the more abundant. The thread of both warp and weft of all the specimens is single-strand and loosely twisted. Thread for binding and sewing is somewhat stouter and is always two or three strand. Plain cloth is made in the simple checkerboard weave (pl. 46, *a*) and is of two classes—that in which the warp and weft are of equal thickness, and that in which the weft is much heavier than the warp. As is shown in the accompanying table of elements to the

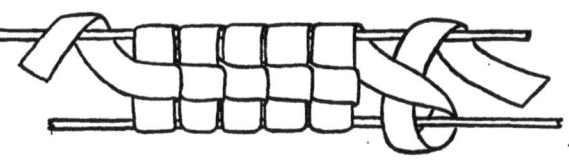

FIG. 43.—Twined splint.

inch in a series of 26 specimens chosen at random, the examples within the groups differ from each other only in fineness of weave. It will be noticed also that the heavy weft cloth averages somewhat coarser than that in which the warp and weft are of equal weight.

EQUAL WARP AND WEFT			HEAVY WEFT		
Warps	Wefts	Examples	Warps	Wefts	Examples
20	24	1	16	20	1
24	24	1	20	24	2
24	28	4	24	24	4
28	32	3	24	28	2
28	36	2	28	28	1
32	34	1	28	32	1
32	56	1			
36	40	2			

Of striped cloth we have only two specimens; the weave in both cases is twilled, in one it is over two under two, in the other over two under one. The former (A–1620, Ruin 8) has alternate stripes of red and natural color, each four threads wide; the latter (A-1709, Ruin 9) three-thread stripes of red, brown, and natural color. The red and brown dyes seem to have rotted the cotton to some extent, as the colored strands are considerably more fragile than the others.

All varieties of cotton cloth were evidently made on the hand loom, an apparatus probably similar to, though lighter than, that in use by the Navaho to-day. The selvage or edge-binding of these ancient fabrics is like that of the better class of Navaho blankets; that is to say, the threads are held in place by a pair of heavy, three-strand strings intertwined as shown in figure 44. For the warp this fastening was probably done at the time of the " set up " outside the loom, according to the Navaho practice.[1] The only difference between the Cliff-house method and that of the Navaho is that the Navaho warp is held by three strings braided together, rather than by two twisted ones, as in the majority of the ancient cotton fabrics. There is one specimen in our collection, however, in which the warp

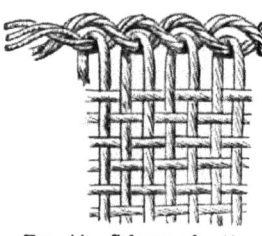

FIG. 44.—Selvage of cotton cloth.

cords are held, as in Navaho blankets, by a braid; a further elaboration is introduced in the form of a row of twined weaving in red threads between the selvage and the body of the cloth (A-1426, Ruin 6). The weft, of course, was worked into its " edge cord " during the weaving, probably again,in the same way as is done by the Navaho, namely, by attaching two strings to the lower beam of the loom on each side just outside the warps and twisting them together as the web grew, including one turn of the weft in each twist (fig. 44). The selvages produced are neat, firm, and considerably heavier than the body of the fabric; they are so much stronger than it that strips of the selvage were usually left after the rest of the cloth was worn out, and these were often reused for sandal ties, pot harness, and other secondary purposes. When cloth was cut across for any reason, it was kept from raveling by rolling up the edge and sewing it over and over with stout thread.

As was stated above, the rags recovered do not give us much idea of the original size of the pieces of cloth produced in the looms. The largest fragment in our collection is 19 inches long. The series of loom attachments observed in the kivas, where presumably these fabrics were produced, average about 4 feet in length.

Other fabrics.—Twined woven textile is represented in the collection by two small specimens. One (A-1398, Ruin 5) is perhaps part of a sandal; it has yucca warp, apocynum (?) weft; there are

---

[1] For Navaho weaving in general and the points here referred to in particular, see Matthews, 1884.

8 warps and 24 pairs of wefts to the square inch. The other piece (A-1138, Ruin 1) is so charred that the fibers cannot be identified; they appear, however, to be yucca warp, apocynum weft, or possibly apocynum both ways. The fabric is much finer than the Ruin 5 specimen, but may also have been part of a very high-grade sandal. The warps are two-cord, 10 to the inch; there are 40 pairs of weft strands, or 80 single strands, to the inch.

Straps.—In the kiva of Ruin 9 was found a long woven strap or headband with a loop at each end (A-1655). It is 19 inches in length, 2½ inches wide. The weft is cotton cord; 24 to 26 yucca strings form the warp. The weft is inserted by twined weaving; a twilled or diagonal effect is produced by inclosing two warp strands, the order of their inclosure being varied from one series to the next. The loops at the ends are made by gathering a number of the warp strands into two rolls, which are strengthened and held together by a continuous figure 8 weaving of cotton cord (pl. 46, *b*). Straps of this sort have often been found in cliff-dwellings and are usually, and probably correctly, called headbands or burden straps. Examples are figured by Nordenskiöld[1] and Fewkes[2] from the Mesa Verde, and by Cummings[3] from Sagiotsosi. There are also several in the Wetherill collection (Mesa Verde) in Denver. Nordenskiöld's specimen bears a

Fig. 45.—Weave of coiled work without foundation.

narrower strap of about the same length attached to one of its terminal loops; the same is true of an example of doubtful location in the Field Museum, Chicago.

Textiles in coiled work without foundation.—This weave, of which the stitch is illustrated in figure 45, is not rare. We have one specimen (A-1708, Ruin 9) made of two-strand human-hair string. There are about 7 coils to the inch, and in the other direction, about 6 loops. A specimen from Sagiotsosi (pl. 46, *c*) is coarser; 4 coils, 5 loops. These hair pieces are so small that their use cannot be ascertained; Cummings, however, figures a hair bag apparently in this technique;[4] and in the Southwest Museum, Los Angeles, there is a sandal from the Canyon de Chelly, the "upper" of which is of hair cloth. Of exactly the same weave, but much finer in texture, is the remarkable little cap from Ruin 2 (see pl. 34, *a*). In this specimen the string is probably of apocynum fiber. Near the edge there are 9 coils and 5 loops to the inch, the stitches nearer the top are deeper and wider spaced. Leggings (see pl. 34, *b*) and sandals (see pl. 40, *a*) were also made in this weave; the former are the coarsest

[1] 1893, pl. xlix. 2.
[3] 1909, figs. 22, 23; 1911, *a*, fig. 4.
[2] 1910, p. 10.
[4] 1910, p. 15.

examples of it we have, the rows being nearly an inch deep and the loops three-quarters of an inch apart.

Feather and fur cloth.—Bits of string wrapped with feathers or strips of fur were found in great quantities. The basis is usually a medium-weight, two-strand yucca cord one-eighth to one-fourth of an inch in diameter. For feather string the plumage of the turkey seems to have been used exclusively; when the heavy wing and tail feathers were employed the pile was usually stripped away from the stiffer part of the quill; small, downy breast feathers were used whole. The wrapping was done spirally, the end of one feather being held under the first few turns of the one following. The finished cord is about the size of the forefinger; a hank of it prepared for use is shown in plate 46, *d.* Fur string is considerably less common than that wound with feathers. It is wound with strips of the untanned skins of small animals, rabbits predominating; in Ruin 6 we found several strips cut to the proper size for wrapping.

The process of making these cords into robes seems to have been to wind a long strand back and forth about a framework until the desired size was reached, and then to make the whole fast by means of twined crossrows of yucca string. The resultant fabric was loosely woven, but must have been light, warm, and soft. Feather-cloth robes were probably the usual overgarment and sleeping blanket, and were very often used as shrouds for the dead. Bits of the cord frequently served for sandal ties, pot harness, and other household purposes where a strong yet soft ligature was needed.

Very clear drawings showing the method of preparing feather and fur string, and the weaving of garments from them, are given by Hough.[1]

WORK IN SKIN

This branch of technology is very poorly represented in our collection from the cliff-houses. We have a few small bits of what is apparently deerskin or mountain-sheep hide, and some strips of rabbit skin for fur cloth. From Ruin 7 was taken a piece of buffalo hide with the hair on; it was found on the top of the ancient rubbish just below the sheep dung, and, therefore, may perhaps be a Navaho importation.

WORK IN WOOD

Processes.—Work in wood was accomplished by chopping, sawing, scraping, and rubbing; traces of all four processes may sometimes be observed on a single specimen. For sawing and scraping the tools appear to have been unhafted flakes of hard stone with rough

---

[1] 1914, pp. 71–73 and figs. 148, 149. See also Fewkes, 1909, fig. 25.

edges; numbers of such flakes are to be found about the ruins. The method of felling trees may be reconstructed by studying the butt ends of house rafters. A groove was first hacked around the trunk with a stone ax, then the tree was bent enough to produce a tension on the fibers, which were finally sawed across with a flake. The butt was commonly trimmed to a roughly conical shape, more rarely rubbed down to a flat surface. Knots were hacked off with the stone ax. The preliminary shaping of implements seems to have been done by whittling or scraping with stone knives and flakes, the finishing by rubbing, first with coarse sandstone, then with closer-grained stone. High polish, presumably acquired in service, is sometimes found on hardwood tools.

Architectural wood.—Under this head come terracing logs, roof beams, logs incorporated in masonry, door lintels, and door staples. Roof beams were usually of cedar, terracing logs and logs in masonry were either cedar or piñon. None of the pieces found were very large, but there were indications in the walls of some of the houses of the use of beams 12 to 14 feet long and 12 inches through the butt. Wooden lintels and staples were made of cedar or oak.

Boards.—Flat wooden objects were taken from Ruin 3 and from the small house near Ruin 2. The former (A–1294) is oval, 10 inches long, 8 inches wide, three-eighths inch thick, well finished and having a drilled hole near the edge in the middle of one of the long sides; the latter (pl. 46 A, *b*) is rectangular, 17 inches long, 6¾ inches wide, one-half inch thick; it has perforations at the corners of one end. The use of these boards is problematical; specimens of the rectangular type (which are not uncommon in cliff-houses) are sometimes called cradle boards without, it seems to us, sufficient justification.

Billets.—In the collection are heavy pieces of worked wood of various sizes and shapes. All of them show wear, and some bear scratches and hacks that suggest use as lapboards. One flat example, 14 inches long, 13 inches wide, 1 inch thick, has at the ends lines of pricked holes, symmetrically arranged and evidently made for some definite purpose (pl. 46 A, *a*, Ruin 1). Found lying together in Ruin 3 were a loaf-shaped block of cottonwood 12 inches long and a bar of the same length, oval in cross section (A–1277, 1278); the two were evidently used together, but in what way is not obvious.

Digging sticks.—There are two types of digging sticks, the long and the short handled. The former have a length of from 3 feet to 3 feet 6 inches, are provided with well-defined pointed or flat blades, round shafts, and sometimes round knobs at the proximal ends (pl. 47, *c*, *d*, *e*). Our best specimens are made of oak. The short type (pl. 47, *f*, *g*) comprises examples 18 inches to 2 feet 6 inches long. They are merely stout sticks, commonly of greasewood, with flat

points that show signs of use in the ground. The exact duplicates
of these specimens in everything except excellence of finish are to be
seen in use by the Navaho at the present day.

"*Seed beaters.*"—This is a conjectural identification applied to a
set of objects found cached behind the rear wall of a small granary
near Ruin 1. As the photographs show (pl. 48, *a, b*), they were
made by lashing together at the butts five or six slim willow twigs
24 inches long in such a way that they all lie in the same plane,
spreading apart from each other a little toward the tips. The twigs
are peeled, except at their butts, where they are fastened together
with sinew bindings and overwrappings of yucca string. The
workmanship is extraordinarily neat. There are three complete
specimens and two pairs of twigs prepared for making a fourth.
Less well-made examples of this type are in the American Museum
and the Field Museum (all, presumably, from Grand Gulch, Utah);
the former are figured by Goddard.[1] Their use is problematical;
they might have served as cotton beaters (American Museum label)
or, as we are inclined to believe, to knock the seeds from grass
plants into gathering baskets.

Skinning knives.—From Ruins 4 and 8 came well-made little tools,
4½ inches long and one-eighth inch thick; their relative widths are
shown in plate 49, *k, l*. One is worked down to a sharp, chisel-like
edge at one end, the other at both ends, and these edges are in each
case stained with a red liquid, apparently blood. The third specimen shown (pl. 49, *m*) was collected by us in Grand Gulch, Utah,
in 1912; it is similar in shape to the single-edged Monument example, and is also stained red at the tip. These delicate little objects could never, of course, have been used for making the first
incision in the hide of any animal, but they might have been useful
in working the cut skin away from the flesh. We can account for
the blood stains, if such they be, in no other way.

Scrapers.—Plate 49, *a–g*, shows various scraping and rubbing implements of oak and cedar. The long specimen seems to have been a
sort of drawknife, as the sharpened edge is on the convexity of
the curve.

Awls.—Although we found no awls of wood during our excavations, they were probably in fairly common use in the district, as
the three fine examples in plate 49, *h–j*, one with two drilled holes in
its butt, were picked up by one of the authors several years ago in
houses in the near-by Sagi Canyon.

Fire-making apparatus.—Fire drills and hearths were recovered
from nearly every dwelling investigated. The former are round
sticks averaging three-eighths of an inch in diameter, the points

---

[1] 1913, p. 50.

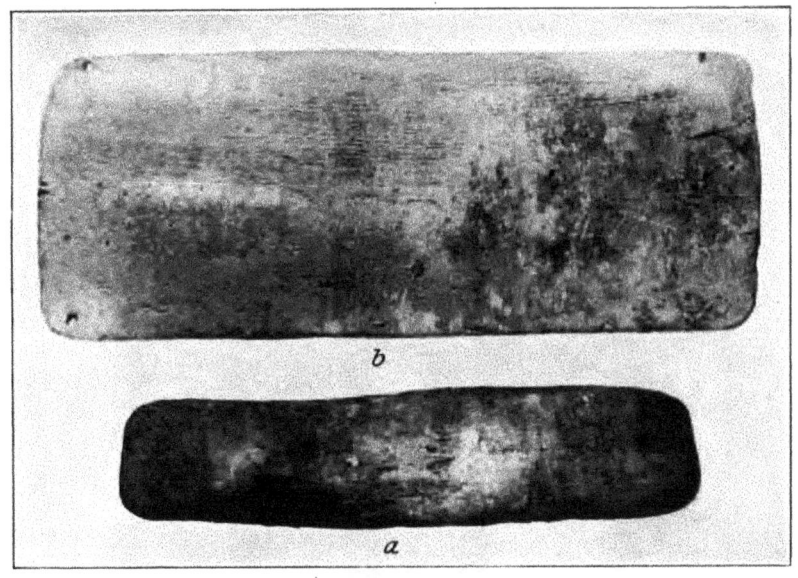

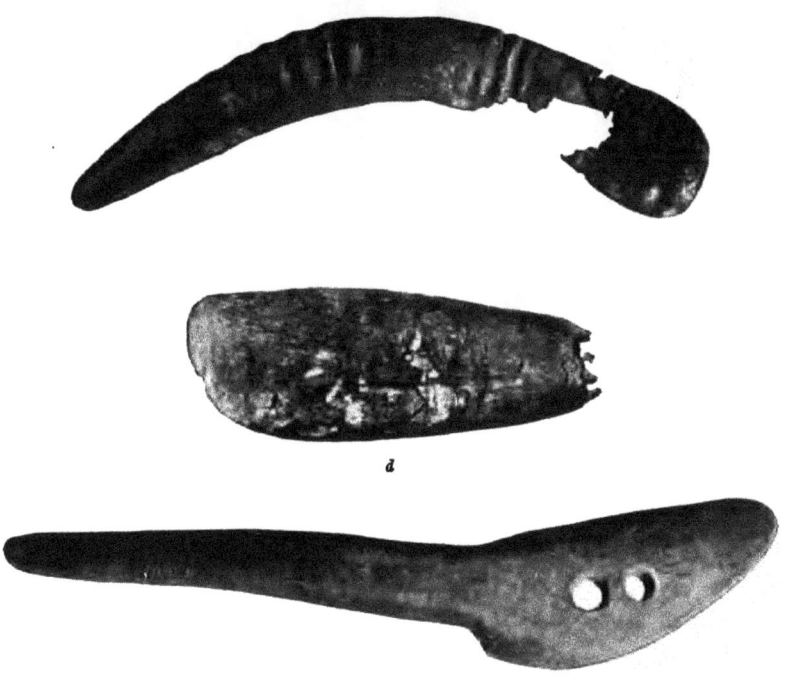

a. BILLET.   *b.* BOARD.   *c, d, e.* IMPLEMENTS OF MOUNTAIN SHEEP HORN

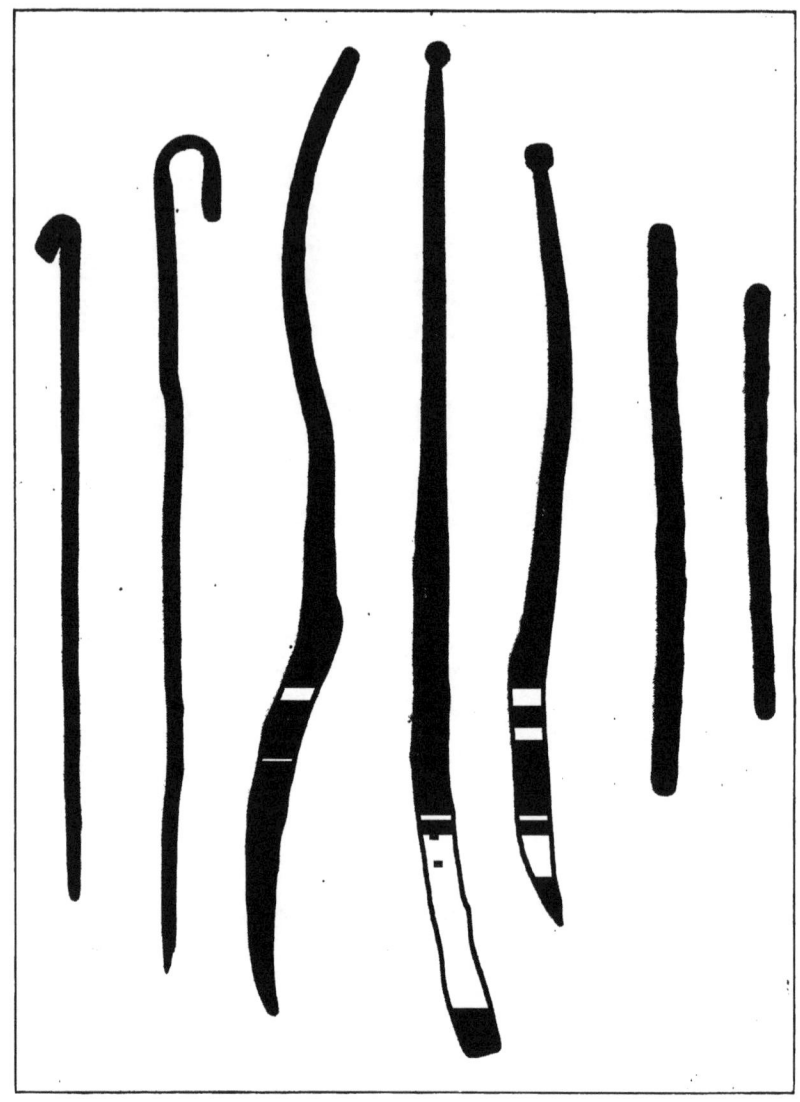

DIGGING STICKS AND CROOKS

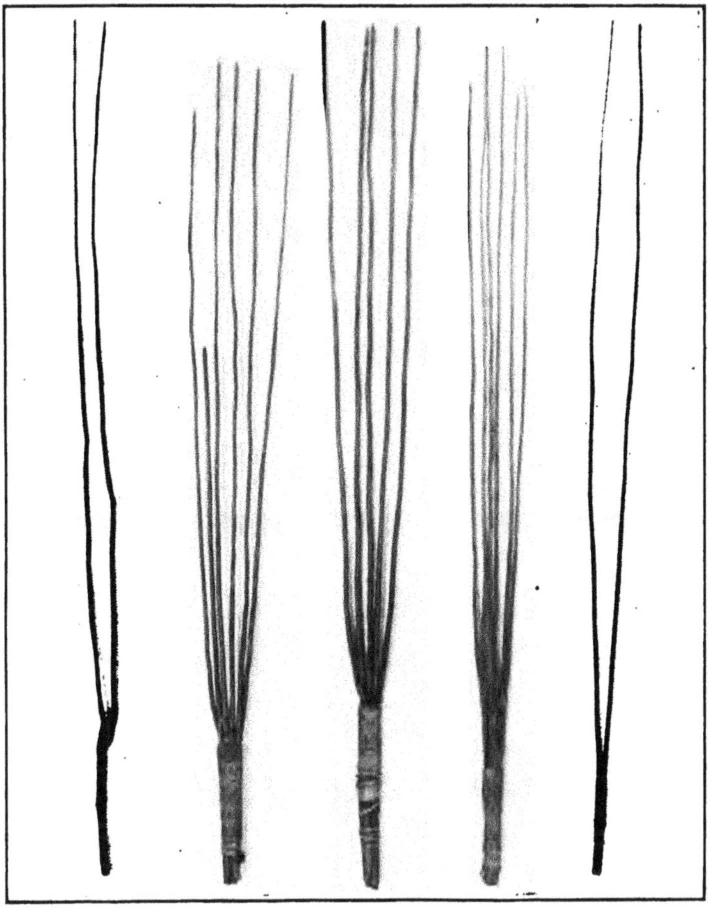

a. SEED BEATERS

b. BUTTS OF SEED BEATERS

k   l   m

j

i

h

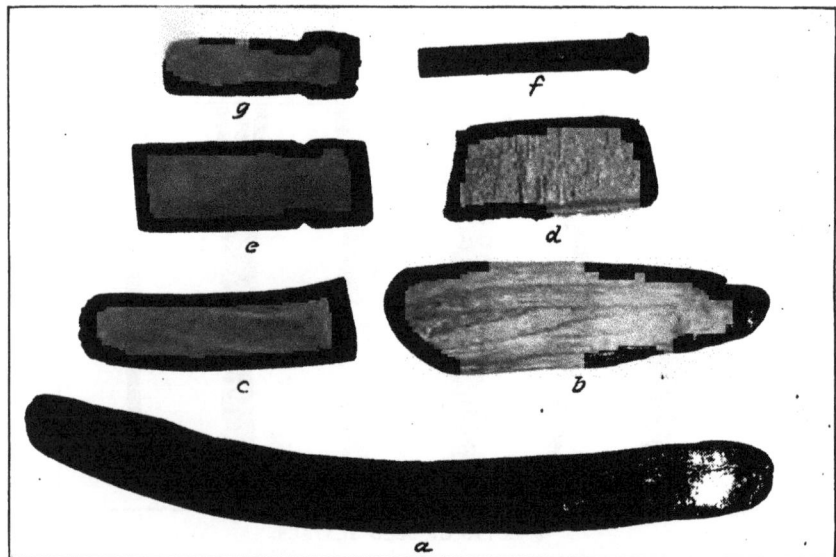

g

f

e

d

c

b

a

a–g, WOODEN SCRAPING AND RUBBING TOOLS.   h–j, WOODEN AWLS.   k–m, SKINNING

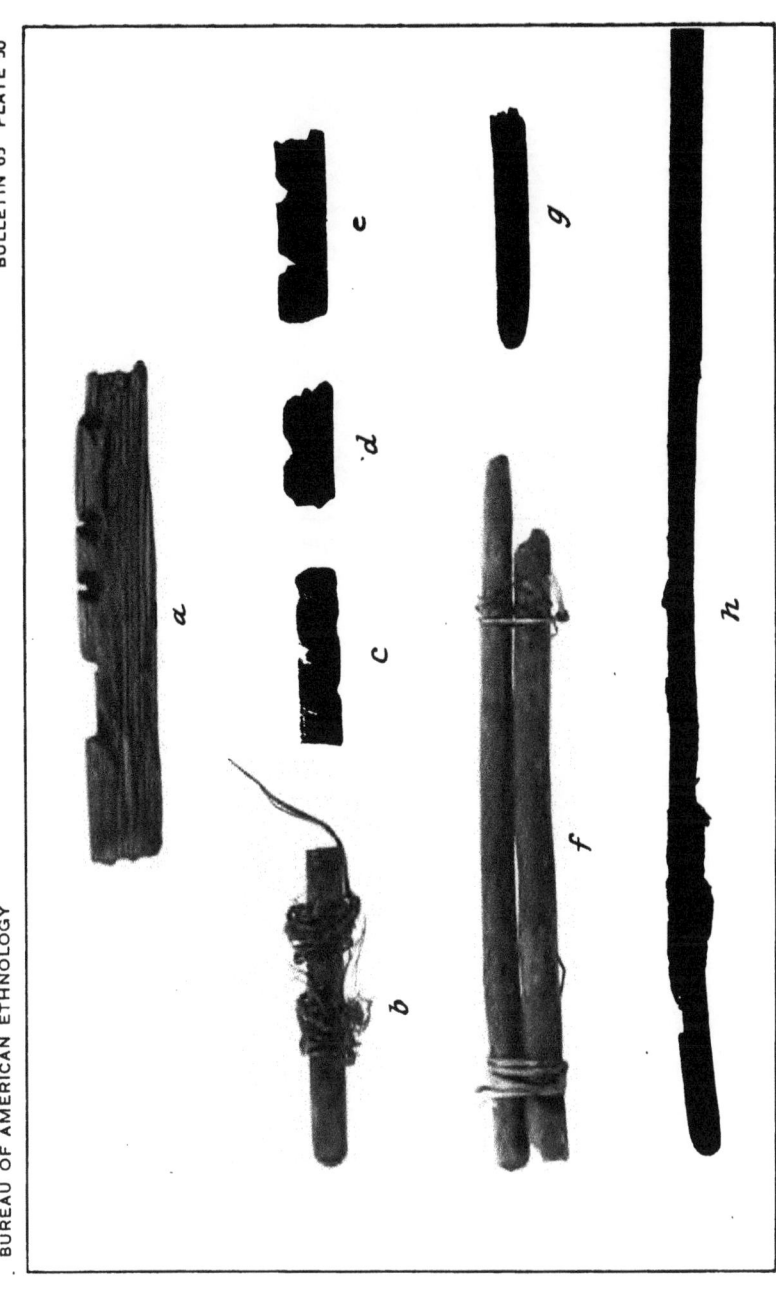

FIRE-MAKING APPARATUS

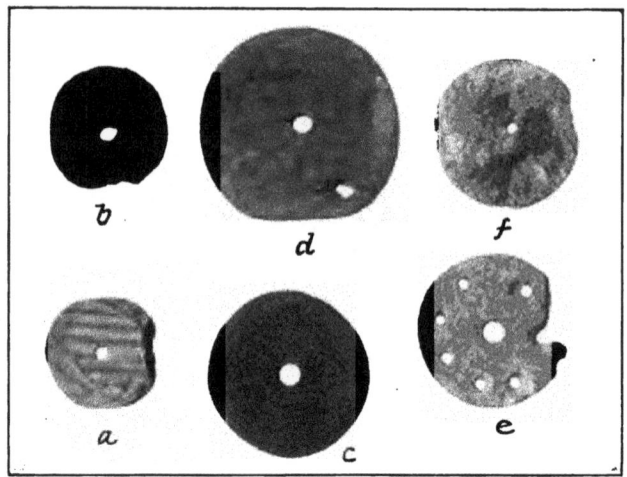

SPINDLE WHORLS

MISCELLANEOUS STONE OBJECTS

rounded and showing traces of charring; some consist of a single stick, others are rather carelessly attached to hafts (pl. 50, *b*, *h*). The hearths, of which only fragments are usually found, are also round sticks with rows of charred sockets in which the drills have been twirled; each socket has a little notch or trough for the engendered spark to fall through onto the tinder (pl. 50, *a*, *c*, *d*, *e*). All the hearths are of soft wood save one (A–1409, Ruin 6), which is made of a sunflower stalk, and all but one (pl. 50, *a*) are round. In Ruin 3 a hearth and drill were found tied together as if for a traveling kit (pl. 50, *f*). Fire pokers were common. They are usually greasewood sticks 18 inches to 2 feet long, smoothed off at one end and charred at the other. The Navaho use exactly similar implements for tending their fires.

Cups and dishes.—These are represented by two fragments of a shallow, traylike, wooden dish from Ruin 1 (A–1162), and by a handsome cottonwood cup found in the kiva of Ruin 8 (fig. 46). It is 3¼ inches high, 2⅜ inches in diameter at the top, 2 inches across the flat base. The interior excavation extends only a little more than halfway to the bottom. About the middle of the outside is an inch-wide band of zigzag decoration, apparently burned in, but now faint and indefinite. This cup, though somewhat broken and rather badly rotted, is still well smoothed, almost polished. An inch below the rim on one side is a hole drilled through to the interior. A similar cup in the American Museum, New York, has a hole of the same nature in the same position; it is from Grand Gulch.

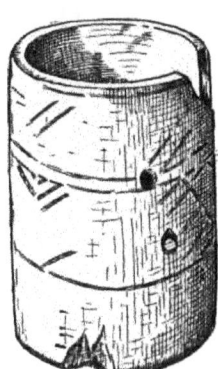

FIG. 46.—Cottonwood cup.

Spindle whorls.—These are all flat and vary from 1⅜ inches to 2⅞ inches in diameter. Besides the wooden examples shown in plate 51, *c*, *d*, there are also illustrated whorls made of squash rind (*f*), mountain-sheep horn (*e*), and pottery (*a*).

Crooks.—Sticks of various lengths, having one end bent back parallel to or even touching the shaft, came to light in several sites. A series of three of these objects was taken from a disturbed burial in Sagi Canyon opposite Kitsiel in 1912 (pl. 47, *b*). They are a little less than 3 feet long and are made of unworked sticks with their hacked ends left unsmoothed. The bend of the crook seems to have been produced by steaming; none of them are worn in such a way as to give a hint as to their use. More carefully made is A–1417 (pl. 47, *a*), both ends of which are neatly finished off and the crook is held down by a lashing of yucca sunk in grooves; the body of the stick is also partly cut away to leave a round opening,

as if for the reception of a cross stick. The length is 28¾ inches.
A-1136, Ruin 1 (not figured), seems to be part of a similar object;

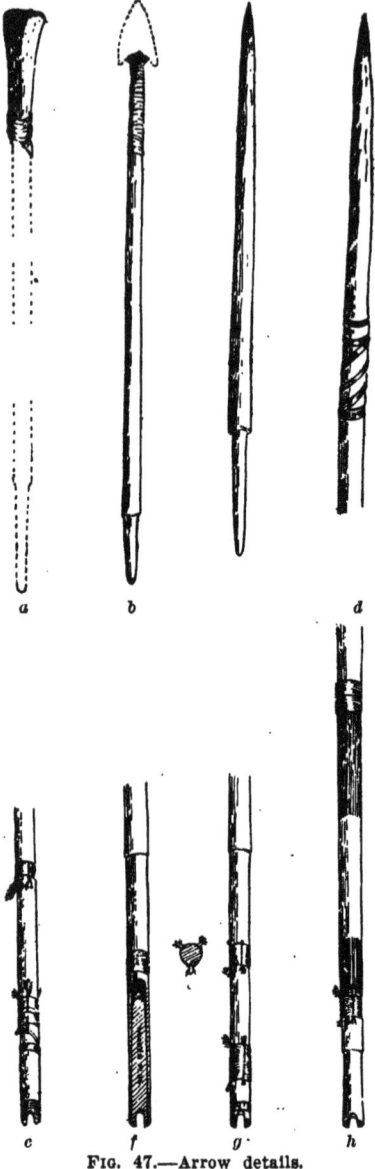

the shaft, however, is burned
away. The crook is held by a
strong yucca tie, but it is less
perfectly made, is larger, and the
body is not so much cut away.

Bow and arrow.—While
neither bows nor whole arrows
were recovered, there came to
light many fragments of the
latter. They are all made of
reeds and fitted with wooden
foreshafts. The reed shafts received no attention beyond the
removal of the leaves and some
smoothing at the joints. They
are from one-fourth to three-
eighths inch in diameter; we
have no data as to their length.
The foreshafts, of tough wood,
oak or greasewood, are 5 to 10
inches long, the majority of
them tapering to a plain and
more or less sharp point (fig.
47, *c, d*). We have only one or
two specimens with notched ends
and sinew wrappings to show
that they were once furnished
with stone tips (fig. 47, *b*).[1]
The only bunt-point was found
in Ruin 7; it is made of a section of hollow bone (fig. 47, *a*).

The foreshaft is always fitted
into the reed shaft just above a
joint, thus reducing the chances
of splitting; it usually has an
abruptly tapering butt that fits
into the reed and a shoulder that
prevents it from being pushed
back into the shaft (fig. 47, *b, c*).

FIG. 47.—Arrow details.

A few examples, having no shoulder, taper less rapidly.[2] Tight sinew
wrappings are applied about the shaft just below the junction (fig.

---

[1] The proportion of stone-tipped arrows was apparently higher in the upper Gila
region; see Hough, 1914, p. 65.

[2] Cf. Hough, 1914, p. 64, fig. 141, *a* and *b*.

47, d), the butt of the foreshaft being further strengthened in its setting by daubing it, before insertion, with piñon or some other adhesive gum. Most specimens seem to have been painted a dull red color.

The ends of the reed shafts are provided with three feathers, held in place by sinew wrappings about their butts and tips (fig. 47, e, g, h). The feathering begins in most cases about 1 inch from the nock, and varies in length from 2 to 5½ inches, the average being about 3 inches. Under the feathers the shaft is usually decorated with broad, equal rings of red and green, sometimes one red and one green, sometimes red at either end and green in the middle. The extremity of the arrow is strengthened and kept from being split by the bowstring by the insertion into it of a tightly fitting wooden plug, held in place by a sinew tie; the nock is cut in this plug (fig. 47, f).

Problematical wooden objects.—From Ruin 3 were taken two small peeled twigs 13 inches long (A–1275). One end of each is brought to a point; the butts are squared. From the butt for a space of 4 inches each twig is painted red, and at the end of the red zone there is a narrow sinew binding. In possession of Mrs. Wetherill there is a large bunch of exactly similar objects tied up with a yucca string; the lot was found by a Navaho in a cliff-house, probably in Sagi Canyon. In the American Museum there are others, from Grand Gulch. The Navahos told Mrs. Wetherill that these twigs were knitting needles, and the New York specimens are catalogued (by Mr. Richard Wetherill, the collector) under the same head. No true knitted textile has, however, yet been found in ancient ruins in the Southwest, so that this identification is doubtful.

In Ruin 8 were discovered two badly rotted wooden tools (A–1598), one sword-shaped, 20 inches long; the other 15½ inches in length, one-half inch wide, and three-sixteenths inch thick. They lay side by side in the débris, so that some connection between them is probable. They may, perhaps, have been weaving tools.

"Strap sticks" is a guesswork title applied to a number of short, cylindrical pieces of wood from 4 inches to 6 inches long by one-half inch in diameter. They were found in several sites, but particularly abundantly in Ruins 7 and 9. Marks about them show that they were once wrapped with some material that kept all but the last inch at either end from becoming worn or soiled. Their size, and the evidence of covering about the middle, suggest their use as the end sticks of such textile bands as the one from the Mesa Verde figured by Nordenskiöld.[1]

---

[1] 1893, pl. xlix–1.

OBJECTS OF STONE

Manos and metates.—Metates were not found in any of the houses, although metate bins, made by setting stone slabs edgewise in the earth, were observed in Ruins 2 and 3. A broken specimen was picked up in an empty cave near Ruin 4, and a small metate accompanied skeleton 5 in the Camp Cemetery at Marsh Pass. The latter is a thin slab of hard sandstone, somewhat hollowed by use on the upper side. The dearth of metates is probably to be accounted for by the rarity in the region of rocks, such as lavas and indurated sandstones, suitable for their manufacture. Hence the people, when moving, probably were induced to go to the trouble of carrying their heavy grinding apparatus with them.

Manos were hardly more common. With the above-mentioned mortuary metate was a small, oval, conglomerate mano (A–1747); and from the rubbish of Ruin 7 were recovered two more normally shaped specimens of crystalline limestone 9½ inches long, 3 inches to 4 inches wide, and wedge-like in cross-section; one of these (A–1543) shows traces of red paint, the other (A–1544) of blue, as if they had been used as convenient surfaces for grinding pigments.

Mortar.—A crude example of mortar (A–1782) was picked up on the surface of the little ruins above the " Pottery Hill " cemetery in Marsh Pass. It is made from a small conglomerate bowlder. The bottom of the stone has been pecked away to provide a flat base, and a cup-shaped depression some 6 inches in diameter and 2 inches deep worked into the top. Mortars such as this are not common in any part of the Southwest, and true pestles are, so far as we know, not found at all north of the Casas Grandes district of northern Chihuahua.

Hammerstones.—These implements are usually rough, battered nodules of quartz or other tough rock. They vary in size from 1½ inches to 3½ inches in diameter, the example shown (pl. 51, *j*) being a rather small one. Example *k* of the same plate is an elongate hammerstone of red jasper, the only one of its kind found.

Rubbing stones.—Rubbing stones are usually small, flat river bowlders, such as occur in enormous quantities along the San Juan; sometimes reduced to convenient size by pecking about the edges, but more often used without modification (pl. 52, *a–f*). They are round or oval, average 3 inches in diameter by 1 to 1½ inches thick, and frequently show signs of long service. One specimen (pl. 52, *e*) has a round, shallow, pecked pit on the upper surface. Another (pl. 52, *f*) is loaf-shaped, 4½ inches long, 2½ inches wide, and 2½ inches thick; the top is rounded, the bottom or rubbing surface flat, and in the two long sides are depressions to fit the fingers of the user. This tool accommodates itself very nicely to the hand; something of the kind must, we imagine, have been employed to rub down to an even surface the faces of the building stones in such walls as those of Ruin A, Marsh Pass.

Small, highly polished pebbles, of the sort commonly found in all parts of the Southwest and generally identified as pot smoothers, were not recovered by us; this, however, is probably of no significance, for the local pottery gives clear evidence of its treatment with the rubber.

Tool grinder (?).—On the surface in Marsh Pass there was picked up a rough piece of soft sandstone (pl. 51, *i*), in one edge of which there were cut two deep grooves, produced perhaps during the process of rubbing down and shaping on it bone or wooden implements.

Pot covers.—Pottery vessels were often found with their orifices closed by rough, flat slabs of sandstone broken off about the edges to bring them to convenient size. The only carefully made pot cover (pl. 51, *h*) is 5½ inches in diameter and one-fourth inch thick. It is apparently a natural slab, the edges worked down by chipping.

Loom weights (?).—In the kiva of Ruin 9 were discovered two contrivances which are believed to have been weights connected in some way with the process of weaving. One (A–1647) is a piece of burned adobe from an old roof, the other (pl. 51, *g*) a small fragment of sandstone; the former has a string tied about it as a means of suspension, the other is notched on the four sides to hold a similar ligature of yucca strips.

Grooved axes and mauls.—The axes in the collection are of surprisingly poor workmanship; this however, is apparently not accidental, but is merely a further demonstration of the seeming lack of good grooved axes throughout the northeastern part of the Southwest. The axes of the Grand Gulch and Montezuma Creek regions, Mesa Verde, Chaco Canyon, and Canyon de Chelly are all, so far as we know, of about the same irregular shape and careless finish as our specimens (pl. 52, *i–k*). Nowhere in the districts mentioned has yet been found anything even remotely approaching in quality the beautiful spirally grooved axes of the Rio Grande,[1] or the black, straight-backed ones of the Lower Gila.[2] Of the specimens here figured, one (pl. 52, *j*) has a plain groove, while the other two (pl. 52, *i*, *k*) are provided with shallow grooves over the butts.

The two mauls (pl. 52, *g*, *h*) are of sandstone; they are not edged, show the effects of battering, and were probably used in breaking out and trimming up blocks of stone for masonry.

Celts.—Plate 52, *l* (No. 88333, Grand Gulch, pl. 52, *m*, introduced for comparison) is our only specimen of a type of celt which is com-

---

[1] See Putnam, 1879, pls. xvii, xviii.
[2] See Fewkes, 1912, pls. 52–56.

mon in the San Juan drainage, but which has not yet been found, so far as we know, on the Rio Grande, the Little Colorado, or the Gila. The present example, like most of the others, is made of yellow hornstone, is broadest just behind the rounded blade, and tapers somewhat toward the butt. It is well polished, particularly at the blade end. At the butt there are several old breaks or nicks, their edges smoothed down by use. These nicks at the butt are found on nearly every celt of this kind that we have seen; but what caused them is doubtful. None of these objects have ever, so far as we know, been found attached to hafts; it is possible that they were used in

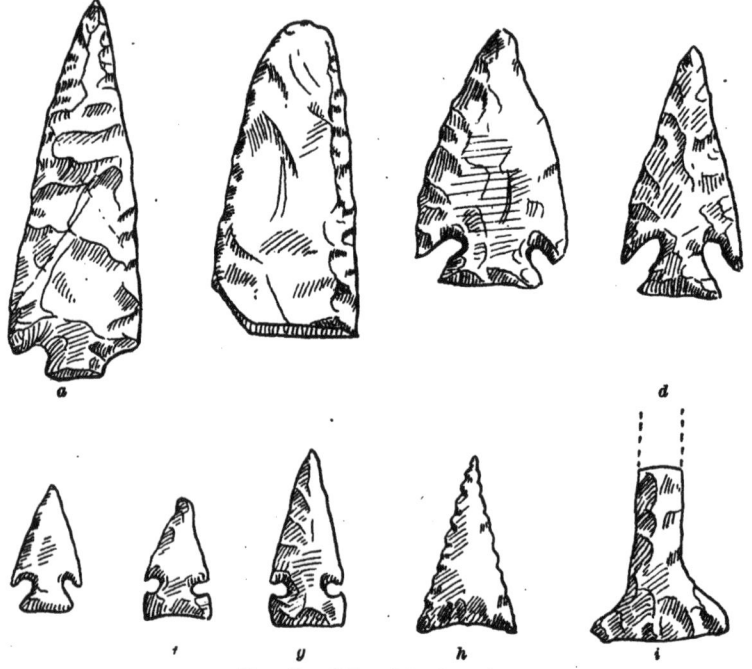

Fig. 48.—Chipped Implements.

the hand, and that the nicks were purposely made to provide a firm grip. Among the whites about Bluff, Utah, they are known as "skinning knives."

Hoe.—An implement of ground stone (pl. 52, *n*) is provisionally identified as a hoe. The marks about the blade look more like the striations produced by work in the ground than the result of any other industry, and certain rubbed areas upon the constricted butt seem to have been produced by the play of an attached handle.

Chipped implements.—Figure 48 gives practically all the examples found during the two seasons. They are knives, arrowpoints, and a drill. No finished stone scrapers were recovered, though many rough chips showed evidence of having been used for scraping or whittling.

Minute drill.—In Ruin 7 was found the tiny drill illustrated in figure 49. The specimen consists of a bent twig about 7 inches long, to the middle of which is attached another shorter bit of twig that holds the very small point. The latter is a sharp-tipped fragment of stone less than one-fourth inch long. It has been retouched a little along one edge, but is otherwise unworked.

Pendants.—Variously shaped pendants of turquoise were taken from the cache pot in Cave I, Kinboko. These are illustrated in plate 62 and figure 68, *d*. Pendants made from thin plates of fine-grained red slate were found in considerable numbers on the surface in Marsh Pass (fig. 50). This style seems typical of the San Juan drainage; the authors have noted it in Chaco Canyon, the Mesa Verde, and on Montezuma Creek. A pendant of selenite was with an infant skeleton in the "Pottery Hill" cemetery.

Pipe.—A small fragment of a highly polished stone cylinder was collected in Marsh Pass near the cemetery (A–1790). It may have been broken from a pipe or possibly from a large bead.

Hematite ball.—A round ball of hematite, three-fourths inch in diameter (A–1650), was taken from the kiva in Ruin 9. It seems to have been originally shaped by water rolling, but bears an added polish as if from long carrying in a bag or from much handling.

Incised slab.—In the little house near Ruin 2 there was found a slab of hard, close-grained sandstone (A–1265) 13 inches long, 4 inches wide, three-fourths inch thick. One side bears criss-cross lines, scratched with a sharp instrument. All the surfaces and edges are of natural cleavage, but the piece has evidently seen long service. Its use is unknown to us.

OBJECTS OF BONE

Awls.—These tools were found at every site; a representative selection is given in figure 51.

FIG. 49.—Stone-pointed drill.

The specimens vary in length, stoutness, and in the sharpness of their points; none offer features of particular interest. Some are made from whole bones, the joints furnishing convenient butts; others are worked from splinters of long-bones.

FIG. 50.—Stone pendants.

Scrapers.—Figure 51 shows the only two scrapers recovered; neither of them is of especially good workmanship. The fine scrapers made from the humeri of the deer and mountain sheep, so common on the north side of the San Juan, do not appear to have been made in this region.

OBJECTS OF HORN

That the mountain sheep played an important part in the lives of the Cliff-dwellers is evidenced by the abundance of its bones in the midden heaps of their ruins, and by the frequency with which it was

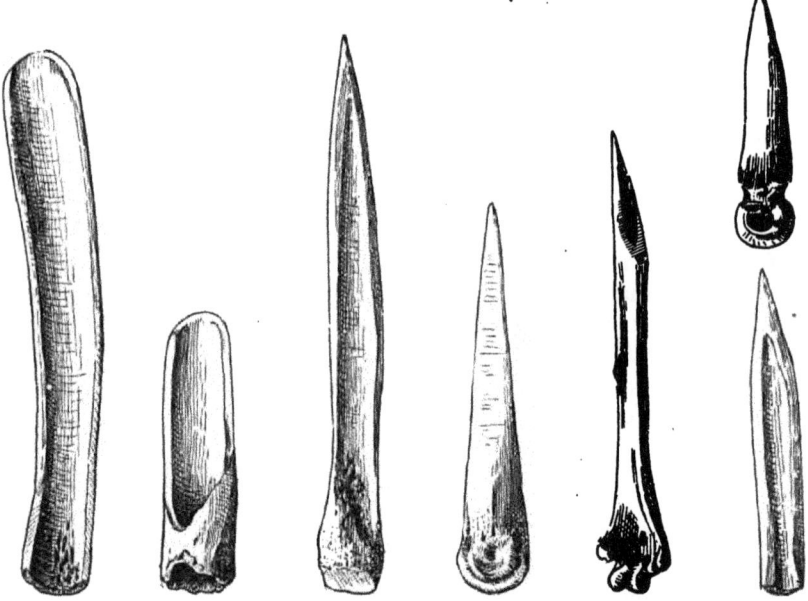

FIG. 51.—Bone tools.

depicted in their rock-cut drawings. Its hair and hide were much used, and its horn found employment for the making of several types of implements.

Scrapers.—The only two specimens of scrapers found in the region are shown in plate 46 A, *c, d*. One is fashioned from the thin horn of a young animal; the other has been split from a large horn steamed and straightened out.

Wrenches (?).—In the possession of Mr. John Wetherill, at Kayenta, there is a piece of mountain-sheep horn pierced by a series of four round holes about three-eighths inch in diameter; their edges are smoothed and beveled as if by much use. In our collection are fragments of two similar objects (A–1270, Ruin 3; A–1643, Ruin 9). From Sunflower Cave there was collected the unbroken specimen illustrated (pl. 46 A, e). Its length is 9⅝ inches, and the workmanship is of a very high order. A guess at the purpose of these specimens is that they served as wrenches to straighten and true up thin, round sticks. Dr. Sterns informs us that tools of similar nature, made from sections of the ribs of large animals, are found in the earth-lodge sites of Nebraska. They may also be compared with the so-called "bâtons de commandement" of the French caves.[1]

OBJECTS OF SHELL

Our finds of shell were limited to an abalone bead (A–1649) and a broken bracelet (88347), both from Ruin 9; and a similar bit of bracelet (A–1397) from Ruin 5. The latter two specimens are of the same type as the bracelets which have been taken in such great quantities from the ruins of the Lower Gila.[2] Examples are also to be seen in the American Museum collection from Pueblo Bonito. The type is recorded by Fewkes from the Little Colorado[3] and by Hough from the Upper Gila.[4] We have not heard of its occurrence in the Rio Grande.

Olivella shell beads were taken from several skeletons in the Marsh Pass cemeteries; the only working which these have undergone is the removal by rubbing of the tips of the spires to permit stringing.

POTTERY

In the discussion of all the other phases of the material culture we have grouped the objects from all the sites together, because we could not make out any differences of classificational value between the specimens from one ruin and those from another. In the case of pottery, however, we are able to see that there are two styles, or perhaps more properly, two substyles of a single main type. As our data are limited, we will, however, describe all the wares together, pointing out in the conclusion the differences which seem to us to justify our belief that two styles are represented in the collection.

---

[1] See Osborn, "Men of the Old Stone Age," p. 131.
[2] Hemenway coll. in Peabody Museum; see also Fewkes, 1912, fig. 48.
[3] Fewkes, 1904, fig. 47.
[4] Hough, 1914, p. 37.

BLACK-AND-WHITE WARE

TECHNOLOGY: The paste is of a clearer white than is common in any other group of black-and-white ware which we have observed, with the exception of that from Chaco Canyon. Tempering normally consists of very minute angular grains of basaltic (?) rock, so fine that they can sometimes be made out only with the aid of a strong hand lens. The slip is always fine and, unless fire-clouded or otherwise marred in baking, is of a clear, even white. Some of the pieces are made of a paste so perfect that the surface, so far as can be ascertained, was not treated with any slip at all, the decoration having been applied directly to the well-smoothed body clay. This procedure is common, so far as the authors know, only in the yellow ware of the ancient Hopi ruins.[1] Where slip is used it is confined, as elsewhere in the Southwest, to the visible parts of vessels. It is brought to an even finish, but is seldom highly polished. The pigment is clear, dull black, with a slightly bluish or slaty cast. Chemical analyses have not yet been made, but it is probable that it is an iron product, as determined by Nordenskiöld for the paint of Mesa Verde black-and-white.[2]

SHAPES: *Ollas.* (1) *Flat upperbody with straight neck.*—The underbody is full, the shoulder abrupt, the upperbody flat and almost horizontal. The neck rises almost straight, but is a trifle smaller just below the orifice than it is at its base. The lip flares slightly. There are three decorative zones—the upper part of the underbody, the upperbody, and the neck. Specimens seem to average about 9 inches high. There is evidently considerable variation in this type, both in details of proportion and in size; our material is all fragmentary. The description given here is of a badly broken example from Ruin 8. Fewkes[3] figures a very fine one from the Little Colorado.

(2) *Globular body with high neck.*—The body is globular, but is usually somewhat elongated vertically (pl. 53, *a*, *b*). There is no true shoulder. The neck is high, but in most cases continues the curving lines of the body without an abrupt break. The lip turns outward rather gradually. Decoration zones are a narrow band about the neck and a field consisting of the whole of the body from just below the neck to well below the point of greatest diameter. Height averages 15 inches, greatest diameter 14 inches.

(3) *Globular body with low neck.*—The body is almost spherical. The orifice is relatively much larger than in the preceding types; the neck very low and abruptly outflaring. A single decorative

---

[1] It has also been reported for the black-and-white ware of Aztec, New Mexico (Morris, 1915, p. 673).
[2] Nordenskiöld, 1893, pl. xxxi.
[3] 1904, pl. xx.

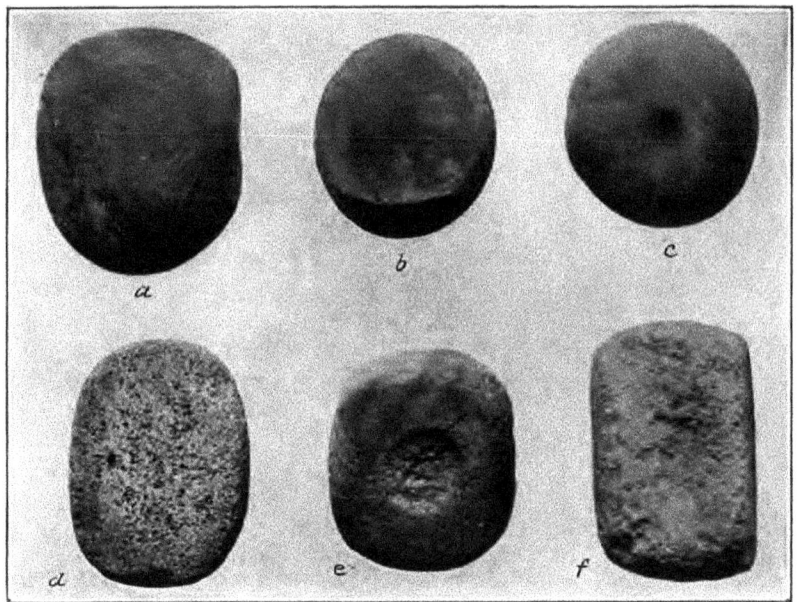

RUBBING STONES

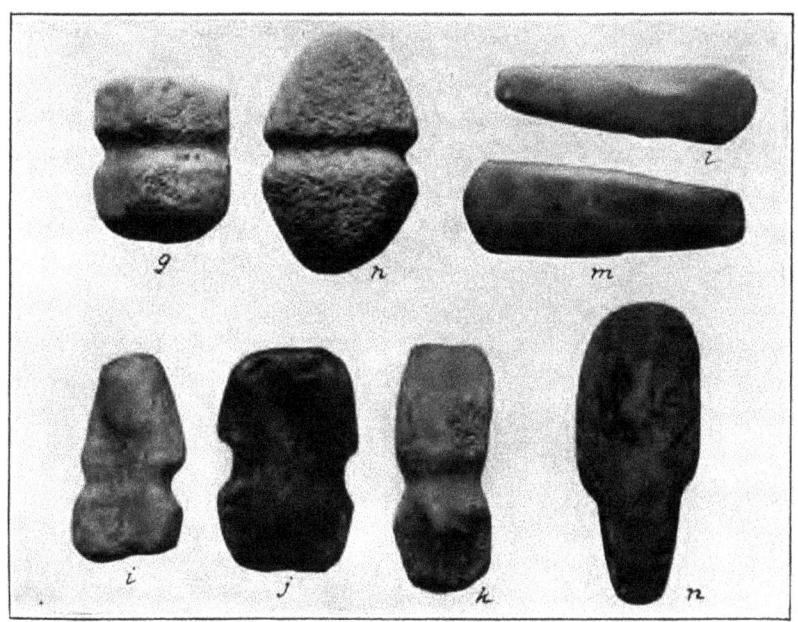

AXES, MAULS, AND CELTS

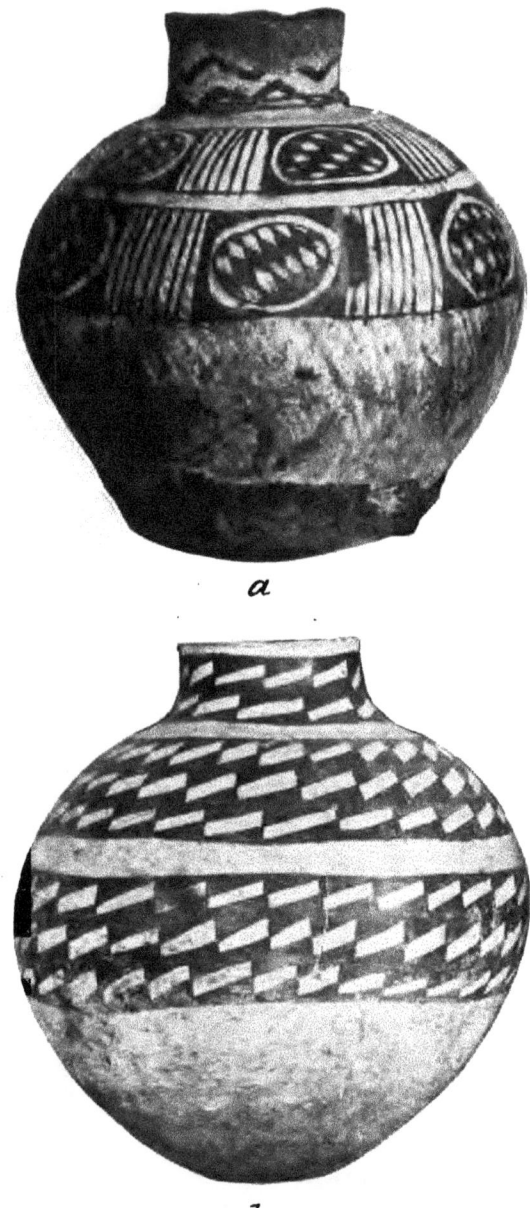

a

b

BLACK-AND-WHITE OLLAS

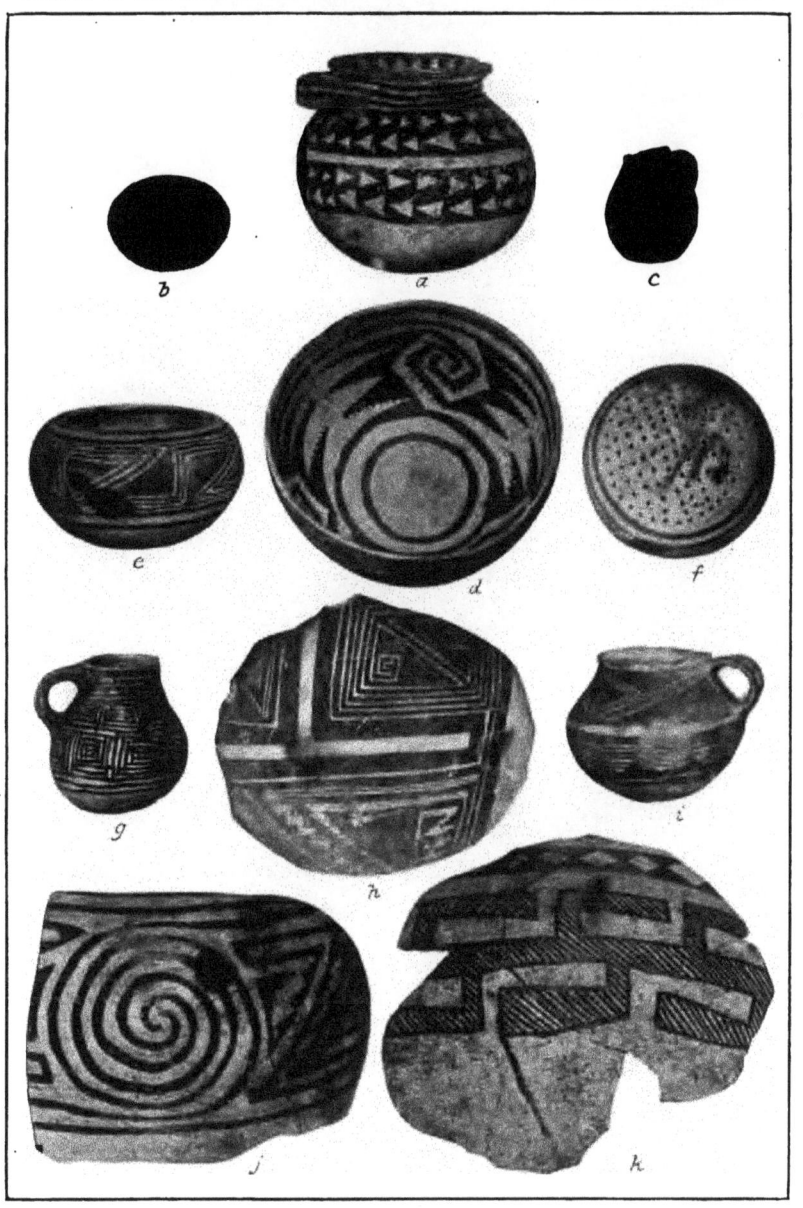

BLACK-AND-WHITE POTTERY

BLACK-AND-WHITE POTSHERDS

zone covers the vessel from just below the neck to well below the point of maximum diameter. Height averages 14 inches, greatest diameter 16 inches (see fig. 55).

It should be noticed that none of these types are provided with handles. Ollas from the Mesa Verde, the McElmo, and the Montezuma Creek regions, on the other hand, regularly have handles.[1]

Seed jars are always of small size, with spherical bodies, flat or rounded tops, and small orifices without necks (see pl. 54, *b*). Holmes calls this form "heart-shaped jar."[2] We have only sherds, so that local peculiarities of shape, if such exist, cannot be pointed out. The tops, however, seem to have been unusually flat.

Colanders are little vessels, usually not more than 6 inches in diameter by 3 inches high; their bottoms are pierced by a number of small holes, as if to fit them for use as sieves. There are two forms, the flat-topped and the flattened-spherical. The former is an exact replica in miniature of the flat-topped olla without the neck; we have no whole specimens. The flattened-spherical type (pl. 54, *e*, *f*) has a single decorative zone running from the orifice to below the point of greatest diameter; the flat-topped style has one zone about the upper surface and another below the abrupt shoulder.

Jugs are small and fat-bellied, much like those of redware (cf. fig. 57). They have a single vertically placed handle running from just below the rim to the upper side of the body (pl. 54, *c*, *g*, *i*). The only instance of a jug with horizontal handle was the cache pot from Cave I (pl. 54, *a*).

Canteens are known to us only through fragments.[3] The body seems to have been spherical, the orifice very small and placed at the top of a short neck without flare at the lip. There are two lugs on the upperbody, perforated vertically for the attachment of a carrying string.

Ladles are all of the bowl-and-handle variety except the single yellowish specimen shown in plate 58, *d*. The handle is usually round and hollow, sometimes solid with a groove along its upper surface; occasionally it consists of a long open loop of clay. The bowl is less than hemispherical and has in all cases an even, rounded rim. Decoration is confined to the interior of the bowl and to a band or a series of dashes along the top of the handle.

Bowls fall into two classes, those with direct rims and those with outcurved rims. The former (pl. 54, *d*) are deep in proportion to their width, the depth being at least half the diameter and occasionally even more (average width 11 inches, a few examples measuring up to 14 inches). The bottoms are rounded and the sides rise steeply. The rims are squarish (fig. 52, *a*), but as the sides are thin,

---

[1] Morley, 1908, pl. xxxix; Cummings, 1910, p. 38; Nordenskiöld, 1893, pl. xxxi.
[2] 1886, p. 330.
[3] But see Cummings, 1910, p. 18.

the square edge is less noticeable than is the case with the heavy-walled Mesa Verde bowls. The second type (outcurved rim) averages smaller than the first, few examples being more than 8 inches in

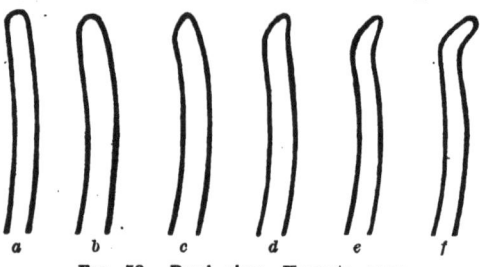

FIG. 52.—Bowl rims, Kayenta ware.

diameter; the pieces are also rather shallower. The rim varies somewhat in the amount of flare; the commonest forms are shown in figure 52, *d*, *e*, *f*. The flare itself is often decorated separately from the main interior design (pl. 55, nos. 1–4, 7, 22–26). We have not noticed this rim treatment developed to any such extent in other southwestern groups. Many, though not all, of the bowls of both classes are provided with single horizontally placed loop handles. Decoration is rigidly confined to the interior.

Pitchers, such as those of Chaco Canyon, Montezuma Creek, and elsewhere, have not been found; nor do mugs, kiva jars, or eccentric forms appear to have been made.

DECORATION: On the basis of the ornament, the black-and-white ware seems to be divisible into two groups; that in which the designs cover most of the background and that in which they cover only a moderate amount of the background. The terms "heavy" and "light," used in the field notes, may perhaps be employed until more suitable ones can be applied. While "heavy" decorations are occasion-

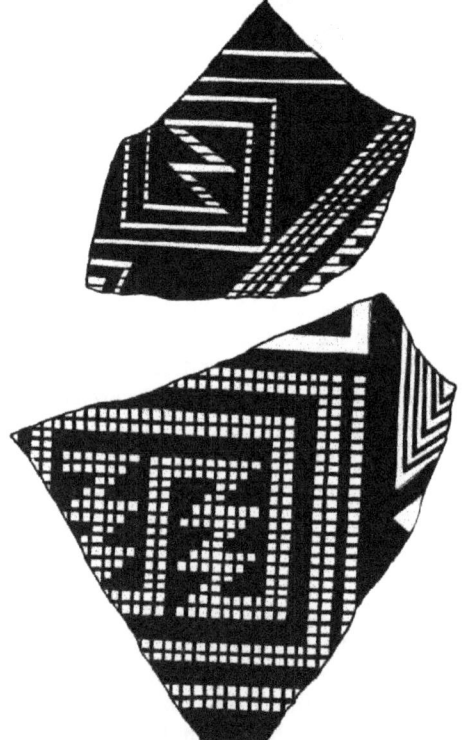

FIG. 53.—Black-and-white designs with "under-framework."

ally set fairly well apart from each other and some "light" ones fairly close together, the difference between the two classes is nevertheless a very real one and rests not only on the relative amounts of background covered, but also on the actual elements of design and their arrangement.

In the "heavy" class, as stated above, the decorative zone is so covered by the black pigment that only very small amounts of the white background are left exposed (pl. 54, *h;* and see Fewkes, 1904, pl. xx, and Holmes, 1886, figs. 327, 328). This gives the impression at first sight that the design is painted in white on a black surface; indeed, in some cases the ancient artist seems to have striven for this very effect. The care which was taken to leave very narrow margins between the black areas resulted in the development of surprising skill and accuracy of brushwork. The most characteristic feature of "heavy" designs is the use of a device which may be called "under-framework." It consists of covering the surface with fine hatching (pl. 54, *h;* fig. 54, *a*) or crosshatching (fig. 53) and

a

b

Fig. 54.—*a*, Black-and-white design with "under-framework." *b*, Black-and-white design, "heavy" type.

then drawing the design over it, locating and measuring its units by means of the underlying lines. In this way were attained great accuracy of spacing and regularity of repetition, and those parts of the preliminary hatching or crosshatching that cross the narrow white spaces between the black figures give to the whole decoration an almost textile appearance.[1] Two decorations not applied over

---

[1] Holmes (1886, p. 342), indeed, refers to examples of this style in support of his theory of the textile origin of southwestern pottery ornament. These pieces, however, are undoubtedly late in the black-and-white evolutionary series, and while they may possibly show textile influence, they surely can throw no light on the ultimate origins of ceramic decoration.

"under-framework," but which are also typical of the "heavy" technique, are scrolls drawn very close together[1] and opposed key figures on the ends of thin interlocking arms (fig. 54, *b*); the latter device is always used to fill diamond-shaped spaces.

"Heavy" designs appear to be confined to certain forms of vessels: the olla with flat upperbody (Type I); the straight-rimmed, square-lipped bowl, and flat-topped colanders. In other words, it is found most commonly on those vessels which are peculiar to this region, and less commonly, or not at all, on forms which have a more general distribution.

The "light" designs, which leave more of the background exposed and in which the entire emphasis is laid on the black lines and figures, are much more varied, less distinctive, and therefore less easily classified than those just described. We have as yet been unable to tabulate and classify the design elements and their framework principles. Perhaps most characteristic, however, is the lavish use of series of small raking triangles set along straight lines in a sort of saw-tooth edge and opposed by like series running in the opposite direction (see pl. 55, 19). Very commonly there is introduced between the two a line saw-toothed on both sides (fig. 55 and pl. 55, 13, 14, 15, 16, 20, 23). This decoration seems to be genetically allied

FIG. 55.—Black-and-white olla.

to ornaments made up of series of raking parallelograms such as that illustrated in plate 53, *b*. Opposed sets of isosceles triangles with their points touching, thus leaving diamond-shaped interspaces, each one of which is occupied by a single dot, are also abundant (pl. 55, 21, 22, 23, 24, 27, 28). Interlocking scrolls (pls. 54, *c*, *j*; 55, 9) and derivative (?) elements (pl. 54, *d*), are common. Where hatching occurs (pls. 54, *k*; 55, 11, 12, 17, 18) it is always, apparently, in the form of current offset designs analogous to those of the redware with dull paint (see fig. 58). Contrasted black and hatching, so typical of the black-and-white wares of the Upper Gila and of the southern side of the Little Colorado, is not found in our collection.

COLORED WARE

(1) Redware with shining paint.   (3) Polychrome ware.
(2) Redware with dull paint.   (4) Plain yellow ware.

---

[1] Holmes. 1886, fig. 325.

The vessels of the groups above mentioned are made of a clay that was originally dull gray; normal firing has turned their surfaces to a warm, yellowish flesh color, hard to describe, but when once seen recognizable at a glance. In cross section there is a central streak of the unchanged gray clay, broader or narrower according to the thoroughness of the firing. Pieces of the plain yellow ware (class 4) were made of this clay and fired without modification; the other three classes were produced by the application of varying slips and pigments; these differences have been used for classification, but there are further differences in the shape of the vessels and in their decoration that will be discussed under the class heads.

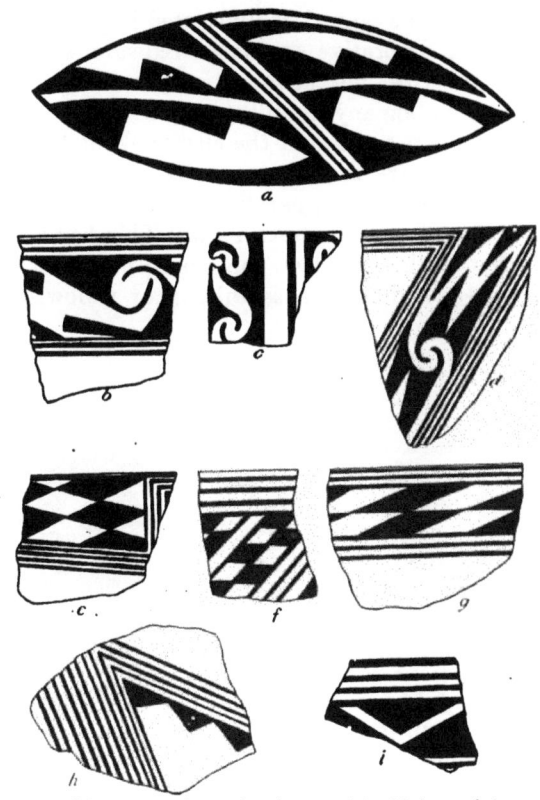

FIG. 56.—Decorations of redware with shining paint.

REDWARE WITH SHINING PAINT: This bears an even coat of fine red slip covering the visible surfaces of the vessels (the interiors of small-mouthed pieces are unslipped); this was worked down, probably with the rubbing stone, to a very smooth, uniform finish which is not exactly polished, yet has a pleasant "slick" feeling to the touch. The most striking feature of the ware, however, is the pigment used in its decoration, a bluish or slaty paint with a distinct sheen or gloss. It is in no sense a glaze, its glossy appearance being due to its susceptibility to mechanical polish. Analyses have not been made, but we suspect that graphite will be found to play some part in its preparation.

Vessels of this ware so far observed are: Bowls, small-mouthed pieces with pitcherlike handles, and seed jars. The *bowls* are characterized by an almost hemispherical form, walls of very uniform thickness, and "direct rims" (neither incurved or outcurved), tending, in most cases, to have square rather than rounded edges (fig. 52, *a*). Handles are uncommon. As only small fragments of the *pitchers* have as yet come to light, nothing can be said as to their form. The only complete *seed jar* found, which from the sherds seems to be typical, is illustrated in plate 34, *c*.

The decorative system of redware with shining paint is difficult to describe, nor have we as yet enough material for an analysis. The accompanying illustrations (fig. 56) plainly show the differences between it and the classes about to be described. Noteworthy features are the exceptionally neat brushwork and the lavish use of sets of narrow, parallel lines.

REDWARE WITH DULL PAINT: This has a paste rather coarser than that of the last class, containing numerous small bits of water-worn quartz and a thick sprinkling of yellowish-white particles (nature

FIG. 57.—Redware jugs.

unknown, ground potsherds ?) which often protrude through the slip and give many of the pieces the appearance of having been sprinkled with very fine sawdust. The slip is thin, particularly on bowl exteriors, where it is generally little more than an unevenly applied wash. The exterior bottoms of bowls and jars are almost always left unslipped. The general surfaces are worked down evenly, but seldom if ever have the perfect texture of class 1. The pigment is a thick, dull black, entirely without luster, contrasting with its background much more sharply than does the slaty bluish paint of class 1.

By far the most abundant specimens of this ware are small, fat-bellied *jugs*, 3 to 6 inches high, with large orifices and single, vertical handles (fig. 57). They have little or no neck and uniformly outcurved lips. A somewhat larger vessel, similar in shape but lacking the handle, was, from the evidence of the sherds, not uncommon.

Canteens are almost globular in shape, have small orifices and two knob-like lugs, perforated vertically for the insertion of carry-

c

FIG. 58.—Decorations of redware with dull paint.

ing strings. *Ladles* are of the "bowl-and-handle" variety.[1] The

---

[1] Except the specimen shown in pl. 58, *d*, which in other ways is not typical of Kayenta pottery.

handles are round, hollow bars, the ends of which are often supplied with a loop of clay as if for suspension. *Seed jars* are full-bodied vessels with flat tops, small orifices, and no necks at all. *Colanders* or sieves are shaped like seed jars, but have in their bottoms many small round perforations one-sixteenth inch in diameter.

Bowls are much less common than the little handled jugs and the jars, their place having seemingly been supplied by black-and-white or possibly by polychrome bowls. They are practically hemispherical, have direct rims and rounded lips (fig. 52, *b*), and are not, so far as we know, ever provided with handles.

The decoration of this class of redware is remarkably uniform. Hatching, particularly in the form of the hatched ribbon, is almost exclusively used. On bowls, and especially on the little handled jugs, there recurs again and again the same ornament, a current design with recurved toothed projections. Its most common form is shown in figure 58, *c;* modifications in *a* and *b*. While other hatched decorations are found, as well as a few in solid black, nine out of every ten small-mouthed vessels, and fully half of all the bowls, carry some form of this type design.

POLYCHROME WARE: While the paste does not differ noticeably from that of the preceding group, the surfaces are so treated as to give an entirely different effect. The yellow paste is used as a background upon which decorations are applied in red, black, and white. Technically the ware is identical with that just described, even to the fine mottling due to protruding of bits of light-colored tempering material. The red pigment is of a bright rich color, but is not thick or particularly tenacious, and rubs away rather easily. The black is dull and apparently of the same nature as that of the last group; like the red, it does not seem to have bitten well into the clay. The white paint is a chalky substance much less permanent than the red and the black; only in very heavily fired specimens does it amalgamate well with the body of the ware; sherds that have been much exposed to the weather are usually found to have lost all but faint traces of it.

Bowls are by far the commonest vessels of polychrome ware. They range in size from 2 or 3 inches to 15 inches in diameter, larger specimens being rare. The average piece is about 10 inches in diameter by 5 inches deep, thus approximating the hemispherical form. While the rim is occasionally direct and rounded, most examples tend to curve or at least to bevel outward (see fig. 52; nos. *e* and *f* are the commonest). On the exterior, half an inch to an inch below the rim, there is usually a single horizontal handle, made of a flat strip of clay and about large enough to admit the tip, but not the first joint, of the thumb. In very small bowls this handle is sometimes set vertically, thus giving them the appearance of cups;

these are, however, quite distinct from the flat-bottomed black-and-white mugs of the northern San Juan.

Ollas were not found by us, though a few sherds from Marsh Pass may perhaps be referred to small examples. *Ladles* are uncommon, that form having been supplied, apparently, by black-and-white specimens. The sherds that do occur all belong to the "bowl-and-handle" variety. *Colanders* are of the same shape as the lusterless paint examples. In our collection are only sherds. No life forms or eccentric shapes were found.

Bowl decoration: Exterior ornament is limited to carelessly drawn lines of red paint that encircle the bowls just below the rim. There are sometimes two or three such lines half an inch wide, sometimes a single line 1 inch to 4 inches in width; occasionally the paint is put on in oblique dashes or, rarely, in the form of a rude meander edged with black. In all cases the paint is merely daubed on, and there is a marked contrast to the neat accuracy of brushwork shown in the decoration of the interior.

The interior designs of polychrome bowls are almost without exception of the "all-over" type; that is to say, they cover, more or less completely, the entire inner surface of the pieces. The framework of all the designs is made up of broad red bands or ribbons outlined in black, often having a second outlining of the chalky white pigment. The simplest figures consist of the bands alone (cf. Fewkes, 1911, pl. 15, *d*). In somewhat more elaborate examples the bands bear angular projections or terminal key figures (pl. 56, *c*).[1] The most ornate and perhaps the most typical specimens have supplementary decorations painted in black over the yellow background between the red framework lines (pl. 56, *a*, *f*). This supplementary decoration is characteristic of the group and is generally carried out in the following manner: The spaces to be ornamented are filled with a coarse hachure of parallel lines; while this may completely fill the field, the lines are usually divided into groups of from three to eight or ten, and the small interspaces thus produced are occupied by elements of a different nature, by far the most common of which are stepped lines (fig. 59, *a*). Others are: fringed or dotted lines (fig. 59, *d*), series of single triangles (fig. 59, *b*), and series of opposed isosceles triangles whose points meet (fig. 59, *e*). Still another "filler," occurring in a number of cases and usually occupying triangular fields, is oblique crosshatching (pl. 56, *f*). Two rather aberrant figures, suggesting certain designs of Rio Grande[2] and Lower Gila pottery,[3] are shown in figure 60. The two paw-like objects in plate 56, *b*, give the only suggestion of a naturalis-

---

[1] In pl. 56 the yellow background of the bowls is represented by white, red fillings are shown by hatching, and white edgings by lines of dots.

[2] See Kidder, 1915, pl. xxiii.

[3] See Fewkes, 1912, fig. 45.

tic motif yet observed in polychrome ware; a similar figure, but with
five projections, is painted on a sherd from the same region (A–1811).

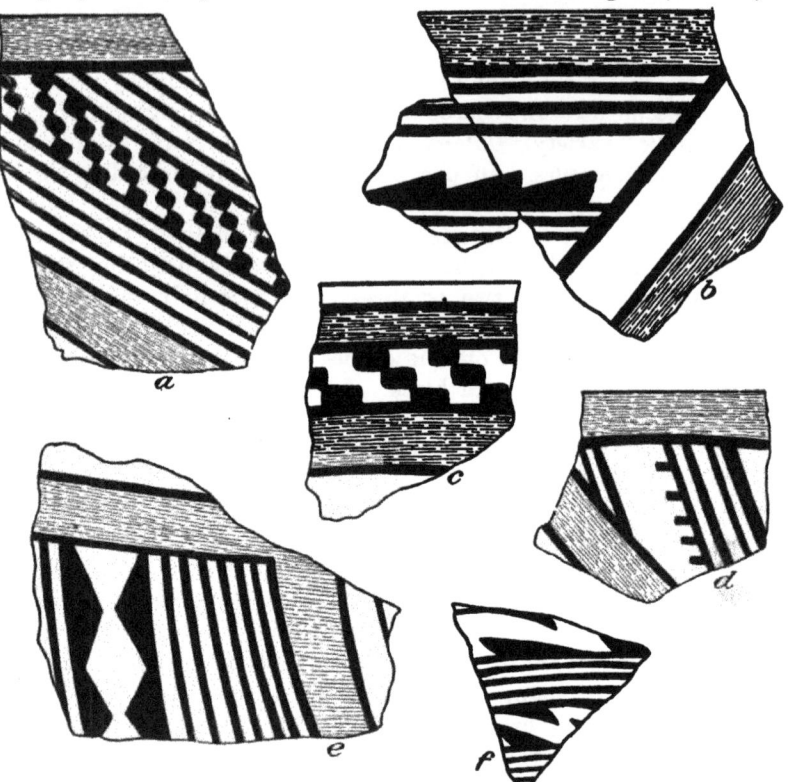

FIG. 59.—Decorations of polychrome redware.

The general method of decoration, as outlined above, can easily
be made out from sherds, but as most of the designs are of the
"all-over" style, and as our
collection contains few unbroken bowls, on which whole
designs may be studied, little
can be said as to the arrangement of the design frame-
works. There seem, however,
to be three principal types,
here given in order of their
apparent abundance: swas-
tika type (pl. 56, c–f), double-
oval type (pl. 56, b), and scroll type (pl. 56, a). On these frame-
works an almost endless number of different patterns were produced.

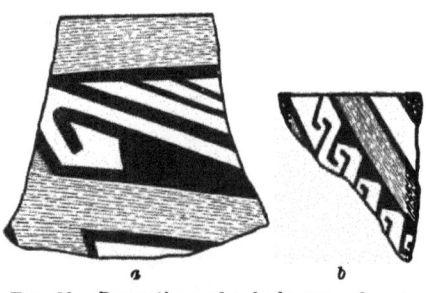

FIG. 60.—Decorations of polychrome redware.

a   b

c   d

e   f

POLYCHROME REDWARE

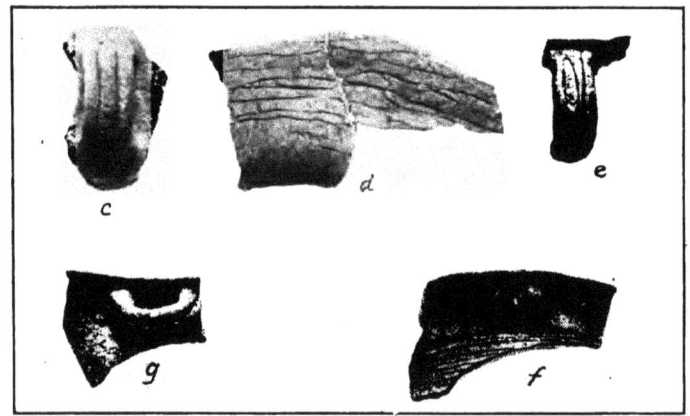

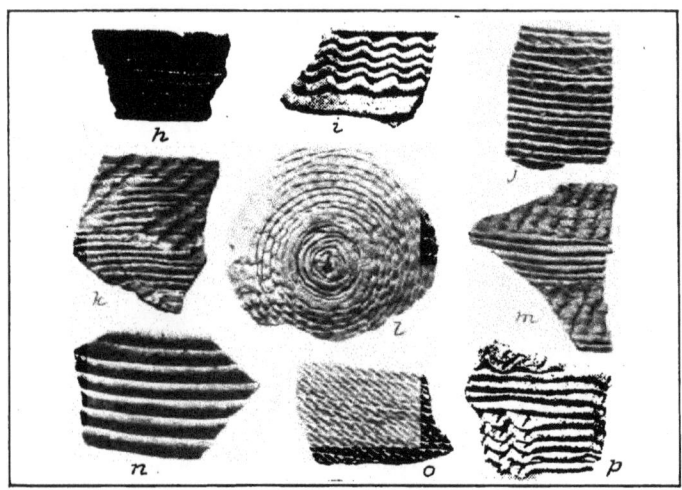

CORRUGATED WARE

PLAIN YELLOW WARE: This is made of the same paste that forms the base of the three preceding classes, but it is entirely unslipped. Pieces of the ware might therefore be considered as unfinished red or polychrome vessels, fired before slipping, were it not for the fact that they are only found, so far as we know at present, in Sagi Canyon and Marsh Pass. The fragments collected by us in the latter locality are of bowls, ladles, and ollas. The bowls are small and deep, have direct rims and single vertically placed handles; a few of them bear one or two lines of dark-brown paint encircling the interior just below the rim. The ladles are "bowl-and-handle" type; nothing definite can be made out as to the shape of the ollas.

CORRUGATED WARE

TECHNOLOGY: The paste of the corrugated vessels is uniformly dull gray; it is coarse, naturally granular, and contains a heavy admixture of tempering material in the form of angular bits of broken (apparently pounded up) rock. The corrugations, which are the original structural coils left unsmoothed on the exterior, vary greatly in size and in the amount of care which was taken to adapt them to ornamental purposes. Examples such as those shown in plate 57, *h–p*, inclusive, are as fine specimens of coiling as may be found anywhere in the Southwest; others (as pl. 57, *d*) are of very crude and careless workmanship; in some cases the coil has been almost completely removed (pls. 57, *a;* 58, *c*).

We have noticed, though we have not accumulated enough data to enable us to make a positive statement, that the finest corrugated ware seems to be associated with the more generalized styles of black-and-white pottery ("light" class) and redware (red with dull paint); and that there appears to be a decided degeneration of the technique in pieces found at sites producing a majority of the highly specialized styles ("heavy" black-and-white and polychrome red). This evidence of a decline in the art of coiling in what we take to be the later stages of the Kayenta culture leads us to present a few speculations on ornamentally coiled pottery in general.

The theory was brought forward by Cushing many years ago[1] that corrugated ware was the earliest form of southwestern pottery and that it was a direct imitation of coiled basketry, the rope of clay taking the place, in the ceramic art, of the fiber bundle which makes the basis or foundation of coiled basketry. This has always seemed doubtful to the authors, for the following reasons. Corrugated pottery is built up by winding round and round on itself a long, thin fillet of clay which, in well-made pieces, is continuous from its beginning at the bottom of the vessel to its termination at the rim;

---

[1] Cushing, 1886.

in some large jars this fillet attains a length of more than 200 feet. The laying up of this coil is in itself a very difficult matter, and when it is considered that it was often also notched, indented, waved, or otherwise-ornamentally modified during the building process, it will be realized how far removed this technique must have been from the first attempts of a nascent art. In the making of smooth-surfaced pottery any irregularity may be rubbed down or filled in, any fault of outline corrected by humoring the plastic walls into shape; in corrugated ware, however, no mistake could be corrected, and from beginning to end the coil must have been laid on with a sure hand and steady eye that must have come from long practice, not only in the handling of clay, but in its mixing to exactly the proper consistency for this delicate work. We think that it is no exaggeration to say that a large, ornamentally indented, corrugated olla required more skill for its construction than any other form of handmade pottery that has ever been produced in ancient or modern times.

In view of these facts we have always considered that corrugated ware was by no means an early type in the general development of southwestern ceramics, and that smooth-surfaced pottery had undoubtedly been made for a long time before its manufacture was commenced. No evidence in support of this idea was, however, forthcoming until we found, at Ruin 5, the remains of an early settlement underlying those of a typical Kayenta cliff-dwelling. The pottery in the lower levels was of two sorts: a well-developed black-and-white ware; and a rough cooking ware the vessel necks of which were encircled by a few heavy, coarse corrugations (see pl. 64, e) of the sort which one would expect to be the forerunners of the finer corrugations which appear on the later jars.

While the ceramic data from the Ruin 5 " slab-houses " is limited, it shows that a good, smooth ware with elaborate decorations had already been evolved before the corrugated technique had passed out of its first tentative stages.

SHAPES: *Ollas* are the most common corrugated form. They are capacious vessels with round bottoms, bodies elongated vertically, large orifices, and slightly flaring uncorrugated lips. They range from 10 to 18 inches high. None have true handles, though some examples are provided at the neck with single or double imperforate lugs (pl. 57, *f*) and others bear added plastic ornaments, such as scrolls (pl. 58, *g*) or "turkey tracks." The ollas were evidently primarily intended for cooking pots, as most of them were heavily coated with soot when found. Cracked pieces were often harnessed with yucca leaves or strings and served as storage jars (pl. 57, *a*, *b*).

Jugs (pl. 58 *e*, *f*) were the only other vessels of corrugated ware recorded by us. They range in height from 4 to 8 inches and are provided with single handles, almost always placed vertically from

a   b   c   d

e

f

g

h

CORRUGATED VESSELS

a

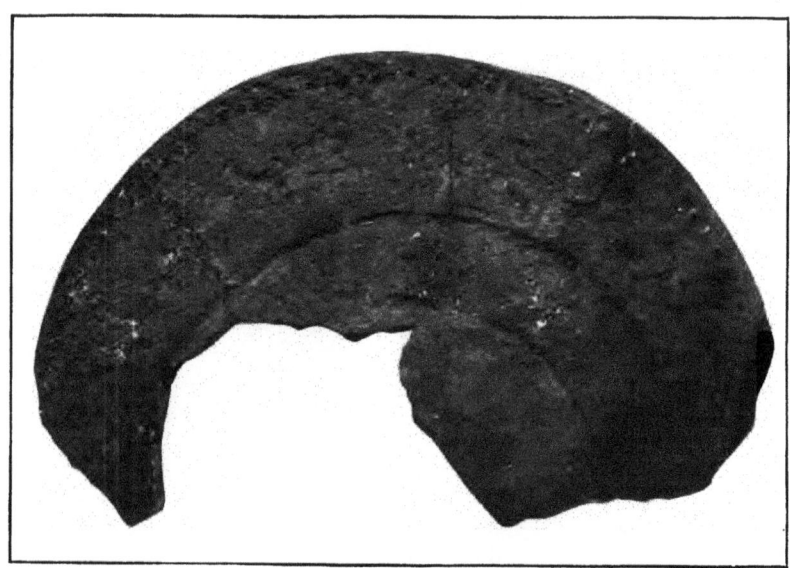

b

POTTERY FROM SUNFLOWER CAVE

the lip, or just below it, to the upper side of the body. These handles are sometimes plain (pl. 58, *e*), but are more often composed of two (pls. 57, *g;* 58), three (pl. 57, *c*), or four (pl. 57, *e*) rolls of clay pressed together. Figure 61 shows an elaborate braid-like arrangement.

UNCLASSIFIED POTTERY OBJECTS

DISHES WITH PERFORATED EDGE: From Sunflower House were taken fragments of a very shallow dishlike pottery tray originally about 13 inches in diameter (pl. 59, *b*). All about its margin are small holes set close together and punched through the rim from the inside before the piece was fired. In some of these perforations are the remains of yucca strips that had been woven back and forth through them, apparently about the entire periphery. Fragments of similar dishes were found on the surface in Marsh Pass; Dr. Fewkes figures others from the same general vicinity.[1] The type is evidently a rather restricted one, but as to its use we are unable to offer a suggestion.

FIG. 61.—Handle of corrugated jug.

Small vessels with raised wavy ridges are illustrated by Fewkes[2] from Peach Spring; fragments of almost identical specimens were recovered by us in Marsh Pass (A–2541). The paste is plain gray and the form is like that of a small, round seed jar; the ridges were evidently pinched with the fingers while the clay was soft.

EFFIGIES: From the surface at Ruin A were collected the two little clay effigies shown in natural size in figure 62. The faces are flat,

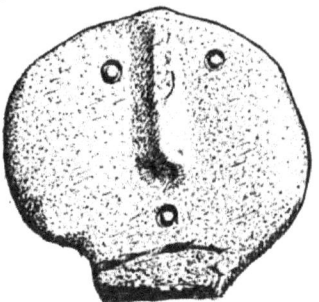

FIG. 62.—Clay effigies.

with the noses in relief; the eyes and mouth of the larger were produced by punching with some small hollow implement; those of the other were made with a sharp-end tool and further emphasized by

---

[1] 1911, pl. 15, *b*.   [2] 1911, pl. 17, *a*.

touches of black paint. The larger head appears to have been originally provided with a "neck" like that of the smaller. Nothing
resembling these figures has ever been found, so far as we know, in
the San Juan drainage, and nothing exactly like them anywhere in
the Southwest.

PIPE: In figure 63 (actual size) are given a drawing and section of

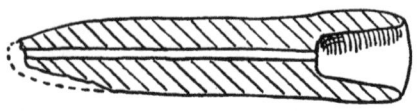

FIG. 63.—Clay pipe.

a clay pipe found on the surface of a small ruin on the top
of the mesa at the mouth of
Sagi Canyon. The surface is
rough, the color reddish-gray.

VESSEL FROM SUNFLOWER
CAVE: The position in which
this pot was discovered (see
p. 95) renders it certain that
it is of an earlier period than
the main sunflower cliff-house. As Basket Maker remains were
noted in the same cave, and as this vessel is unlike any normal
Cliff-house product with which we are familiar, it is possible that
it may have belonged to that culture. No other pottery identifiable
as Basket Maker was, however, found either here, in Kinboko, or at
Sayodneechee. The form is sufficiently illustrated by the photograph (pl. 59, a). The dimensions are: Height, 9¾ inches; greatest

FIG. 64.—Ceremonial object.

diameter, 10 inches; orifice, 4⅞ inches. The base clay is a very dark
gray, the exterior black with soot. The surface is rough, but shows
the marks of a finishing tool applied vertically with a scraping move-
ment.

CEREMONIAL OBJECTS

"OWLS"

From Ruin 7 came the two little specimens figured in figures 64 and
65. The former is 8½ inches long, the latter 3 inches across the
points of the cross. Identical objects are illustrated in the Fran-

SUNFLOWER CACHE

OBJECTS FROM SUNFLOWER CACHE

ciscan Fathers' "Ethnologic Dictionary of the Navaho Language," page 475, and described as owl bugaboos to subdue insubordinate children. Whether or not the present examples, which are undoubtedly ancient, had the same use, we can not tell.

"SUNFLOWER CACHE"

The finding of this extraordinary collection of what we must suppose to have been ceremonial paraphernalia is described on page 94. The fact that it was contained in a vessel of normal Cliff-house corrugated ware makes it reasonably safe to assign it to that culture.

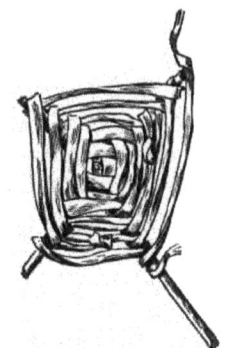

The deposit consists of a wooden bird, 21 yellow and 5 white wooden sunflowers, 2 leather sunflowers, and 25 wooden cones.

The *Bird* (pls. 60, 61) is made of cottonwood and is 9⅜ inches long. The breast, belly, back, neck, and throat are painted yellow; the tail, wings, crown, and cheeks are light cobalt blue with black edgings; each wing bears 10 yellow dots arranged in 2 rows of 5 each. The forehead is a dull salmon pink. There is a small hole in the head, which has cemented into it with

FIG. 65.—Ceremonial object.

piñon gum a fragment of feather quill. This quill once protruded, butt-end out, to simulate, presumably, the beak of the bird. On either side of the belly is a hole three-sixteenths inch in diameter; the two run inward and slightly upward, meeting at a very obtuse angle in the middle of the body. If these holes were intended as sockets for legs, the latter would have protruded in a rather unnatural attitude. In the very similar, though unpainted, birds found by Cummings in the Monument country [1] the leg holes are placed in the same way. The present specimen is of very graceful proportions and of perfect workmanship. It was made, or at least finished, entirely by rubbing, probably with coarse sandstone; nowhere on it, or on the other objects about to be described, is there the least sign of breaking, cutting, or whittling.

The *Wooden Sunflowers* number 26, of which 21 are yellow and 5 white. The largest one is 6⁷⁄₁₆ inches in diameter across the petals, the smallest 3 inches. There is an almost perfect gradation between the two extremes, so that the specimens do not fall into size groups.

All are made as follows: The body (fig. 66) is a section of a small round branch, apparently cottonwood, cut almost square across the bottom, more or less rounded on the top; a small hole perforates it vertically through the center. Just below the top the body is ringed by a narrow groove, cut inward and downward; this groove

[1] 1915, fig. 55.

is filled with a black, pitchy gum, in which are set the petals; the gum is also smeared about the bases of the petals above and below where they emerge from the groove. Each petal is neatly cut out in the general form shown in the drawing (fig. 66). Individual examples in the same flower vary little. The least number of petals in any specimen is 19 (this is also the smallest specimen); there are 2 of 20, 1 of 21, 2 of 23, 4 of 25, 4 of 26, 6 of 28, 1 of 29, 4 of 30, and 1 of 35.

After having been set in the grooves, the petals were painted. Either the upper and lower surfaces were given a first coat of dull yellow and then the upper side was treated with a second, heavier, and more brilliant lemon-yellow coat; or, as seems more likely, the upper surface was freshened by repainting some time after the original manufacture of the specimens. Three of the white flowers show traces of having been originally yellow; in the other two the white pigment is applied directly to the wood. The tops of the central cylinders, or bodies, in all but three cases are colored black.

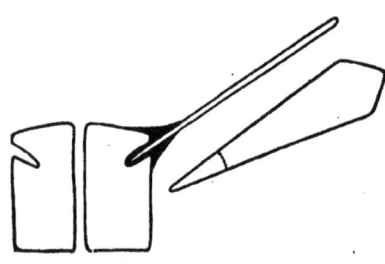

FIG. 66.—Cross section of sunflower.

The two *Skin Sunflowers* (pls. 60, 61) are made of tanned leather, probably deerskin or mountain-sheep hide. The larger is 6¾ inches across and has 23 squared-off tips. It is dull yellow below; the top is brighter and has, in the middle, a round black spot 2½ inches across. In the center is a small hole, through which runs a piece of yucca string 1½ inches long, knotted at each end so that it cannot be withdrawn. The smaller is 4½ inches across and has 19 points, all but 4 of which are square tipped. It is of an ochry shade of yellow, somewhat darker than the other. In the middle there is the same large black spot, and also the central perforation; the string, however, is missing.

The *Cones* (pls. 60, 61) are 25 in number, or one fewer than the sunflowers; the material is the same as that in the bodies of the latter. They are very uniform in shape and size, the tallest being 2 inches in height, the shortest 1¾ inches. Although they differ slightly in proportions, the average specimen has its point of greatest diameter (1¼ inches) about one-quarter inch above the base; thence to the rounded or slightly flattened top the taper is gradual. The base is concave, and from it to the top runs a small vertical perforation, similar to those which traverse the bodies of the sunflowers. In three of these holes are bits of string, apparently knotted cords, the knots of which became bound in the holes and caused the strings to break when they were being pulled out.

The color of the cones is a rich, dark red; this was produced by covering their sides and tops (the bases are uncolored) with a thick coat of red ochre, and then washing over this a thin coat of some transparent, resinous varnish which has kept the ochre from rubbing off, and has also somewhat toned down its original bright shade.

Dr. Fewkes has kindly examined the above material and tells us that he believes the bird to have formed part of an altar equipment similar to that of the Hopi flute altar. The "sunflowers" were perhaps attached to the sides of helmet masks like those worn by the personators of Hopi Kachinas. As to the function of the cones, Dr. Fewkes is in doubt.

CAVE I CACHE

The inclusion of this material in the section on ceremonial objects is open to question. The careful burial of such a heterogeneous collection of oddments in so small a vessel and the nature of the objects themselves, however, both smack of ceremonialism. The entire contents of the pot are described together here, rather than under their proper headings in the Material Culture section, in order that the reader may obtain a clearer idea of the variety and richness of the cache. There is also a possibility that the collection may not be a ceremonial deposit of the Cliff-dwellers at all, but merely a selection of the richer loot taken from the near-by Basket Maker cists by some Cliff-dweller, inclosed in a contemporary vessel, and buried for safe keeping. The container is, however, surely of Cliff-dweller make (see pl. 54, *a*). It was found, as was described in the narrative (p. 77), close below the surface at the rear of the cave. Just under the lid lay two flat leather objects, one of them made of three, the other of four, layers of dressed deerskin sewed together at the edges (A–1847). While they are both so badly decayed that their exact nature can not be made out, they appear to have been oval in outline. They are about 6 inches long by 3 inches wide.

Under the leather objects, and bottom up, was a very small black-and-white seed jar (pl. 54, *b*); its lower side was for some unknown reason much disintegrated, the surface had partly scaled off, and on removal more fragments came away. This little jar rested on a large polished lignite button, and packed about it were three small but beautifully woven bags, their mouths closed by draw strings. Between two of the bags lay a long strip of dried flesh or sinew folded on itself several times.

The contents of the cache pot had in some way become very much decayed, apparently more by a sort of dry rot than by moisture;

the woven bags were so fragile that though they were lifted out with the greatest care their lower sides fell away and the objects in them dropped out of their own weight and were mixed together in the bottom of the pot. For this reason the exact list of what was in each sack cannot be given, although a few light specimens were not disturbed in moving. This much may be said: Everything in the pot, except the pieces of leather, the strip of flesh, and the button, was contained in one or another of the three bags or in the little seed jar. We give a list of objects known to have come from particular bags, a second list of those which had been held in one or another of them, but which cannot be more particularly assigned, and a third list of specimens from the seed jar.

I. OBJECTS FROM INDIVIDUAL BAGS:
    Bag A-1848—
        Necks of two small paint sacks.
    Bag A-1849—
        Bundle of herbs (?) wrapped with string.
    Bag A-1850—
        2 shell beads (A-1851).
        Bundle of herbs much decayed (A-1852).
        14 squash seeds (A-1853).
        2 disks of green stone (A-1869).

II. OBJECTS FROM THE THREE BAGS:
    Small leather bag containing (?) (A-1854).
    Necks of 4 small leather paint bags (A-1855).
    Bundle of herbs (?) much decayed (A-1856).
    Small leather bag containing turquoises (A-1857).
    Lump of rough turquoise partly worked (A-1858).
    Three bits of iron pyrites (A-1859).
    Bit of malachite (A-1860).
    Meal (?) (A-1861).
    Eight olivella shells (A-1862).
    Cylinder of manganese ore (A-1863).
    Five turquoise pendants (A-1864-1868).
    Purple shell bead (A-1870).
    Three double-lobed white stone beads (A-1871).
    Bead of impure turquoise (A-1872).
    Seven minute black stone beads (A-1873).
    Red paint (A-1874).
    Pollen (?) and part of corn-husk container (A-1876).
    Small piece of charcoal (A-1894).
    Dried wild gooseberry (crushed in packing).

III. OBJECTS FROM THE SEED JAR:
    Decayed small woven strip (A-1881).
    Seven kernels of corn (A-1883).
    Neck of red-paint bag (A-1884).
    Red paint from broken bag (A-1885).
    Small leather bag with pendant (A-1886).
    Small leather bag containing red paint (A-1887).
    Turquoise pendant (A-1888).
    Jadeite pendant (A-1889).
    Three beads of serpentine (A-1890).

Twelve minute black stone beads (A–1891).

Four bits of malachite (A–1892).

Three bits of azurite (A–1893).

Description of Objects

The textile bags (pl. 62, a–c) are twilled-woven, seamless sacks originally about 5 inches long. How their bottoms were formed can not be determined from the badly decayed specimens, but the bodies seem to have been cylindrical with unconstricted mouths. The fabric at the apertures was turned in and sewed down to form tunnels for the heavy, round draw strings, which were neatly braided of many strands. The material of the bags is apparently cotton,

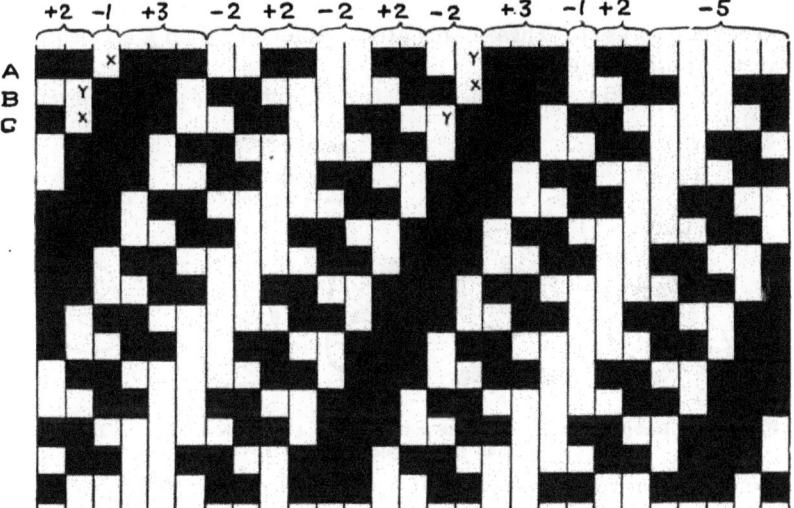

FIG. 67.—Diagram of weave of twilled bag.

the warp in natural color, the weft dyed dark to bring out the complex twilled pattern.

Two of the bags are so much rotted that the details of the weave cannot be ascertained; a part of the third (pl. 62, a) is in sufficiently good condition to allow of the threads being counted. The following twill formula was determined for a series of eight or nine rows: plus 2, minus 1, plus 3, minus 2, plus 2, minus 2, plus 2, minus 2, plus 3, minus 1, plus 2, minus 5, and repeat (see fig. 67). The order of pluses and minuses is not changed from row to row, but the twill is "set over" to produce the diagonal effect in the following manner: beginning with the row lettered A, it will be seen that there are two plus 3's, one (which we will call x) coming between minus 1 and minus 2, the other (called y) coming between minus 2 and minus 1. In the second row (B) the plus 3 lettered x is set directly below the plus 3 lettered $y;$ in the third row (C) the plus 3 called y is placed below the plus 3 called x of the row (B) above, but is set one step to the left. In the fourth row x comes directly below y, etc.

The weave as here given is from the middle of the bag, and the pattern is diagonal. Some change in the arrangement of the rows at a higher level seems to throw the pattern in the other diagonal direction, and there are some indications that the design as a whole was made up of diamond-shaped figures. How these changes were effected cannot be ascertained, but enough has been said to make clear the extraordinary elaborateness of the weave. A bit of fine textile, apparently of twilled work and possibly part of one of the bags, had sewed to it a tiny black stone bead of the same sort as those found loose in the jar and the seed jar; it is probable that the others were once so used. These beads are a trifle more than a sixteenth of an inch in diameter.

The little skin sacks (pl. 62, e, f, h, $i;$ fig. 68, a) were eleven in

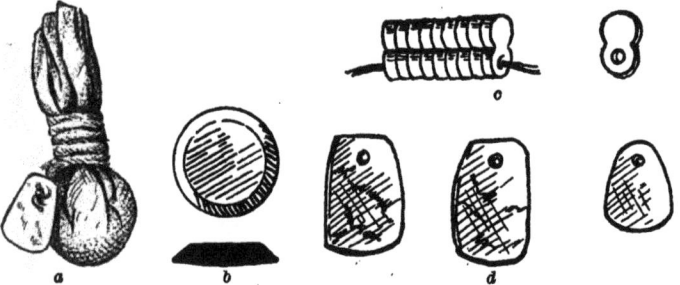

FIG. 68.—a, Red-paint sack from cache pot. b, Inlay (?) of greenstone. c, Double-lobed beads. d, Turquoise pendants.

number. Each one was made of a round piece of soft leather. The contents were placed in the center and the edges puckered together and tied with a cotton string. The puckered parts have resisted decay better than the tightly stretched bodies, so that seven of the specimens are represented by the necks only; four are perfect. All seven of the necks have particles of bright red paint adhering to their inner surfaces, and a considerable amount of the pigment in the form of fine grains was shaken out of them; more was recovered by sifting the rotting material in the bottom of the large jar. One of the perfect bags (pl. 62, h) has split a little, disclosing as contents two turquoise beads; another (pl. 62, f), the largest of the lot, is very heavy (it has not been opened). The remaining two (pl. 62, e, i) were found in the small seed jar; pinholes driven into their sides show that they hold the same red paint as did the broken sacks. To the neck of A-1886, the only one whose pucker string is preserved complete, is attached a small turquoise pendant (fig. 68, a). We think it probable that each of the red-paint sacks once had a

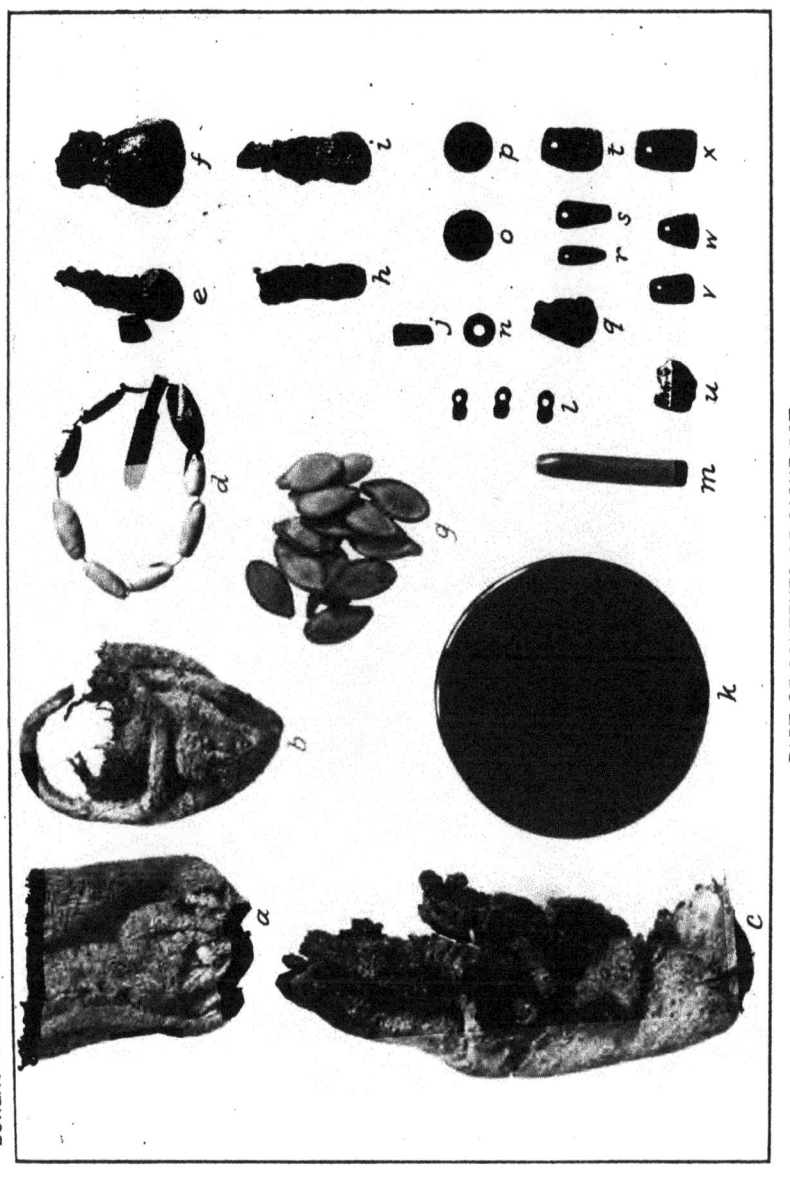

PART OF CONTENTS OF CACHE POT

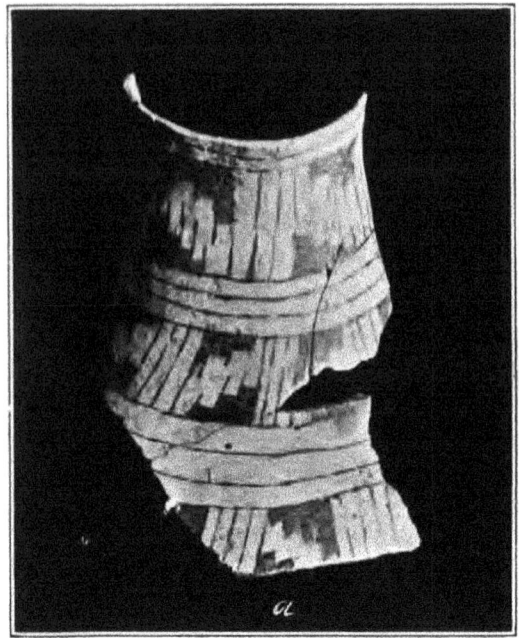

SLAB-HOUSE OLLA FRAGMENT

SLAB-HOUSE BLACK-AND-WHITE FRAGMENTS

similar appendage, for six necks were found in the large jar, also six pendants and beads of turquoise; in the small seed jar were two paint bags (besides the one that retains its turquoise), and here also were found two loose pendants—one of turquoise and one of jadeite.

The red paint itself is a rather coarse powder, the grains of which under a strong lens have a waxy appearance; in color it is an extremely brilliant scarlet. According to Professor Wolff, the substance is realgar (arsenic monosulphide), a material to be found at volcanic vents or hot springs. It would be interesting to know where the nearest place is at which such phenomena occur; we know of none in the immediate region.

The lignite "button" (pl. 62, *k;* fig. 69) is not quite 3 inches in diameter by one-fourth inch thick. All its surfaces are beautifully polished. A ridge has been left on the back, and two holes have been drilled in slantingly from its sides, meeting in the middle.[1]

The little cylinder of manganese ore (pl. 62, *m*) is 1¾ inches long; it shows great care in shaping, and one end is worn down all around as if by much rubbing, perhaps for the extraction of paint from it. As the two disks of greenstone, or prase (pl. 62, *o, p;* fig. 68, *b*), have no means of attachment, it seems likely that they were designed for inlays; their larger surfaces are very slightly convex. The three two-lobed beads of white stone are of an unusual shape; strung together, they give the effect of a double string

FIG. 69.—Lignite button.

(fig. 68, *c*). Identical specimens, collected at Pueblo Bonito by Prof. W. K. Morehead, are in the Musuem of Phillips Academy, Andover.

All the stone pendants save one are of turquoise, their front surfaces streaked with a gray trachyte matrix, while the backs of some of them consist entirely of layers of this material (see pl. 62, *r–t, v–x;* fig. 68, *d*). The exception (pl. 62, *j*) is a small, highly polished bit of jadeite, perforated for suspension. The color is a deep green and the specimen is slightly translucent. This is the only case of the occurrence of jadeite in the Southwest of which we have knowledge.

The other objects from the cache pot need no particular description; they are interesting because of their variety—olivella shells, pieces of azurite and malachite, squash seeds, kernels of corn, pollen in little corn husk (?) containers, bundles of herbs, a bit of charcoal, and a dried gooseberry. The association of things of such diverse nature appears to us to indicate that the cache was ceremonial in nature.

---

[1] Fewkes, 1904, fig. 45, records a fragment of a similar "button" from the Little Colorado.

B. SLAB-HOUSE CULTURE

As was stated in the description of the site, the lower levels of the débris in Fluteplayer House (Ruin 5) contained pottery quite different from the normal Kayenta wares of the upper strata. Unfortunately the lower deposits had been so soaked by seepage that all perishable material in them had rotted away; our characterization of the culture is, therefore, necessarily based, until other and drier sites shall be discovered, upon the architecture (see pp. 42–44), the pottery, and the utensils of stone and bone.

POTTERY

Two wares make up the body of the collection: black-and-white and black; besides these there are three sherds of a redware, very

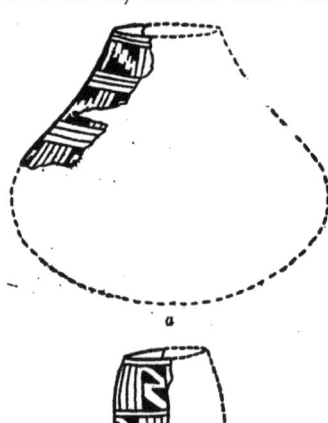

FIG. 70.—Slab-house vessels.

similar to if not identical with the redware with shining paint described in the cliff-house section. As it is possible that these red sherds may have worked down from above, it is perhaps best to accept them only provisionally as belonging to the slab-house group.

BLACK-AND-WHITE WARE.—The body of this pottery is markedly granular in cross section and contains considerably more tempering material than does Kayenta black-and-white. The slip is yellowish white and the pigment a slaty shade of black. Sherds were found of ollas, bowls, and of a single specimen of a sort of goblet.

Ollas appear to have had a full but rather "squatty" body and a high, gracefully curved neck (fig. 70, *a;* pl. 63, *a*). There is no evidence of handles. Decoration, in the specimens at hand, consists of several horizontal bands about the neck and body.

Bowls.—Little can be said as to shape, as all the bowl sherds recovered are too small to permit of even tentative reconstruction. The rims are direct (*i. e.* with no incurve or outcurve), and have rounded edges which are left plain (not painted black, as in Chaco Canyon bowls; nor "ticked" with dots, as in Mesa Verde examples). There seem to have been no handles. The slip covers the whole interior and, as nearly as one can tell, the whole exterior as well. Decoration, in all but one piece, is confined to the interior.

Goblet.—The form of this piece is shown in figure 70, *b*, and plate

b   *c*

BONE IMPLEMENTS FROM RUIN 5

e

SLAB-HOUSE CORRUGATED WARE

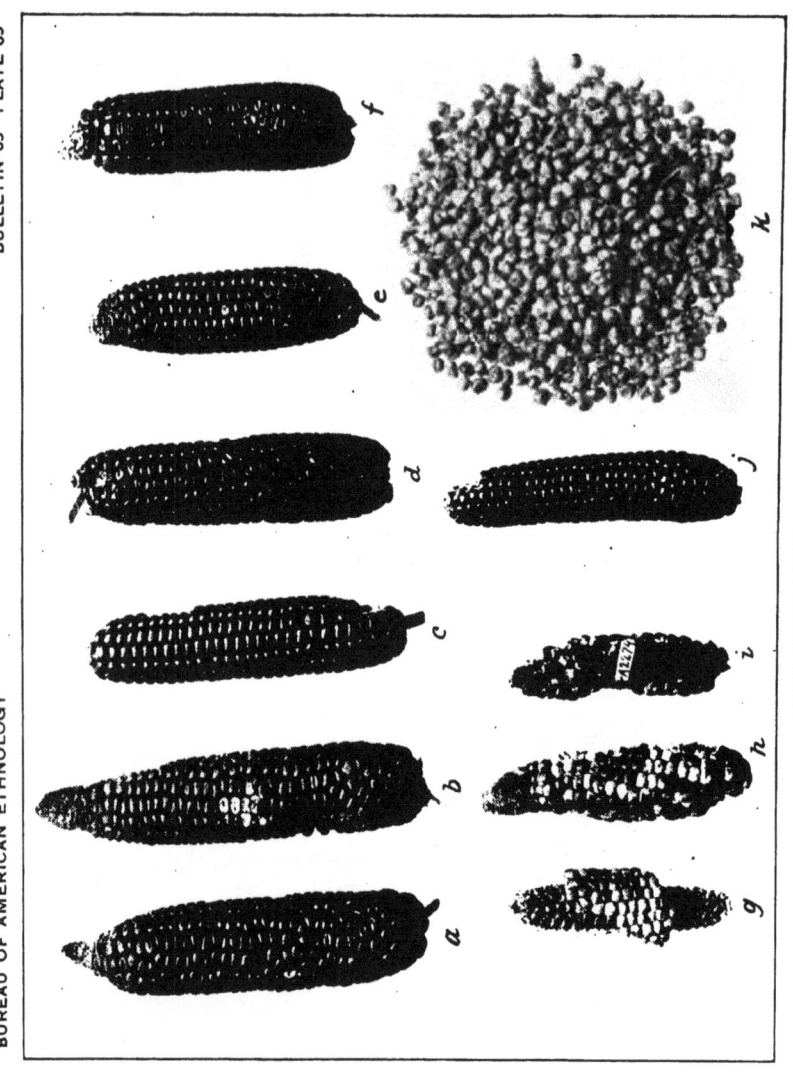

CORN FROM BASKET MAKER CAVES

63, *d*. There is a pair of suspension holes on one side near the rim; the design is in horizontal bands.

No sherds identifiable as belonging to such other forms as pitchers, seed jars, mugs, canteens, or ladles were recovered; the last named, however, as well as some of the others, may be expected to appear in future excavation of Slab-house sites.

Decoration.—The designs on Slab-house black-and-white are strikingly different; both in elements and in execution, from those of the corresponding Kayenta ware. As a representative selection is given in the accompanying figures (pl. 63, *b–h*), we will not attempt a verbal description, but merely point out the prevalence of sets of thin lines rather widely spaced and used: (1) vertically, to mark off panels of design (pl. 63, *a, d*); (2) horizontally, to mark off separate bands (pl. 63, *a, e*); (3) as edging lines following the contours of triangular (pl. 63, *e*) or stepped (pl. 63, *g*) elements. This use of thin lines set wide apart, and particularly their use in edging, is highly typical of one of the most important subgroups of the black-and-white ware of Chaco Canyon.

BLACKWARE.—The body of this pottery is, as always, gray clay heavily tempered with sand. The original color of the vessels was probably dull gray, but all the sherds found were blackened by use over fire. Although we have no whole pieces, it can easily be seen that the preponderating form was a high-bodied olla with a distinct neck and slightly flaring rim. While some of the jars were smooth over the whole surface, the majority had broad, flat coils, one-fourth to one-half inch wide, covering the neck from the orifice to the beginning of the body proper (see pl. 64, *e*). These corrugations are easily distinguished from the narrow, ridge-like, and often indented coils of the Kayenta cooking pots.

In the blackware collection are two handles, one round in cross section, the other figure 8 shaped; they were apparently applied vertically and seem to have formed parts of small pitchers with large orifices.

The pottery from the bench and sand hill near Ruin 7 (see p. 54) corresponds very closely to that just described; the black-and-white has the same peculiar decoration and the black the same broad, flat coils. There are also a few sherds of redware with shining paint.

STONE AND BONE

Our stone and bone material is very scanty. Stone is represented by half a dozen rather crude chipped points (more flakes were found in the lower levels of Ruin 5 than in normal cliff-dwelling rubbish); and bone by the implements shown in plate 64, *a–d*. The eyed needle, of which we recovered three specimens, is a very rare type in the

Southwest. The hollow bone tool (pl. 64, a) was taken from the floor of the round room. It is, so far as we know, unique. It shows the polish of long use; it is slightly curved, and has on its convex side a number of narrow, parallel grooves that look as if they had been made by the play of strings pulled back and forth around that side of the specimen. We can offer no suggestion as to its use.

SANDALS

Certain slab-built ruins described by Professor Cummings from Sagiotsosi[1] and stated by him to be definitely earlier than the cliff-dwellings of the region, would seem to be closely similar to our Slab-house type. From one of them he recovered a number of scallop-toed cord sandals. This style of footgear is represented in many un-located collections (Peabody, American, Southwest, and Brooklyn Museums), but was not encountered by us in either the cliff-houses or the Basket Maker caves; we venture to suggest, therefore, that it may be characteristic of the Slab-house culture.

C. BASKET-MAKER CULTURE[2]

FOOD

VEGETAL

Corn.—The Basket Makers, like the Cliff-dwellers, were a corn-using people. We have some evidence, however, that this important cereal was less highly developed among the former than among the latter. Our corn specimens fall, according to provenience, into three classes: (1) from cliff-dwellings proper; (2) from Basket Maker caves and directly associated with Basket Maker remains; (3) from the general digging near the surface in Cave II. On samples from these three groups we have the following notes from Mr. G. F. Will, of Bismarck, North Dakota, a gentleman who has given much study to the different varieties of Indian-grown corn.

(1) *From the Cliff-dwellings.*—"Specimen A–1588 (Ruin 7) is a mixed sample. It contains several kernels of a large, white, flint corn which differs in type from any other lot, as well as from the modern type of the Pueblo region. In fact the kernels might be from an ear of Mandan white flint so far as appearance is concerned. The sample also contained one kernel of a blue flour corn similar to the modern one, and some white or yellow corn of the usual Pueblo type. Sample A–1172 (Ruin 1) contained one kernel of blue flour

---

[1] 1910, p. 10 and figure on same; Sagiotsosi lies only a few miles southwest of the "Monuments."

[2] Based on finds from the Sayodneechee Burial Cave (1914); and from Caves I and II, Kinboko (1915).

corn and several of red flour corn. The other four samples from various cliff-houses are all of flour corn showing a predominance of the type that at present exists in the Southwest."

(2) *From Basket Maker caves directly associated with Basket Maker remains.*—"Sample A–2483 (cache in Cave II; pl. 65, *k*) is a yellow flint corn; it has very small kernels, so small as to be taken for popcorn were the shape a bit different. There is one red kernel and two others that seem to be red. A–2274 (pl. 65, *h, i;* cist area, Cave I) are yellow and white flints."

(3) *From near surface and in general digging, Cave II.*—" Sample A–2481 (pl. 65, *j*), a very small white flint, smaller than the other samples; both from the appearance of the kernels and of the ear it might be called popcorn, though it probably is not. There is very little superficial difference between a small-kernel flint and a pop-corn. Sample A–2482 (pl. 65, *d*) is a flour corn. The color was probably a white, partly shaded with red, a color which is very common in the soft corns of the Pueblo area at the present time. This specimen also has the relatively small kernels that distinguish the modern corn of the Pueblo region from that of any other locality, and so far as can be determined, resembles the Zuñi, Hopi, and Navaho corn of the present day. I find that in size the Zuñi is nearest. Sample A–2480 (pl. 65, *f*) looks very much like an ear of dent corn, as do the kernels from it; however, the flour corn is so apt to show occasional dented ears that this ear is more likely to be one of dented flour corn. A–2480, B and C, are also flour corns of the modern type (pl. 65 *b, c*)."

Summarizing these data, we find that the cliff-house corn is variegated (white, yellow, red, blue) flour corn and a large form of white flint; the surely Basket Maker specimens are small flints; of the doubtful specimens (general digging, Cave II), some are flints, some flour. This would appear to indicate that the Basket Makers had only the small flints, while the Cliff-dwellers had a varied assortment of more highly developed types. This fits in very well with our theory that the Basket Maker is an earlier culture than the Cliff-dweller, but there is no sure way of telling that the flour-corn ears from Cave II were not of Basket Maker origin. We believe that they were left in the cave by later people, as were without much doubt the pieces of pottery which were also found in the surface sand. There is, nevertheless, a strong possibility that they may after all be Basket Maker, and we do not wish to state, therefore, without further exploration, that the apparent difference in corn types is a real one.

Squash of apparently the same species as that from the cliff-dwellings was present in both Cave I and Cave II, where seeds and many fragments of rind were recovered.

Acorns (A-2485) were found mixed with the corn in the Cave II cache.

Piñon nuts were discovered in the rubbish of Cave I and a considerable quantity of them (A-2448) lay loose in the grass filling of a large cradle from Cave II (A-2447).

Coreocarpus seeds (A-2309), in quantity about a peck, were taken from the bottom of Cist 4, Cave I.

Dried fruit.—A substance resembling pulverized dried fruit of some kind was found mixed with meal in a woven bag (A-2313) from one of the Cave I cists.

Beans were not encountered in either year's digging in Basket Maker caves. Whether or not this is the result of chance can only be told by further excavations in such sites.

ANIMAL

The débris in Caves I and II contained, queerly enough, very few animal bones, and these were all slivers too small for positive identification. The abundance of pieces of deerskin and mountain-sheep hide, bunches of prepared sinew, and fragments of bird skin and feathers shows, however, that hunting must have furnished the people with a considerable part of their sustenance. A complete list of the bird identifications is given in the section on feather-work; the species most likely to have been used as food were the greater yellowlegs and Hutchins' wild goose.

In regard to the domestication of the turkey we are in doubt. We found no beds of turkey droppings and feathers such as form part of the rubbish of nearly every cliff-house. Furthermore, the normal Cliff-house turkey-feather cloth is not represented in our Basket Maker collection. As in the case of beans, however, further investigation is necessary before we can state positively that turkeys were not domesticated.

DRESS

BODY CLOTHING

Robes of fur cloth were evidently the standard overgarment for cold weather. They were commonly used to wrap up the bodies of the dead for interment; fragments of them came from almost every burial cist. Nothing approaching a complete example, however, was collected.

Skin robes were found over the two child "mummies" recovered in Cists I and C, Cave I (see pl. 73, *a*). They were made of mountain-sheep hide tanned with the hair on. While both were of small size, it is probable that larger ones were in use by adults.

String skirt (pl. 66, *a*).—The specimen consists of a waist cord to which is attached a pendent fringe like a small apron; it is incomplete. The waist cord is a two-strand hair rope, each strand made up of six two-strand hair strings; over it are looped the fine brown apocynum (?) strings of the fringe. Each of these is about one thirty-second inch in diameter and averages 32 to 36 twists to the inch. They are gathered in bundles of about 300 and held in place close under the waist cord by a double twined weaving of hair string. The length of the fringe is approximately 12 inches. Still attached to the waist cord are five bundles, and it seems as if there had once been at least four more. A conservative estimate allows 300 12-inch strings to the bundle and counts nine bundles. This gives 2,700 feet of string, and as each string is two-stranded, a total length of 5,400 feet of the filament. When it is considered that the necessary fiber had to be extracted from its parent leaves or stalks, sorted, cleaned, combed, and twisted, it can be realized what a vast amount of labor was put into this garment.

Although the present specimen was not found in place on a body, its identification as a skirt is made certain by the finding of fragments of a similar one at the waist of the young female "mummy" in Cist 16, Cave I. Bundles of string, not, however, attached to a waist cord, lay in the lap of an infant "mummy" (pl. 66, *b*).

Tasseled sash (A–2185, Cave I).—A length of only about 14 inches remains. The piece consists of 36 yucca strings held together in a flat band 3½ inches wide by a continuous back-and-forth weaving of two twined strings. At the remaining finished end (the other is missing) the strings are gathered into two tapering braids, knotted at their terminations.

"Gee-string" (?) (A–2310, Cave I).—This specimen is a soft, loose cord made by twisting together 30 thin strings of fine, gray, animal wool (species not determinable). It is about half an inch in diameter and a little less than 7 feet long. The two ends are provided with small tie strings.

FOOTGEAR

No leggings or moccasins were recovered, but sandals were found in considerable quantities—loose in the débris of occupancy, tied together in pairs and deposited in the cists as mortuary offerings, and still in place on the feet of "mummies." A classification follows:

Type I: *Yucca leaf.*
  a, Whole leaf.
  b, Crushed leaf.
Type II: *Cedar bark.*

Type III: *Cord.*
  a, Plain sole.
  b, Reinforced sole.
Type IV: *Hide.*

Type I, a.—Cross weaving of whole yucca leaves over yucca leaf warps (pl. 67, *a*). There are only two specimens of this style in the collection; they are both made in the same general manner as the corresponding type of Cliff-dweller sandal (I, *b;* p. 103, and pl. 38, *a, b, c*), viz, by lacing the leaves back and forth across the warps and bringing out the large ends on the underside, where they are shredded into a pad. They have four warps, each one made of one yucca leaf; the small ends are brought to the heel, where they are tied together in the triple knot shown in figure 71, *b*. The attachment at the toe is made by shredding out a bunch of the fiber of each leaf and fastening these bunches together (fig. 71, *a*). The rest of the

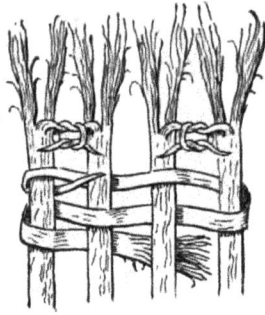

ends protrude to form a toe fringe. The type differs from the analogous Cliff-dweller one in the toe and heel warp ties, and in the presence of a toe fringe.

Type I, b.—Cross weaving of crushed yucca leaves over warps of the same material (pl. 67, *b*). The leaves appear to have been rolled or crushed before they were woven; although this process did not entirely remove the parenchyma, it rendered the elements fibrous and easy to manipulate; the completed article, too, was probably softer to the foot than a sandal made of natural leaves. Each one of the four, sometimes six, warps consists of two leaves; they are fastened at the toe and heel in the same manner as in the simpler type described above (fig. 71). The heel is often

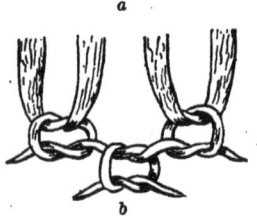

Fig. 71.—Toe and heel warp ties of Type I, *a*, sandal.

somewhat rounded, but the toe is usually square, and is again provided with a fringe made by the protruding warp ends. The weft strands are tightly woven in, and the butts form, as before, a pad on the sole (pl. 67, *b*).

Type II.—Cross weaving of thick cedar-bark string over warps of the same material (pl. 67, *c, d*). The string of which these sandals are made is a thick, soft, loose, two-strand twist of shredded cedar bark. The weft is continuous, running across and across. The warps, three, four, or five in number, are attached to each other at the rounded heel and at the rounded (pl. 67, *d*) or square (pl. 67, *c*) toe, in some manner which cannot be made out without destroying the specimens. There is no toe fringe. Sandals such as these could not have had great wearing qualities, as cedar bark goes to pieces rapidly under friction; but they were thicker, softer, and probably more comfortable than any of the other types, and may possibly have been worn as inner soles.

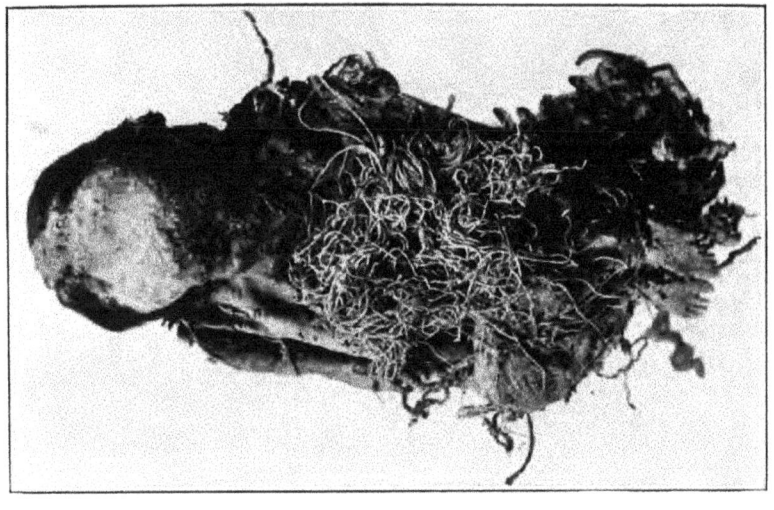

BUREAU OF AMERICAN ETHNOLOGY

a. BREECHCLOTH OR APRON

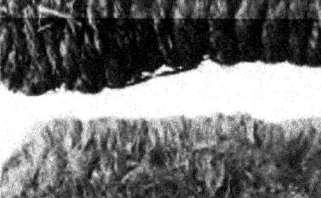

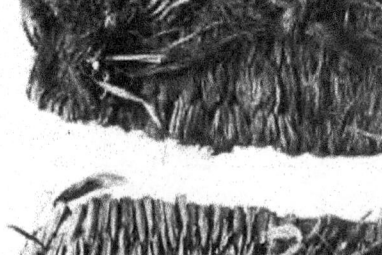

a. TYPE I, a, SANDAL   b. TYPE I, b, SANDAL   c. TYPE II SANDAL   d. TYPE II SANDAL

Type III, a.—Cross-woven cord sandals with plain soles (pl. 68, *a*). These specimens are square heeled and square toed. They have ten or, more commonly, twelve warps consisting of stout, two-stranded yucca-fiber cord. The weft is thin one-strand cord, also of yucca, and the body is of the same simple cross weave used in the foregoing type, except that on reaching the outer warp on either edge the weft is wrapped twice about it before being started back across the sandal. This double wrap at the edges is also seen in the fine-cord Cliff-house sandal (Type II, b; fig. 38); but in that case the weaving is of the twined variety. The warps of the present type are looped at the toe, where they are held in place by three rows of twined weaving. Under these are caught short bunches of fiber that protrude in front to form a toe fringe; in other cases the fiber is wound round and round between the warps and behind the twining strands so as to produce a sort of bolster across the toe (pl. 68, *a*). At the heel the warps are knotted together and the ends are tucked back, probably with the aid of an awl, into the fabric. This knotting provides, across the heel, a strong, heavy ridge well fitted to resist the particularly severe wear to which that part of a sandal is subjected.

Type III, b.—Cord sandals with reinforced soles (pl. 68, *b–d*). All the specimens of this group have square toes, fringed with bunches of fiber or of deerskin strips; the heels are also square. The yucca-cord warps, twelve to thirty in number, depending on the size and fineness of the sandal, are laid out parallel, looped at the toe, and there held in place by twined cross strands, as in the preceding class. The weft is sometimes of yucca, sometimes of a softer fiber (apocynum?), more rarely of human hair; in some of the coarser examples it is run in by simple over-and-under cross weaving; more commonly it is twined. The most characteristic feature is the extra layer of knots or folds which forms a reinforcement for the soles. It will be remembered that the fine-cord Cliff-dweller sandals (Type II, b) were reinforced on the bottom with series of knots tied in the wefts. The reinforcement of these Basket Maker specimens, on the other hand, is produced by means of extra strands extending the length of the sandals. One or more such strands accompany each warp, are turned about it for attachment at every two or three weft intervals, and are knotted, twisted, or twined about each other as they emerge on the underside (from their periodical warp attachments), there to form a sort of "pile" (pl. 68, *c*). In the most elaborate specimens the extra strands are held by secondary warps and themselves hold what might be called secondary wefts. Lack of specimens suitable for the necessary dissections has prevented us from making at this time an analysis of these exceedingly complicated weaves. The superficial appearance of the type is shown by the photographs. Points that should be noticed in comparing it to the jog-toe and scallop-toe (Cliff-house and Slab-house (?) types, respectively), are: square toe with fringe; side bindings, often in red; reinforcement covering the whole sole instead of being in the form of knots arranged in patterns and covering only part of the sole. Further study will undoubtedly serve to subdivide the type into several subgroups.

In concluding this brief description of the textile sandals of the Basket Makers, it may be noted that the plaited over-two-under-two weave in yucca leaves, in which three-quarters of all Cliff-dwelling sandals are made, is not represented at all in our Basket Maker collection.

Type IV.—Hide sandals. These are much less common than textile ones. They consist of pieces of rawhide cut to conform roughly to the sole of the foot. One fragmentary specimen (A–2356, Cave I) is made of two thicknesses of mountain-sheep skin with the hair on, sewed together around the edges with a narrow leather thong. The holes which hold the toe loop can be made out, and part of a human hair heel loop is still in place.

SANDAL TIES

· The method of attachment of sandals seems to have been simpler than among the Cliff-dwellers, for in our collection we have no examples of the side-loop tie (see pl. 41, *a*), or of the crisscross tie (pl. 41, *c*). The only hitch represented (pl. 69, *a*, *b*) is the regular heel-and-toe-loop variety with a long tie string. The example which we figure is apparently typical; in it the heel loop consists of a two-strand cord of human hair, carried back and forth across the heel of the sandal ten times; the toe loop is made up of two pairs of somewhat larger and more loosely twisted hair cords. Both are permanently fastened to the sandal. The second and third toes are inserted in the toe loop, and the heel loop is pulled up over the back of the foot. The tie string (a small two-strand hair cord about 30 inches long) is tied at one end to the top of the toe loop. It is then brought back and around the heel loop on the outside of the foot, carried over the instep and around the heel loop on the opposite side of the foot; it is then brought back again, caught around the original stretch from toe loop to heel loop, and pulled tight. The remaining length of cord is looped back and forth four times between the toe loop and the instep crossing; finally, the end is wrapped once about these loops near the toe loop and is made fast by a single hitch.

A rather constant feature, which seems to differentiate Basket Maker from Cliff-dwelling sandals, is the use of heel and toe loops of multiple strands (pls. 68, *d*; 69, *a*). These loops are also very commonly made of human-hair string. The tie cords again are often made of human hair, a feature not noted in the Cliff-dwellings.

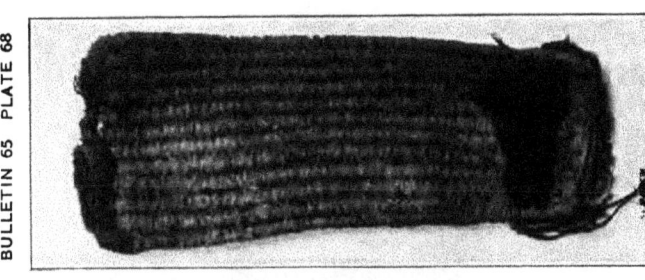

d. TYPE III, b, SANDAL

c. TYPE III, b, SANDAL, SOLE

b. TYPE III, b, SANDAL, UPPER SIDE

a. TYPE III, b, SANDAL

a. SANDAL ON FOOT

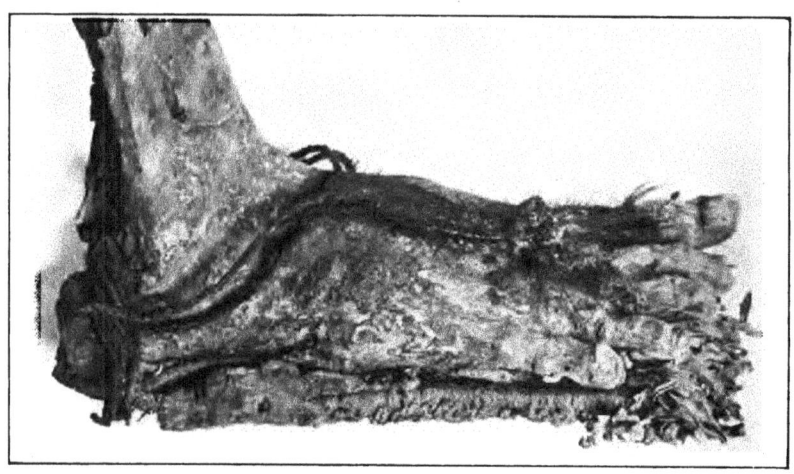

b. SANDAL ON FOOT, SIDE VIEW

PERSONAL ORNAMENTS

Necklaces of various kinds were evidently much worn, as almost every undisturbed Basket Maker skeleton yet found by us was pro vided with one. We are inclined to believe, indeed, that the cists of Cave I were plundered primarily for the beads accompanying the interments in them.

In the Sayodneechee cave the bodies were so badly decayed and so closely packed together that the make-up of individual necklaces could seldom be noted. From the neck of one skeleton (Nó. 7, Cist A), however, we recovered in its original order a string of heavy stone beads with a short pendant of similar beads (pl. 70, *l*). Like

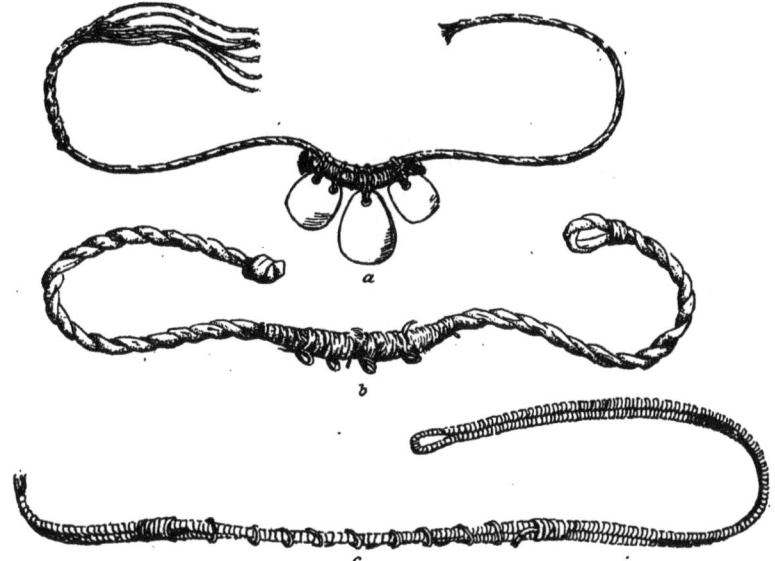

Fig. 72.—Necklace and neck cords.

strings were with several of the bodies in Cist B, but could not be collected in order. Another common arrangement was a string of olivella shells passing once or twice about the neck. An ornament of this sort was found at the throat of the "mummy" in Cist 16, Cave I; it consisted of a double string of olivella shells (pl. 70, *a*) with a pendant of white limestone, through the middle of which there runs vertically a natural band of red color (pl. 70, *e*).

The method by which many of the single pendants and pairs of pendants from Sayodneechee were probably once attached to the persons of their wearers is shown by a necklace taken from a little trinket basket in Cave I. This specimen is shown in figure 72, *a;* three white limestone pendants are hung to a short piece of heavy cord by means of sinew wrappings that pass through the perforations in their upper ends. The short, heavy cord is all that remains of a neck cord such as will be described in the next paragraph. The ends of the original cord have been cut off close to the pendants, and a new string has been installed and tied to the fragment of the old one by fine yucca ligatures which also pass through the holes in the pendants, reinforcing their old sinew attachments.

This arrangement was more or less a makeshift; the original neck cord was undoubtedly like the specimen shown in figure 72, *b*, which, however, has lost its pendants. It is a two-strand twist of rawhide, 16 inches long, with a loop for an eye at one end and a knot for a toggle at the other. The central 2½ inches is wrapped with sinew, overwrapped with yucca strings, and holds four small loops for the attachment of the missing pendants.

A third specimen (fig. 72, *c*) is less complete, but is surely also a fragment of a necklace. It is made of two light yucca strings held together by a close figure 8 weaving of fine sinew. The loop or eye is present, the toggle missing; in the middle are remains, in the form of loops and broken ends of string, of a central attachment

FIG. 73.—Detail of shell necklace.

device similar to those described above. In this connection it is interesting to note that in the Peabody Museum collection from the caves of Coahuila, in northern Mexico, there are long strings for necklaces or bandoleers, made in much the same way as these, but holding in place of pendants the vertebræ of some species of snake.

A fourth necklace from Cave I, but, unfortunately, very fragmentary, is shown in plate 70, *c*, and figure 73. It consists of the shells of *Pyrimidula strigosa* var. *cooperi;* twelve of these are still in place, and five more were found in the earth near by. They are so strung together by a fiber cord running through holes in the upper parts of their whorls that they fit closely into each other. The attachment string is fastened to the neck cord by a third small string, which takes a double hitch about it between each shell (see fig. 73). Nordenskiöld [1] figures identical shells from the Mesa Verde; they were found loose, but are perforated for suspension in the same way as these.

Pendants that once probably formed parts of ornaments such as the above, but which were discovered loose in the Sayodneechee cists, are made of various materials. Some stone examples are shown in

[1] 1893, pl. lx, fig. 2.

SHELL, STONE, AND BONE ORNAMENTS

ACORN CUP AND STONE BEADS

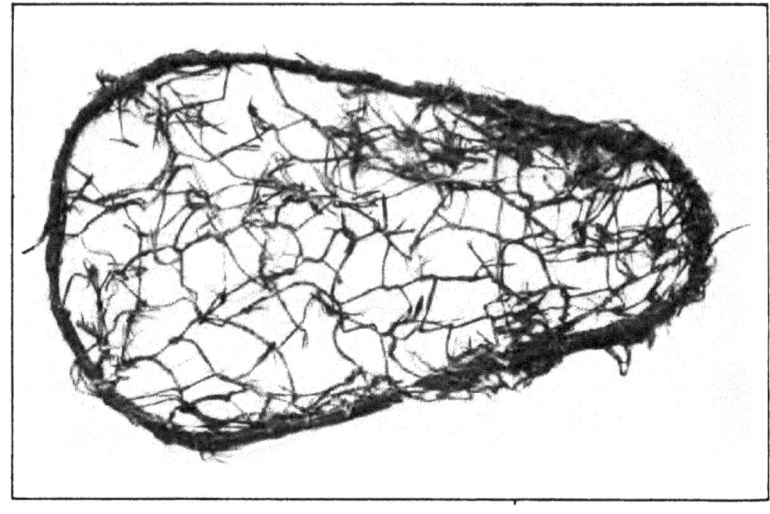

b. GRASS-RIMMED CRADLE

a. FRAGMENT OF REED-BACKED CRADLE

figure 74—*a* is actinolitic schist, *b* red jasper, *c* satin spar. No turquoise pendants were found. The pointed lignite objects (fig. 75)
were taken from the two sides of the skull of an infant in Cist D, and
presumably were worn as ear ornaments. Shell pendants were common, but are less varied
in shape than those of
stone, being plain round
or oval plates of abalone
(haliotis), one-half to
three-fourths inch in diameter, perforated for sus-
pension.

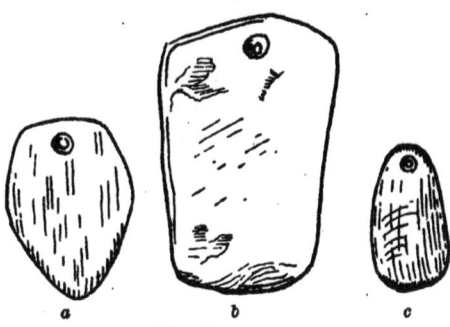

FIG. 74.—Stone pendants.

Beads are of stone, shell,
and bone. That great
quantities of them were
found in the undisturbed
cists at Sayodneechee, and that practically none was recovered from
the rifled burial places in Cave I, Kinboko, seems to lend color to
our theory that beads were the principal object of the plunderers.

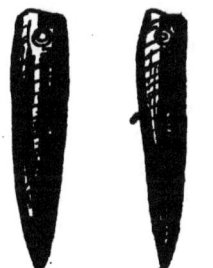

FIG. 75.—Lignite ear
ornaments.

The stone beads are made of lignite, limestone, serpentine, pic-
rolite, hematite, albatite, and calcareous tufa.[1]
Particularly striking is the large number of lignite
beads, some highly polished and still retaining
their fine black luster (pl. 70, *l, m, o*).

There are two kinds of beads: the cylindrical
and the hemispherical. The former are all made
of black albatite, a phase of asphaltic shale; they
are a little less than three-sixteenths inch in diameter, with fine straight bores not more than one
thirty-second inch across (fig. 76, *d*). They vary
somewhat in length, but are of uniform diameter and cylindrical in form.

Hemispherical stone beads are much larger, averaging seven-
sixteenths inch in diameter. The biconical nature of the large bore
is shown in figure 76, *a, b* (see also pl. 70, *l*). Hematite and serpentine

FIG. 76.—Hemispherical and cylindrical stone beads.

are the commonest materials, though the minerals mentioned above
all occur. These large beads were all found at the necks of the skeletons, but from the small number of them usually accompanying each

---

[1] For the identifications we are indebted to Profs. J. E. Wolff and Charles Palache
of Harvard University.

body it would appear that a cord encircled the throat with a few beads hung or strung at its middle.

Most of the shell beads were made from olivellas by simply cutting off the end of the spire. They occurred in great quantities in all the Sayodneechee cists (a single specimen came from the general digging in Cave I). A string of 53 shells was taken from the neck of a skeleton in Cist B (A–1915); another (pl. 70, *b*) from the same cist has single shells alternating with pairs of the little albatite cylinders. Besides olivellas we have specimens of a larger similar shell (pl. 70, *j*) prepared for threading by the removal of the spire and part of the body; there are also seven small, thin, discoidal examples cut from an unidentifiable bivalve (A–1902). A single bead of this nature is attached to the left ear of the infant "mummy" from Cist I, Cave I.

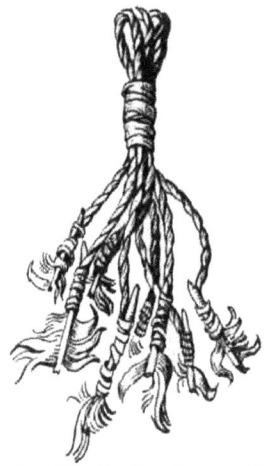

FIG. 77.—Feathered pendant.

There are a few hemispherical bone beads in the Sayodneechee collection (A–1947), of about the same size and shape as those of stone. They are fashioned from the solid part of the shaft of a long-bone of some large animal. Two short, cylindrical tubes of bird bone, highly polished, probably also served as beads (see pl. 86, *c*, *d*), as did some similar tubes recovered in their original order (pl. 70, *f*). A string of acorn cups used as beads is shown in plate 70, *k*.

Feathered pendant (fig. 77).—This object may or may not have been for personal ornament. It is from Cave I. It is made of four tightly twisted fiber strings, doubled to form loops and bound together for a space of three-eighths inch by sinew. To each of the eight loose ends there are bound with sinew two small feathers, the greater part of which have been broken off. The total length of the specimen is 2 inches.

HOUSEHOLD APPURTENANCES

CRADLES

RIGID TYPE: Our data as to this style is very scanty. We have only fragments of three very badly decayed examples from the cists of Cave I (pl. 71, *a*). They seem to have had an outer frame made from a single stick bent into a sort of guitar shape. This outer frame appears to have sometimes been inclosed by an ornamental wrapping of twilled yucca leaves. The filling, as may be seen in the figure, is of crisscrossed reeds (not twigs as in the

Ruin 7 Cliff-dwelling example, pl. 42) held together by decorative lashings. In one case these are of hair, in another of leather thongs, in the third a mixture of the two.

FLEXIBLE TYPE: *Grass.*—Plate 71, *b*, illustrates one of three examples from Cave I; it is made of grass and yucca leaves. The rim, or what corresponds to the wooden hoop of the rigid type, is a continuous roll of coarse grass stalks bound up tightly with yucca; the average thickness of the roll is three-fourths inch. The front and back consist of coarse-meshed, carelessly woven yucca nettings attached to the grass rim. A little shredded grass and some corn husks, with which the cradle was originally padded, are still held by the netting at the small end. It is 33 inches long and 21 inches in maximum width.

The second specimen (A–2293, general digging, cist area, Cave I) has a very firmly rolled grass rim 1¼ inches in diameter. The yucca netting on what is apparently the back is of a uniform large mesh; what remains across the front appears to have been close meshed at the small end, while the upper portion is more like a lacing than a net. The cradle holds for padding a quantity of beaten or shredded grass and shredded cedar bark. A fragment of a third cradle (A–2294) consists of the lower or small end with a double net of yucca like the specimens just described. It also held some of the soft padding.

While it is possible that these objects were not cradles, they are assumed to be such because of their shape (pl. 71, *b*) and because of their contents of soft grass and bark, substances commonly used by the Indians as bedding for infants. Furthermore, they are of such flimsy construction that they would have been of little use as carrying devices, the only other logical service assignable to them. One of the infant "mummies" from Cave I was found lying on grass and cedar bark, the latter embedded in the adobe in which the remains were encased.

Professor Cummings [1] reports "bags of loosely woven yucca lined with cedar bark" and "bags of cedar bark fiber held together with interlacings of yucca cord." Hough [1] mentions finding in Tulerosa cave, New Mexico, "bed heaps rudely constructed, though in a definite manner, of soft grass inclosed in a mat-like net of yucca leaves; bundles of leaves and grass served as pillows."

Cedar bark.—Ten cradles of cedar bark were found, three in Cave I, seven in Cave II. The two best examples are here described and figured. No. A–2446 (Cave II) is 27 inches long and 16 inches wide (pl. 72, *a*). It was apparently made by weaving a mat of cedar-bark strips, laid parallel to each other and held together by twined

---

[1] From Sagiotsosi, 1910, p. 14.
[2] 1907, p. 21.

rows of yucca leaves 3 inches apart; figure 78 shows the manner in
which the latter were carried along the edge before reentering the
mat, and at the same time providing loops for the attachment of the
yucca netting which drew up the sides of the mat and inclosed the
cradle. At one end the mat is turned up at a sharp angle and is
held thus by a mesh of yucca leaves attached at several points to
the front netting. The other end is formed in the same manner,
but with less care.

The second specimen ("grass area," Cave II, pl. 72, *b*) is 30 inches
long, 18 inches wide. It was filled with crushed and shredded bark
in which were a number of piñon nuts. It is made of thick ¾-inch
strips of cedar bark running its whole length; these are held close

together by tightly twisted
yucca-leaf twining elements
irregularly spaced but carried along the edge as in
figure 78.

The bottom is turned up
and attached as in the cradle
described above. The top is
either unfinished or broken,
loose and frayed ends of the
bark strips extending some
10 inches beyond the last

FIG. 78.—Edge binding of cedar-bark cradle.

twining. The V-shaped
opening from the top to within 4 inches of the bottom is laced across
with a rude netting caught into the twining elements of the body.

The shapeless appearance of these cradles when found, crushed
down by the sand in the cists and in the débris, at first deceived us
as to their nature, and in the field we referred to them as panniers.
It was not until they had been cleaned in the laboratory and had
regained something of their original shape that their true purpose
became evident. The identification was rendered certain when the
infant "mummy" from Cist 1, Cave I, was unwrapped and found to
lie in the somewhat tattered remains of one of them, the yucca netting still fastened across the body (pl. 73).

Toy cradle (?).—In plate 29, *a*, under the "mummified" foot will
be seen what appears to be a small grass bag, but which proves, on
closer examination, to have all the essential features of the cradles
just described. The back or body is made of grass bundles instead
of cedar-bark strips; the netting, however, is of yucca as in the larger
specimens. When whole it was apparently about 18 inches long by
8 inches wide. We judge that this little object was a toy cradle.
The bones of a child, 6 or 7 years of age, found in the same cist,
lend color to the theory.

a

b

CEDAR-BARK CRADLES

INFANT'S "MUMMY," PART OF CEDAR-BARK CRADLE, AND WRAPPINGS

e. BRUSH, NATURAL SIZE   *f.* BRUSH, ENLARGED.

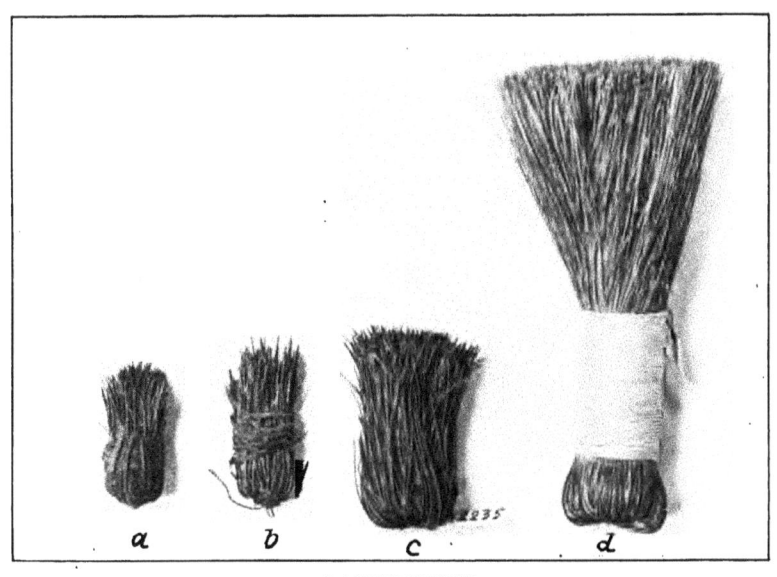

a-d, HAIRBRUSHES

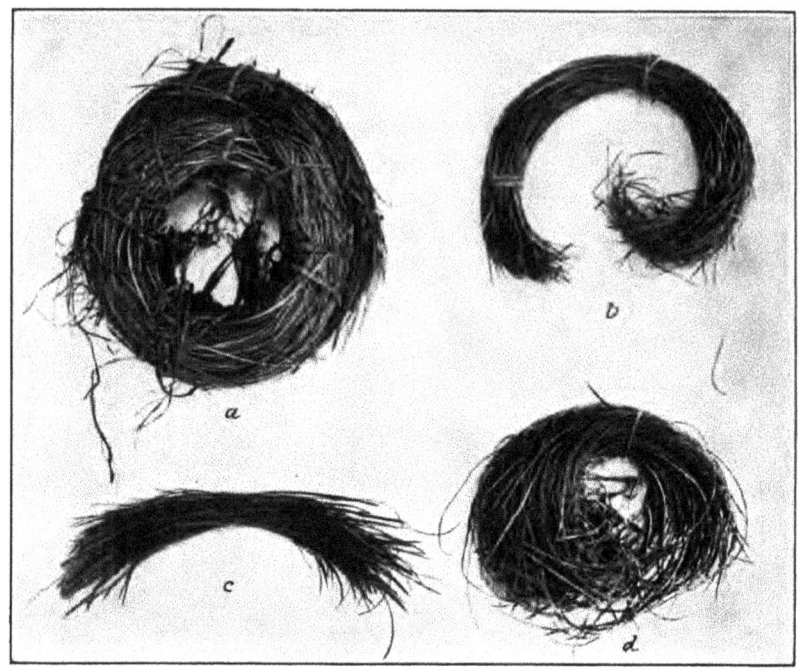

BUNDLES OF BASKET SPLINTS

e. COIL OF ROPE

TORCHES

Our few specimens do not differ from the Cliff-dwelling examples, being merely rolls of cedar bark tied up with yucca and charred at the ends. Two of them are shown in plate 80, *a*, *b*.

BRUSHES

From Cave I came three brushes quite different from the simple bunches of stiff fibers found in the cliff-houses. They are tiny little contrivances made in the following manner: A bundle of stiff plant fibers was bound together a little to one side of the middle, the short end of the bundle forming a core over which the long end was folded back until the tips of both ends were even with each other; this was done in such a way as completely to surround the core, to which the folded-back portion was firmly bound by a second wrapping (see fig. 79). In one example (pl. 74, *e*, *f*) an extra tie was applied, running vertically from the butt and through the bristles; this specimen is the smallest, 1⅝ inches in length; the other two are 2 inches and 2¼ inches long, respectively. These little objects were evidently used as hair brushes, as strands of human hair are still entangled in their bristles. The type, though not found so far in the cliff-dwellings, is a widespread one among the Indians of northern Mexico, the Pima of Arizona, and various California tribes. The accompanying illustration (pl. 74, *a–d*) shows our three specimens and one of similar construction from San Luis Potosí.

FIG. 79.—Section of fiber brush.

BASKETRY

TWILLED BASKETRY

We do not know whether twilled ware, in the form of the yucca ring basket so common in the cliff-dwellings, was or was not produced by the Basket Makers. No specimens were found in excavating the two caves if we except the somewhat doubtful example from Cist 9, Cave I (p. 79). In the Grand Gulch collections in the American Museum, however, there are numerous ring baskets, as well as a small-mouthed twilled basket of yucca. These are figured by Pepper as of Basket Maker origin,[1] but it should be remembered that this lot of Grand Gulch material is a mixture of both Basket Maker

---

[1] 1902, pp. 23–25.

and Cliff-dweller products. It is safe to state on the basis of our explorations that even if the ring basket was used by the Basket Makers on the southern side of the San Juan, it was very much less common than among the Cliff-dwellers, for no Cliff-dweller collection as large as our Basket Maker one would fail to contain the fragments of several dozen specimens of this type.

COILED BASKETRY

The relative frequency of coiled basketry in Cliff-dweller and Basket Maker sites is best illustrated by the following statistics: our Cliff-dwelling collection contains in round numbers 1,100 specimens, of which four are of basketry; 580 specimens are catalogued from the three Basket Maker caves, and of these about 175 are basketry. Owing to decay at Sayodneechee and to looting in Cave I, the majority of our specimens are fragmentary; we have, however, a few whole baskets and large pieces to help us in our study of forms, while the quantities of shreds and worn-out bits from the débris of occupancy and the plundered cists are particularly useful for technological details.

Weave.—With the exception of one very crude example (pl. 76, *a*) in which a single rod is used, every piece in the collection is made over a two-rod-and-bundle foundation. The rods, varying in thickness according to the fineness of the product, are thin, round twigs with pithy centers;[1] the bundles consist of fibers, usually from the yucca leaf, more rarely of what appears to be some sort of shredded root; the sewing elements are thin wooden splints (except in the very rough piece referred to above, where they are yucca leaf). Several bunches of these splints prepared for use were found buried in Cave I (pl. 75, *a–d*); the individual elements are from three thirty-seconds to one-eighth inch wide, and vary from 12 to 16 inches long. Three of the bunches contain both light- and dark-colored splints; one (pl. 75, *c*) is composed entirely of dark ones.

As is shown in figure 80, the two rods are set side by side and the fibrous bundle is laid above them. The sewing element, in inclosing this foundation, takes in the rods and the bundle above them, and also passes through about half of the bundle of the coil below (fig. 80, *b*). It is this gripping of the bundle of the lower coil which alone holds the fabric together. While careless manipulation of the awl has sometimes caused the sewing elements to split each other (pl. 76, *f*), they do not, so far as we can discover, ever interlock. Mason's[2]

---

[1] We have not yet been able to have made the botanical identification of the rods and splints.

[2] 1904, p. 244.

definition of coiled basketry reads as follows: " [It] is produced by an over-and-over sewing with some kind of flexible material, each stitch interlocking with the one immediately underneath it." The present type, whose sewing elements do not interlock, does not accord with the above description, and we have here, apparently, a fundamental difference between Basket Maker and Cliff-dweller coiled basketry and what we must suppose, on the authority of Mason, to be the more general style. We have not had an opportunity to follow this line of investigation, although it promises much of classificational value; we have noted, however, that Navaho basketry (probably made by Paiute women) is made in the same way as our cave material. That from the Coahuila (northern Mexico) burials, on the other hand, has interlocked sewing elements.

While all the specimens in our collection conform exactly to the description given above, they vary considerably in fineness of weave and excellence of materials (see pl. 76). The coarsest pieces have foundation rods one-quarter inch in diameter and run 2½ coils and

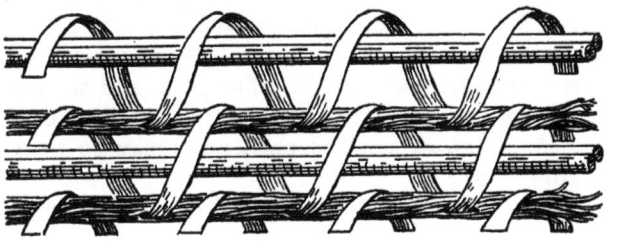 

a   *b*

FIG. 80.—Detail of coiled basketry weave.

6 to 7 stitches to the inch; the finest have 7 coils and 12 stitches; the great majority have 5 coils and 9 to 11 stitches. This is comparatively coarse weaving (our few Cliff-dwelling examples have 5 coils and 17 to 20 stitches to the inch), and results in the exposure, between the stitches, of the foundation rods which, in the Cliff-dwelling pieces, are hidden because the splints are narrower and are pulled closer together. The edge bindings are all simple.

In regard to the manufacture of these baskets (or at least those of bowl-like form), it seems probable that they were held right-side up, that the foundation was steadied by the left hand and the awl and sewing splint manipulated from the inside with the right hand. Looking from above, the coil, in all the bowl-like specimens, is seen to run counterclockwise.

SHAPES

Shallow trays are the commonest form. They range from 3 inches to 3 feet in diameter, the smaller ones (pl. 76, *m*) being relatively deeper and more bowl-like than the larger. Our collection contains none of the latter, although we have fragments of many (pl. 76, *a–g*); for their shape and general appearance reference should be had to the illustrations in Pepper's paper.

A second form, represented by small bits only, is the *large carrying basket* with flaring sides and small, pointed bottom.[1]

Less common are *baskets with restricted orifices.* These little pieces are very neatly made (pl. 76, *l, n*), and seem to have served as trinket holders and workbaskets, for specimen *l* contained the three-pendant necklace described in the section on personal ornaments (fig. 72, *a*) and *n* (see also pl. 77) held pieces of bird skin, a leather bag, and a basketry disk.

The most interesting piece of basketry found was taken from Cave II (pl. 78). It has an elongated base, oval in cross section; the upper part flares out and becomes round; it is constricted again at the top, and the orifice is small.[2] There does not seem to have been a neck, but there is some evidence that there was once a string-hinged cover. On opposite sides, just below the point of greatest diameter, are pairs of carrying loops made by twisting into a heavy cord eight or ten 2-strand human-hair strings. The entire inner surface of the basket is thickly pitched with piñon gum, and the same material has been daubed on such parts of the exterior as had begun to wear through. A design of small stepped units may be faintly made out on the upper curve.

There can be little doubt that this specimen is a *water-carrying basket.* The pitched interior is really sufficient proof, but the identification is further borne out by the peculiar shape, which permits the piece to fit snugly against the shoulders of the bearer, and by the incurved top, which would effectually have prevented the contents from splasing out during transportation.

A number of small basketry *plaques or disks* were taken from the cists and rubbish (pl. 76, *i, k*), and one was found in the basket shown in plate 77. These appear to be beginnings of baskets, as all are clearly unfinished and all conform closely in shape and weave to the bottoms of one or another of the types described above. While the majority are round, there are a few which, by their oval shape and sharply rising sides, indicate that they were intended to be completed in some form similar to the water carrier.

MATTING

We do not know whether or not rush mats such as have been described from the cliff-houses (p. 111) were used by the Basket

---

[1] See Pepper, 1902, p. 8.
[2] Dimensions: Total height 17 inches, greatest diameter 14¾ inches, orifice 4½ inches.

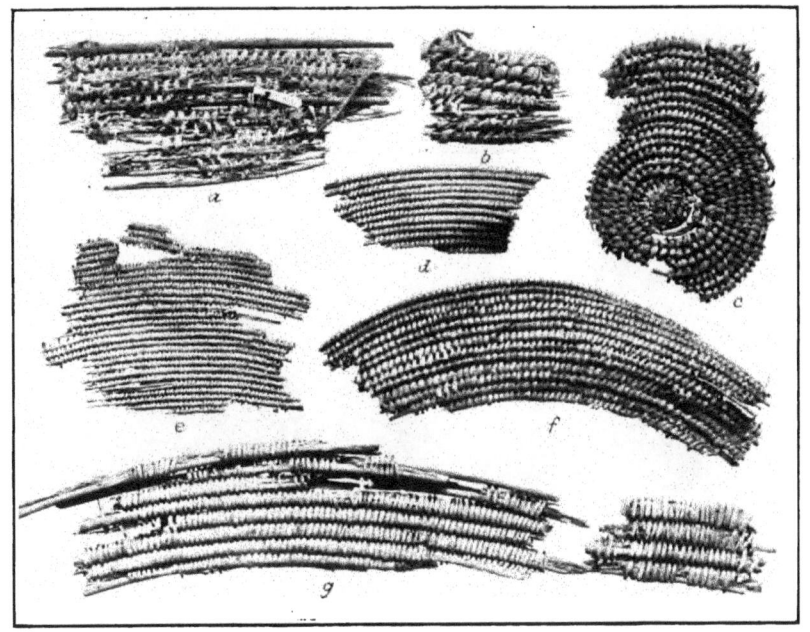

FRAGMENTS OF COILED BASKETRY

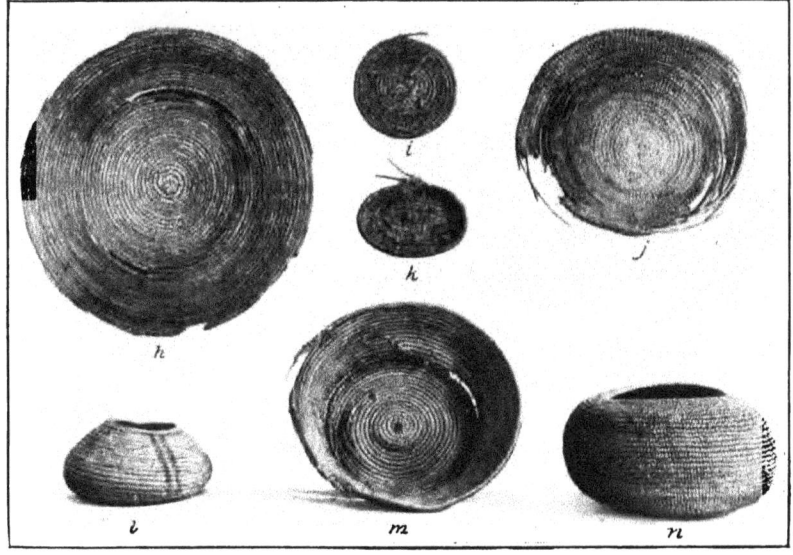

COILED BASKETRY

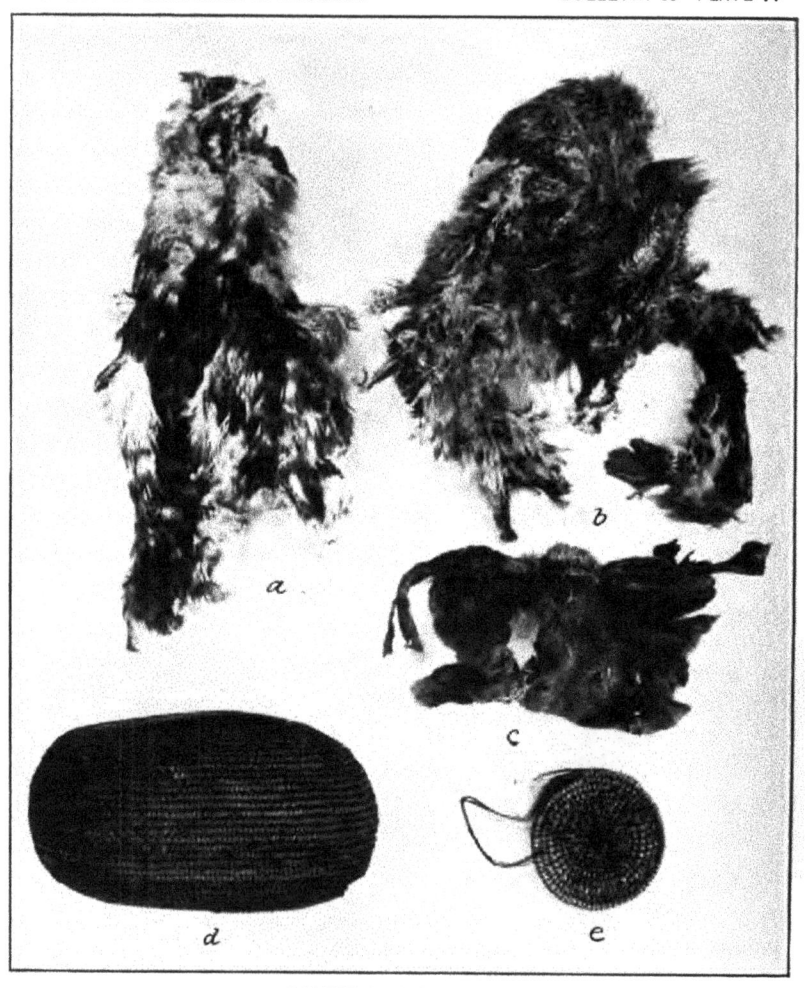

BASKET AND CONTENTS

a

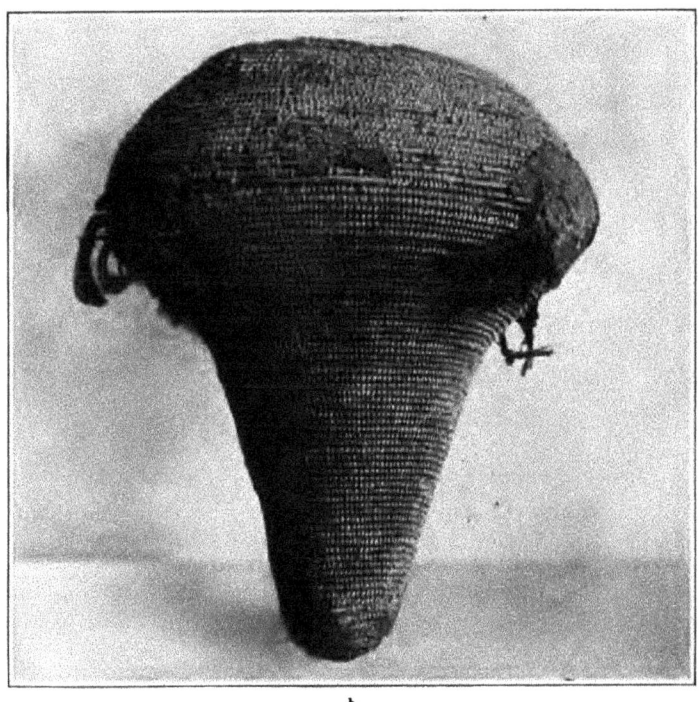

b

WATER-CARRYING BASKET

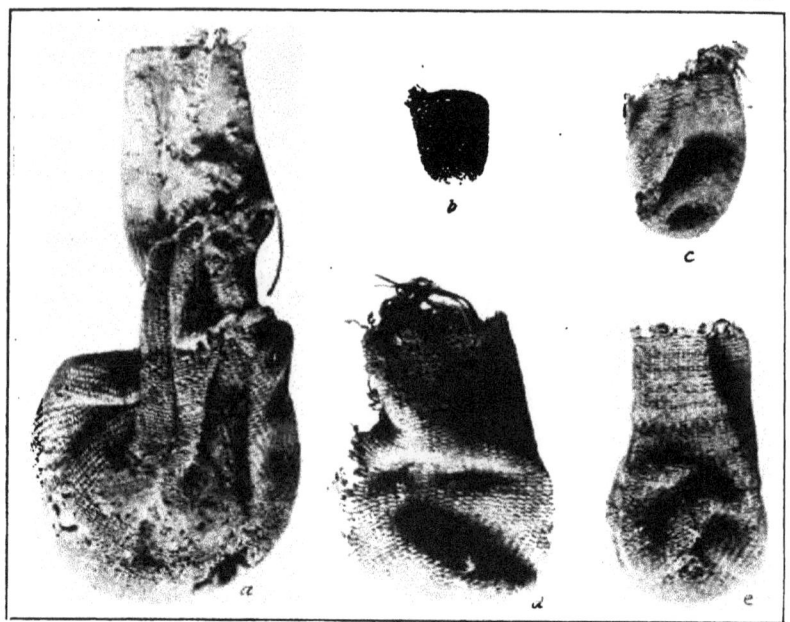

TWINED WOVEN BAGS

ƒ. FRAGMENT OF LARGE TWINED WOVEN BAG

Makers. A fragment of twilled work was taken from Cist 9, Cave I, but it was so badly decayed that it was impossible to tell whether the material was tule or yucca; the object, therefore, might be either a twilled basket or a mat. It is safe to state, however, as we did in the discussion of ring baskets, that rush matting was infinitely less common among the Basket Makers than it was among the Cliff-dwellers.

TWISTED CORDS AND THREADS

Cotton.—No trace of cotton was found by us in the Basket Maker caves. Pepper[1] states positively, however, that an atlatl in the Hazard collection bears a wrapping of cotton yarn. Furthermore, he figures[2] a small coiled basket closed with a piece of cotton cloth; this specimen, like several others in the American Museum collection from Grand Gulch which have already been referred to in this paper, must be regarded as doubtful Basket Maker material until the original field catalogues can be carefully examined.

Yucca and apocynum (?).—Strings of these fibers do not differ in any way from those of the Cliff-dwellers; great quantities of both were made, particularly of apocynum (?), the material employed in the manufacture of the fine twined bags so characteristic of the Basket Maker culture. Our only notable specimen is a coil of stout yucca-fiber cord or thin rope taken from Cist 7, Cave II (pl. 75, *e*). It is a two-strand clockwise twist one-fourth inch in diameter; the total length is about 70 feet.

Human hair.—Very characteristic of this culture seems to be the extensive use of human hair for all sorts of strings. The examples run from single-strand twists not more than one thirty-second inch in diameter to 40 and 50 strand cord nearly one-half inch thick. The commonest style is a tight twine made by twisting together four to six 2-strand strings, the whole being from three thirty-seconds to five thirty-seconds inch in diameter. Several bundles of hair, cut into short lengths and tied up ready for use, were found in Cave I; one very interesting specimen (A–2304, Cist 4) consists of an unfinished string, partly twisted and running off at one end into a bunch of loose hair; it is wrapped up in a neat bundle and tied with a yucca strip.

The following are some of the uses to which hair string was put: Sandal toe and heel loops; sandal tie strings; as secondary warps in sandal weaving; woven into narrow bands; as tie strings in hairdressing; as a single ornamental element in yucca straps; as loops for carrying baskets; as netted haircloth; as ornamental cradle lashings; as a waistband to hold a breechcloth.

---

[1] 1905, p. 118. [2] 1902, p. 23, and text, p. 25.

Wool of various animals (not specifically identifiable) was also twisted into cords, but much less commonly so than was human hair.

BRAIDED CORDS

Our material on this branch of technology is very scanty, consisting of a large strap of raw yucca leaves that bears evidence of use as a carrying strap (A–2167); a similar straplike object of raw yucca leaves with a bit of human hair string attached to one end (A–2472, Cave I); and an 8-inch length of flat-braided yucca fiber about half the thickness of a lead pencil (A–2176, Cave I).

FINE-CORD TEXTILE FABRICS

No cotton cloth was found, nor was there observed any trace of loom weaving in any other fiber.

TWINED WEAVING: *Bags.*—This technique was used in the manufacture of sandals (described above) and of bags. The latter, ranging in size from tiny specimens 1½ inches long to large flexible sacks 2 feet or more deep and 18 inches in diameter, are highly characteristic of the Basket Maker culture; we have found no trace of them in the Cliff-dwellings.

From the smallest examples (pl. 79, *b*) to the largest (of which we have only fragments, see pl. 79, *f*), all are made in the same way over warps of yucca or apocynum (?) which vary in number according to the size of the bag. These warps radiate from the bottom, new ones being introduced between the original ones as the body flares, and being dropped out again toward the neck to allow for the necessary constriction. The weft is of fine apocynum (?) string of a yellowish color, the paired strands running round the bag, beginning at the bottom. Decoration consists of horizontal bands in red, black, and the natural shade. The texture of the bands is varied by changing the color of one or both of the paired elements and thus producing a number of stepped, offset, and recurring oblique patterns (pl. 79, *f*). As was the case with the twined sandals, lack of material suitable for dissection prevents at this time an adequate study of weaves and decorations. It may be noted, however, that in the large specimen figured, there are about 10 warps and 17 pairs of wefts to the square inch of fabric.

The range in size of these bags indicates a wide variety of uses. A number of small ones from the cists in Cave I were found empty, and may have been despoiled of their former contents by the looters, or simply buried as offerings. The medium-sized one shown in plate 79, *a*, held corn meal and a substance resembling dried fruit. The large bags, some of the fragments of which appear to have been cut with a knife, may perhaps have been split open and used for mortuary wrappings. The body of a very young infant, discovered in Cave II, had almost certainly been interred in a bag.

COIL WITHOUT FOUNDATION: We have only two examples of this technique. One (A–1969) is from the Sayodneechee burial cave; it is a badly decayed fragment the size of one's thumb-nail. The rows are close together and the loops are very small; the nature of the material is not determinable. The other (A–2325, Cist 3, Cave I) is a piece of haircloth rather crudely woven of loosely twisted strings of human hair; it is precisely similar to the Cliff-dwelling bit shown in figure 45 and plate 46, c.

FIG. 81.—Detail of band.

WOVEN BANDS: These are of two varieties—the coarse and the fine. The coarse type, of which we have three specimens from Cave I, is made in all cases by lacing back and forth a single string across a series of strings laid parallel to each other. This is best explained by the diagrammatic drawing (fig. 81). It will be noticed that there are seven parallel elements and that the " binder " is continuous; a decorative effect is introduced by making the central string of hair; this contrasts effectively with the dark-yellow apocynum (?) of which the rest of the band is woven. The width is three-eighths inch. The other two specimens differ only in detail: one (A–2184) is one-half inch wide, has 10 parallel elements forming five loops at one end, and is entirely of hair; the other (A–1836) is five-eighths inch wide, 20 inches long, and has 16 parallel strands of hair; the " binder " is apocynum (?). As all these objects are fragmentary, and do not give us much evidence as to how they were finished off at the ends or of their original length, we can not tell anything as to their use. They might have been headbands, burden straps, or possibly cradle carriers. A very similar band is attached to a woven bag in the modern Maya collection in the Peabody Museum.

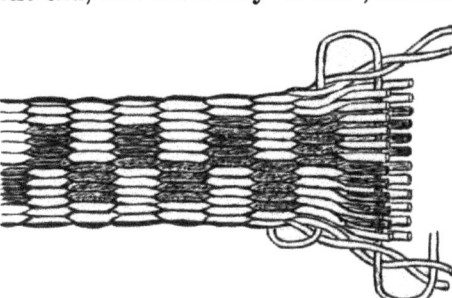

FIG. 82.—Detail of narrow band.

The finer type, which is represented by one short piece only three-eighths inch in width, is of excellent workmanship. The general principle of manufacture is the same as in the coarser specimens, viz, parallel elements are held together by a " binder " which crosses back and forth and thus holds them together. Again recourse must be had to the enlarged drawing (fig. 82) to explain the weave. The parallel elements consist of fourteen pairs of very fine strings; each pair twines about the successive crossings of the "binder." The two outer pairs of elements on each edge are yellow (apocynum?); each of the ten inner pairs is made up of one yellow and one black (human hair) string. As the two elements (of a single pair) twine about each other and about the "binder," there are, of course, successive emergences (on the surface) of the two strings, yellow, black, yellow, black, etc. The strands are so arranged as to work these alternating emergences into the decoration shown in figure 82.

FUR AND FEATHER CLOTH

As was stated in the section on Dress, we have no complete garments of either fur or feather cloth, but from the cists in Cave I a great enough number of fragments and strings was recovered to enable us to judge of the quality of the cloth and to learn that there are important differences between it and the corresponding Cliff-

FIG. 83.—Detail of feather string.

dweller fabrics. Of the latter, fully nine-tenths of the specimens are made of feather string (i. e., yucca cord wound with feathers); of the Basket Maker specimens, on the other hand, at least as large, if not a larger percentage is woven of fur string. Furthermore, Cliff-dweller feather string is practically always wound with the stripped pile from the large wing and tail feathers of the turkey; while the few Basket Maker examples which do occur are wound, not with stripped or whole individual turkey feathers, but with narrow strips of the skins of small birds with the downy feathers upon them.[1] Two methods of attaching these little strips are shown in figure 83. A still further difference between the two classes is that while feather string was generally used by the Cliff-dwellers to form the body of their fabrics, the Basket Makers employed it generally, if not always, for ornamental edgings, tassels, bands, or lashings for cradles, and wove the body of their cloth from fur string.

---

[1] More rarely with tufts of feathers caught between the twists of the cord after the manner of "fluff string."

The fur string was generally produced by wrapping yucca cords with thin strips of rabbit skin, the end of one strip being caught under and held in place by the beginning of the next. The hides of other small animals as well as that of the mountain sheep also served; the latter seems generally to have been tanned before use, all the others to have been applied raw. Ribbons of very tough skin, like that of the badger, were sometimes merely twisted on themselves instead of being wound about a cord base; and occasionally two strips, one light colored and one dark, were twined together to produce a spirally striped effect. Ornamental tassels were made by catching bits of the thick, dark fur from rabbits' feet through the strands of yucca string in the same way as was done with some of the pieces of feather string (see fig. 83).

For weaving the fur strings into cloth they were laid side by side and held in that position by widely spaced rows of twined yucca cords.

CEDAR BARK

Cedar bark was a very important raw material in Basket Maker industry; more so, apparently, than among the Cliff-dwellers. It was used for making cradles, sandals, torches, and as padding in bed nets and baby carriers.

Bags of cedar bark, whole and fragmentary, were found in both caves. The best specimen (fig. 84) is a nearly complete sack 11 inches long and 9 inches wide. Its foundation is of bundles of partly shredded bark running from the top down across the bottom and up the other side; they are held in position by twined rows of yucca string. The piece is light and strong, and, while of too open a mesh to have held corn or small nuts, it must have made a serviceable receptacle for larger objects.

Plate 80 shows other articles of cedar bark: *a* and *b* are torches; *d* is a ring, presumably used when carrying burdens on the head; *c*, *e*, and *f* are problematical objects, the latter a queer T-shaped bundle unlike anything that we have seen in southwestern collections.

LEATHER

Uses of leather and hide noted under other heads are: robes, sandals, cradle lashings, cover for ball (p. 192), and fur string.

Pollen pouch.—Figure 85 represents a small, bottle-necked sack of soft-tanned skin 5 inches long. It is made of two pieces cut to match and sewed together with a running stitch. The seam is on the inside and the orifice will just admit the little finger. When squeezed the bag throws out a fine dust of pollen as if it had once been used as a container for that substance. Also from Cave I came half of a similar pouch (A–2240).

A flat *skin wallet*, 11½ inches wide, made of pieces of the hides of small animals, was found in Cave I (A–2397). It is sewed together with fiber string and the hair sides are out.

"*Double-head*" *bags* (fig. 86).—Both our examples of this type are fragmentary, but their nature can be determined with certainty. Each was made by sewing together the trimmed pelts of two prairie

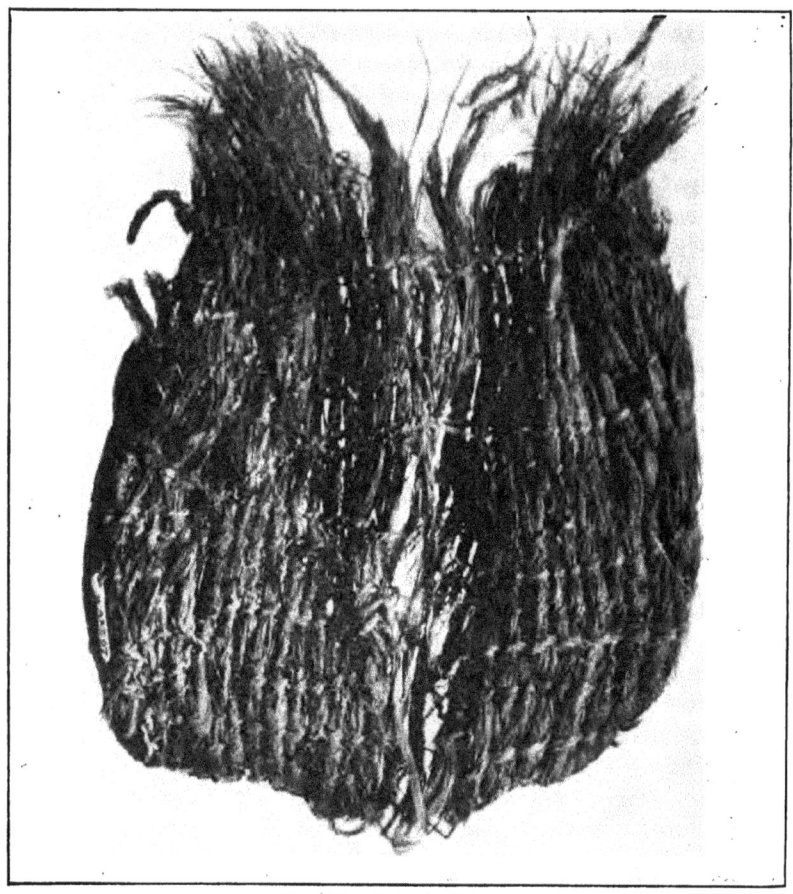

FIG. 84.—Cedar-bark bag.

dogs in such a way that the neck of the bag was formed by the heads of the animals, its mouth by their mouths. The two skins had originally been laid hair side to hair side and sewed together with coarse fiber thread in a wide running stitch. The whole had then been turned inside out to hide the seam and bring the fur to the exterior. Hough[1] notes (from Tulerosa) " the skin of a small animal having the loops of yucca fastened to the margin by which it

[1] 1914, p. 86.

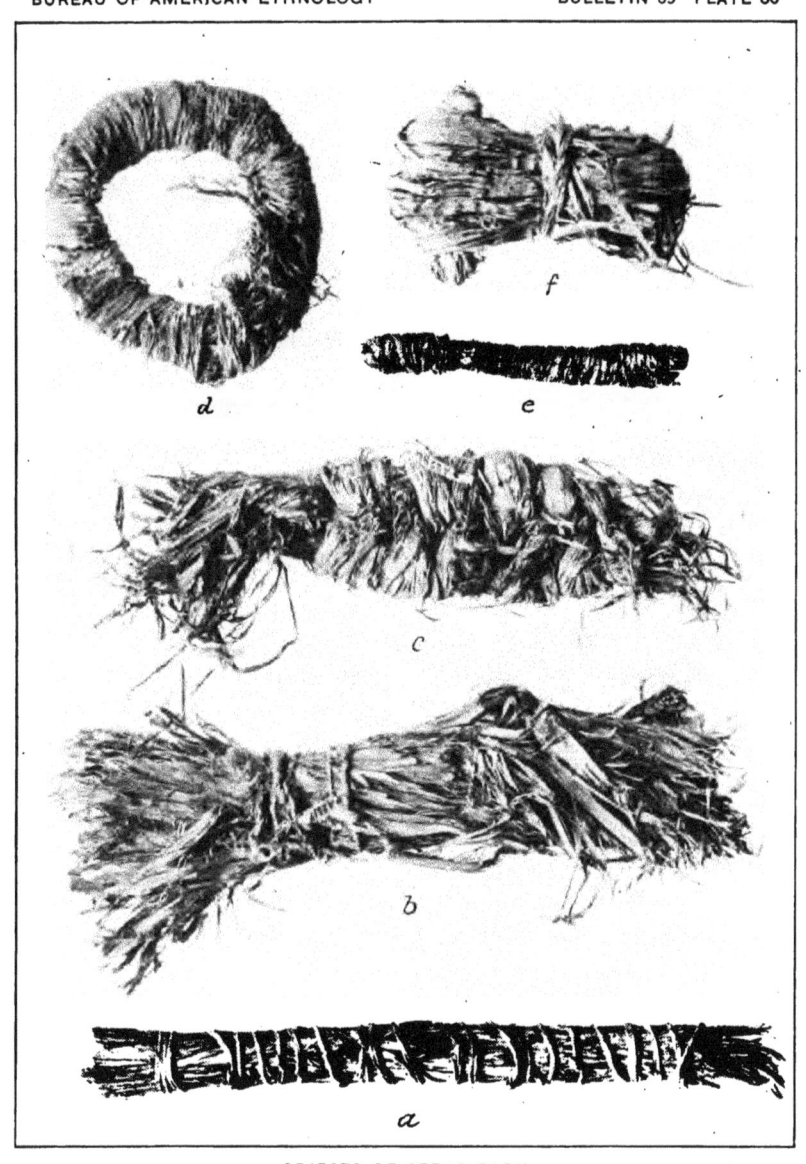

OBJECTS OF CEDAR BARK

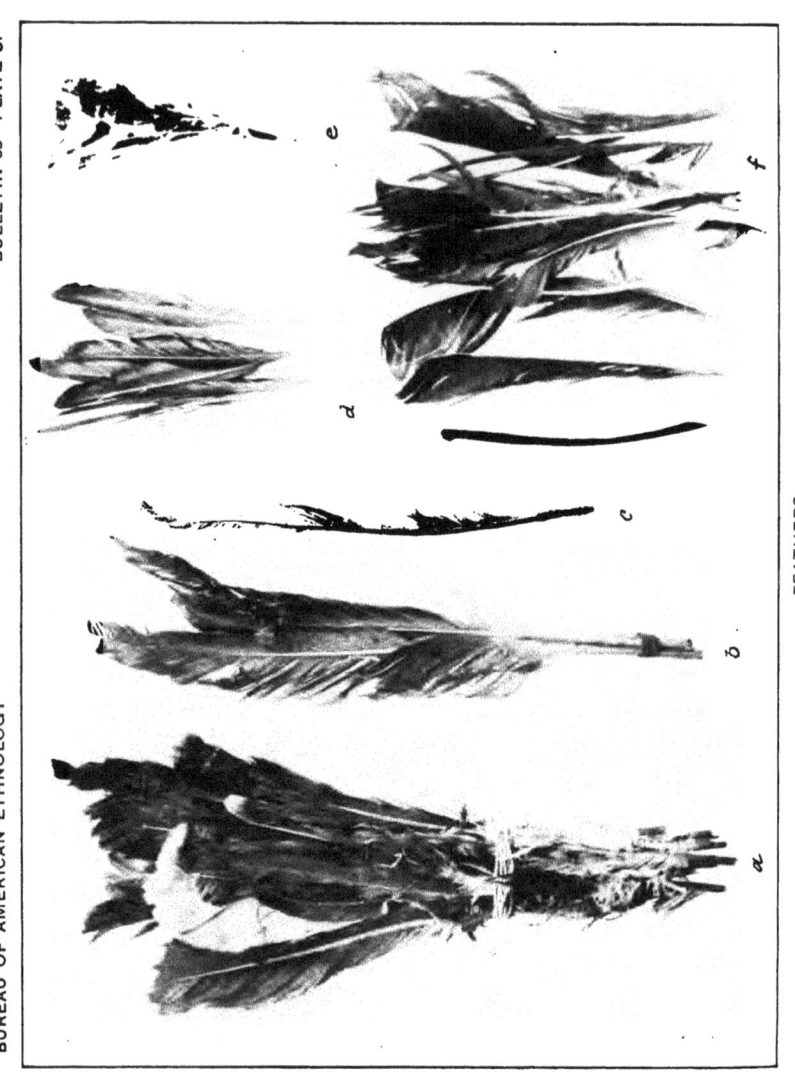

FEATHERS

was stitched in drying." This might perhaps be one-half of a bag such as the above.

Paint container (pl. 77, *c*).—What seems to have been a "roll-up" to hold pigments was found in a basket in Cave II. It consists of two pieces of skin of deer or mountain sheep sewed together in an overcast stitch with yucca string. At either end of the seam there project little rolled tags of hide, one of which is tied with cord. The flesh side of the object is heavily coated with red paint and the skin under the hair on the other side shows traces of the same.

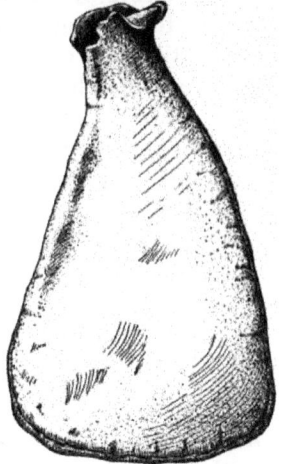

FIG. 85.—Leather pollen pouch.

FEATHERS

Uses of feathers under other heads are: in feather string, pendants, and in atlatl dart feathering (p. 181). Loose feathers and feathers tied in bundles are shown in plate 81, *a–f*, and bird skins in plate 77. The specific identifications, kindly made for us by Mr. Outram Bangs, of the Museum of Comparative Zoology, Harvard University, follow:

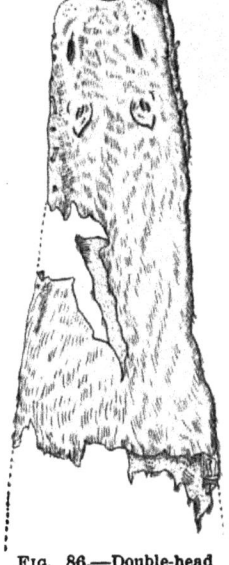

FIG. 86.—Double-head sack.

Western red-tailed hawk (*Buteo borealis calurus*), plate 81, *a.*

Swainson's hawk (*Buteo swainsoni*), plate 81, *f.*

Western great horned owl (*Bubo virginianus pollescens*), plate 81, *e.*

Raven (*Corvus corax sinuatus*), plate 81, *f.*

Crow (*Corvus brachyrhynchus hesperis* or *C. cryptolenca*), (A–2197), not figured.

Hutchins' (?) wild goose (*Branta canadensis hutchinsi*), plate 81, *b.*

Greater yellowlegs (*Tringa melanoleuca*), plate 81, *d.*

SINEW

Sinews were much used for seizings as in feathering atlatl darts and making brushes. In these cases the material was split into thin, narrow, tape-like strips. As a substitute for string it served to tie up bunches of feathers, for attaching pendants to neck cords, etc.;

used thus it is usually roughly shredded out and of varying length. We have several specimens in which fine, round filaments were employed for sewing, as in the case of a mended rent in a skin robe, in the stitchings of some leather bags, and in fastening the skin cover about a stuffed ball (see p. 192).

A bunch of raw sinew (A–2187, Cave I) is made up of two bundles, each tied with yucca strips and the two tied together. The length of the pieces is about 16 inches, and they have the appearance of being the two tendons of Achilles taken from a deer or mountain sheep and carried home " in the rough " for the preparation of thread.

WOOD

PROCESSES

These do not differ, so far as we have observed, from those noted in the cliff-dwelling section, which indeed comprise about all the methods available for a people ignorant of metals. As will be seen in the following descriptions of specimens, the finished articles are in no way inferior to those from the cliff-dwellings.

ARCHITECTURAL WOOD

Architectural wood was practically absent if our investigations give a fair sample of the dwellings of the Basket Makers (but see p. 206 in the general discussion of the culture). The only instances we recorded were the rough sticks worked into the roofs of covered cists in Caves I and II.

SPEAR THROWER, OR ATLATL

This interesting weapon is represented in our collection by one almost perfect specimen and three or four fragments. The atlatl is a device which serves to add greater length and therefore greater propulsive force to the arm of the thrower in launching a spear or dart. It consists of a long, thin stick with a grip for the hand at one end, and a hook-like spur to hold the butt of the spear at the other. In throwing, the butt of the spear was placed against the spur at the end of the atlatl and lay flat along it with the head projecting in front of the user's hand (fig. 87); it was held in this position, probably near its middle, by the second (fore) and third fingers which passed through loops on the sides of the grip (fig. 88, b). The fourth and fifth fingers were clenched upon the atlatl shaft below the loops, holding it firmly against the palm and heel of the hand. The base of the thumb served to solidify this grip on the atlatl shaft, and the thumb proper aided to steady the spear in its resting place between and upon the second and third finger (fig. 87).[1]

For the actual throw the arm was brought forward and the atlatl whipped over; at the same time the thumb and the fore and second fingers released the dart, which was propelled by the pressure upon its butt of the engaging spur.

Our most complete atlatl was found in Cist 10, Cave I (pl. 82, *c. d*). Owing to its having been pressed down into the bottom of the burial cist by the weight of the body above it, it is now somewhat bent and twisted; although in places the wood (a close-grained variety, possibly oak) is slightly shrunken, the stick has for the greater part retained its original proportions and still shows a smooth, careful finish. Its length over all is 26 inches; width of spur end 1⅜ inches; of grip end ⅞ inch. As the photograph shows, the spur is a little rounded projection carved in the end of a groove sunk into the upper or flat side of the shaft. The last two or three inches of the spear fitted into this groove and a little shallow cup in its butt engaged the spur (fig. 87).[2] The groove, together with the cup and spur arrangement, must have held the dart perfectly steady, yet without in the least hampering its release at the instant of throwing; there could have been no possibility of side-slip.

The spur is 3 inches from the end; from it to the handle the front of the shaft is flat; the edges are rounded, the back slightly convex. The handle proper begins 4 inches from the butt; at that point there are shallow notches on the edges for the reception of the seizing which once held in place the now missing finger loops (see fig. 88, *b*). Marks of the binding can still be seen. Just below these notches are deeper and broader ones, so cut, apparently, that the loops might set more closely together (fig. 88).

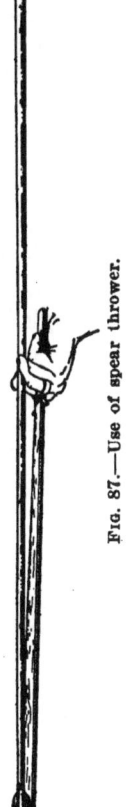

Fig. 87.—Use of spear thrower.

---

[1] This reconstruction of the method of gripping the atlatl and spear is the result of practical experiment and of observation of the grip on the atlatl as depicted on the sculptures of Chichen-Itza, Yucatan. The grip as figured by Pepper (1905, pl. I), in which the spear is held by the thumb and forefinger, makes it difficult to accomplish a straightaway throw; that of Cushing (1895, fig. 32) is much like ours, except that the little finger is not in use; as a matter of fact, the little finger aids greatly in holding the atlatl firmly in the hand.

[2] This atlatl is, therefore, "mixed," according to Krause's classification of spear throwers into male, female, and mixed (1905, p. 620).

One other feature of this atlatl remains to be described. Seven inches from the butt, on the flat side (pl. 82, *d*), are the marks of wrappings. These correspond exactly to the position 'in which there was found, lying below the atlatl and in contact with its convex side, the curious stone object shown in plate 83, *b* (placed as found in pl. 82, *c;* with restored wrappings in fig. 88, *b*). This object is of fine-grained white limestone with bands of natural red color encircling, or rather running through, a projection which rises from one end (pl. 83, *b*). In the top of the projection and in the upper surface of the other end are shallow round depressions that appear to have been made for the reception of inlays (fig. 88, *b*). Running through it below the projection is a drilled hole which held the bindings that attached it to the atlatl shaft; its weight is one ounce. Two objects from the Sayodneechee burial cave are, on the basis of the above specimen, identifiable as atlatl stones. One (pl. 83, *c*) is of indurated shale; its peculiar shape, with flat bottom, square ends, and high, loaf-like top, is best shown in the photograph. It weighs 2½ ounces. The other (pl. 83, *a*) is smaller, thinner, and lighter

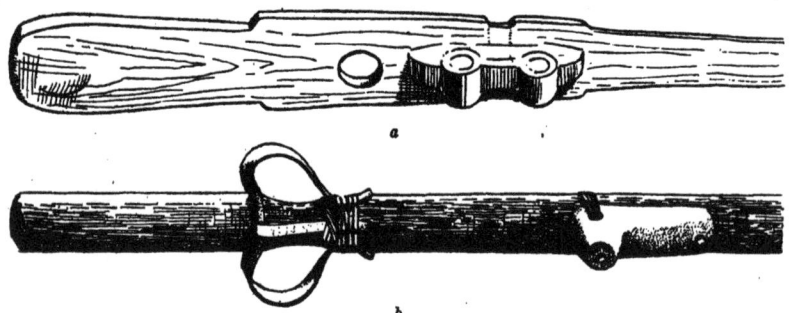

a

b

Fig. 88.—Spear throwers.

(one-half ounce); its material is mica schist. Both show distinct traces of lashings on their upper or convex sides, but not on their lower or flat surfaces. This bears out the theory that they were once bound against sticks (presumably atlatl shafts), for had they been suspended as ornaments or for any other purpose, the lashing marks would run all the way round them.

For what reason these stones were attached to the back sides of atlatl shafts is not obvious; they may have served as weights to give a proper balance or to lend added power to the apparatus. The peculiar shape of the Cave I specimen, and the very fine finish of all three, make it seem possible, however, that they may have had other than a utilitarian purpose. That the practice of binding a stone to the back of the atlatl was a common, if not universal, one among the Basket Makers, is shown by an example from Grand Gulch in the Field Museum, Chicago, which bears a small, beauti-

SPEAR THROWER

a

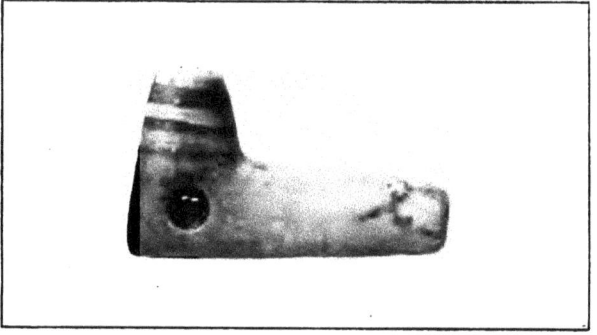

b

c

SPEAR-THROWER WEIGHTS

fully worked piece of limestone;[1] and by another in the Free Museum of Science and Art, Philadelphia (a replica is on exhibition in the Brooklyn Institute of Arts and Sciences), which, according to Cushing's label,[2] has: "wild-cat tooth fastening of finger loops with 'Feather Cleaver' Lightning stone (knife or arrow of chalcedony), war fetish stone, and 'Blood Clot' of limonite, and wrappings of dyed cotton yarn originally decorated with bright-feather work."

Even after making due allowance for Cushing's bias toward the mystic, it seems clear that the attached objects in this particular case must have been ceremonial in nature, but as to the others we are still in doubt.

It has occurred to the authors that the stones might perhaps be, so to speak, ceremonialized relics of former useful parts of the atlatl, but their researches in this direction brought out very little evidence. Traces of attached objects, apparently inlaid, are to be seen on an ancient atlatl from Yucatan in the Peabody Museum, and on an example from Bering Sea there is a small ivory figure fastened to the back. To throwing sticks from New Guinea are tied carved figures, but these are placed on the edge of the shaft where they served to keep the dart from slipping sideways.[3] Peruvian throwing sticks bear attached pieces of stone or bone that were used to form a handgrip.[4] Neither of these cases is, however, really comparable to ours; the nearest approach is seen in a throwing stick from the upper Rio Negro, Brazil (Peabody Museum), which has carved in high relief on its back a curious double-ended contrivance; there are also notches at the sides as if for wrappings (see fig. 88, *a*).

DARTS

As to the length of the projectiles thrown with the atlatl we have no data; their general make-up, however, is well illustrated by a number of broken darts found in the general digging in Cave I. The main shafts are of some light but strong wood with a small pith "heart." The butt of each is provided with a shallow cup to engage the spur of the throwing stick (fig. 89, *b*, *c*), and the ends are wrapped with a fine sinew seizing to keep the spur from shoving too far into the cup and thus splitting the shaft.

The feathering method is indicated, but not wholly made clear, by the two specimens reproduced in figure 89; *b* seems to show a double attachment similar to that of Lower Yukon darts (fig. 89, *a*, introduced for comparison).

---

[1] Krause, 1905, pl. iv, 34. [3] Krause, 1905, pl. i, fig. 12.
[2] Quoted by Pepper, 1905, p. 113. [4] Uhle, 1909, passim.

The tip of the spear was, apparently always, provided with a foreshaft; this, as the drawing shows (fig. 89, *f*), was set into a hole drilled in the end of the main shaft. The holes in the two socketed specimens recovered by us are 1 inch deep by seven-sixteenths inch in diameter at the mouth. Traces of red staining are visible on the example illustrated at *f*.

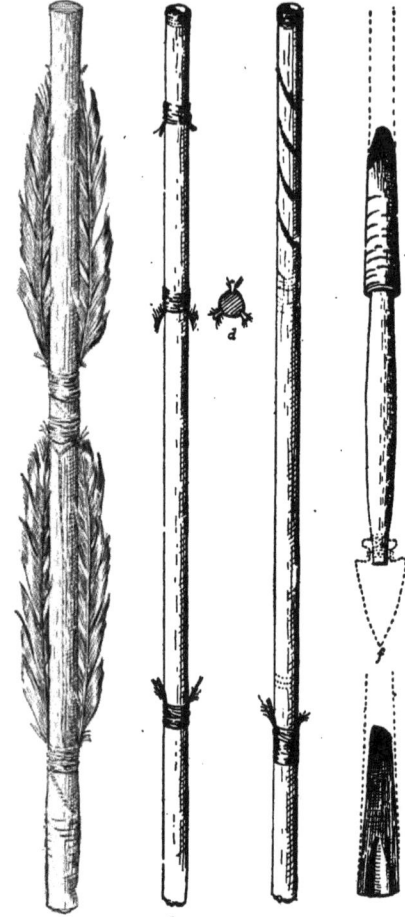

As to foreshafts we have more data, four specimens having been taken from the débris in Cave I (pl. 84, 18–21). It will be noted that, although they differ somewhat in length (longest 6¾ inches, shortest 4⅜ inches), they are all made in the same way. Each has the butt tapered to fit the socket of the main shaft, the taper being sometimes roughed a little to provide a grip. The tips are deeply notched to receive the stone points, which were made fast with seizings and gum. The chipped heads were apparently of two types, the tanged and the plain. The only example recovered in its foreshaft (pl. 84, 18) is of the former variety. From the cists of the Sayodneechee cave, however, came a number of points whose size makes it seem certain that they were atlatl dart tips.[1] A number of these are shown in figure 90; the majority

FIG. 89.—Details of atlatl dart.

are untangled and have more or less square bases. The workmanship is fine and in cross section they are markedly thinner than the majority of southwestern chipped heads.

Bunt points were not found by us, unless the specimen in figure 92 is to be regarded as such. Pepper, however, shows several in his paper on the atlatls from Grand Gulch.[2]

---

[1] By comparison with the data on fore shaft tips given by Pepper, 1905, p. 127.
[2] 1905.

MISCELLANEOUS WOODEN OBJECTS

Implement of unknown use.—Figure 91, *a*, illustrates the specimen, which is 14 inches long, 1⅜ inches wide, eleven-sixteenths inch thick at the center, and 1¹⁄₁₆ inches thick at the ends. It is made from a cottonwood limb and its two edges show no work beyond the removal of the bark. The two sides are exactly alike, flat with a small

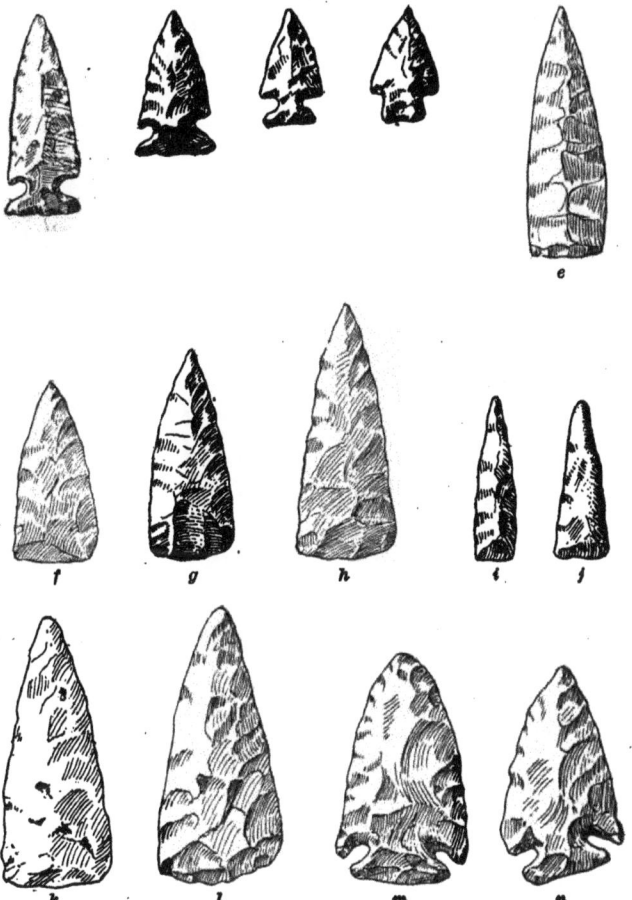

FIG. 90.—Atlatl tips and other implements of chipped stone.

raised projection left at either end. The fashioning of the surfaces seems to have been accomplished by rubbing with coarse sandstone; none of them shows the wear of use or any other markings which might furnish a hint as to the purpose of the object.

Fiber and grass shredders or beaters (?).—This is a conjectural identification of the two cleaver-shaped tools shown in figure 91, *c*, *d*.

The original form of both seems to have been produced by burning and was presumably accidental; both, however, exhibit much wear on their edges as if they had been used in pounding on some hard yet somewhat yielding material. As we found quantities of beaten and shredded grass and cedar bark in the caves, we think it possible that these pieces, with their convenient handgrips, might have been employed as pounders.

Worked slab (fig. 91, *b*); this is of cottonwood, 11¼ inches long and about three-eighths inch thick; one side is slightly convex, the other concave. Top, bottom, and sides retain marks made by the

d

a   *b*   *c*   *e*

FIG. 91.—Wooden objects.

rough stone rubber with which it was shaped. There are no indications of wear by service. The specimen might have been a lapboard, or even possibly a last for shaping moccasin soles.

End of wooden implement (pl. 84, 1); present length 14 inches. It is made of very heavy, tough, close-grained wood, perhaps mountain mahogany. The end and shaft are carefully worked. It is probably the handle of a digging stick or possibly part of a club.

Unfinished (?) *implement* (pl. 84, 2); length 14½ inches. The bark has been removed from a portion of this stick and the surface scraped; one end is carefully cut, the other shows the original break and still retains some of the outer bark.

Fire pokers (*?*) (pl. 84, 3', 4); these are both fragments of peeled sticks whose ends are pointed and somewhat hardened by fire.

Flat-pointed sticks (pl. 84, 14, 15); these again are fragmentary. Their ends are brought to flat points which show the polish of long use. One of them is broken off roughly; the other was partly sawed through, apparently with a flint flake, before breaking.

Sticks tied together (pl. 84, 13). Two twigs fastened to each other by a sinew binding about their middles. One end of each is cut off square and further finished by rubbing; the other is rough.

Spindle shaft (*?*) (pl. 84, 17); this is a fragment of a well-made, tapering implement with a sharp point, much like the spindle shafts of the Cliff-dwellers. We found no spindle whorls of wood or of any other material.

Problematical object (pl. 84, 9, and fig. 92); a stick five-eighths inch in diameter and 2½ inches long, from which the bark has been removed, one end whittled to a sharp point, the other hacked off round and a trifle " burred ". This may be

FIG. 92.—Wooden awl (?).

a rough awl-like implement or possibly a bunt head for an atlatl dart.

Short pointed sticks (pl. 84, 5–8, 16). These are peeled twigs, mostly of greasewood, with carelessly sharpened ends; they range in length from 3 inches to 5½ inches. They are the only objects from the Basket Maker caves which even remotely resemble arrow fore-shafts, but as all other evidence of the use of the bow and arrow is lacking, they should probably not be recognized as such.

Bent twig (pl. 84, 11). The shape is shown by the illustration. One end appears to have been broken off by twisting, the other by pulling the branch from the tree. A strand of yucca fiber is tied across the crook. Except for some wear or battering at the bend the object is unworked. The specimen is not unlike several of the " crook pahos " figured by Hough[1] from the upper Gila, but in this case some utilitarian purpose seems more likely.

Longitudinally bored sticks. There are two examples of this type. The larger (pl. 84, 3) is 8 inches long and five-eighths inch in diameter. It is drilled completely through, the holes having been made from either end and meeting in the middle, where they show a conical cross section. The boring is very neatly done and, save at the middle, there is left so thin a shell of the outer wood that the piece, which is really a peeled twig, has the weight and appearance of a hollow reed. One end exhibits faint traces of yellow paint, the other is stained dark. The smaller specimen (pl. 84, 24) is $3\frac{7}{16}$ inches long, one-half inch in diameter. Like the other, it is a plain peeled stick; the bore, however, is smaller and leaves more of the original wood. The ends are slightly tapered, neatly rounded off, and each is encircled with a single narrow line burnt into the wood. The purpose of these objects is unknown, but the decorative lines about the ends of the smaller example give it a certain resemblance to the specimens next to be described.

Gaming (?) sticks. The six specimens illustrated in plate 84, 25–30, are provisionally identified as such. Three of them (28, 29, 30) are exactly alike, 3⅛ inches long, nine-sixteenths inch broad; they were made by splitting lengths of peeled cottonwood twigs so as to leave one flat (28) and one arched side (29, 30); the flat sides have been rubbed down smooth, the round sides are unaltered save for the removal of the bark and the drawing of a pair of incised lines at each end. The other three sticks (25, 26, 27) are plain, round cylinders, again made from lengths of peeled branches. Their ends are carefully worked down flat with rounded edges.

The only two wooden objects recovered from the Sayodneechee burial cists are of these same types. One (A–1965) is three-fourths inch long by three-eighths inch wide, has one flat and one convex side like the three from Cave I; it also shows faint traces of incised

FIG. 93.—Stick with grooved end.

markings on the convex surface. The other (A–1964) is a bit of stick with the bark on, but with nicely finished ends; its length is 1 inch, diameter one-fourth inch.

Ball and billet (pl. 84, 22, 23). Both specimens illustrated are made of cottonwood; the former was once a round ball of excellent workmanship, but has lost part of one side; the latter is a short section of a branch with one end cut off square, the other slightly arched. The ball might perhaps have been used in a kicking game like that of the Pima.[1]

Reed whistles (pl. 84, 31–34). These range in length from 4 inches to 4¾ inches. They are made from sections of reed, and each is provided with a single "stop," burned, not cut, into one side.[2] In the two longer examples (33 and 34) the "stop" is placed at a joint in the reed; that of 34 is bound about and partly covered by a wrapping of sinew and fine fiber. The shaft of 34 is decorated with burned-in bands and with longitudinal and scroll-like patterns of burned dots.

[1] Russell, 1908, fig. 87.
[2] Hough (1914, p. 127, fig. 328) mentions burning of flute holes in the Tularosa district.

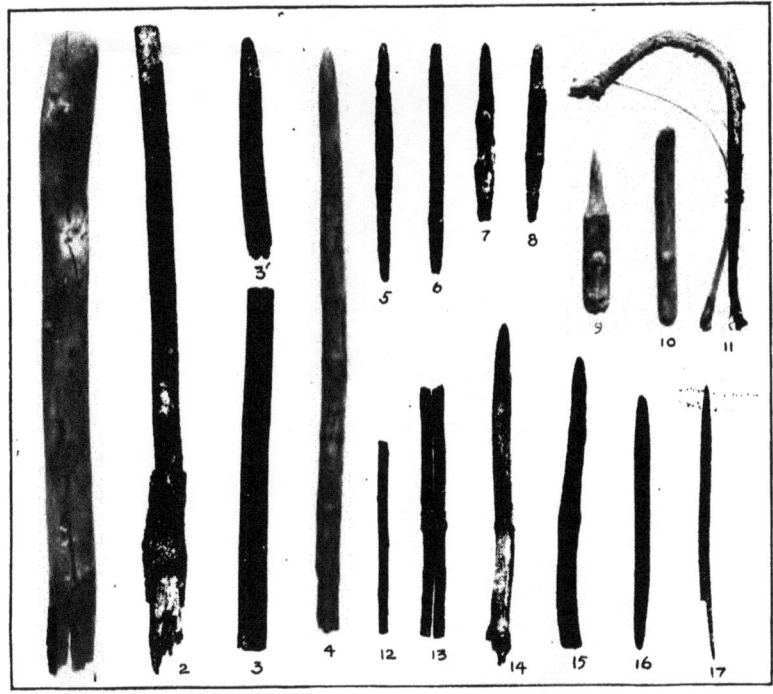

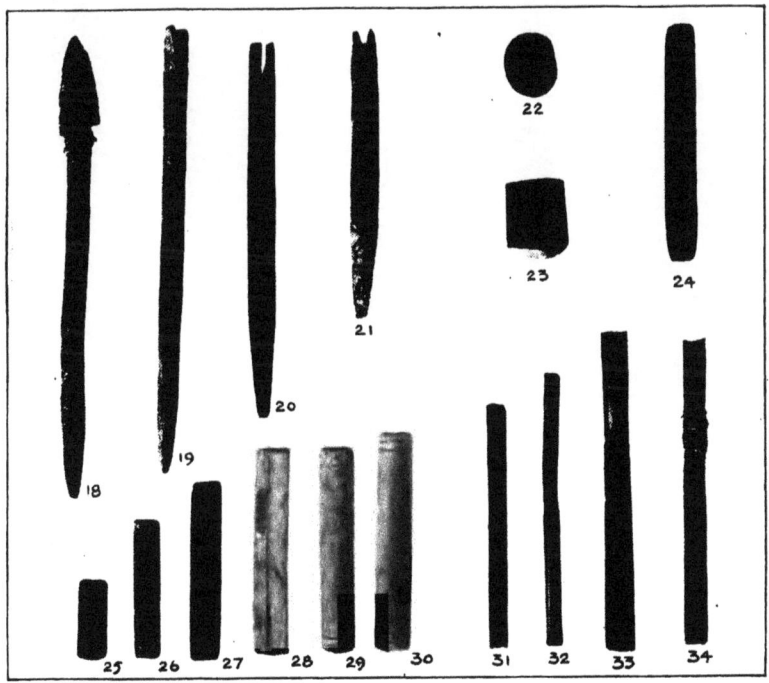

WOODEN OBJECTS

a. PAINTED BARK OBJECT

b. BARK OBJECT OF UNKNOWN USE   *c.* BONE AWLS

Stick with grooved end (fig. 93). A carefully worked piece of twig with a small groove encircling one end. In the American Museum collection from Grand Gulch are a number of sticks of this nature, tied together in pairs with strings which set into the grooves; we can hazard no guess as to their use. Length 6¾ inches.

Problematical bark object (pl. 85, *b*). This specimen is 7 inches long, 5 inches wide, and seven-eighths inch thick. It is made from a piece of yellow-pine (?) bark and in shape very roughly resembles a shovel blade. The flat surfaces show no marks of work or wear, but the edges and ends appear to have been rubbed down with some rough implement, probably a piece of coarse sandstone.

Painted bark object (pl. 85, *a*). This is a fragment broken from some larger specimen, the nature of which is not obvious. It consists of a piece of the bark of a deciduous tree, 3¾ inches wide, bent in a loop over a twig 10¼ inches long. The loop is held together by several turns of yucca string, which also engage the twig and prevent it from slipping out. One surface of the bark is decorated with zigzag vertical lines, alternating red and white; they seem to have been made by a finger dipped in wet paint.

STONE [1]

Chipped drills and scrapers, rubbing stones, hammerstones, celts, and axes; none of these types are represented in our collection. Whether or not this is of any significance we can hardly judge, our excavations in Basket Maker sites being as yet too limited; for data on this subject we cannot safely draw on other Basket Maker collections such as those in the American Museum and the Field Museum, for until the catalogues of those collections have been more thoroughly collated than is at present possible one cannot be certain which objects were taken from cliff-dwellings and which from Basket Maker caves. A few large chipped blades, perhaps knives, are shown in figure 90.

Flat pebbles, six in number (A–1930), averaging 2 inches in diameter by three-eighths inch thick, were found in a little cache with a skeleton in Cist B, Sayodneechee. They are apparently of natural shape, and show no wear of any kind nor any traces of paint.

Pipes of stone were found at Sayodneechee (two examples), and in Cave I (one example). One of the Sayodneechee pipes is of very soft, red sandstone and is in fragmentary condition (A–1911). The shape is very squat and the walls thick; what is left of the bowl is lined with a heavy "crust" deposited by the smoke. The stem hole, very small in proportion to the size of the bowl, holds the rotted remains of a wooden mouthpiece. The other Sayodneechee pipe

---

[1] For chipped points and atlatl stones see under atlatl (p. 178); for beads and pendants pp. 162–164.

(fig. 94, *b*) and the one from Kinboko (fig. 94, *a*) are much alike in size, shape, and material. The bowls are made of fine-grained limestone, banded horizontally and darkened by long use. The outer surfaces are polished, but not highly enough to obliterate entirely the marks of the pecking tool with which they were originally roughed out. The rims are thick, in one case flat, in the other rounded. The bowl of each is heavily encrusted with the carbonized remains of the smoking mixture. The relative size and shape of bowl and stem hole is best shown in the illustration. In the stem hole of the Kinboko specimen may be seen remnants of the gum that once fastened the stem in place, and the same material was used to mend an incipient crack in the bowl. The dimensions of this example are: Length, $1\frac{7}{16}$ inches; greatest diameter, $1\frac{1}{4}$ inches; thickness of rim, three-sixteenths inch; diameter of stem hole, one-eighth inch

 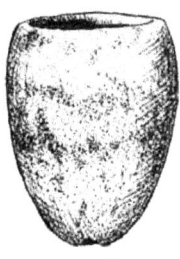 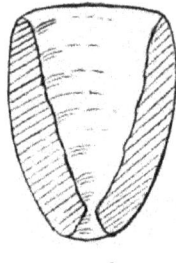 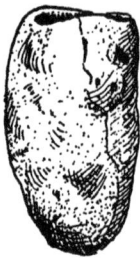

a　　　　　　　　b　　　　　　　　c　　　　　　　　d

FIG. 94.—Stone and clay pipes.

Two pipes of clay may perhaps best be described here. They were the only pottery objects found by us that are surely identifiable as Basket Maker products. One (fig. 94, *d*, Cave I) is crudely modeled from a bit of dark-gray clay; the surface is lumpy and carelessly finished. The second (A–1967, Sayodneechee) is also very poorly made and the surface is irregular. While both these specimens are longer and slimmer than the stone pipes, they are, nevertheless, much squatter than the long, tubular cliff-dwelling type; they differ from it also in having a distinct bowl much larger than the orifice which receives the stem. Although we recovered no example with the mouthpiece preserved, its nature is illustrated by a pipe in the Deseret Museum, Salt Lake City, probably from Cottonwood Canyon, Utah, which has a short, straight stem made from a 2-inch section of hollow bird bone. The bowl is of horizontally banded limestone, heavy, squat, and flat-lipped; in every way similar to our specimens. A Basket Maker pipe with wooden stem is figured by Montgomery in Moorehead's " Stone Age in North America," vol. II, p. 38, fig. 436.

PAINTS

In the cache with a skeleton in Cist B, Sayodneechee, there was a small lump of red ochre (A–1934). At the bottom of the same cist was a mass composed of yellow ochrous sandstone (A–1970) that had been ground, wet, and made into a flat cake (see p. 30 and pl. 9). Both of these finds may be presumed to represent the raw colors employed in painting such objects as the butts of the atlatl darts, the problematical bark contrivance (pl. 85, *a*), the prepared scalp (pl. 87 *a*), etc. White, seen on the scalp and on the bark object, is not present in its raw state in our collection.

BONE

Awls were not recovered in that abundance which the amount of basketry present in the caves would lead one to expect. We have but two specimens, both from Cave I; these are particularly interesting because of the string and string-and-fur wrappings which encircle them and provide a firm grip for the hand (pl. 85, *c*). It is probable that many bone implements were once so equipped, but these are, so far as we know, the only examples that have been preserved in their original condition. Somewhat awl-like, but perhaps designed for other purposes, are the three carefully made and sharp-pointed little instruments shown in plate 86, *e*.

Bone "whistles" were found, one in each of the caches with skeletons in the Sayodneechee cave (pl. 86, *a*, *b*). They are short tubes, cut from hollow bird bones, nicely finished on the ends, and provided with single "stops." Above and below the "stop" of one of them can be seen faint traces of ligatures.

Bone tubes, probably for beads, are figured with the "whistles" (pl. 86, *c*, *d*); their ends are cut off rather roughly, but their surfaces are highly polished as if by long use. The pair of larger tubes illustrated in plate 86, *f*, are of probable but not of certain Basket Maker origin, having come from a cist in Sunflower Cave (No. 4, see p. 96); their length is 7¼ inches, and each one of them is decorated at its heavier end by an encircling incised line and row of dots.

Bone dice (?). A set of small bone objects (pl. 86, *g*) was contained in a pouch of thin skin found in the general digging in Cave I. The bag was sewed up at one side and tied at the neck with fiber string. The set of "dice" consists of eight lenticular pieces eleven-sixteenths inch long and one-fourth inch wide, and three discoidal ones one-fourth inch in diameter; all have one flat and one rounded surface. The circular examples have their flat sides heavily coated with pitch; their convex sides are clear except for a single small, pitch-filled hollow (or possibly perforation) in the center. The flat sides of the long pieces are also coated with pitch, through which show transverse marks or scorings; one has two narrow lines incised across the center of its convex side.

A single lenticular "die," identical with the above, was found in the neighborhood of Cist I in this cave (A–1842); another (A–1306) in a small empty cave in the "Monuments." In the American Museum there is a larger, though otherwise similar specimen, from Pueblo Bonito; Culin [1] describes others from the vicinity of Tanner's Spring, Arizona. Small circular "dice" found in Tulerosa Cave are figured by Hough,[2] and these are said to be coated on one side with "gray mud."

The identification of these objects as dice is open to question. The heavy pitching and the careless scoring of the flat sides makes it seem possible that they were used as inlays, in which case the pitch would have served as an adhesive and the scorings have acted to give it a firmer hold on the smooth bone.

SHELL.

The only use recorded for this material is in the making of beads and pendants.

CEREMONIAL OBJECTS

"SCALP"

This specimen was found under the shoulders of the "mummy" in Cist 16, Cave I (pl. 87, a, b). It is the entire head skin of an adult, with the hair carefully dressed. In its preparation the scalp proper, including the ears, was removed from the skull in one piece; the face to the mouth in another; and the chin with the lower cheeks in a third. After drying or curing, the three sections were sewed together again, one seam running across the forehead and one down each side in front of the ears; the horizontal seam which joins the upper and lower face pieces crosses at the region of the mouth, but the skin along this sewing has been so trimmed, probably in order to insure a straight seam, that no sign of the lips remains. The eyes and nose, though shriveled, are plainly recognizable; the eyebrow and eyelash hairs are still in position. Although thorough examination under the brittle "side-bobs" of hair is impossible, one can make out the shrunken ears; through the lobe of each there runs a bit of yucca string, the attachment cords presumably for pendants which have now disappeared.

<hr>

[1] 1907, p. 48, fig. 7.   [2] 1914, p. 128, pl. 25.

a   b   c   d

BONE TUBES AND WHISTLES

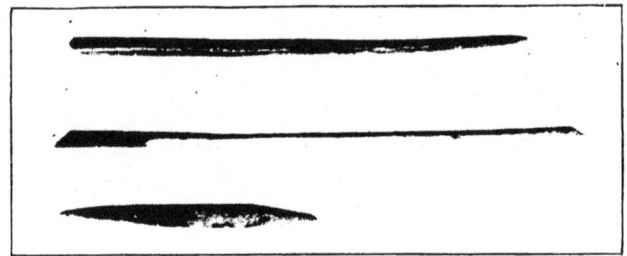

e. BONE IMPLEMENTS

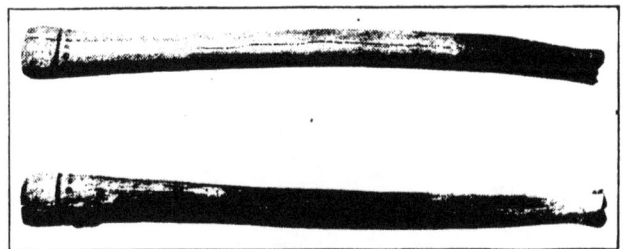

f. DECORATED BONE TUBES

g. BONE DICE AND CONTAINER

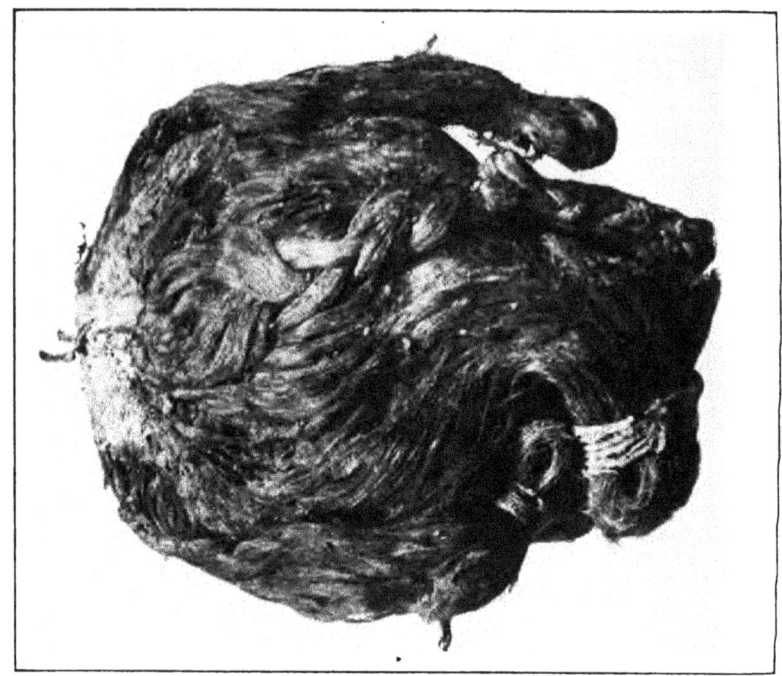

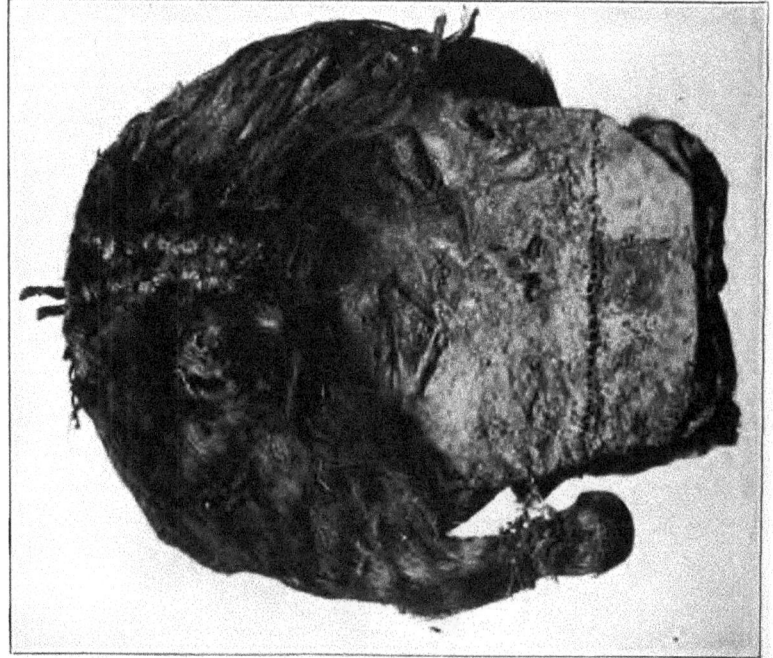

SCALP

The hair is arranged as follows: a " part " 1 inch wide, from which the hair has been clipped, runs up to a large semilunar tonsure at the crown. The brow tresses on either side are gathered together in "bobs " that fall in front of or over the ears and are tied up with wrappings of apocynum (?) string. The long hair from just behind the tonsure is braided into a thin plait, whose lower, end is doubled back on itself and bound with hair string. The remainder of the back hair is made into a single short fat "bob," string-wrapped, that falls to the nape of the neck. Plate 88, *a*, *b*, are photographs of a restoration based on this specimen.

The face has been colored rather elaborately: the "part " and tonsure are painted with a pasty, greenish-white pigment; up the center of the "part " and across the tonsure runs a narrow streak of yellow. Just under the forehead seam there is a thin, horizontal band of red. From this to a line drawn across the face half an inch below the eyes is a zone of white. A band left in the natural color of the skin extends from here to just below the nostrils, whence to the bottom the white paint is continuous, except for a broad median band of red running downward from the mouth seam.

Rove through two small holes in the tonsure is a narrow thong for suspension. In this part of the scalp there is a short rent carefully sewed up, probably a wound or a cut made in skinning.

This interesting specimen seems to have been prepared and used as a trophy. The dressing of the hair was probably done after the skin had been cured; its arrangement is peculiar and, so far as we know, is not similar to any known style used in recent times in the Plateau. Partial head shaving and the long, braided scalp lock are suggestive of Plains coiffures. The head was presumably that of an enemy, though there is no way of telling whether it was an enemy of the same or of a different stock. It may be mentioned, however, that in what are apparently Basket Maker pictographs in the " Monuments " (fig. 100) and in Grand Gulch, some of the figures are represented as wearing " side-bobs " very like those of the present specimen. As to the clipping or tonsuring of the hair nothing definite can be said. It may have been done post-mortem in the preparation of the trophy. The forehead of the " mummy " with which it was found, however, shows distinct signs of clipping, the hair having been removed forward of a line drawn over the crown of the head from ear to ear. Montgomery also states[1] that a " mummy " from the Grand Gulch district (which, from the description of its grave and the nature of the objects found with it, we take to be Basket Maker) had "the hair closely cut from the front half of the head, thus leaving the back hair only." If hair cutting was a

---

[1] 1894, p. 230.

common practice, it may account for the extraordinarily abundant use of human hair in the various arts of the Basket Makers.

PROBLEMATICAL OBJECT

Figure 95 illustrates a pointed stick; 1½ inches from its broken-off end there are tied with yucca-leaf wrappings the dried hind feet and middle leg bones of a small animal. From the stained appearance of the pointed end it would seem that the animal's body had been impaled on the stick and held thus by tying the hind legs in the position they now occupy.

BALL

The specimen (A–2377, Cave I) is an oval ball, 5½ inches long, made by winding cedar bark about a flat piece of sandstone and covering the whole with prairie-dog hide, skin side out. There is no definite evidence for placing this object, or the one previously described, among the ceremonial material; we are unable, however, to assign to either of them any utilitarian purpose.

FIG. 95.—Problematical object.

D. PICTOGRAPHS

In the Southwest the development of pictographic art is always dependent on the presence or absence of rock faces suitable for the reception of the figures. Thus, in the upper Pecos Valley of New Mexico, where there are few cliffs and those of coarse and uneven texture, drawings are rare, while in the Galisteo Basin, only a few miles to the west, the many smooth exposures of rock have led to the production of a wealth of graphic representations. The San Juan drainage in general, with its even, vertical, sandstone cliffs, was a singularly favorable region for the growth of the art, and in the Marsh Pass–Monuments district, in particular, the abundance of pictographs is very striking. They occur for the greater part in the immediate vicinity of the archeological sites, usually at the entrances to caves or at the mouths of canyons that contain dwelling places, occasionally on side or back walls of inhabited caves; conversely, they are seldom found at any great distance from ruins.

It is idle to speculate on the purpose or meaning of the pictographs. Whether they were made for religious reasons, as records of war or the chase, or whether they were done merely for amusement, can not be told without further material and a study of the motives which have led other people in other regions to produce like inscriptions.[1] Some of the examples, such as the so-called "flute-players" (p. 194), are found many miles apart, yet represent identical personages; others are apparently meaningless combinations of lines. At all events, the pictographs may be expected to have a definite classificational value which will become evident when they have been collected from other parts of the Southwest. We reproduce, accordingly, all the examples recorded by us.

The material falls into two groups, the rock-cut and the painted. The former is by far the larger, possibly because rock-cut drawings are little affected by exposure to sand scouring and other forms of weathering and have therefore been preserved in greater numbers, but more probably because their production required no paraphernalia beyond sharp-pointed stones such as are present at the foot of every cliff. The vast majority were made by pecking away the darkly weathered surface of the rock, the figures thus being of a lighter color than their surroundings. While even to-day the contrast of tone between figure and background is discernible, it is not nearly so much so as when the pecking is fresh; the ancient figures have themselves been weathered to a considerable extent, and there is seldom danger of being deceived as to the age of any examples.

The subject matter of the drawings is rather limited, mountain sheep and human figures predominating; there are also a number of four-legged creatures with short tails, and a few birds. No vegetal forms can be recognized. As to the meanings of the labyrinth-like peckings and the concentric circles of dots, it is not profitable even to guess. Although the execution of all these pictographs seems to us crude and conventional, they are for the greater part obviously naturalistic in motive; much more so than, for instance, those of the Rio Grande drainage. In most cases the figures bear no apparent relation to each other, mountain sheep, human forms, labyrinths, spirals, and the like, being pecked haphazard on the rock faces, often running over and partly or wholly obliterating each other; in some instances, however, grouping is evidently intentional, and we seem to see attempts at narrative representation. This and other features will be brought out in the following notes.

PECKED PICTOGRAPHS [2]

SINGLE FIGURES

Mountain sheep (pl. 89) are perhaps the commonest of all depictions. They range in size from 6 inches to 5 feet or even 6 feet in

---

[1] We saw a Navaho boy of 6 or 7 years drawing pictures of horses on the rocks with a bit of charcoal while his father was working in a near-by field.

[2] In each drawing of a pictograph there is introduced a bar representing a length of one foot.

length. Realism depends largely on size, no attempt having been made in the smaller examples to show such details as the division of the hoofs or the mouths and the ears. No two are exactly alike, but all conform to a very definite style, which is more easily made out from the illustrations than from description.

Anthropomorphic figures are scarcely less common than sheep. They approach true realism particularly in the hunting scenes (see below), the isolated or single examples (pl. 90) being usually rather conventional, though hairdressing (resembling the Hopi girl's style, pl. 90, *f, h*) and headdress (*l, n*) are shown. Whether the creatures with tails (*g, j, k, o, p*) are animal or human (with dance paraphernalia such as pendent foxtails) is uncertain.

Birds are rare, much more so than in the Grand Gulch–Montezuma Creek country to the north of the San Juan. The two most striking examples are shown in plate 91, *a, b*. The species is, of course, doubtful. It should be remarked that the appendage with an arrowhead-like termination on the neck of one and the small projection from the breast of the other may be the remains of earlier drawings, the latter possibly the head of a mountain sheep.

Aside from the above types and a few snakes and hand prints, the rest of the single figures recorded are of unknown nature.

GROUPS

Plate 93, *b*, figure 96, and plate 94 show groupings of figures that were presumably made with narrative intention. Each one of these sets occupies a single rock face that contains no drawings other than those reproduced.[1] Plate 93, *b* (Ruin 5 Canyon, Hagoé) records the largest lot; in it are a number of mountain sheep, some of which are accompanied by series of hoof marks. There is also a set of barefoot human tracks following the ithyphallic sheep on the left. The individual who made the tracks evidently came to a stop behind the sheep, as right and left foot are placed side by side instead of in the alternating order in which they approach the spot. In the upper right-hand corner is another series of human footprints made by a man who seems to be lassoing a sheep (compare also the sheep at center bottom with footprints and with reata about horns). In the same quarter is a partly obliterated humpbacked figure holding a long object to its mouth; the reclining position should be noted.[2]

Figure 96, *b* (from the opposite side of the same canyon) has obvious similarities to the foregoing; there are the same tracks lead-

---

[1] Except that the large bird (pl. 91, *b*) was placed a few feet below and to the right of the group (pl. 93, *b*).

[2] The act of holding something to the mouth will be referred to for convenience as "flute-playing," though it is by no means certain that some other performance is not indicated, such as stick-swallowing, cloud-blowing, or even, though less probably, shooting with a blowgun.

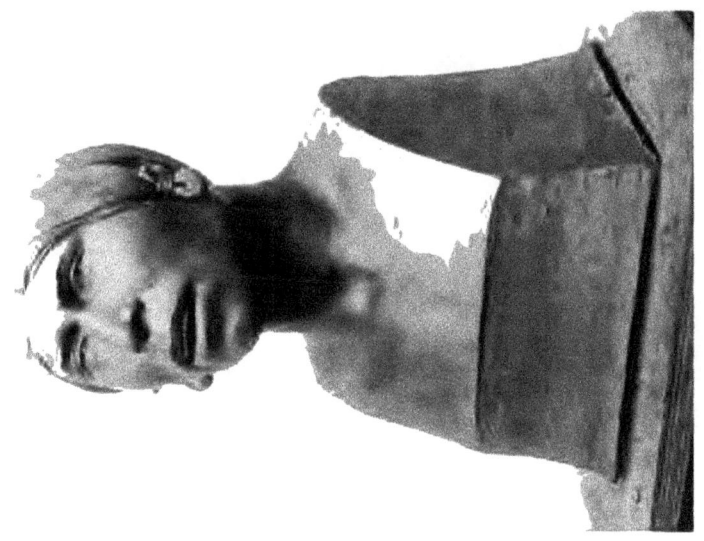

a

b

RESTORATION FROM SCALP

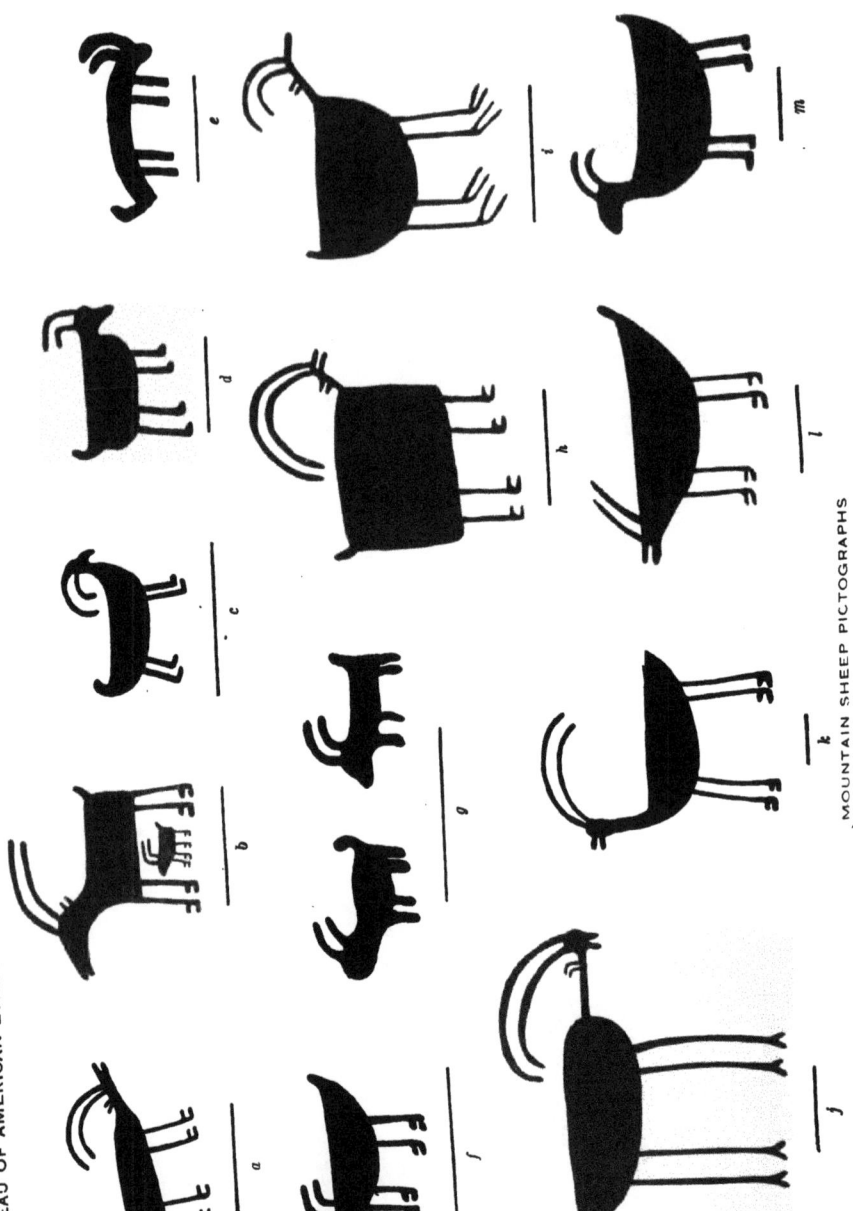

MOUNTAIN SHEEP PICTOGRAPHS

a   b   c   d

e   f   g   h

i   j   k   l

m   n   o   p

HUMAN AND OTHER PICTOGRAPHS

MOUNTAIN SHEEP PICTOGRAPHS

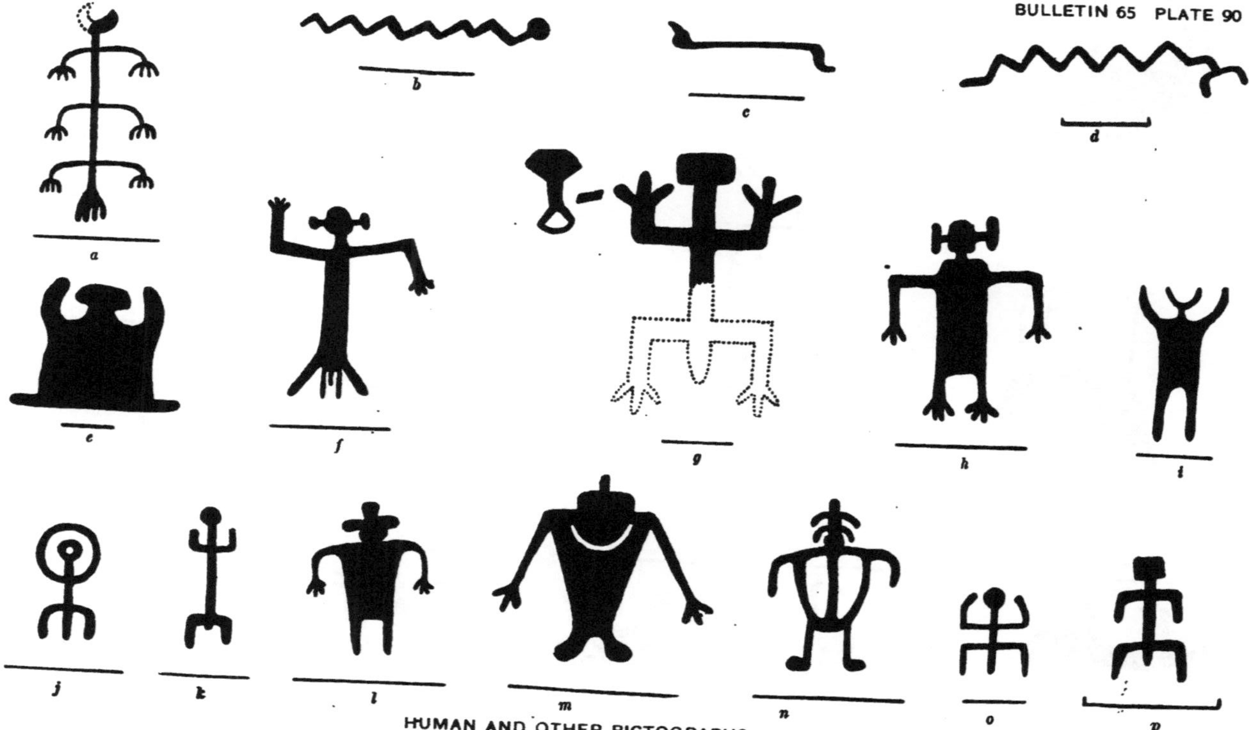

HUMAN AND OTHER PICTOGRAPHS

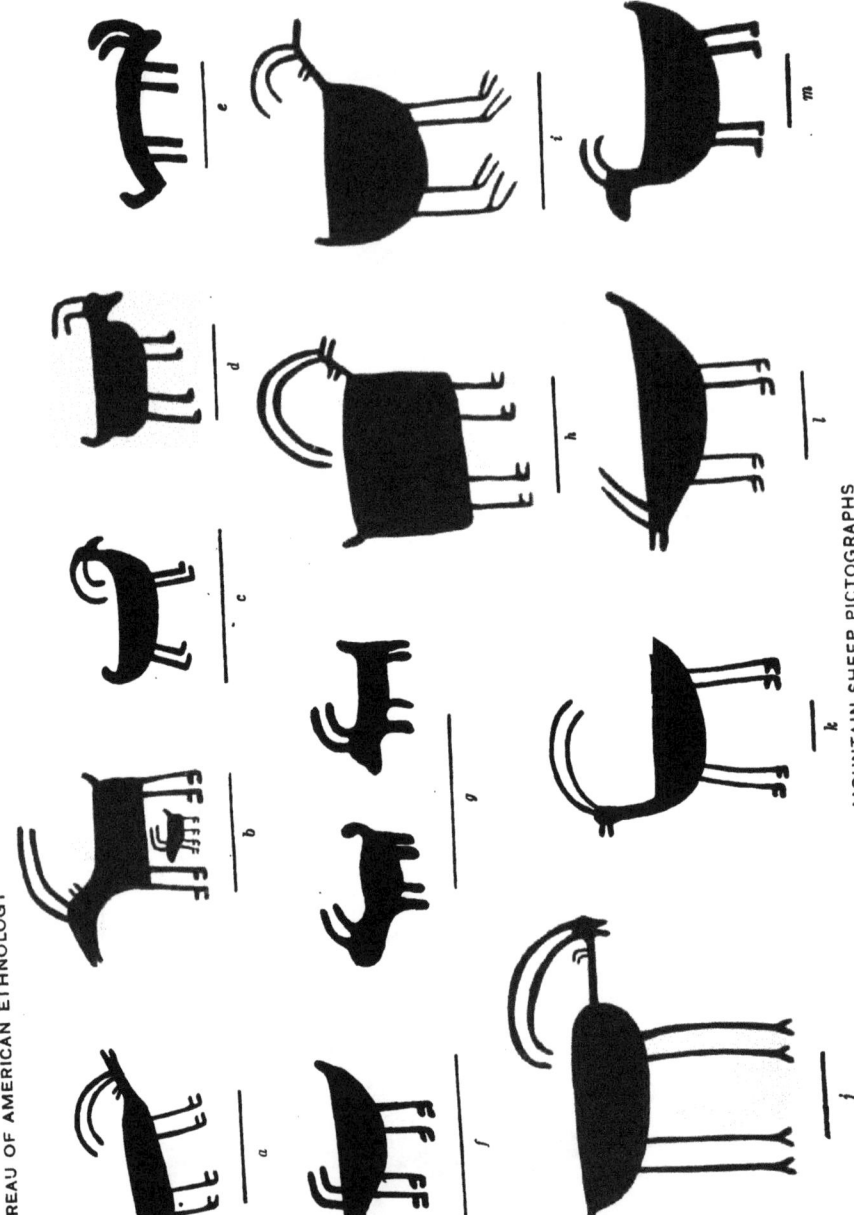

MOUNTAIN SHEEP PICTOGRAPHS

HUMAN AND OTHER PICTOGRAPHS

MISCELLANEOUS PICTOGRAPHS

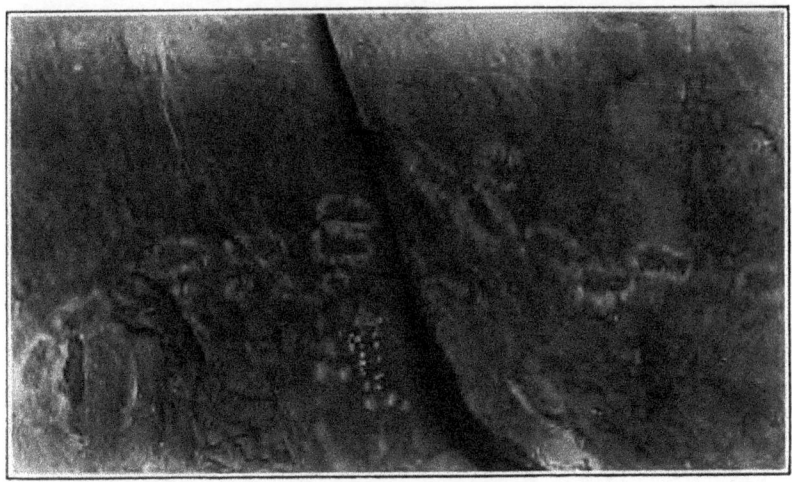

a. SANDAL PRINTS IN RUIN 6

b. PECKED HAND PRINTS IN CAVE I

a. PECKED MOUNTAIN SHEEP

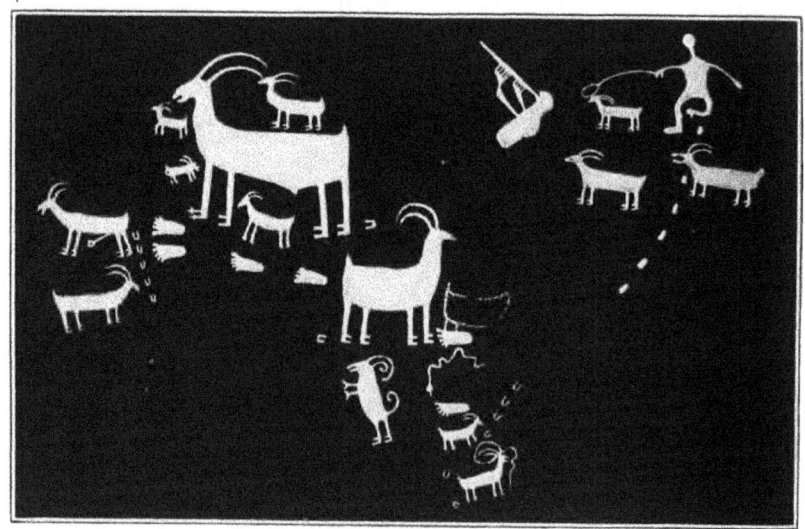

b. GROUP OF PECKED FIGURES

ing to an ithyphallic sheep and also human footprints following after and coming to a full stop behind the animal. In front is a humpbacked individual with an object held to its mouth. Under a large barefoot track at the right is a small "flute-player" in a peculiar position on his back with his legs in the air.

Figure 96, *a*, from a hundred yards or so higher up the canyon, shows five "flute-players," four of whom are humpbacked, lie on their backs, and show the peculiar leg position noted above. The fifth is upright and phallic. There is also a series of footprints.

Plate 94, *d–f*, are perhaps not true groups; they are included in the series because they occur on rock faces free from other drawings. Examples *a–c*, however, are of interest for comparison with the Hagoé groups just discussed. Of these, *a* shows a pair of "fluteplayers" analogous in attitude to, and with the same humped

FIG. 96.—Pictograph groups near Ruin 5.

backs as, the ones from Hagoé. These two formed part of a large agglomeration of pictographs in a cave near Ruin A, Marsh Pass, but the majority of the others, among which were sheep, were too much time-worn for certain recording. Pictographs *b* and *c* are from the lower reaches of Kinboko just above Ruin A. In one a humpbacked individual is shooting a sheep; in the other a humpbacked figure is associated with two sheep, and in front of him is a single sandal print.

The one common element in all these groups is the humpbacked figure. He is associated with sheep (hunting concept?) in all but one (fig. 96, *a*); in four with footprints (tracking or hunting concept?); in three with phallic manifestations; in four with "flute-playing" and the reclining attitude. This personage may therefore be defined as a humpbacked creature connected in some way with hunting, with phallicism, and with "flute-playing." That this particular conception, in some of its phases at least, was a very definite one is shown by the close similarity in shape and attitude between the figures from Hagoé and those from Marsh Pass, sites a number of miles apart. That it was exceedingly widely disseminated in the Southwest is proved by the following instances: In Fewkes Canyon,

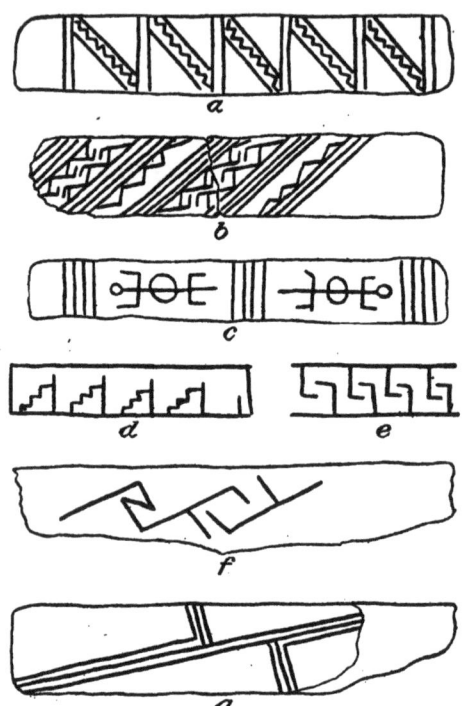

Mesa Verde, there are painted on the wall of a room in what seems to be a ceremonial building humpbacked phallic individuals shooting mountain sheep;[1] in a caveate cliff-room on the Pajarito Plateau, in central New Mexico, is carved a series of humpbacked phallic figures lying on their backs and "playing flutes"; a still more distant example may perhaps be recognized in the humpbacked male figures of the erotic figurine groups from Casas Grandes, Chihuahua, Mexico.[2]

FIG. 97.—Incised designs on building stones, Ruins 8 and A.

INCISED PICTOGRAPHS

These are distinctly rare, the only example in graphic pitography being the bowstrings of the hunter in plate 94, *c*. Incised decorations on building stones were found at Ruins 8 and A (fig. 97), and the authors have seen similar ones on the walls of Betatakin, Sagi Canyon. With the exception of figure 97, *c*, all of them are geometric and suggest the decorations of pottery. Comparison should be made

---

[1] See Fewkes, 1916, *a*, fig. 2 and pl. vii; in the latter there seems also to be a semi-reclining "flute-player" (*d*).

[2] See Kidder, 1916, p. 259, and pl. iii. As is there pointed out, some connection with Kokopelli, the Hopi humpbacked phallic deity, is to be suspected. Cf. Fewkes, 1903, pl. xxv.

with incised building stones recorded by Dr. Fewkes from Sun Temple, Mesa Verde.[1]

PAINTED PICTOGRAPHS

The statement has been made[2] that painted pictographs were characteristic of the Basket Maker culture and rock-cut ones of the Cliff-dwellers. It is true, indeed, that most if not all of the rock-cut examples collected by us were found at or near cliff-dwellings and were probably a product of that culture, and also that certain painted figures are probably Basket Maker. The general distinction, however, does not hold good, for we have seen painted pictographs so placed on cave walls that they could have been made only by people sitting or standing on the roofs of the cliff-houses themselves. Such a series, representing sheep, tailed anthropomorphic

FIG. 98.—Painted pictograph.

creatures, and snakes, was present in Ruin 7 (these were recorded, but were unfortunately lost in the field). Also in cliff-dwellings are seen hand prints in red or white paint, generally slapped on with the wet hand (pl. 33, a), less commonly " stenciled " by laying the hand on the rock and dabbing about it with paint (pl. 92, a). The latter figure illustrates an interesting series of stenciled sandal prints; the imaginary individual is shown by his tracks to have walked to a little projection in the vertical wall, to have jumped down from it, landing with both feet together, and then to have continued his journey.

FIG. 99.—Painted pictograph.

All the foregoing are presumably Cliff-house; a second class comprises painted pictographs the cultural affiliations of which can not as yet be definitely determined. They are shown in figures 98 and 99 and plate 95.[3] The first two are from the upper walls of the cave near Ruin A that held the hump-backed figures described above (pl. 94, a). The large white sheep conforms rather closely to the pecked examples; the red foot-shaped objects with it and those in figure 99 are of a type which we have not noted elsewhere; the red, white, and yellow spirals are also peculiar. White hand

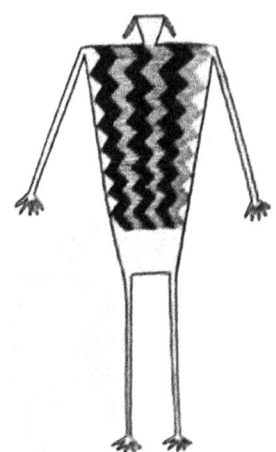

FIG. 100.—Square-shouldered painted figure.

[1] 1916. p. 12 and fig. 11.
[2] Pepper. 1902.
[3] In the drawings of painted pictographs outlined spaces represent white, black represents red, and shading yellow.

prints are associated with both these groups. Plate 95, *a*, shows two
long snakes, a small sheep, an anthropomorph (?), and some hand
prints, all done in white paint; plate 95, *b*, is a circular red painting
accompanied by two other objects of unknown meaning. The former
has been much battered and is also touched up with charcoal, presumably by Navaho.

SQUARE-SHOULDERED FIGURES

These large and very peculiar anthropomorphic representations we
believe to be of Basket Maker origin, because we found them on
the walls of the strictly Basket Maker Cave II and because at

FIG. 101. — Square-shouldered
painted figure.

Ruin 4, where they are very abundant,
they and their attendant hand prints are
obviously older than the Cliff-house structure. Similar figures are also common in
Butler's Wash, Grand Gulch, and other
typically Basket Maker canyons, and are,
so far as we know, absent from the Mesa
Verde and other localities which the
Basket Makers do not seem to have inhabited. These paintings are all much
alike (figs. 100, 101, and pls. 96, 97, *a*);
full-front human forms with triangular
bodies, long arms and legs and small
heads. They range in height from 1 foot
to 5 feet, and are usually roughly daubed on the rocks in chalky
white paint. The bodies of a number of them bear zigzag decorations in red and yellow (figs. 100, 101), and some show headdresses
or perhaps hairdressing. In plate 97, *a*, may be seen two series of
small red squares arranged in step formation; these appear to be of
the same period as the white paintings.

NAVAHO PICTOGRAPHS

During the course of our explorations we collected a few drawings
which, because of their freshness and of the nature of their subjects,
we can assign to a very recent period. We saw some of them being
drawn by Navaho children, and all are probably of Navaho origin.
Charcoal seems to be the favorite medium, the walls of many caves,
particularly those of Cave I, being decorated with scrawly pictures
of men on horseback, sheep, cattle, wagons, and deer; some of these
charcoal sketches can be made out overlying the large white square-
shouldered pictographs in plate 97, *a*. Incised, or rather scratched,
drawings of the same nature are shown in plate 97, *b*, *c*.

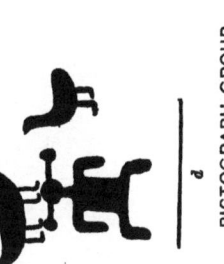

PICTOGRAPH GROUP

a .

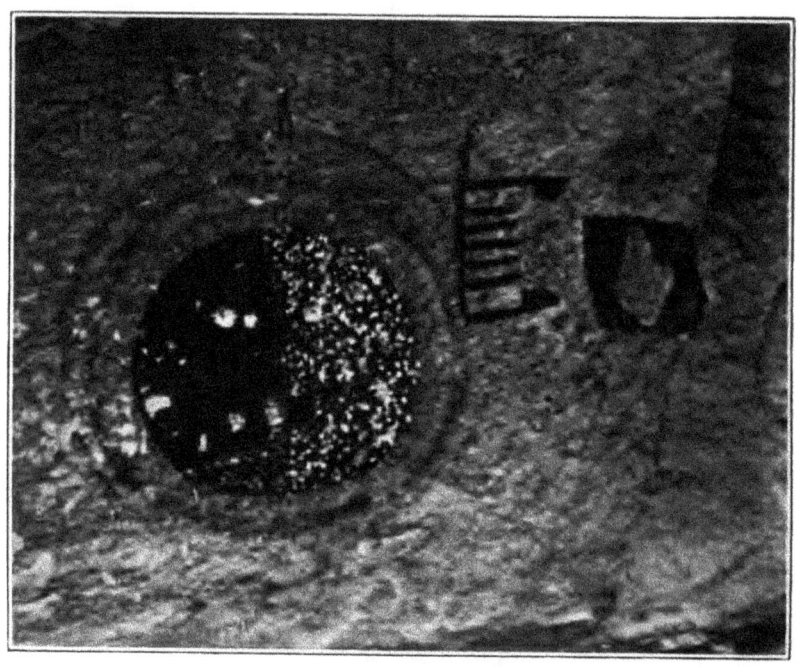

b

PAINTED PICTOGRAPHS

a

b

SQUARE-SHOULDERED PAINTED FIGURES

a

b

c

a. SQUARE-SHOULDERED PAINTED FIGURES. *b, c.* NAVAHO INCISED DRAWINGS

Of quite different style, but surely recent and probably also made by the Navaho, are the strange creatures reproduced in figure 102. Some of these are incised, some drawn in charcoal. They presumably depict dance characters or mythical personages, but we were unable

FIG. 102.—Navaho drawings.

to collect any information as to whether they were the work of children (like the charcoal drawings), or whether they were made with some more serious purpose by adults. It will be noticed that the bodies are of hourglass shape, a feature not observed in any of the ancient examples.

III. CONCLUSION

AS was pointed out in the introduction to the section on Material Culture, our explorations yielded remains of what we consider to be two distinct cultures—the Cliff-house [1] and the Basket Maker. There is some evidence also of a third culture, the Slab-house. In this concluding section we present certain notes and speculations based on the data gathered from these groups.

CLIFF-HOUSE

To summarize: We have abundant remains, in the form of cliff-dwellings and surface ruins, of a fairly homogeneous culture occupying the whole region. It is characterized by stone houses built above ground, specialized ceremonial rooms or kivas, and high development of pottery. Corn, beans, and squash were cultivated, cotton was grown, and the turkey was domesticated. The textile arts were well developed, particularly in loom weaving, twilled work (matting, baskets, cotton bags), and twined work (cord sandals). Very good coiled basketry was produced, but apparently in rather limited quantities. Stone implements, both polished and chipped, were not remarkable either for abundance or for excellence of workmanship.

All the cliff-dwellings and pueblos examined were enough alike in architecture, kiva construction, and pottery to warrant their being assigned to a single culture period. There are, however, differences between the pottery of some of the small settlements (Ruins 2, 3, 4, 5, and 7) on the one hand, and a group consisting of small houses 6 and 8 and the pueblos of Marsh Pass on the other, that seem to show a variation of some sort within the culture, and therefore point to a fairly extended period of occupancy. The wares of the former division lack in general the features characteristic of high specialization (shapes such as the flat-topped ollas and colanders; intensively elaborated decorations as, "under-framework" in black-and-white; white-edged designs in polychrome) which are found so commonly in the wares of the second group. This would seem to indicate that the ruins of the first group were somewhat earlier than those of the second, and also that they were of somewhat wider distribution;

---

[1] Including, of course, the pueblos in the open; a better term is, perhaps, "Kiva culture," cf. Kidder, 1917.

also that toward the end of the period of occupancy of this district the population withdrew to the vicinity of Marsh Pass, where the culmination of the culture, so to speak, was reached in the pueblos of the pass and the great cliff-houses of its tributary Sagi Canyon.[1]

Regarding the culture as a unit, it may be assigned a position as a subgroup of the great northeastern Kiva-culture.[2] That branch of southwestern civilization has not yet been clearly delineated, but it appears to have comprised all the true cliff-dwellings and pueblos of the San Juan drainage, with outposts running down and across the Colorado and, in somewhat later times, down the Rio Grande. At present, in addition to the division under discussion (which we may term the Kayenta), we can recognize in the San Juan district two definite subgroups: Chaco Canyon and Mesa Verde-McElmo. The position of two other groups is less certain: The Montezuma Creek, which should perhaps be classed with Mesa Verde; and the Aztec-Bloomfield, whose ruins, so far as we can tell from surface indications, are allied architecturally to Chaco Canyon and ceramically to Mesa Verde.

This very general classification of San Juan sites leaves unaccounted for the great and important mass of remains in the Canyon de Chelly and the lower Chinlee. Of these the authors have no personal knowledge beyond their very brief examination of the Nockito cliff-house.

The Kayenta group differs from the others most strikingly in pottery and in kiva construction. Its redwares are much more abundant than are those of any other San Juan region, the polychrome redware being, so to speak, its trade-mark. Black-and-white also differs in its shapes (handled bowls, colanders; lack of mugs and pitchers) and decorations ("heavy" designs, etc.) from that of the other groups.

The kivas are characterized, to permit ourselves a paradox, by their lack of character; they do not show the strict orthodoxy of form displayed by the six-pilastered Mesa Verde and Montezuma Creek type,[3] or of the low-benched style which appears to belong to the larger Chaco Canyon ruins.[4] As was brought out in the text, they vary greatly in size and interior arrangement, some having small recesses, some very large ones, many none at all.

---

[1] This process—i. e., early diffusion in small sites, later concentration in large centers with high cultural specialization, and lastly more or less abrupt abandonment of whole regions—is a common phenomenon in southwestern archeology. Examples are: Chaco Canyon, Mesa Verde, Lower Gila, Casas Grandes. It has not yet been satisfactorily explained, though an attempt to account for it on the basis of climatic change has been made by Huntington (1914).

[2] Kidder, 1917. The arrangement there given is somewhat different from the present one; final classification is not yet possible.

[3] See Fewkes, 1908, 1909, 1911, a; Morley, 1908; Kidder, 1910.

[4] Pepper, 1899.

. Further differences between Kayenta ruins and those of other groups will undoubtedly be brought out by close studies of the architecture and of the minor arts.

Having established, to our own satisfaction at least, that the Kayenta type is a real one, we must consider its range and its place in the general archeological scheme. For this we are at present almost wholly dependent on the evidence afforded by pottery.

The Canyon de Chelly and its tributary Del Muerto produce, if the many collections said to have come from them are correctly labeled, a certain percentage of Kayenta ware, and we found a good deal of it at Nockito in the lower Chinlee. This is so far our eastern and southeastern limit for seemingly home-made pieces. Vessels of Kayenta type are fairly common in the cliff-houses of Grand Gulch and White Canyon to the northeast. What the wares to the north and west, in the Navaho mountain country, may be, we do not know; nor have we as yet any knowledge of the pottery of the numerous large ruins of Nitsi Canyon. In the southwest the type seems to crop out in the vicinity of the Hopi towns and at certain sites on the Little Colorado.[1] Dr. Fewkes states[2] that the pottery of the Black Falls pueblos is similar to that of Marsh Pass, but as to this opinion we cannot pass judgment, no pieces from those sites having been figured.

We have found small sherds of Kayenta polychrome ware without white edgings at the following places: Pueblo Bonito and Hungo Pavie in Chaco Canyon; Cliff Palace in the Mesa Verde; Alkali Ridge in the Montezuma Creek drainage. At none of these sites was there noticed white-edged polychrome or "heavy" designed black-and-white. As these two styles are considered by us to belong to the later stage of the Kayenta culture, we infer that the earlier Kayenta ruins were roughly contemporaneous with the Mesa Verde and Chaco Canyon periods. This supposition is still further borne out by the finding in Ruin 7 of a typical Mesa Verde bowl sherd.

Going rather farther afield, a certain distant resemblance may be pointed out between Kayenta wares and the polychrome pottery of the lower Gila (Casa Grande, etc.). This is seen in the use of the current offset toothed decoration (fig. 58), the stepped line, and the prevalence of white edgings. Such comparisons as this are, however, rather unprofitable in the present stage of our investigation.

Turning to the kivas, we find that those examined by us are all round and subterranean, all possess the ventilator and fire pit, probably all had the deflector and perhaps all had sipapus, though several of them were in so ruinous a condition that the latter features could not surely be identified. Although some had recesses (pre-

---

[1] Consult plates in Fewkes, 1898 and 1904.
[2] 1911, p. 11.

sumably corresponding in function and surely in some way related to the recesses between the pilasters of Mesa Verde–McElmo–Montezuma Creek kivas) none of them had pilasters. Their variable character is marked. In relation to the Mesa Verde–McElmo–Montezuma Creek type they must be either early and unformed, late and degenerate, or peripheral. More than this can not be decided, but we incline to believe that the orthodox six-pilastered kiva is a product of the northern side of the San Juan and that our specimens are probably the result of a southwestern spread of the subterranean kiva cult. The earlier examples in our district would, in that case, be considered as peripheral.

One interesting and at present inexplicable point is that in Turkey House, Sagi Canyon, there is a six-pilastered kiva. This ruin has pottery which is quite different from, and evidently earlier than, that of Kitsiel, though the two houses are only a few hundred yards apart.

A further peculiar state of affairs is to be observed in the Sagi ruins: some of the houses have only round kivas, very similar, apparently, to the ones excavated by us; others have only rectangular ceremonial rooms which, however, seem to show round kiva influence in a form of deflector placed opposite the lateral entryway.[1] The former class is well illustrated by Kitsiel, the latter by Betatakin. The pottery from these two ruins is of the highly specialized Kayenta style, and all the evidence leads to the belief that they were very nearly if not actually contemporaneous. While we can offer no explanation of this phenomenon, it emphasizes the fact that although the archeological problems of northern Arizona are very complex, there is a wealth of material available for their solution.

SLAB-HOUSE

To name a culture on so slight a body of evidence as that uncovered in Ruin 5 is perhaps unwise. It is certain, however, that the remains both of houses and of pottery brought to light in the lower levels of that site differ markedly from those found at the top; their position also renders it certain that they are older.

It is probable that the Slab-house remains are intermediate in time between the developed Cliff-houses and the Basket Maker habitations, but their cultural affinities to the two cannot be determined until we have more data. The similarity between Slab-house black-and-white pottery decoration and that of some of the Chaco Canyon black-and-white is another problem about which it is idle to speculate at the present time. As to the range of the Slab-house type of culture we are ignorant; we found it a few miles to the east near Ruin

---

[1] See Fewkes, 1911, and Cummings, 1915.

7, traces of it at Ruin 9, and Cummings's older houses in Sagiotsosi seem to us to be surely Slab-house. Dr. Kroeber has recently discovered in the Zuñi Valley sherds which are very similar to the Ruin 5 specimens.[1]

BASKET MAKER

That the finds made in the Kinboko caves and at Sayodneechee are the products of a culture different from that of the cliff-dwellings and pueblos of the region, the authors are entirely convinced. There is also no doubt in their minds that the objects are of the same culture as that discovered in Grand Gulch, Utah, by the Wetherill brothers and called by them "Basket Maker." This name was adopted by Pepper in his short paper[2] on the Wetherill and the McLoyd and Graham collections; as it has undoubted priority, we continue its use.

This culture, as reported by Pepper, differed from that of the Cliff-dwellers in various particulars: skull deformation was not practiced; houses were round, subterranean chambers; the atlatl was used to the apparent exclusion of the bow and arrow; pottery was rare, crude, and basket-marked; basketry, on the other hand, was extremely abundant. Our investigations served to confirm most of these statements;[3] we have also been able to add to the list a number of other differences, the more important of which are shown in the accompanying tabulation. It should be remembered, however, that our knowledge of the Basket Maker culture is still far more scanty than our knowledge of the Cliff-dweller. Further field work may prove that some of the stated differences do not exist; it will also probably add others not now recognized.

TABLE OF DIFFERENCES—CLIFF DWELLER AND BASKET MAKER

CLIFF DWELLER	BASKET MAKER
HOUSES	
Square-cornered, masonry rooms built above ground.	Little data; perhaps only semisubterranean cists.
BURIALS	
In individual graves, in the open, or in the rubbish of houses.	In cists, rock lined, or dug in hardpan of caves, often more than one body in a cist.

[1] See Kroeber, 1916, p. 37. The type also occurs in the Hopi country (author's explorations in 1917).

[2] 1902.

[3] In Kidder, 1917, it was stated that we were able to confirm them all. Further study, however, inclines us to reserve opinion on basket-marked pottery, round subterranean rooms, and proved greater antiquity for Basket Maker remains.

CLIFF DWELLER	BASKET MAKER

CRANIA

Strongly deformed back.	Undeformed, long, scaphoid.

FOOD

Turkey domesticated.	Apparently no domestication of turkey.
Corn of various well-developed types grown.	Flint corn only (?).
Beans abundant.	Beans apparently not grown.

SANDALS

Twilled types of whole yucca leaves very abundant.	Absent.
Side-loop tie.	Absent.
Fine-cord type has pointed toe and bottom reinforcement of raised decoration covering only part of sole.	Fine-cord type has square, fringed toe and bottom reinforcement covering whole sole.
Hair-cord ties rare or absent.	Hair-cord ties abundant.

CRADLES

Rigid (twig-backed) cradles of oval shape.	Rigid (twig-backed) cradles of guitar shape.
Absent (?).	Grass-edge and cedar-bark cradles abundant.

BASKETRY

Twilled yucca ring baskets abundant.	Very rare or absent.
Coiled basketry rare, but very fine.	Extremely abundant, but somewhat coarser.

MATTING

Twilled rush mats abundant.	Rare or absent.

CORDS AND THREADS

Cotton common.	Absent (?).
Hair string rare.	Very common and used for a great variety of purposes.

FINE-CORD FABRICS

Loom cloth common.	Absent.
Absent.	Twined bags common.
Turkey feather cloth common.	Absent.
Fur cloth rare.	Common.

WEAPONS

Bow and arrow.	Spear thrower.

CLIFF DWELLER	BASKET MAKER
	PIPES
Long and slim.	Short and squat.
	POTTERY
Very abundant.	Rare, perhaps even absent.

A few elements of the Basket Maker culture may be somewhat more fully discussed.

HOUSES

Our information on this important subject is still very meager. The Sayodneechee cave was a burial place pure and simple, containing no sign of occupancy as a dwelling other than a large ash bed, which, as was stated in the description, may perhaps be the product of crematory fires. In the case of Cave I, Kinboko, we found a great number of small, stone-lined cists. All these, however, had been so pulled about and ransacked by their ancient despoilers that we were unable to determine positively whether they had all been used for burial or whether they were originally made for shelters, storage, etc., and used secondarily for sepulchers as occasion required. It should be remembered, in this connection, that such close proximity to the dead was not repugnant to the Pueblo people; we have instances without number of burial in the rooms, under the floors, and in the courts of buildings which we know to have been inhabited after the interments were made. In Cave I there was some but not a great deal of rubbish of Basket Maker occupancy.

The second Kinboko cave was without much doubt domiciliary, for it contained a considerable amount of ash and other débris; furthermore, no burials were found in it with the exception of parts of the skeleton of a very young baby.

The structures in these caves are of three kinds: (1) The large, shallow oval pit with nests of grass disposed about its edge (Cave II). (2) Small cists made by lining the sides of holes in the loose sand with stone slabs (Caves I and II). (3) Jar-shaped excavations in hardpan with little or no reinforcement (Sayodneechee).

As to the purpose of these constructions, the most natural supposition is that the large oval pit was used as a sleeping place, the grass nests serving as beds. The stone-lined cists are more puzzling; their small size excludes them from consideration as regular dwellings, though if the people did not object to lying curled up in a rather squirrel-like position they might have been utilized as sleeping places. In some cases they served as graves. Jar-shaped cists excavated in hardpan contained only burials at Sayodneechee. Similar cists, though smaller, were described to us by Clayton and John Wetherill as having been used in the Grand Gulch region, primarily for storage, secondarily for burial. The examples cited by Cummings[1] from Sagiotsosi are probably Basket Maker products, the square-toed sandals found in one of them making, to our minds, the identification almost certain.

Round subterranean rooms, some as large as 22 feet in diameter (construction not specified) and containing Basket Maker remains, are reported from Grand Gulch by McLoyd and Graham.[2] We found nothing resembling these.

Summing up the above information, it would appear that the Basket Makers used caves to some extent as dwelling places, but that they seldom if ever erected in them any houses worthy of the name. The stone-lined cists may have been used for sleeping places, storage bins, and, perhaps, secondarily, sometimes even primarily, for burial. The caves were presumably inhabited, but seemingly not for long periods (comparative thinness of débris of occupancy). It seems probable, therefore, that the people lived during a large part of the year in the open, where they presumably erected temporary houses analogous to the summer shelters of the Navaho; that they used the caves only in winter, perhaps even only during particularly severe weather. Whether burial was always in caves or, as among the cliff-dwelling people, sometimes in caves, sometimes in the open, we have at present no means of knowing. If the Basket Makers lived for a large part of each year outside the caves, we may expect eventually to find traces of their summer encampments. The identification of such sites will not be an easy matter as, with the exception of pipes and the hemispherical type of bead, neither likely to be abundant in mere dwelling places, we have so far been unable to identify any objects characteristic of the Basket Makers, which are made of imperishable substances and which are therefore likely to be found in the open.

THE SPEAR THROWER, OR ATLATL

The spear thrower with two-finger grip (made either by attaching loops, by cutting holes in the shaft, or by deeply notching its sides) has a very interesting distribution.[3] It occurred most commonly, apparently, in central Mexico, but ranged outward to the north into Coahuila, to the south as far as Panama, and probably east into the Antilles.[4] Examples were recovered by Cushing at San Marcos, Florida. A specimen, presumably of this type, represented by a

---

[1] 1910, pp. 13, 14.
[2] Quoted by Pepper, 1902, p. 7.
[3] We leave out of consideration the usually asymetrical Eskimo type, the Amazonian single finger-hole type, and the Peruvian style with tied-on gripping piece. None of these can be believed to have more than a very distant relationship to the class under discussion. See Krause, 1905, p. 636.
[4] Krause, p. 632.

bone spur tip only, was found by Peabody and Farabee in a mound in Mississippi.[1]

Beyond Coahuila the spear thrower has not been recorded south of northern Arizona and southeastern Utah, except from caves on the upper Gila.[2] In the Utah-Arizona district, however, the atlatl was in very common use among the Basket Makers; but it has never yet been reliably reported from any true cliff-dwelling or pueblo site.

The extreme northerly occurrence of the two-finger spear thrower is from the guano caves of Churchill County, Nevada;[3] while the farthest west is from Santa Barbara, California, in the form of a specimen collected by Vancouver and now in the British Museum.[4]

What conclusions are to be drawn from this very extended yet partially disconnected range? It can hardly be believed that so peculiar and highly specialized a device could have originated independently in the several different regions. It is possible that it spread outward from Mexico; to Florida and the Gulf coast, via the Antilles; to Utah via northern Mexico and the Rio Grande, and from Utah north and west into Nevada; to California via the lower Colorado River and the coast, perhaps thence inland to Nevada. Further exploration of caves, where the atlatl, being a wooden implement, is only likely to be preserved, may serve to fill some of the gaps in these seemingly improbable migration routes.

A second supposition, and in some ways a more reasonable one, is that the spear thrower was an implement of very wide distribution in early times, that it was superseded throughout most of its range by the development or introduction of the bow, and that it persisted only in certain regions where local conditions favored its retention. That the spear thrower is a device not out of place in very primitive forms of culture is shown by its appearance in the French caves and among the aborigines of Australia and New Guinea; that it was capable of persisting into much higher civilizations is proved by its use among the Nahua and Maya.

POTTERY

We found potsherds and whole vessels in each of the three Basket Maker caves examined; they were in every case, however, of the wares typical of the cliff-dwellings and pueblos of the region; and they occurred in all instances in the surface sand overlying the levels from which the Basket Maker remains were taken. In the Basket Maker débris of occupancy and in the cists proper no single sherd was recovered. The only pot which might be assigned to that

---

[1] *Peabody Museum Papers*, vol. III, no. 2, pl. xx.
[2] Hough, 1914, p. 21, and pl. 20, fig. 2.
[3] Information from Mr. Loud of the Affiliated Colleges Museum, San Francisco, Cal.
[4] Krause, 1905, fig. 37.

culture was the spherical black vessel from below the floor of the Sunflower Cliff-house (p. 95, and pl. 59, *a*).

As against this seeming absence of pottery, we have the following statement of McLoyd and Graham:

The third kind of pottery is very valuable, less than fifty pieces having been found up to date, and those in the underground rooms that have been mentioned as being underneath the cliff-dwellings and in the same caves. It is a very crude unglazed ware, some of the bowls showing the imprint of the baskets, in which they were formed.[1]

It is possible that the Basket Makers of Grand Gulch produced more pottery than did those of the Kayenta district; it should be remembered, however, that basket-marked pottery, though rare, is to be found in many cliff-dwellings and pueblos, and it may be that McLoyd and Graham, knowing basketry to be typical of the Basket Maker culture, concluded that basket-marked pottery must be associated with it. We have not been able to examine the pieces referred to.

The question of the presence or absence of pottery is still, then, an open one. That a corn-growing people should not have made pottery is extraordinary, for in America the two have usually migrated together; in fact pottery has often spread, as in southern California, beyond the limits of corn growing.

In any case it may safely be inferred that pottery was infinitely less abundant among the Basket Makers than it was among the Cliff-dwellers, and was probably, if present, of a crude type.

RELATIVE AGE

As to the relative age of the Basket Maker and Cliff-dwelling cultures, we are able to make no conclusive statement. The Wetherills, the accuracy of whose statements on other points we have had many opportunities to corroborate, were sure that the Basket Maker remains in Grand Gulch underlay those of the Cliff-dwellers. McLoyd and Graham were of the same opinion. Although we were unable to find any such case of direct superposition, we noted in Sunflower Cave cists of undoubted Basket Maker origin which had apparently been destroyed during the building or occupancy of the cliff-house. We also found in the same cave an undoubted Basket Maker sandal lying in otherwise straight Cliff-dweller rubbish, as if it had been pulled from one of the rifled cists. The other caves offered no direct evidence; the cliff-house walls in Cave I were founded on hardpan in a corner that contained no Basket Maker remains. In this cave, as in Cave II and at Sayodneechee, however, the surface sand contained Cliff-house potsherds and a few cached

---

[1] Quoted by Pepper, 1902, p. 9.

vessels. The position of these finds makes it practically certain to our minds that they could have been deposited in their observed positions only after the Basket Maker cists had been abandoned. We assume, therefore, as a working hypothesis that the Basket Maker culture antedates that of the Cliff-houses in the region studied.

RELATION OF THE TWO CULTURES

When we come to the question of the relation of the two cultures we are on even less firm ground. Was the Basket Maker culture the product of a people inhabiting the region before the coming of the Cliff-dwellers, and later on displaced by them; or was the Basket Maker the prototype of the Cliff-dweller, and did a gradual growth take place in the region from the Basket Maker through the Slab-house to the Cliff-dweller? Certain lines of evidence seem to favor this latter hypothesis. From the Basket Maker cist to the Slab-house semisubterranean room seems a logical development, the latter being little more than a slab cist with an adobe top to carry the walls a little higher than could be done with stone slabs of reasonable size. The masonry cliff-house or pueblo room, with its square corners, would be but another step in advance, the kiva perhaps being a ceremonial reminiscence of the earlier subterranean type of dwelling. In sandals, too, a possible development may be suggested: from the square-toed Basket Maker type, with its more than necessarily elaborate weave, through the scallop-toe style (tentatively identified as Slab-house) with somewhat simpler weave but still unpractical toe, to the naturally shaped pointed toe and further simplified weave of the Cliff-dweller sandal.

Whether the Basket Maker culture is parent to that of the cliff-dwellings and pueblos of the region; whether it died out entirely; or whether it still persists among such seminomadic people as the Ute and Paiute cannot be definitely stated. We know much too little about the comparative technology of the Southwest.

As to the origin of the Basket Maker culture itself, we are again in doubt. The fact that corn was grown points, of course, to the South; for corn is without question southern in origin.[1] The fact that the people had corn without pottery, or at least with little pottery, indicates that it had not reacted very strongly on their method of life and therefore that they probably had not had it long. The atlatl may or may not be considered as showing Mexican influence. The basketry bears a strong resemblance to that of California, but the similarities are perhaps superficial rather than real; contact with California, however, is proved by the presence in the Basket Maker caves of Pacific coast shells such as the abalone.

Corn (and perhaps the atlatl) from the South, and shells from California, do not, of course, prove anything more than trade re-

---

[1] Harshberger, 1893.

lationships; it is not necessary to postulate migrations, nor is there any good reason for supposing that the Basket Maker remains as we find them are not those of an early, generally diffused, and basically indigenous Plateau culture that was just beginning to be influenced by the use of a cereal, but that had not yet developed the permanent, well-built houses and high ceramic art that are usually the concomitants of an agricultural life in an arid environment. ·

These various questions cannot be in any way decided until we have a great deal more information as to range, culture, and somatology.

RANGE

The Basket Maker culture is found in Grand Gulch (the type locality), Comb Wash, Cottonwood, Butler, and White Canyons—all tributaries of the San Juan or the Colorado in southeastern Utah. To the south of the San Juan we have found it in the Monuments and in Marsh Pass, and there can be little doubt that it occurs also in Sagiotsosi. Here definite knowledge ceases.[1] Pepper believes, on the evidence of an atlatl reported to have been found in Canyon de Chelly, that the culture extended to that region, and there is no good reason that it should not have done so. One of the authors saw in Bluff, Utah, a "mummy" and some Basket Maker sandals which were said to have been found by a Navaho in the lower Chinlee somewhere near Nockito.

The Chinlee enters the San Juan almost directly opposite the typical Basket Maker canyons—Butler Wash and Cottonwood Wash—and not far above Grand Gulch itself; Canyon de Chelly is a tributary of the Chinlee. Thus the Basket Maker culture has been found, or suspected, over a single continuous and rather restricted area. Its relation to the Cliff-house–Pueblo culture can hardly be understood until we know whether this restriction is real or whether the culture was actually much more widely distributed. As was pointed out in the paragraph on the house type, Basket Maker remains are probably not easily identifiable in open sites, but there is still a vast amount of cave country from which they have not been reported, but where they would be easily recognized if present. Such districts are the McElmo and Mesa Verde, the canyons to the north of the Colorado in arid Utah; the Rio Verde, Walnut Creek, and the upper Gila and Salt. In the latter locality, at Tulerosa Cave, we find some traits of culture suggestive of the Basket Maker.[2]

The caves of Coahuila produce spear throwers analogous to those from Arizona and Utah, and many other specimens show a sort of

---

[1] It will probably, however, be discovered in Sagi Canyon and perhaps also in Nitsi to the west, these valleys being close to Marsh Pass.

[2] See Hough, 1914, plates and figures. The more striking resemblances were pointed out in the footnotes to the section on Material Culture.

family resemblance to Basket Maker material; Coahuila coiled basketry, however, is of the locked stitch variety.

CULTURE

It of course goes without saying that we need more data before we can attempt to draw any certain conclusions as to the affinities of the Basket Maker culture. Something may, however, be done in tracing out various lines of inquiry for which we already have the material. One such is offered by basketry. It has been shown above that Basket Maker coiled work, as well as that from the cliff-houses, is made without interlocking stitches. Mason states that all coiled basketry has interlocking stitches, so that we must suppose that to be at least the usual type in other districts. If the unlocked style is unusual, it should provide a good classificational item. We have in the museums of the country a great amount of coiled basketry from the Shoshonean tribes of the Southwest; also from the Apache, the Pima, etc.; as well as from the different Californian and north Mexican stocks. There are, moreover, archeological specimens from caves in southern New Mexico and Arizona, Coahuila, Nevada, and California. A thoroughgoing study of the designs and weaves of these groups may be expected to bring out much suggestive information.

Similar comparative investigations should be carried out along other lines—sandals, matting, dice, pipes, beads, twined work, coil without foundation, etc. The correlation of these branches of cultural inquiry, taken together with somatological researches and a consideration of the geographical range of the Basket Makers, can hardly fail to throw much light on the questions of who they were and whence they derived their culture, whether or not it was parent to that of the Cliff-dwellers or whether it was the forerunner of some other culture, possibly that of the modern Ute and Paiute.

SOMATOLOGY

The question of whether the Basket Maker culture was or was not parent to that of the Cliff-dwellings would be simplified if we knew something of the racial affinities of the people who produced it. This, of course, can only be accomplished by means of somatological studies. Basket Maker crania are undeformed, dolichocephalic, and of a rather markedly scaphoid type; those of the Cliff-dwellers are so strongly deformed posteriorly that we are quite unable to tell what their natural form might have been. It is probable, however, that competent physical anthropologists will be able to reconstruct, at least approximately, the true form of the Cliff-dweller cranium, and thus comparative studies may yet be made. All the living peoples of the Southwest, particularly the Ute and the Paiute, should be brought into comparison somatologically with the Basket Makers.

APPENDIX I

Provenience and Catalogue Numbers of Objects Illustrated

Figure Number	Peabody Museum Catalogue Number	Locality	Figure Number	Peabody Museum Catalogue Number	Locality
Pl. 34, c	A–1252.......	Ruin 2.	Pl. 45, 3	A–1295.......	Ruin 3.
d	A–1272, 1273..	Ruin 3.	4	A–1195.......	Ruin 2.
Pl. 34, a	A–1260.......	Ruin 2.	5	A–1203......	Do.
b	A–1706........	Ruin 9.	Fig. 43	A–1248......	Do.
Pl. 35, a	A–1216.......	Ruin 2.	Pl. 46, b	A–1655.......	Ruin 9.
b	A–1217.......	Do.	Fig. 45	88325........	Sagiotsosi.
c	Same as above	Do.	Pl. 46, c	88325.........	Do.
Pl. 36, a	A–1482.;.....	Ruin 7.	d	A–1280......	Ruin 3.
b	A–1311.......	Ruin 4.	Pl. 46A, a	A–1135.......	Ruin 1.
c	A–1682.......	Ruin 9.	b	A–1263.......	Cave near ruin
Pl. 37, a	A–1312.......	Do.			2.
b	Same as above	Ruin 9.	Pl. 47, a	A–1417.......	Ruin 6.
Pl. 38, a	A–1503.......	Ruin 7.	b	88318.........	Sagi Canyon.
b	A–1504.......	Do.	c	88317.........	Do.
c	Same as above	Do.	d	A–1158..;....	Ruin 1.
Pl. 39, a	A–1657...:....	Ruin 9.	e	A–1157.......	Do.
b	A–1153.......	Ruin 1.	f	A–1460......,	Ruin 7.
c	Same as above	Do.	g	A–1673.......	Ruin 9.
Pl. 40, a	A–1497.......	Ruin 7.	Pl. 48, a	A–1187–91....	Cave near
b	A–1484.......	Do.			Ruin 1.
Pl. 42	A–1574.......	Do.	b	Same as above	Do.
Pl. 43, a	A–1576.......	Do.	Pl. 49, k	A–1592.......	Ruin 8.
b	A–1587.......	Do.	l	A–1314.......	Ruin 4.
c	A–1577.......	Do.	m	88337.........	Grand Gulch.
Fig. 40	A–1362.......	Ruin 5.	a	A–1416.......	Ruin 6.
Pl. 44, f	A–1257.......	Ruin 2.	b	A–1293.......	Ruin 3.
a	A–1508.......	Ruin 7.	c	A–1594.......	Ruin 8.
b	A–1519.......	Do.	d	A–1371.......	Ruin 5.
c	A–1519.......	Do.	e	A–1595.......	Ruin 8.
d	A–1515......	Do.	f	A–1640......	Ruin 9.
e	A–1579......	Do.	g	A–1326......	Ruin 4.
Pl. 45, 1	A–1151.......	Ruin 1.	h	88316.........	Sagi Canyon.
2	A–1194.......	Ruin 2.	i	88342.........	Do.

Figure Number	Peabody Museum Catalogue Number	Locality	Figure Number	Peabody Museum Catalogue Number	Locality
Pl. 49, j	88303.........	Sagi Canyon.	Pl. 52, k	A–1344.......	Ruin 5.
Pl. 50, a	A–1603.......	Ruin 8.	l	A–1776.......	Marsh Pass.
b	A–1368.......	Ruin 5.	m	88333.........	Grand Gulch.
c	88279.........	Ruin 9.	n	A–1267.......	Near Ruin 2.
d	A–1369.......	Ruin 5.	Fig. 48, a	A–1786.......	Marsh Pass.
e	A–1410.......	Ruin 6.	b	A–1601.......	Ruin 8.
f	A–1288.......	Ruin 3.	c	A–1787.......	Marsh Pass.
g	A–1161.......	Ruin 1.	d	A–1991.......	Chinlee Valley.
h	A–1202.......	Ruin 2.	e	A–1839.......	Cave 1.
Fig. 46	A–1597.......	Ruin 8.	f	A–1785.......	Marsh Pass.
Pl. 51, a	A–1800.......	Marsh Pass.	g	A–1372.......	Ruin 5.
b	A–1462.......	Ruin 7.	h	A–1775.......	Marsh Pass.
c	A–1600.......	Ruin 8.	i	A–1782.......	Do.
d	A–1212.......	Ruin 2.	Fig. 49	A–1461.......	Ruin 7.
e	88346.........	Sagi Canyon.	Fig. 50, a	A–2497.......	Marsh Pass.
f	A–1462.......	Ruin 7.	b	A–2499.......	Do.
Fig. 47, a	A–1468.......	Do.	Fig. 51, a	A–1469.......	Ruin 7.
b	88301.........	Sagi Canyon.	b	A–1224.......	Ruin 2.
c	A–1440.......	Ruin 7.	c	A–1778.......	Marsh Pass.
d	A–1356.......	Ruin 5.	d	A–1154.......	Ruin 1.
e	A–1200.......	Ruin 2.	e	A–1644.......	Ruin 9.
f	Ideal drawing.........		f	A–1774.......	Marsh Pass.
g	.....do........		g	A–1676.......	Ruin 9.
h	A–1320.......	Ruin 4.	Pl. 46A, c	88309.........	Sagi Canyon.
Pl. 51, g	A–1646.......	Ruin 9.	d	A–1399.......	Ruin 5.
h	A–1400.......	Ruin 5.	e	A–2565.......	Sunflower Cave
i	A–1783.......	Marsh Pass.	Pl. 53, a	A–1256.......	Ruin 2.
j	A–1780.......	Do.	b	A–1255.......	Do.
k	A–1779.......	Do.	Pl. 54, a	A–1845.......	Cave I.
Pl. 52, a	A–1279.......	Ruin 3	b	A–1879.......	Do.
b	A–1279.......	Do.	c	A–1759.......	Marsh Pass: Pottery Hill Cemetery.
c	A–1184.......	Ruin 1.			
d	A–1628.......	Ruin 8.	d	A–2525.......	Marsh Pass Cemetery.
e	A–1184.......	Ruin 1.			
f	A–1149.......	Do.	e	A–1716.......	Marsh Pass: Camp Cemetery.
g	A–1186.......	Mound near Ruin 1.			
h	A–1627.......	Ruin 8.	f	A–1716.......	Do.
i	A–1437.......	Ruin 6.	g	A–2525.......	Marsh Pass Cemetery.
j	A–1315.......	Ruin 4.			

Figure Number	Peabody Museum Catalogue Number	Locality	Figure Number	Peabody Museum Catalogue Number	Locality
Pl.54. h	81813.........	Betatakin.	Pl.56. f	K cam. 50....	Locality unknown.
i	A-1719.......	Marsh Pass Cemetery.	Fig.59,a	A-1811.......	Marsh Pass, surface.
j	A-2522.......	Do.	b	A-1438.......	Ruin 6.
k	A-1760.......	Marsh Pass: Pottery Hill Cemetery.	c	A-1438.......	Do.
			d	A-1811.......	Marsh Pass, surface.
Fig.52	All A-1811....	Marsh Pass, surface.	e	A-1266.......	Cave near Ruin 2.
Fig.53	81813	Betatakin.			
Fig.54,a	A-1631.......	Ruin 8.	f	A-1342.......	Ruin 4.
b	A-1631.......	Do.	Fig.60,a	A-1811.,.....	Marsh Pass, surface.
Fig.55	A-1770.......	Marsh Pass.			
Pl.55	A-1811.......	Do.	b	A-1811.......	Do
Fig.56,a	A-1757.......	Marsh Pass: Pottery Hill.	Pl.57, b	A-1585.......	Ruin 7.
			a	A-1978.......	Ruin 2.
b	A-1811.......	Marsh Pass, surface.	c-p	....	Various sites.
			Pl.58, a	A-2486.......	Cave II.
c	A-1404.......	Ruin 5.	b	A-2487.......	Do.
d	A-1572.......	Ruin 7.	c	A-2488.......	Do.
e	81814.........	Sagi Canyon.	d	A-2489.......	Do.
f	81814.........	Do.	e	A-2523.......	Marsh Pass.
g	A-1811.......	Marsh Pass, surface.	f	A-2299.......	Cave I.
			g	A-2538.......	Sunflower Cave.
h	A-1572.......	Ruin 7.			
i	A-1632.......	Ruin 8.	h	A-1582.......	Ruin 7.
Fig.57,a	A-1732.......	Marsh Pass Cemetery.	Fig. 61	A-1131.......	Ruin 1.
			Pl. 59, a	A-2539.......	Sunflower Cave.
b	A-1768.......	Do.	b	A-2533.......	Do.
c	A-1748.......	Do.	Fig,62,a	A-2502.......	Ruin A.
d	A-1733.......	Do.	b	A-2502.......	Do.
Fig.58,a	A-1802.......	Do.	Fig. 63	A-1813.......	Mesa at Segi mouth.
b	A-1811.......	Do.			
c	A-1811.......	Do.	Fig. 64	A-1539.......	Ruin 7.
Pl.56, a	A-1735.......	Do.	Fig. 65	A-1540.......	Do.
b	A-1750.......	Do.			
c	Keam-249....	Locality unknown.	Pl. 60	A-2606 to A-2610.	Sunflower Cave.
d	A-1729.......	Marsh Pass Cemetery.	Pl. 61	A-2606 to A-2610.	Do.
Pl. 56, e	A-1734.......	Marsh Pass Cemetery.	Fig. 66	A-2606.......	Do.
			Pl. 62, a	A-1850.......	Cave I.

Figure Number	Peabody Museum Catalogue Number	Locality	Figure Number	Peabody Museum Catalogue Number	Locality
Pl. 62. b	A–1849.......	Cave I.	Pl. 65, j	A–2481.......	Cave II.
c	A–1848.......	Do.	k	A–2483.......	Do.
d	A–1862.......	Do.	Pl. 66, a	A–2224.......	Cave I.
e	A–1887.......	Do.	Pl. 66, b	A–2410.......	Do.
f	A–1854.......	Do.	Pl. 67, a	A–2164.......	Do.
g	A–1853.......	Do.	Fig. 71	A–2164.......	Do.
h	A–1857.......	Do.	Pl. 67, b	A–2165.......	Do.
i	A–1886.......	Do.	c	A–2376.......	Do.
j	A–1889.......	Do.	d	A–2375.......	Do.
k	A–1880.......	Do.	Pl. 68, a	A–2439.......	Do.
l	A–1871.......	Do.	b	A–2591.......	Sunflower
m	A–1863.......	Do.			Cave.
n	A–1870.......	Do.	c	Same as above	Do.
o	A–1869.......	Do.	d	A–2438.......	Cave I.
p	A–1869.......	Do.	Pl. 69, a	A–2311.......	Do.
q	A–1892.......	Do.	b	Same as above	Do.
r	A–1867.......	Do.	Pl. 70, a	A–2386.......	Do.
s	A–1866.......	Do.	b	A–1912.......	Sayodneechee.
t	A–1864.......	Do.	c	A–2111.......	Cave I.
u	A–1858.......	Do.	d	A–2111.......	Do.
v	A–1888.......	Do.	e	A–2671.......	Do.
w	A–1868.......	Do.	f	A–2131.......	Do.
x	A–1865.......	Do.	g	A–1948.......	Sayodneechee.
Fig. 67	A–1850.......	Do.	h	A–1948.......	Do.
Fig.68,a	A–1886.......	Do.	i	A–2411.......	Cave I.
Fig. 69	A–1880.......	Do.	j	A–2116.......	Do.
Fig.68,b	A–1869.......	Do.	Fig.72,a	A–2383.......	Do.
c	A–1871.......	Do.	b	A–2341.......	Do.
Fig.68,d	A–1865.......	Do.	c	A–2186.......	Do.
Fig.68,d	A–1864.......	Do.	Fig. 73	A–2111.......	Do.
Fig.68,d	A–1868.......	Do.	Fig.74,a	A–1959.......	Sayodneechee.
Fig.70,a	A–1405.......	Ruin 5.	b	A–1956.......	Do.
b	A–1405.......	Do.	c	A–1907.......	Do.
Pl. 63, a	A–1405.......	Do.	Fig. 75	A–1950.......	Do.
b–h	A–1405.......	Do.	Pl. 70, k	A–2112.......	Cave I.
Pl. 64, e	A–1405.......	Do.	l	A–1898.......	Sayodneechee.
Pl. 64, a	A–1345.......	Do.	m	A–1895.......	Do.
b	A–1350.......	Do.	n	A–1932.......	Do.
c	A–1349.......	Do.	o	A–1933.......	Do.
d	A–1351.......	Do.	Fig.76,a	A–1898.......	Do.
Pl.65,h,i	A–2274.......	Cave I.	b	A–1898.......	Do.
f	A–2480.......	Cave II.	c	A–1898.......	Do.

Figure Number	Peabody Museum Catalogue Number	Locality	Figure Number	Peabody Museum Catalogue Number	Locality
Fig.76,d	A–1932.......	Sayodneechee.	Pl. 78, a	A–2490.......	Do.
Fig. 77	A–2194.......	Cave I.	b	Same as above	Do.
Pl. 71, a	A–2226.......	Do.	Pl. 75, e	A–2476.......	Do.
b	A–2292.......	Do.	Pl. 79, a	A–2313.......	Cave I.
Pl. 72, a	A–2446.......	Cave II.	b	A–1822.......	Do.
Fig. 78	A–2447.......	Do.	c	A–2212.......	Do.
Pl.72, b	A–2447.......	Do.	d	A–2207.......	Do.
Pl. 73, a	A–1816.......	Cave I.	e	A–2208.......	Do.
b	A–1818.......	Do.	f	A–2213.......	Do.
c	A–1816.......	Do.	Fig. 81	A–2408.......	Do.
Fig. 79	A–2209.......	Do.	Fig. 82	A–2204.......	Do.
Pl. 74, a	A–2209.......	Do.	Fig.83,a	A–2428.......	Do.
Pl.74,e–f	A–2209.......	Do.	b	A–2428.......	Do.
b	A–2236.......	Do.	Fig. 84	A–2367.......	Do.
c	A–2235.......	Do.	Pl. 80, a	A–2214.......	Do.
d	17687.........	San Luis Po-tosi.	b	A–2317.......	Do.
			c	A–2286.......	Do.
Pl. 75, a	A–2253.......	Cave I.	d	A–2218.......	Do.
b	A–2252.......	Do.	e	A–2217.......	Do.
c	A–2252.......	Do.	f	A–2215.......	Do.
d	A–2252.......	Do.	Fig. 85	A–2238.......	Do.
Fig. 80	Ideal drawing.		Fig. 86	A–2379.......	Do.
Pl. 76, a	A–1827.......	Do.	Pl. 81, a	A–2202.......	Do.
b	A–2257.......	Do.	b	A–2203.......	Do.
c	A–2357.......	Do.	c	A–2200.......	Do.
d	A–2246.......	Do.	d	A–2197.......	Do.
e	A–2247.......	Do.	e	A–2198.......	Do.
f	A–2246.......	Do.	f	A–2201.......	Do.
g	A–2250.......	Do.	Fig. 87	Restoration from A–2088.	
h	A–1817.......	Do.			
i	A–2264.......	Do.	Pl. 82, a	A–2087.......	Do.
j	A–2343.......	Do.	b	A–2087.......	Do.
k	A–2363.......	Do.	c	A–2088.......	Do.
l	A–2382.......	Do.	d	A–2088.......	Do.
m	A–2262.......	Do.	Fig.88,a	A–2088.......	Do.
n	A–2457.......	Cave II.	b	85323.........	Brazil.
Pl. 77, a	A–2461.......	Do.	Pl. 83, a	A–1952.......	Sayodneechee.
b	A–2460.......	Do.	b	A–2089.......	Cave I.
c	A–2459.......	Do.	c	A–1972.......	Sayodneechee.
d	A–2457.......	Do.	Fig.89,a	63521.........	Bering Sea.
e	A–2458.......	Do.	b	A–2092.......	Cave I.

Figure Number	Peabody Museum Catalogue Number	Locality	Figure Number	Peabody Museum Catalogue Number	Locality
Fig.89,c	A-2091.......	Cave I.	Fig. 92	A-2083.......	Cave I.
d	A-2092.......	Do.	Pl.84,18	A-2095.......	Do.
e	A-2090.......	Do.	19	A-2096.......	Do.
f	A-2090.......	Do.	20	A-2096.......	Do.
Fig.90,a	A-1921.......	Sayodneechee.	21	A-2096.......	Do.
b	A-1920.......	Do.	22	A-2103.......	Do.
c	A-1918.......	Do.	23	A-2102.......	Do.
d	A-1924.......	Do.	24	A-2101.......	Do.
e	A-1925.......	Do.	25	A-2099.......	Do.
f	A-1940.......	Do.	26	A-2099.......	Do.
g	A-1940.......	Do.	27	A-2099.......	Do.
h	A-1940.......	Do.	28	A-2098.......	Do.
i	A-1913.......	Do.	29	A-2098.......	Do.
j	A-1926.......	Do.	30	A-2098.......	Do.
k	A-1899.......	Do.	31	A-2107.......	Do.
l	A-1899.......	Do.	32	A-2104.......	Do.
m	A-1899.......	Do.	33	A-2106.......	Do.
n	A-1899.......	Do.	34	A-2105.......	Do.
Fig.91,a	A-2065.......	Cave I.	Fig. 93	A-2076.......	Do.
b	A-2066.......	Do.	Pl. 85, b	A-2057.......	Do.
c	A-2063.......	Do.	Pl. 85, a	A-2231.......	Do.
d	A-2064.......	Do.	Fig.94,a	A-2135.......	Do.
e	A-2061.......	Do.	b	A-1936.......	Sayodneechee.
Pl. 84, 1	A-2068.......	Do.	c	A-1936.......	Do.
2	A-2069.......	Do.	d	A-2136.......	Cave I.
3	A-2084.......	Do.	Pl. 85, c	A-2142.......	Do.
4	A-2072.......	Do.	d	A-2143.......	Do.
5	A-2075.......	Do.	Pl. 86, e	A-2145.......	Do.
6	A-2075.......	Do.	Pl. 86, a	A-1937.......	Sayodneechee.
7	A-2075.......	Do.	b	A-1931.......	Do.
8	A-2075.......	Do.	c	A-1948.......	Do.
9	A-2083.......	Do.	d	A-1948.......	Do.
10	A-2085.......	Do.	Pl. 86, f	A-2590.......	SunflowerCave.
11	A-2081.......	Do.	g	A-2133.......	Cave I.
12	A-2077.......	Do.	Pl. 87, a	A-2389.......	Do.
13	A-2079.......	Do.	b	A-2389.......	Do.
14	A-2071.......	Do.	Pl. 88, a	Restoration from A-2389.	Do.
15	A-2071.......	Do.			
16	A-2074.......	Do.	b	.....do........	Do.
17	A-2082.......	Do.	Fig. 95	A-2465.......	Cave II.

APPENDIX II

LOCALITIES OF PICTOGRAPHS

Fig. No.	Locality.	Fig. No.	Locality.
Pl. 89, a	Cliffs at mouth of Sagi Canyon.	Pl. 91, a	Cliffs at mouth of Ruin 5 Canyon.
b	Ruin 8.		yon.
c	Lower falls of Laguna Creek.	b	North wall of Ruin 5 Canyon.
d	Cliffs at mouth of Sagi Canyon.	c	Cliffs below mouth of Marsh
e	Chinlee Valley, 5 miles above		Pass.
	Ruin 9.	d	Chinlee Valley, 5 miles above
f	Cliffs at mouth of Sagi Canyon.		Ruin 9.
g	Ruin 2.	e	Cliffs below mouth of Marsh
h	Cliffs below mouth of Marsh		Pass.
	Pass.	f	Do.
i	Do.	g	Do.
j	Peach orchard, Hagoé.	h	Half a mile above Ruin 9.
k	Above Ruin 5, Hagoé.	i	Mouth of Kinboko.
l	Cliffs at mouth of Sagi Canyon.	j	Lower falls of Laguna Creek.
m	Ruin 1.	Pl. 92, a	Ruin 6.
Pl. 90, a	Chinlee Valley, 5 miles above	b	Cave I.
	Ruin 9.	Pl. 93, a	Near Ruin 1.
b	Cliffs at mouth of Sagi Canyon.	b	North wall Ruin 5 Canyon.
c	Ruin 9.	Fig. 96, a	South wall Ruin 5 Canyon.
d	Mouth of Kinboko.	b	Do.
e	Lower falls of Laguna Creek.	Pl. 94, a	Cave near Ruin A.
f	Ruin 9.	b	Kinboko just above Ruin A.
g	Lower falls of Laguna Creek.	c	Do.
h	Half a mile above Ruin 9.	d	Ruin 9.
i	Cave near Ruin A.	e	Near Ruin 5.
j	Lower falls of Laguna Creek.	f	Cave I.
k	Cave near Ruin A.	Fig. 97, a	Ruin 8.
l	Lower falls of Laguna Creek.	b	Do.
m	"South Comb," 8 miles north	c	Do.
	of Ruin 7.	d	Ruin A.
n	Lower falls of Laguna Creek.	e	Do.
o	Do.	f	Do.
p	Do.	g	Do.

Fig. No.	Locality.	Fig. No.	Locality.
Fig. 98	Cave near Ruin A.	Fig. 101	Ruin 4.
Fig. 99	Do.	Pl. 97, b	Near Ruin 1.
Pl. 95, a	Near Ruin 2.	c	Do.
b	Blue Canyon.	Fig. 102a	Do.
Pl. 96, a	Ruin 4.	b	Do.
b	Do.	c	Lower falls of Laguna Creek.
Pl. 97, a	Cave II.	d	Ruin 4.
Fig. 100	Ruin 4.	e	Do.

BIBLIOGRAPHY

CULIN, STEWART.
　1907. Games of the North American Indians. *Twenty-fourth Report of the Bureau of American Ethnology*, Washington, 1907.
CUMMINGS, BYRON.
　1910. The ancient inhabitants of the San Juan Valley. *Bulletin of the University of Utah*, 2d Archeological number, vol. III, no. 3, pt. 2, Salt Lake City, 1910.
　1915. The kivas of the San Juan drainage. *American Anthropologist*, n. s. vol. XVII, pp. 272–282, Lancaster, Pa., 1915.
CUSHING, FRANK HAMILTON.
　1886. A study of Pueblo pottery as illustrative of Zuñi culture growth. *Fourth Report of the Bureau of Ethnology*, pp. 467–521, Washington, 1886.
　1895. The arrow. *American Anthropologist*, vol. VIII, no. 4, pp. 307–349, Washington, 1895.
FEWKES, JESSE WALTER.
　1898. Archeological expedition to Arizona in 1895. *Seventeenth Report of the Bureau of American Ethnology*, pt. 2, pp. 519–742, Washington, 1898.
　1903. Hopi katcinas drawn by natives artists. *Twenty-first Report of the Bureau of American Ethnology*, pp. 3–126, Washington, 1903.
　1904. Two summers' work in Pueblo ruins. *Twenty-second Report of the Bureau of American Ethnology*, pp. 3–195. Washington, 1904.
　1908. Ventilators in ceremonial rooms of prehistoric cliff-dwellings. *American Anthropologist*, n. s., vol. X, no. 3, pp. 387–398, Lancaster, Pa., 1908.
　1909. Antiquities of the Mesa Verde National Park: Spruce-tree House. *Bulletin 41, Bureau of American Ethnology*, Washington, 1909.
　1911. Preliminary report on a visit to the Navaho National Monument, Arizona. *Bulletin 50, Bureau of American Ethnology*, Washington, 1911.
　1911, a. Antiquities of the Mesa Verde National Park: Cliff Palace. *Bulletin 51, Bureau of American Ethnology*, Washington, 1911.
　1912. Casa Grande, Arizona. *Twenty-eighth Report of the Bureau of American Ethnology*, pp. 25–179, Washington, 1912.
　1914. Archeology of the Lower Mimbres Valley, New Mexico. *Smithsonian Miscellaneous Collections*, vol. 63, no. 10, Washington, 1914.
　1916. Excavation and repair of Sun Temple, Mesa Verde National Park. Department of the Interior, Washington, 1916.
　1916, a. The cliff-ruins in Fewkes Cañon, Mesa Verde National Park, Colorado. Holmes Anniversary Volume, pp. 96–117, Washington, 1916.
GODDARD. PLINY EARLE.
　1913. Indians of the Southwest. *American Museum of Natural History*, Handbook Series, no. 2, New York, 1913.

HARSHBERGER, J. W.
1893. Maize: a botanical and economic study. *Contributions from the Botanical Laboratory of the University of Pennsylvania*, vol. I, no. 2, Philadelphia, 1893.

HOLMES, WILLIAM HENRY.
1886. Pottery of the ancient Pueblos. *Fourth Report of the Bureau of Ethnology*, pp. 257–360, Washington, 1886.

HOUGH, WALTER.
1907. Antiquities of the upper Gila and Salt River valleys in Arizona and New Mexico, *Bulletin 35, Bureau of American Ethnology*. Washington, 1907.
1914. Culture of the ancient Pueblos of the upper Gila River region, New Mexico and Arizona. *Bulletin 87, U. S. National Museum*, Washington, 1914.

HUNTINGTON, ELLSWORTH.
1914. The climatic factor as illustrated in arid America. *Publications of the Carnegie Institution of Washington*, no. 192, Washington, 1914.

KIDDER, ALFRED VINCENT.
1910. Explorations in southeastern Utah. *American Journal of Archeology*, 2d ser., vol. XIV, pp. 337–359, Norwood, Mass., 1910.
1915. Pottery of the Pajarito plateau and of some adjacent regions in New Mexico. *Memoirs American Anthropological Association*, vol. II, pt. 6, pp. 407–462, Lancaster, 1915.
1916. The pottery of the Casas Grandes District, Chihuahua. Holmes Anniversary Volume, pp. 253–268, Washington, 1916.
1917. Archeology of the San Juan drainage. *International Congress of Americanists, 19th Session, 1915*, Washington, 1917.

KRAUSE, F.
1905. Sling contrivances for projectile weapons. *Annual Report of the Smithsonian Institution for 1904*, pp. 619–638, Washington, 1905.

KROEBER, ALFRED L.
1916. Zuñi potsherds. *Anthropological Papers of the American Museum of Natural History*, vol. XVIII, pt. 1, New York, 1916.

MASON, OTIS TUFTON.
1897. The cliff-dweller's sandal, a study in comparative technology. *Popular Science Monthly*, vol. L, pp. 676–679, New York, March, 1897.
1904. Aboriginal American basketry: studies in a textile art without machinery. *Annual Report of the U. S. National Museum for 1902*, pp. 171–548, Washington, 1904.

MATTHEWS, WASHINGTON.
1884. Navajo weavers. *Third Report of the Bureau of Ethnology*, pp. 371–391, Washington, 1884.

MONTGOMERY, HENRY.
1894. Prehistoric man in Utah. *The Archaeologist*, vol. II, nos. 8, 9, 11, Waterloo, Ind., Aug.–Nov., 1894.

MORLEY, SYLVANUS GRISWOLD.
1908. The excavation of the Cannonball ruins in southwestern Colorado. *American Anthropologist*, n. s., vol. X, pp. 596–610, Lancaster, Pa., 1908.

MORRIS, EARL.
1915. The excavation of a ruin near Aztec, San Juan county, New Mexico. *American Anthropologist*, n. s. vol. XVII, no. 4, pp. 666–684, Lancaster, Pa., 1915.

NORDENSKIÖLD, GUSTAV.
  1893. The cliff-dwellers of the Mesa Verde. Translated by D. Lloyd Morgan. Stockholm, 1893.
PEPPER, GEORGE H.
  1899. Ceremonial deposits found in an ancient Pueblo estufa in northern New Mexica. *Monumental Records*, vol. I, no. 1, pp. 1–6, New York, 1899.
  1902. The ancient basket makers of southeastern Utah. *American Museum Journal*, vol. II, no. 4, suppl., New York, April, 1902.
  1905. The throwing stick of a prehistoric people of the Southwest. *International Congress of Americanists, 13th Session, New York, 1902*, pp. 107–130, Easton, Pa., 1905.
PRUDDEN, T. MITCHELL.
  1903. The prehistoric ruins of the San Juan watershed in Utah, Arizona, Colorado, and New Mexico. *American Anthropologist*, n. s., vol. V, no. 2, pp. 224–288, Lancaster, Pa., 1903.
PUTNAM, FREDERIC WARD, *and others*.
  1879. Reports upon archaeological and ethnological collections from the vicinity of Santa Barbara, California, and from ruined pueblos of Arizona and New Mexico, and certain interior tribes. *U. S. Geographical Surveys West of the 100th Meridian*, vol. VII, Archaeology, Washington, 1879.
RUSSELL, FRANK.
  1908. The Pima Indians. *Twenty-sixth Report of the Bureau of American Ethnology*, pp. 3–389, Washington, 1908.
SNYDER, J. F.
  1897. The cliff-dweller's "sandal last." *The Antiquarian*, vol. I, pp. 128–130, Columbus, Ohio, 1897.
  1899. The "sandal last" of the cliff-dwellers. *American. Archaeologist*, vol. III, pp. 5–9, Columbus, Ohio, 1899.
UHLE, MAX.
  1909. Peruvian throwing-sticks. *American Anthropologist*, n. s., vol. XI, no. 4, pp. 624–627, Lancaster, Pa., 1909.
WETHERILL, RICHARD.
  1897. Sandal stones. *The Antiquarian*, vol. I, p. 248, Columbus, Ohio, 1897.
WINSHIP, GEORGE PARKER.
  1896. The Coronado expedition, 1540–1542. *Fourteenth Report of the Bureau of Ethnology*, pt. 1, pp. 329–613, Washington, 1896.

INDEX

Lightning Source UK Ltd.
Milton Keynes UK
UKHW012223110219
337137UK00006B/1306/P